D0393135

THE REWRITING
OF AMERICA'S
HISTORY

THE
REWRITING
OF
AMERICA'S HISTORY

Catherine Millard

Horizon House Publishers
Camp Hill, Pennsylvania

Horizon House Publishers
3825 Hartzdale Drive
Camp Hill, PA 17011

ISBN: 0-88965-092-6
LOC Catalog Card Number: 91-73175
© 1991 by Catherine Millard
Printed in the United States of America

93 94 95   5 4

Cover illustration © by Karl Foster

Unless otherwise noted, Scripture quotations are from the
New American Standard Bible, © The Lockman Foundation 1960, 1962,
1963, 1968, 1971, 1972, 1973, 1975, 1977.

Contents

ACKNOWLEDGEMENTS

To my wonderful dad, who encouraged and supported me during the formulation of this book. Gratitude is expressed to Almighty God for allowing Dad to read its contents.

I am indebted to John W. Wrigley, a superb photographer, who has served our God and country selflessly by giving of his gifts and talents. Without his help this ministry would not have been possible.

To Mr. John G. Talcott, Jr., of Plymouth, Massachusetts, for his expert guidance on the 1620 Pilgrims and their monuments.

To Helen Weir, a beautiful sister in Christ, whose illustrations, done to the glory of God, have greatly enhanced this book.

FOREWORD

Catherine Millard points the way out of the frustration which so many Americans have felt during the latter half of the 20th century. To reclaim our beloved nation from the destructive forces of humanism, secularism, atheism and false religions, we must first retrieve the true history from those who have almost hidden it beneath an avalanche of lies, distortions and misinterpretations.

By relearning the facts that a righteous new government came from righteous people seeking to advance the kingdom of Christ, it will be possible to reverse the ungodly laws of this generation that even now are condoning the destruction of millions of lives. Starting with Columbus and his discovery of the new world, Millard presents from the priceless documents themselves convincing evidence of the Christian foundations of America.

These bulwarks of faith as recorded by the founding fathers and woven into the fabric of our national life must be brought to light once more in the schools and colleges of America, the author argues convincingly, in order that young people can know again the pride and the assurance of providential guidance and the gratitude that every American citizen should experience firsthand. That, after all, is what it means to be an American—to have experiential knowledge of national blessings which are the envy of the whole world.

I would like to see this book read by educators and students, by politicians and voters, by church leaders and lay people, and by every citizen who desires to know the truth about the real beginnings of this wonderful country of ours.

Dr. D. James Kennedy
Coral Ridge Presbyterian Church

INTRODUCTION

Rewriting a nation's history is frequently one of the first strategies taken by a conquering nation. Why? Because a people who do not know from where they came also do not know where they are going. Thus, they become easy prey for a conquering nation.

While this phenomenon has occurred repeatedly throughout history and throughout the world, today it is happening to our beloved United States!

It's happening through the rewriting and/or reinterpretation of American historical records: in our national parks, monuments, memorials, landmarks, shrines and churches. In some cases, changes are subtle, and in others, blatant. It's done through removal of key historic pieces that do not support the current ungodly bias. It's even been done architecturally, through the physical removal of valuable stained-glass windows in a key national church.

And it's also done through emphasis and de-emphasis of historical periods according to what fits a mode. In fact, the history of our founding period has been eroded and eliminated, almost to the point of oblivion. A nationwide phenomenon has occurred, whereby there is an emphasis upon history from the Civil War onwards, or even as recent as the early 1900s, to the deliberate exclusion of the founding period, which in itself, is an incredible testimony to the hand of Almighty God upon this land, and His intricate involvement in the affairs of our nation, from its earliest beginnings.

For over seven years, Christian Heritage Tours in Washington, D.C.—the city's only tour service, private or government-sponsored, whose sole purpose is to help people rediscover the rich Judaic-Christian heritage of our nation—has been conducting tours of our national monuments, landmarks and memorials. From many thousands of people, schoolchildren included, whom we have shepherded through our tours, we have received numerous strange, contradictory reports of the degeneracy and general idiocy of our founding fathers, and other men and women who helped fashion the way of life in *this nation under God*. It grieves my heart to hear such naive and outrageous falsehoods from the lips of well-meaning and intelligent Americans. Truly they have been victims of the rewriting of America's history. It is for these reasons I write this book, *The Rewriting of America's History*. It is dedicated to the glorious truth that this nation was established upon biblical principles: its founders were men of Christian nobility; her freedoms and liberties stemming from amazing and miraculous answers to prayer in the face of sure failure and disaster (as in the case of Valley Forge); and God's faithful blessings are upon a people who confidently placed themselves under the protective banner of His care.

And my hope for this book is that it will awaken Americans to rediscover who we are as a nation, and that God will raise up a faithful remnant of modern-day patriots who will accept the challenge of steering this nation back onto its original, godly course.

Catherine Millard

" . . . and as one small candle may light a thousand, so the light here kindled hath shone unto many, yea in some sort to our whole nation; let the glorious name of Jehovah have all the praise."

Governor William Bradford

Chapter I

WHERE HAVE WE COME FROM?

(i) Who was Christopher Columbus?

While conducting Christian Heritage Tours, I frequently ask the question: "Who do you believe Christopher Columbus was?" Answers vary from "an adventurer" to "a sailor" to "the discoverer of the New World." He was in fact, all of the above, but the most important aspect of his life—his Christianity, is never mentioned. Not many people are aware of Christopher Columbus' deep faith in God and His Son, Jesus Christ. Furthermore, very few people realize that it was this faith which was the impetus that initiated his whole voyage. Columbus wrote a book entitled *Book of Prophecies*, in which he copied down Scripture pertaining to bringing the gospel to unknown coastlands. The book was only recently translated into English from the original Latin and Spanish versions by a great scholar, Dr. August Kling. It was my privilege to spend several fascinating hours sharing research finds with Dr. Kling prior to his death in 1986.

Columbus' entire voyage was funded and made possible through Queen Isabel and King Ferdinand of Spain—uniquely in light of its missionary outreach. Isabel herself having a strong Christian world view, the populace accepted and embraced Columbus' tenuous expedition primarily for evangelistic reasons.

His real name, early history books disclose, was Cristobal Colon. His writings show a strong thread of Christianity. Even his signature is encased in a triangular pattern, with the beautiful names of Almighty God—El Shaddai (Almighty God); Adonai (Lord God) abbreviated, written above his signature, Christopher Ferens (Christ Bearer):

"X.p.o. Ferens," was meant to represent Columbus as the cross-bearer or the Christ-bearer:

$$.S.$$
$$.S. \quad A \quad .S.$$
$$x \quad m \quad y$$
$$: \overline{Xpo} \; FERENS. /$$

When the expedition found its first nugget of gold, it was carefully wrapped and sent back to Columbus' son, Don Diego, to deliver to Queen Isabel. It included detailed instructions in writing, telling him "to return it to her so that she may see the miracle of the Lord and remember to whom she ought to thank for it." [1]

Six years after Columbus' discovery of the New World we see that the spiritual welfare of the native people was still of primary importance to him. In his famous mayorazgo *(Testament of Founding Hereditary Family Estate)*, dated Thursday, 22nd February, 1498, he states:

> Also I order to said Don Diego, my son, or to him who will inherit said mayorazgo, that he shall help to maintain and sustain on the Island Espanola four good teachers of the holy theology with the intention to convert to our holy religion all those people in the Indias, and when it pleases God that the income of the mayorazgo will increase, that then also be increased the number of such devoted persons who will help all these people to become Christians. And may he not worry about the money that it will be necessary to spend for the purpose . . . [2]

Through the ages of history, many great inventors, scientists and visionaries have acknowledged the Bible and the leading of the Holy Spirit as the basis for their contributions which revolutionized the world of their day. Columbus was no exception. The following lengthy quotation from the Introduction of Christopher Columbus' *Book of Prophecies* summarizes not only his deep commitment to the gospel mandate, but also points to the Bible as the very source of his inspiration:

> At a very early age I began to sail upon the ocean. For more than forty years, I have sailed everywhere that people go. I prayed to the most merciful Lord about my heart's great desire, and He gave me the spirit and the intelligence for the task: seafaring, astronomy, geometry, arithmetic, skill in drafting spherical maps and placing correctly the cities, rivers, mountains and ports. I also studied cosmology, history, chronology and philosophy.
>
> It was the Lord who put into my mind (I could feel His hand upon me) the fact that it would be possible to sail from here to the Indies. All who heard of my project rejected it with laugh-

ter, ridiculing me. There is no question that the inspiration was from the Holy Spirit, because he comforted me with rays of marvelous illumination from the Holy Scriptures, a strong and clear testimony from the 44 books of the Old Testament, from the four Gospels, and from the 23 Epistles of the blessed Apostles, encouraging me continually to press forward, and without ceasing for a moment they now encourage me to make haste.

Our Lord Jesus desired to perform a very obvious miracle in the voyage to the Indies, to comfort me and the whole people of God. I spent seven years in the royal court, discussing the matter with many persons of great reputation and wisdom in all the arts; and in the end they concluded that it was all foolishness, so they gave it up. But since things generally came to pass that were predicted by our Savior Jesus Christ, we should also believe that this particular prophecy will come to pass. In support of this, I offer the gospel text, Matt. 24:25, in which Jesus said that all things would pass away, but not his marvelous Word. He also affirmed that it was necessary that all things be fulfilled that were prophesied by himself and by the prophets.

I said that I would state my reasons: I hold alone to the sacred and Holy Scriptures, and to the interpretations of prophecy given by certain devout persons.

It is possible that those who see this book will accuse me of being unlearned in literature, of being a layman and a sailor. I reply with the words of Matt. 11:25: "Lord, because thou hast hid these things from the wise and prudent, and hath revealed them unto babes."

The Holy Scripture testifies in the Old Testament by our Redeemer Jesus Christ, that the world must come to an end. The signs of when this must happen are given by Matthew, Mark and Luke. The prophets also predicted many things about it.

Our Redeemer Jesus Christ said that before the end of the world, all things must come to pass that had been written by the prophets.

The prophets wrote in various ways. Isaiah is the one most praised by Jerome, Augustine and by the other theologians. They all say that Isaiah was not only a prophet, but an evangelist as well. Isaiah goes into great detail in describing future events and in calling all people to our holy catholic faith.

Most of the prophecies of Holy Scripture have been fulfilled already . . . I am a most unworthy sinner, but I have cried out to the Lord for grace and mercy, and they have covered me completely. I have found the sweetest consolations since I made it my whole purpose to enjoy His marvelous presence.

For the execution of the journey to the Indies I did not make use of intelligence, mathematics or maps. It is simply the fulfillment of what Isaiah had prophesied. All this is what I desire to write down for you in this book.

No one should fear to undertake any task in the name of our Savior, if it is just and if the intention is purely for His holy service. The working out of all things has been assigned to each person by our Lord, but it all happens according to His sovereign will even though He gives advice. He lacks nothing that it is in the power of men to give him. Oh what a gracious Lord, who desires that people should perform for Him those things for which He holds Himself responsible! Day and night moment by moment, everyone should express to Him their most devoted gratitude.

I said that some of the prophecies remained yet to be fulfilled. These are great and wonderful things for the earth, and the signs are that the Lord is hastening the end. The fact that the gospel must still be preached to so many lands in such a short time—this is what convinces me. [3]

I have shared this information with many different school groups. The responses have always been amazement and surprise—even resentment at the truth having been withheld from them. In talking with the students, it became apparent that they were being taught sterile, dry facts, devoid of the spiritual values which motivated Columbus' great achievements, galvanizing him to action. That is maybe why they were being turned off to education in general and history in particular. The problem is, the very inner life has been stripped away from our history. Students are not exposed to the life-changing and motivating forces at the core of these heroes' lives. As so many giants of history testify, it is God who gave them the talents and the enablement to change their world for His glory.

Of 10 modern biographies by major publishers consulted, none makes mention of Christopher Columbus' faith in Christ and his motivation for the furtherance of the gospel. This phenomenon conforms with the style and content of the vast majority of history books, textbooks, dramatic presentations and exhibitions promoted throughout America on the life and adventures of Christopher Columbus. Let us take a look at what recent biographers are teaching children in regard to the discoverer of America:

From a 1989 Children's Press publication entitled, *Christopher Columbus, the Great Explorer* we read:

> . . . He sailed to Cuba
> He found more islands.
> But when he got back
> he found sick, angry men.
> Then Columbus did some cruel things.
> He sent island people to
> Spain as slaves.
> He made others look for gold.
> If they didn't find enough
> he punished them.[4]

Another publication, bearing the name, *Columbus Day*, published in 1990, teaches children the following about this noted personage:

> . . . Columbus liked the Indians. But when he saw that their jewelry was made of gold, he began making evil plans. He decided that the Indians should be the slaves of the Europeans who would settle in this region. The Indians would mine gold for the Europeans and do their other work. Columbus also hoped the Indians would become Christians. He felt they would gain more from Christianity than they would lose by becoming slaves. Before leaving the island, Columbus kid-

napped a few Indians. He wanted them to guide him to other islands. And he wanted to show them off back in Spain.[5]

The above two children's books portray a cruel, evil, money-grubbing and materialistic slave-driver. This is the opposite to Christopher Columbus' true identity, which has been documented from original sources, as discussed above.

What a tragic legacy to pass on to our nation's children—an evil report on the character of a godly hero, the discoverer of America!

Even in the following dramatic presentation, *Columbus Discovers America*, written in the 1930s, Columbus' motivation is said to be slaves, gold, ivory, jewels and land. No mention is made of the true, spiritual purpose and motivation for his voyage:

> . . . Herald. He comes!
> (There is a slight stir outside and Columbus plainly dressed, a man of about fifty-six, white-haired, tall, well-formed and dignified, enters, followed by Father Juan, Sebastian, and goes at once to the King, kneels, kisses his hand, and then to the Queen the same. He presents Father Juan, who makes obeisance, and then Sebastian.)
>
> Columbus: Your Majesty—your humble servant. My lieutenant. Sebastian! Father Juan!
>
> Ferdinand: Well, my good sir, what have you to say to us? More, I trust, than you have said at other times!
>
> Columbus: (As always, with great dignity) I have more to say, may it please your Majesties. It is this. I have lingered long about the outskirts of your Majesties' court. I have forborne to wait upon the kings of other lands. I have hoped without hope, waited with no end in view. I have been exposed to scoffs and indignities, ridiculed as a dreamer, scorned as an adventurer, and why? Because I have hoped to make this united kingdom of Aragon and Castile the greatest in the world! And your Majesties still keep me cooling my heels like any needy beggar at your gates.

Ferdinand: Bold words these, Senor Christopher!

Isabella: Oh, Senor, is this the way to gain favor with princes?

Columbus: I do not try to gain favor with princes. I confer favor on them! I am filled with wonder that Your Majesties, who have jointly undertaken so many great and perilous enterprises, should hesitate where the loss is so trifling and the gain so great.

Isabella: Indeed?

Columbus: And that a queen so devout forgets how much may be done to the glory of God.

Ferdinand: The gain so great, you say? And how?

Columbus: I offer Your Majesties boundless lands and wealth, unnumbered subjects, and everlasting fame!

I ask only to go forth in your name to risk my own life, to encounter great hardships and certain peril, only that I may plant the flags of Aragon and Castile on virgin soil, and return to you, my ships laden with slaves, with gold, with ivory, and jewels! . . .[6]

In conclusion to this section on Christopher Columbus, I quote again from Columbus' *Book of Prophecies*, as to his motivation and enablement. As he said, it was simply the fulfillment of Isaiah's prophecies in the Old Testament:

. . . I am a most unworthy sinner, but I have cried out to the Lord for grace and mercy, and they have covered me completely. I have found the sweetest consolations since I made it my whole purpose to enjoy His marvelous presence. For the execution of the journey to the Indies I did not make use of intelligence, mathematics or maps. It is simply the fulfillment of what Isaiah had prophesied. All this is what I desire to write down for you in this book. No one should fear to undertake any task in the name of our Savior, if it is just and if the intention is purely for His holy service . . . the fact that the gospel must still be preached to so many lands in such a short time—this is what convinces me. [7]

And let it be so.

Above: "Embarkation of the Pilgrims at Delft Haven, Holland, July 22, 1620" by Robert W. Weir. Elder Brewster holds the Bible open to the book of Matthew. Pastor Robinson prays with outstretched hands. Photo by John W. Wrigley. Below: "The First Thanksgiving at Plymouth, Massachusetts" by Jennie Augusta Branscombe. Courtesy of Pilgrim Society.

(ii) William Bradford, the Pilgrims and the Mayflower Compact

William Bradford was born in 1590 at Austerfield, an obscure town in Yorkshire, England. "Here and in some other places," writes Cotton Mather, to whom we are indebted for what is known of Bradford's early life,

> he had a comfortable inheritance left him of his honest parents who died while he was yet a child and cast him on the education, first of his grandparents, and then of his uncles, who devoted him, like his ancestors, into the affairs of husbandry. Long sickness kept him as he would afterwards thankfully say, from the vanities of youth and made him the fitter for what he was afterwards to undergo. When he was about a dozen years old, the readings of the Scriptures began to cause great impressions upon him; and those impressions were much assisted and improved when he came to attend the ministry of Reverend Mr. Richard Clifton, not far from his abode; he was then also further befriended by being brought into the company and fellowship of such as were then called professors. Nor could the wrath of his uncles, nor the scoff of his neighbors, now turned upon him as one of the Puritans, divert him from his pious inclinations.

When about 18 years of age, Bradford, with the company who had separated from the established church, went to Holland. He was twice arrested for having fled from England; but an explanation of his reasons secured his early release, and he was permitted to join his friends at Amsterdam. While there, he became apprenticed to a Frenchman engaged in the manufacture of silks. On coming of age, he promptly converted the property left him in England into money and engaged in business for himself at Leyden. Here he continued until, with a portion of Mr. Robinson's church, he embarked on the Mayflower for New England. No doubt Bradford was an equal sharer in the many trials of the colonists on land. He was chosen the second governor of the colony in 1621, and continued in that office with the exception of five years, until his death in 1657. Mather continues:

> He was a person for study as well as action; and hence, not withstanding the difficulties through which he passed in his

youth, he attained unto a noble skill in languages. He was also well skilled in history, in antiquity; and in philosophy and for theology, he became so versed in it, that he was an irrefragable disputant against the errors, especially those of Anabaptism, which with anxiety he saw rising in his colony; wherefore he wrote some significant things for the confutation of those errors. At length he fell sick, and so continued through a winter and spring, and died on the 9th of May, following, in the 69th year of his age. The opportunities which governor Bradford had for writing the history of the Plymouth Colony were superior to those of any other colonist and although his duties as Chief Magistrate would seem to afford him little leisure for writing, yet he thereby acquired an entire familiarity with every subject of a public nature in any way connected with the colony. This, taken in connection with the high character which he has always enjoyed, has caused this work to be regarded as of the first authority, and as entitled to take precedence over anything else relating to the history of the Pilgrims.

The history of Plymouth Plantation is fascinating. After the death of its author, the manuscript written by Bradford passed into the hands of his nephew, Nathaniel Morton, who drew quite copiously from it for the facts in his "New England's Memorial." It afterwards came into the possession of Thomas Prince, who made use of it in his *Chronological History of New England*. On the death of Prince, it was left in the New England Library, in the tower of the Old South Church, Boston. When Boston was occupied by the British in 1775-76, the church was used by the British soldiers for a riding school, and it is quite likely that Bradford's manuscript history was among the spoils carried to Nova Scotia. In 1855, the manuscript, which had long been given up for lost, was found in Fulham Library, among a rare collection belonging to the Bishop of London. How it ever got from Boston to London still remains a mystery. The original manuscript was returned to Massachusetts in 1897.[1]

Bradford's history *Of Plimoth Plantation*[2] commences with the following interesting commentary, in a triangular pattern:

Though I am growne aged, yet I have had a longing desire, to see with my own eyes, something of the most ancient lan-

guage, and holy tongue, in which the Law, and oracles of
God were write; and in which God, and angels, spoke to the
holy patriarchs, of old time; and what names were given to
things, from the creation. And though I cannot attaine to
much herein, yet I am refreshed, to have seen some glimpse
hereof; (as Moses saw the Land of Canaan afarr off) my aime
and desire is, to see how the words, and phrases lye in the holy
texte; and to dicerne somewhat of the same for my owne con-
tente.

Excerpts from Governor William Bradford's moving account
of the inception, motivation, trials and reasons for his little band of
Pilgrims' embarkation upon their arduous journey on the Mayflower, to these inhospitable and danger-strewn foreign shores, are
here quoted. There are many opinions as to why the first settlers
came to America, but why should we take anyone's educated
opinions, when we have the first governor of Plymouth Plantation's
detailed historical account? The purpose is to show the reader that
the historian Bradford, unlike today's secular historians, understood
that all history is simply the outworking of God's majestic plans, in
and through the lives of His people in opposition of Satan's working in the lives of those he controls and deceives. It is interesting that
in Bradford's history *Of Plimoth Plantation*, the first nine chapters are
devoted to the history of the Christian church prior to their arrival
at Cape Cod in November, 1620. As Bradford states, it was essential
that he begin with the very root. And that he did. We see this in
chapter one, as he discusses the opposition that took place following the Reformation and the downfall of popery:

> It is well knowne unto ye godly and judicious how since ye
> first breaking out of ye lighte of ye gospell in our Honourable
> Nation of England, (which was ye first of nations whom ye
> Lord adorned ther with, after the grosse darkness of popery
> which had covered and overspred ye Christian world), what
> warrs and opposissions ever since, Satan hath raised, main-
> tained, and continued against the Saints, from time to time, in
> one sort or other. Some times by bloody death and cruell tor-
> ments; other whiles imprisonments, banishments, and other
> hard usages; as being loath his kingdom should goe downe,
> and trueth previale, and ye churches of God reverte to their
> anciente puritie and recover their primative order, libertie

and bewtie. But when he could not prevaile by these means, againste the maine trueths of ye gospell, but that they began to take rootting in many places, being watered by ye blooud of ye martires, and blessed from heaven with a gracious encrease; he then begane to take him to his anciente strategeme used of old against the first Christians. That when by ye bloody and barbarous persecutions of ye heathen Emperours, he could not stop and subvert the course of ye gospell, but that it speedily overspred with a wonderfull celeritie the then best known parts. . . ye professours themselves, (working upon their pride and ambition, with other corrupte passions incidente to all mortall men, yea to ye saints themselves in some measure), by which wofull effects followed; as not only bitter contentions, and hartburnings, schismes, with other horrible confusions, but Satan tooke occasion and advantage therby to foyst in a number of vile ceremoneys, with many unproffitable cannons and decrees, which have since been as snares to many poore and peacable souls even to this day. So as in ye anciente times, the persecutions by ye heathen and their Emperours, was not greater than of the Christians one against other; . . .

Bradford documented the split that took place among professing Christians as follows:

The one side laboured to have ye right worship of God and discipline of Christ established in ye church, according to ye simplicitie of ye gospell, without the mixture of men's inventions, and to have and to be ruled by ye laws of God's word, dispensed in those offices, and by those officers of Pastors, Teachers, and Elders, etc. according to ye Scriptures. The other partie, though under many colours and pretences, endevored to have ye episcopall dignities (affter ye popish maner) with their large power and jurisdiction still retained; with all those courts, cannons, and ceremonies, togeather with all such livings, revenues, and subordinate officers, with other such means as formerly upheld their antichristian greatnes, and enabled them with lordly and tyranous power to persecute ye poore servants of God. This contention was so great, as neither ye honour of God, the commone persecuton, nor ye mediation of Mr. Calvin and other worthies of ye Lord in those places, could prevaile with those thus episcopally minded, but they proceeded by all means to disturbe ye peace of this poor persecuted church, even so farr as to charge (very unjustly, and ungodily, yet prelatelike) some of their cheefe opposers, with rebellion and high treason against ye Emperour, and other such crimes . . .

Governor Bradford goes on to give the lamentable results of this schism:

...Religion hath been disgraced, the godly greeved, afflicted, persecuted, and many exiled, sundrie have lost their lives in prisones and otherwys. On the other hand, sin hath been countenanced, ignorance, profannes, and atheisme increased, and the papists encouraged to hope againe for a day . . . so that in England at this day the man or woman that begins to profes Religion, and to serve God, must resolve with him selfe to sustaine mocks and injuries even as though he lived amongst ye enimies of Religion . . .

The historian weighs all these cataclysmic happenings in the scales of Scripture, and concludes:

. . . but it is ye Lord's doing, and ought to be marvelous in our eyes! . . . Every plante which mine heavenly father hath not planted (saith our Saviour) shall be rooted up. (Matt. 15:13) . . . Behold, I come unto ye, O proud man, saith the Lord God of hosts; for thy day is come, even the time that I will visite thee. Jer. 50:31 . . .

and:

When the Lord brougt againe the captivitie of Zion, we were like them that dreame. Psa: 126:1. The Lord hath done great things for us, wherof we rejoyce. v. 3. They that sow in teares, shall reap in joye . . .

Bradford gives much credit to the preachers and true men of God, such as John Robinson, William Brewster, Richard Clifton and others. Through them, people saw their sinful conditions, repented and received God's grace to change their lives. But they soon met with persecution and scorn which, Bradford tells us, they bore with much patience. Furthermore, God revealed to them that the "lordly and tyrannous power of ye prelates ought not to be submitted unto: which was contrary to the freedome of the gospell, would load and burden men's consciences, and by their compulsive power make a prophane mixture of persons and things in ye worship of God."

The afflictions took a turn for the worse; Bradford likens their former problems to "fleebites" in comparison to their latter sufferings. In 1607, concluding that it was impossible to continue the worship of God in England, they agreed to resettle in Holland where they had heard they would have freedom of religion. It was not an easy undertaking, as Bradford describes below:

> Being thus constrained to leave their native soyle and countrie, their lands and livings, and all their friends and famillier acquaintance, it was much, and thought marvelous by many. But to goe into a countrie they knew not (but by hearsay), wher they must learne a new language, and get their livings they knew not how, it being a dear place, and subjecte to ye miseries of warr, it was by many thought an adventure almost desperate, a case intolerable, and a miserie worse than death. Espetially seeing they were not acquainted with trade nor traffique, (by which ye countrie doth subsiste), but had only been used to a plaine countrie life, and ye inocente trade of husbandrey. But these things did not dismay them (though they did sometimes trouble them) for their desires were sett on ye ways of God and to enjoye His ordinances; but they rested in His Providence, and knew whom they had believed . . .

Life in Holland was very difficult. There were extremely long hours for the adults and the children alike. They feared the corruption of their children by the native youth. Difficulties finally drove them to leave Holland.

After much prayer and the consideration of various resettlement locations, it was decided it would be best to live as a distinct body by themselves, under the government of Virginia.

Bradford describes their departure from Holland being rooted in their love of God:

> So being ready to departe, they had a day of solleme humiliation, their pastor taking his texte from Ezra 8:21: "And ther at ye river, by Ahava, I proclaimed a fast, that we might humble

ourselves before our God and seeke of Him a right way for us, and for our children, and for all our substance." Upon which they spente a good parte of ye day very profitably and suitable to their presente occasion. The rest of the time was spent in powering out prairs to ye Lord with greate fervencie, mixed with abundance of tears. And ye time being come that they must departe, they were accompanied with most of their brethren out of ye citie, unto a towne sundrie miles off called Delfes-Haven, wher the ship lay ready to receive them. So they lefte ye goodly and pleasante citie, which had been ther resting place near 12. years; but they knew they were pilgrimes (Hebrews 11), but lift their eyes to ye heavens, their dearest cuntrie, and quieted their spirits . . .

What could now sustaine them but ye spirite of God and His grace? May not and ought not the children of these fathers rightly say: Our fathers were Englishmen which came over this great ocean, and were ready to perish in this wilderness; (Deuteronomy 26:5,7) but they cried unto ye Lord, and He heard their voyce, and looked on their adversitie, etc. Let them therefore praise ye Lord, because He is good, and His mercies endure for ever. (107 Psalm: v. 1,2,4,5,8) Yea let them which have been redeemed of ye Lord, show how He hath delivered them from ye hand of ye oppressour. When they wandered in ye deserte wilderness out of ye way, and found no citie to dwell in, both hungrie, and thirstie, their sowle was overwhelmed in them. Let them confess before ye Lord His loving kindnes, and His wonderful works before ye sons of men.

They arrived at Cape Cod, Massachusetts, on November 11, 1620. Ocean storms had blown them off course. Thus, they arrived in Massachusetts rather than their originally intended Virginia destination, King James having granted a charter to the Virginia Company for its incorporation. (See First Charter of Virginia, April 10, 1606, page 307.)

It is interesting to note that these Pilgrims had written up an agreement entitled *The Leyden Agreement* of 1618 subscribed by John Robinson and William Brewster. The following excerpt clearly establishes their priorities.

Seven articles which the Church of Leyden sent to the Counsel of England to be considered of their judgment occasioned about their going to Virginia
Anno 1618.

1. To the confession of faith published in the name of the Church of England and to every article thereof we do with the reformed churches where we live and also elsewhere assent wholly. 2. As we do acknowledge the doctrine of faith there taught, so do we the fruits and effects of the same doctrine to the begetting of saving faith in thousands in the land (conformists and reformists as you are called) with whom also as with our brethren, we do desire to keep spiritual communion in peace and will practise in our parts all lawful things. 3. The King's Majesty we acknowledge for Supreme Governor in his Dominion in all causes and over all persons, and none may decline or appeal from his authority or judgment in any cause whatsoever, but in all things obedience is due unto him, either active, if the thing commanded be not against God's Word, or passive if it be, except pardon can be obtained. 4. We judge it lawful for his Majesty to appoint bishops; civil overseers, or officers in authority under him, in the several provinces, dioses, congregations or parishes to oversee the churches and govern them civilly according to the Laws of the Land, unto whom you are in all things to give an account, and by them, to be ordered according to Godliness. 5. The authority of the present bishops in the land, we do acknowledge so far forth as the same is indeed derived from his Majesty unto them and as you proceed in his name, whom we will also therein honor in all things and him in them. 6. We believe that no sinod, classes, convocation or assembly of Ecclesiastical officers has any power or authority at all but as the same by the Magistrate given unto them. 7. And lastly, we desire to give unto all Superiors due honor to preserve the unity of the Spirit, with all who fear God, to have peace with all men what in us lieth, and wherein we err to be instructed by any.
Subscribed by John Robinson and William Brewster.[3]

The *1618 Leyden Agreement* only further validates the Christian identity and purpose of the 1620 Pilgrims, who subsequently finding themselves about to arrive upon land with no established form of government as it would have been, had they landed in Virginia, saw the necessity to establish some type of governmental order among themselves before landing. The result was the *Mayflower Compact*, a charter which they drew up and signed, electing their own officers, and binding themselves to work together for their common Christian faith and their common good. From this simple mutual agreement, took form the first American Commonwealth, the beginning "of government of the people, by the people, for the people." This document, establishing the Pilgrims' priorities, read as follows:

THE COMPACT

In the Name of God, Amen. We, whose names are underwritten, the loyal subjects of our dread sovereign Lord King James, by the grace of God, of Great Britain, France and Ireland King, defender of the faith, etc., having undertaken, for the glory of God, and advancement of the Christian faith, and honor of our king and country, a voyage to plant the first colony in the northern parts of Virginia, do, by these presents, solemnly and mutually, in the presence of God and one of another, covenant and combine ourselves together into a civil body politic, for our better ordering and preservation, and furtherance of the ends aforesaid; and by virtue hereof to enact, constitute and frame such just and equal laws, ordinances, acts, constitutions, and offices, from time to time, as shall be thought most meet and convenient for the general good of the colony; unto which we promise all due submission and obedience. In witness whereof we have hereunder subscribed our names at Cape Cod the 11 of November, in the year of the reign of our sovereign lord, King James of England, France, and Ireland and the eighteenth, and of Scotland the fifty-fourth, Anno Dom. 1620.[4]

It had been a difficult journey. Bradford tells us that, of the 103 Mayflower Pilgrim disembarking passengers, 51 of these died during the first New England winter. However, this stalwart band of settlers who had braved the dangerous seas and inhospitable New England shores, to live their lives in harmony with God's Holy Scriptures, persevered in prayer, obedience and praise to Almighty God.

Above: "Faith"—The Monument to our Forefathers, Plymouth, Massachusetts. Courtesy of Pilgrim Society. Below: "Morality" holding the Ten Commandments in her left hand and the Scroll of the book of Revelation in her right.

Having devoted most of his book to the origins of the Pilgrims, Bradford continued his history, giving brief highlights of life in Plymouth Plantation.

This priceless document, *Of Plimoth Plantation*, was lost for many years to America, until in 1858, the Reverend Dr. John Waddington, having borrowed the manuscript from Fulham, England, showed it to an audience in Southwark, saying:

> So far as we know, not a person now living in the land of the Pilgrims has ever seen this manuscript. It has been kept at Fulham among the papers of no use to the See. It is not in the catalogue of the library, and probably is not reckoned in any inventory of the property. No one can tell how it came to Fulham.[5]

A March 25, 1897 article which appeared in the *London Times*, commits the manuscript "to his Excellency, the American Ambassador, for safe transmission to the President and Senate of the United States, upon such conditions and security as the court may determine." It is now a jealously cherished and guarded item of our American Christian heritage, at Plymouth, Massachusetts.

National Monument to the Forefathers

There are many outstanding monuments and memorials in Plymouth which glorify God. In stone, marble, granite and bronze, they relate a heroic Christian past, worthy to be passed down to succeeding generations of Americans, vibrantly exuding the gospel message of eternal life, the Pilgrims' main concern.

The predominant and most impressive of these is the National Monument to the Forefathers. A poem read at the dedication of this monument on August 1, 1889, reads thus:

> This Monument, where Virtue,
> Courage, Law and Learning sit
> Calm Faith, above them, grasping Holy Writ;
> White hand upraised o'er beauteous trusting eyes, and pleading finger pointing to the skies.
> —John Boyle O'Reilley.

Towering high in its majestic splendor, the central figure of the monument is *Faith*. She stands upon a main pedestal, one foot resting upon a replica of Plymouth Rock, and holds an open Bible in her left hand. Her right hand points heavenward. The symbolism is trust in God and His unfailing words, written down for us in the Bible.

Four smaller, seated figures represent the Christian values and principles promulgated by the Pilgrims themselves. They are *Morality*, *Law*, *Education* and *Liberty*.

Morality holds the Ten Commandments in her left hand and the scroll of Revelation—the last book of the Bible, in the right. She is flanked by an Old Testament *Prophet* on one side, and the *Evangelists* on the other.

Law is tempered with *Justice* on the one hand, and *Mercy* on the other.

Education is represented with the *Wisdom of maturity* on one side and *Youth following Experience* on the other.

Liberty is accompanied by *Peace* on one side and the *Overthrow of Tyranny* on the opposite side.

The main pedestal has four polished façades. Two of these bear the names of the Mayflower Pilgrims, while another bears the inscription "National Monument to the Forefathers. Erected by a grateful people in remembrance of their labors, sacrifices and sufferings for the cause of Civil and Religious Liberty." The upper half of the fourth panel was, in June, 1989, inscribed with the moving words from William Bradford's account *Of Plimouth Plantation*, found in the dedication to this book.

This inspiring statue is made of Maine granite. Its cornerstone was laid on August 1, 1859. Designed by Hammatt Billings, her height is 81 feet from the ground to the top of her head. The total weight of the National Monument to our Forefathers is 180 tons.

Burial Hill

The most striking monument at Burial Hill is that to Governor William Bradford. A marble obelisk marks his grave, with a Latin inscription bearing the phrase: "What our fathers with so much difficulty attained, do not basely relinquish."

The inscription on the south side reads: "H.I. William Brad-ford of Austerfield, Yorkshire, England. Was the son of William and Alice Bradford. He was Governor of Plymouth Colony from 1621 to 1633; 1635 to 1637; 1639 to 1643; 1645 to 1657."

An inscription to the north side follows: "Under this stone rest the ashes of William Bradford, a zealous puritan and sincere Chris-tian Governor of Plymouth Colony from 1621 to 1657, (the year he died) aged 69, except 5 years, which he declined."

Since Bradford was a student of Old Testament Hebrew, it is appropriate that a Hebrew inscription, beautifully reiterating his life, is engraved upon his tombstone: "Let the right hand of the Lord awake."

Other Memorials

A radiant stained-glass window in First Church, Plymouth, depicts John Robinson delivering his Farewell sermon to the Pil-grims before their departure from Holland.

Not far from Plymouth Rock, another moving statue is that of a Pilgrim woman standing next to a tall granite fountain. She por-trays the courage and Christian virtues exemplified by Pilgrim wives, who stood firm in their faith, withstanding great trials and tribulations for the cause of the gospel. She holds a Bible in her right hand. An inscription on the back of the fountain reads: "They brought up their families in sturdy virtue and a living faith in God without which nations perish."

A moving and inspirational painting entitled: *Thanksgiving— And so instead of famine God gave them plenty*, graphically portrays the origins and true significance of America's present-day "thanks-giving" celebration. The original can be seen in Pilgrim Hall, Ply-mouth, Massachusetts.

In spite of this great weight of evidence pertaining to the Christian origins of our nation and the Pilgrims' stalwart faith and trust in Almighty God and His Son, Jesus Christ, it is once again flabbergasting to read current historical accounts of the Mayflow-er Pilgrims and Plymouth Colony. Some of these are excerpted below, as follows:

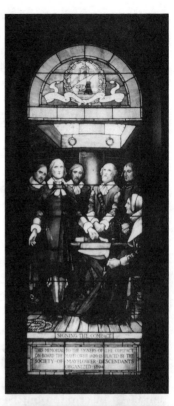

Stained-glass windows in First Church, Plymouth Massachusetts. Above: The Pilgrims signing the *Mayflower Compact* in a cabin of the Mayflower before disembarking on American soil, November 1620. Below: Pastor John Robinson's farewell sermon to the 1620 Pilgrims at Delft Haven, Holland.

Influence and Reputation of William Bradford as an Author
I The Genesis of a Myth

. . . A myth was early created involving the settlement of Plymouth; and, rightly or wrongly, the myth has not been totally banished from the national consciousness, despite the strenuous and salutary efforts in the twentieth century of numerous debunkers or "realists" . . . As a result, the elementary-school version of the Plymouth story, centering about the first Thanksgiving Day and drawing a romantic aura from Longfellow's wholly fictional "The Courtship of Miles Standish," has been undermined, and rightly so. We now regard the Pilgrims more as human beings who enjoyed their beer and stronger drink, who were guilty at times of greediness, who occasionally cheated one another, and who were not always kindly disposed toward the Indians. In fact the humanized version of the settlement and early years of Plymouth is precisely the one to be found in *Of Plimmoth Plantation*, and the idealized one may be traced to such users and revisers of Bradford's manuscript as Nathaniel Morton and especially, Cotton Mather—persons who were even more intent than Bradford on proving that the Pilgrims, along with the other Puritans, were God's people. . . . [6]

And again:

. . . With Mather's effusion, the legend of Plymouth as a colony based solely on a spiritual foundation became firmly established in American folklore. But the seed of the legend was obviously planted by Bradford, who, as leader of a band of seekers of a New Canaan, was soon being compared to Moses, most notably so by Cotton Mather.[7]

And another account:

A strong wind pushed the "Mayflower" across the ocean, and as they sailed it grew stronger. Rain swept across the deck in sheets. The ship tossed up and down. The passengers had to crowd into the little cabin or the dark hold. When the ship rolled, cups and dishes slid across the table and crashed on the floor. When it tossed, mountains of sea water broke over the deck. The boards in the cabin ceiling worked loose. Cold water poured down on William and Dorothy and the other passengers. Surely the ship could never live through such a storm . . .

"See!" William Bradford helped Dorothy to the rail. She had been sick like most of the passengers. She was still too weak to stand alone. "There it is—our new home. America! We'll be ashore soon, then you'll feel better."

But it was another month before the Pilgrims found a place to settle. First the "Mayflower" anchored off the end of Cape Cod. For days William Bradford and Miles Standish and the other leaders explored the land. They found fresh water. They found corn buried by the Indians. They exchanged shots with Indians.

One day while William Bradford was marching through the woods he walked straight into an Indian deer trap. It caught him by the leg and left him hanging up in a tree head down until Miles Standish cut him loose. Still they found no place that looked good . . . On Christmas Day, twenty men went ashore to begin the building of Plymouth. All the rest stayed aboard the "Mayflower," a mile and a half out in the harbor.

The Pilgrims didn't believe in celebrating Christmas, except by working harder than usual. But then the weather grew so bad they couldn't work at all.

At last they put up a few little buildings. The walls were made of twigs and mud. The roofs were thatched. Little by little as buildings were finished, families came ashore to live in them. . . . William Bradford nearly died too. When he recovered, they made him governor. . . . [8]

The above account depicts the elements, the crashing of table utensils upon the floor, the sickness of Mrs. Bradford on board ship, the exploration of the new land by Bradford and Standish, an encounter with the Indians, Bradford's dilemma in a tree, work undertaken on Christmas Day and the putting up of buildings. The Pilgrims' sustaining faith, their zeal and love of God, has been totally eliminated in the above narrative. This excerpted quote from a recent history book on Bradford and the Pilgrims shows how Christianity has been virtually extracted from their lives.

Another contemporary book writes in a fictional conversational style, relating a dialogue between William Bradford and other members of the Pilgrim band, such as Edward Winslow, as follows:

> William Bradford returned to his chair and leaned forward toward his friend. "America," he said, "is a land of promise. Don't you agree?" "The colonists in Virginia have not found it so," Edward answered. "Only a few of them remain alive." "But we will go as more than colonists for England," William said. "We will go as one large family who seeks a good life for one another. We will get away from the temptations and wars of the old world. Like pilgrims, we will begin a new kind of life in a new world. . . ." Edward seemed surprised. "You sound as though the congregation had already made a decision to go." William Bradford smiled. "I do get excited when I think of such an adventure," he said. "To cross the ocean. To walk over vast lands and forests unpeopled except by a few savages. We are holding a meeting next week to talk about leaving Holland for America. Would you come too, Edward, if we decide to go?" "I'd like to come to the meeting," Edward said . . . The men said that great sums of money would be needed for a ship, and for supplies and necessities to begin life in a wilderness country where there was no place to buy anything. "We have thought of that," Elder Brewster said. "If we vote to go, we will send two trusted men to England to borrow money from certain companies which were formed by men to invest in the new world, where they hope to make a profit from furs and gold. . . ."[9]

This account majors on the good life, departure from the temptations and wars of the old world, a great adventure, large sums of money, buying commodities, borrowing money, investing in the New World and making a profit from furs and gold. This is alien to Bradford's own account which emphasizes the spiritual dimension of their voyage.

Plimoth Plantation

Plimoth Plantation, in Plymouth, Massachusetts, is a reenactment of the first settlement founded by Governor William Bradford, Pilgrim father, and his band of Christian followers. My visit to this national historic site, on September 4, 1989, disclosed the following:

The Plimoth Plantation Visitors' Guide literature concentrates upon externals—the dress, costumes, crafts, dwellings, manners, dialect, 17th-century style of furniture and "world view" of the English colonists and the Wampanoag Indian tribe, leaving out the true identity of Plimoth Plantation: the quest of the Pilgrim fathers and their followers for biblical freedom in America. They had braved the hazardous ocean for the cause of gospel truth—away from religious persecution by the established state church in England—in order to establish Plimoth Colony. The whole concept and meaning of Plimoth Plantation is entirely by-passed, leaving out the Pilgrims' exemplary day-to-day Christian lives, culture and manner of worship, together with their zeal to evangelize the Indians.

Their education programs offer "classroom visits, on-site workshops and educational resources" of the above vintage, which further strengthens my premise that foremost American historic sites and shrines are being powerfully used in a classroom format, to teach millions of students history that has been poured into a secular mold; in this case devoid of Bradford's scriptural emphasis.

To reach Plimoth Plantation, one has to enter through a building which now serves as a thoroughfare for all tourists entering and exiting this sacred site. No markers, plaques or literature within or without the structure indicated its true identity—that of the *Meeting House*, or place of worship, which was the beacon and center of life for these Pilgrims, who had risked their lives to abide by God's Words. Pew benches were pushed to either side, being used as a waiting room. The pulpit was in the shade, to the left as one walked through, and hardly decipherable, with no plaque or informative historic literature explaining its great value and significance in the daily life of the Pilgrims at Plimoth Plantation.

After the harvest crops were gathered in November, 1623, it was of this very Meeting House that Governor William Bradford spoke when he ordered that: "All ye Pilgrims with your wives and little ones, do gather at the Meeting House, on the hill, . . . there to listen to the pastor, and render thanksgiving to the Almighty God for all His blessings."[10]

Historic Reenactment

The Plimoth Plantation historic reenactment of the 1621 Pilgrims is alien to the true history of these Christians and their lives of cleanliness, godliness and obedience to the Word of God; as borne out by the original manuscript accounts of this settlement. Part of the collection at the Library of Congress, is a book entitled *Pilgrim Possessions as told by their Wills and Inventories,* by Richard Briggs Bailey. It factually identifies the items owned by the Plimoth settlers. Under the subtitle *Table Utensils,* it states:

> A considerable amount of pewter appears. Pewter probably was highly regarded as the chief prize of many a household, kept highly polished to make a proud display. Bottles, cups, flagons, platters, pots, salts and vessels of pewter are found among the table utensils mentioned.[11]

Pewter used in abundance in the 17th century denoted nobility in daily living. This is contrary to the actual impression given in the reenactment of these Pilgrims' homes and customs at Plimoth Plantation.

In the same publication under the subtitle *Furniture,* numerous chairs, chair tables, oak chests, cupboards, tables, carpets and boxes are listed; "chests, trunks and boxes were all necessary pieces of furniture in the early colonial home."[12]

A further inventory on Pilgrims' *Clothing* lists numerous caps, cloaks, coats, bands, boots and breeches for the gentlemen; bonnets, caps, ribbons, lace and clothes of distinction being listed for the women. This negates the impression given at Plimoth Plantation that the Pilgrim fathers and their families experienced a subsistence-level existence, similar to that of peasant settlements. Their Wills and Inventories denote gentility and a simple, but gracious, and godly way of life.[13]

Under a further subheading entitled: *Bedding,* a profusion of beds, bed upholstery, featherbeds and bolsters, curtains, bedspreads, blankets (of different colors), rugs, valances, sheets and warming pans find their place. The following is quoted from the text:

> . . . for warmth, two or three blankets and or rugs of different colors would be used, as well as a set of curtains. The bedstead

probably had a laced bedcord to provide support for the feather beds. It was of simple construction with a moderately high headboard. It might have drapery hung about it, so that during the day, with the curtains pulled loosely back and the best coverlet carefully smoothed over the bedding, a handsome focal point was achieved. . . . Every bed had sheets as well as blankets, the latter being of various colors: red, blue, yellow and white. Here is the first evidence against the cold, colorless Pilgrims of so many history books. Pillows were in abundance with plenty of pillowcases to go with them.[14]

Numerous Bibles and Psalmbooks are listed for each Pilgrim home:

The Bible was the Geneva Bible of 1560, while the Psalmbook was Henry Aintworth's Book of Psalms, Englished both in prose and meter, first published in Amsterdam in 1612. The Psalmbook furnished the material for the Pilgrims' Hymns, sung without accompaniment or musical notation.[15]

The Bible, together with many other Christian works, is listed in every Pilgrim household, showing indisputably that their lives revolved around the Word of God and its teachings. This is borne out by Governor William Bradford's scriptural account: *Of Plimoth Plantation*.

Of further interest is the godliness exemplified in the Last Will and Testament of William Palmer, Pilgrim, dated 7 November, 1637:

Money: Next my debts being payd I would have myne Executors to give somewhat to Stephen Tracy and somewhat towards the Meetinghouse at Plymouth, also I would have yeong Rowly to be placed with Mr. Partridge that hee might bee brought up in the feare of God, and to that end if his father suffer it I give Mr. Partridge five pounds. And if in case my sonne Henry or daughter Bridgitt be liveing if they demand it, I give them fourty shillings a peece if they be liveing . . .

Miscellaneous: My desire is that my estate consisting of land, houseing goods, chattells &c mooveables as my Executors

aforesaid shall thinke meete to give her (his wife) for her present comfort . . .'[16]

The way that Plimoth Plantation currently reenacts the
lifestyle of these Pilgrims is clearly false. It is also dangerous in
terms of a nation's foundational Christian history being wrongly
interpreted and passed down to succeeding generations of impres-
sionable American youth. For example:

William Bradford's House:

A visit to Governor William Bradford's one-room house disclosed no bedclothes, sheets or blankets upon his bed. When questioning this unusual condition at 4 p.m. on a sunny Monday afternoon, his costumed wife replied that they were outside, on the
front fence, drying. I commented upon the old four-poster bed, asking whether it was Bradford's original bed, upon which his wife
quickly replied: "It is *my* bed, I brought it with me from England."
The floors were dirty and unswept; the furniture dusty. Unpleasant
odors diffused throughout the house, while the bleating of sheep
could be heard continually.

The above reenactment of William Bradford's home and family life reminded the visitor of a peasant settlement. This is a far cry
from the godliness, cleanliness and orderliness of the homes kept by
our Pilgrim fathers and their families.

Elder Brewster's House:

Upon entering Elder Brewster's house, the visitor was struck
by a pungent odor of dead fish. A glance around the one-roomed
house disclosed the head of a dead fish lying in a bowl upon a side
table. I asked Brewster's wife whether it was, indeed, a dead fish.
"Oh yes," she replied, "it's been there for two days!" Bedspreads
and eiderdowns lay crumpled up against a wall. The floors were
dirty; the beds unmade; bedclothes unkempt, worn, torn and
disheveled. No bedspreads covered the beds. Elder Brewster's
costumed wife told me that seven people lived and slept in the one-
room house. The parents slept in a four-poster bed; Elder Brewster
and his wife slept upon the crumpled-up eiderdown, which was
pulled out and spread upon the floor at night; their two sons slept

on another eiderdown spread out in the center of the room, while their daughter slept at the feet of Elder Brewster and his wife.

Quite in keeping with this false portrayal of the Pilgrims, is a Plimoth Plantation reenactment in book form, entitled: *The First Thanksgiving Feast*, a 1984 publication,[17] which acknowledges dependence on the Plimoth Plantation staff for the interpretation and understanding of the Pilgrims' lives.

The Introduction to *The First Thanksgiving Feast* claims that it is based on the firsthand historical accounts: *Of Plimoth Plantation* and *Mourt's Relation*.

Unfortunately, there are a number of serious flaws in this reenactment of the foundational history of Plymouth Plantation. Straw farm hats are worn by the Pilgrim woman, as depicted throughout the book's copious photography. This is a contradiction to the factual account of *Pilgrim Possessions as told by their Wills and Inventories*. Straw farm hats were never a part of the ladies' apparel.

The introductory section to this book states:

> In September, 1620, a sturdy ship called the Mayflower left Plymouth, England with 102 passengers aboard. Half of these men, women and children were Separatists, so called because they had broken away from the national Church of England to worship in their own way. The others were members of the Church of England who were looking for greater economic opportunity in the New World. In November, the Mayflower arrived at Cape Cod in New England. The passengers, later known as the Pilgrims, decided to establish a permanent home there. The Separatists called themselves "saints" and referred to others as "strangers" . . .

Throughout the body of the text of this book, John Alden, Peter Brown, George Soule, Miles Standish and Richard Warren are termed "Strangers." However, these five men were among the 41 signers of this original Christian document; "a civil body politick under God for the furtherance of the Christian faith." Stephen Hopkins' wife, Elizabeth, and John Billington's wife, Eleanor, are also termed "Strangers" in the text of this book. These two Pilgrim men, however, were also signers of the *Mayflower Compact*, incorporating their wives and children in its terms, and thereby establishing themselves as a *Christian Pilgrim Colony*.

The author of the book, *The First Thanksgiving Feast*, acknowledges that the dialogue of her book is fictional. However, it appears that the fiction does not stop with the dialogue. For example, in the section depicting general recreation of the Pilgrims, there is an outlandish account of pillow-fighting among the Pilgrim women, which certainly is not found in either *Of Plimoth Plantation* or *Mourt's Relation*. Following is a quote:

> . . . Pillow pushing was a favorite of the children. Straddling a log, high off the ground, two young women pounded away with pillows until one or the other fell off. "Tis very good for exercising the muscles," one of the Pilgrim men shouted. . . . A group of men and women engaged in a tug of war. "Come Mistresses, try your strength," the men beckoned. "Are ye ready?" shouted the leader. "Are ye set? Gooooooo." There were grunts and giggles and then cheers as one side finally pulled the other over the line. It was a sight to behold, with men and women tumbling about on the ground.[18]

Photographs accompanying the above text depict the Pilgrim women engaging in pillow fights, one of these women lying on her back on the ground with her leg in the air.

Being appalled at these grievous untruths of this reenactment of the lives and activities at Plimoth Plantation, I wish to quote excerpts from the original text *Of Plimoth Plantation* by William Bradford and *Mourt's Relation* formerly entitled *A Relation or Journal of the English Plantation settled at Plymouth, 1622* for the reader to compare America's true, 1621 history with the above rewritten account.

Mourt's Relation:

This book, attributed to Bradford or Winslow, begins with the author's statement that the Pilgrims' foremost desire was to carry the gospel of Christ into these foreign parts, among a people which as yet had no knowledge or taste of God. Once again it is clear that the furtherance of the gospel was a primary goal of these Pilgrim Fathers.

The body of *Mourt's Relation* calls for the Scriptures as the voice and Word of God guiding and directing their every action. The author likens this Pilgrim band to God's people in the Old Testament being given the promised land. He further explains the true significance of the biblical terms "strangers" and "pilgrims" for God's people as follows:

> ... But now the ordinary examples and precepts of the Scriptures, reasonably and rightly understood and applied, must be the voice and word that must call us, press us, and direct us in every action. Neither is there any land or possession now, like unto the possession which the Jews had in Canaan, being legally holy and appropriated unto a holy people, the seed of Abraham, in which they dwelt securely and had their days prolonged, it being by an immediate voice said, that he (the Lord) gave it them as a land of rest after their weary travels, and a type of eternal rest in heaven but now there is no land of that sanctimony, no land so appropriated, none typical, much less any that can be said to be given of God to any nation as was Canaan, which they and their seed must dwell in, till God sendeth upon them sword or captivity. But now we are all in all places strangers and pilgrims, travellers and sojourners, most properly, having no dwelling but in this earthen tabernacle; our dwelling is but a wandering, and our abiding but as a fleeting, and in a word our home is nowhere, but in the heavens, in that house not made with hands, whose maker and builder is God, and to which all ascend that love the coming of our Lord Jesus. (II Cor. 5:1,2,3.) ... [19]

Bradford's overriding theme throughout *Of Plimoth Plantation* is that of God's immeasurable grace and His guiding hand upon the lives and endeavors of the Pilgrim settlers. *Of Plimoth Plantation*:

> ... What could now sustain them but ye spirite of God and His grace? May not and ought not the children of these fathers rightly say: "Our fathers were Englishmen which came over this great ocean and were ready to perish in this wilderness; (Deut. 26:5,7) but they cried unto ye Lord, and he heard their voyce, and looked on their adversitie, etc. Let them therefore praise ye Lord, because He is good, and his mercies endure forever (107 Psalm v. 1,2,4,5,8)." Yea, let them which have been redeemed of the Lord show how he hath delivered them

from ye hand of ye oppressour. When they wandered in ye desert wilderness out of ye way, and found no citie to dwell in, both hungrie and thirstie, their sowle was overwhelmed in them. Let them confess before ye Lord his loving kindnes and his wonderfull works before ye sons of men . . . [20]

and

. . . Thus it pleased God to vanquish their enemies and give them deliverance; and by his spetiall providence, so to dispose that not any one of them were either hurte, or hitt, though their arrows came close by them, and on every side of them, and sundry of their coats, which hunge up in ye barricade, were shot throw and throw. Afterwards they gave God sollamne thanks and praise for their deliverance. . . . [21]

and

. . . and thus they found ye Lord to be with them in all their ways and to bless their outgoings and their incomings for which let his holy name have ye praise for ever to all posteri-tie . . . [22]

Further to these original documents on the mind-set and value-system of the 1620 Pilgrims at Plimoth Plantation, what does the term "Pilgrim fathers" really mean? Who were these people whose lives and deeds so thoroughly influenced and permeated the entire course of America's history? Quoting from a publication of the Colonial Society of Massachusetts, reprinted under the title *The Term Pilgrim Fathers*, we read that President Roosevelt, in his August 20, 1907 address commemorating the landing of the Mayflower Pilgrims, said:

The coming hither of the Pilgrims 300 years ago, followed in far larger numbers by their sterner kinsmen, the Puritans, shaped the destinies of this Continent, and therefore pro-foundly affected the destiny of the whole world. . . . [23]

William Penn's leatherbound Bible and Psalter. Penn Mutual Collection, Philadelphia. Photo by John W. Wrigley.

(iii) William Penn—Separation of Church and (from Interference by) the State

> Pennsylvania may well be proud of such a founder and law-giver as William Penn, and an obligation be felt by her enlightened citizens to cherish by commemorations of his exalted philanthropy and his beneficient institutions, their expanding influence in the cause of civil and religious liberty.
>
> James Madison,
> Fourth U.S. President, 1826[1]

William Penn was an English nobleman whose father, Admiral Penn, aspired to a great military career for his son. At age 22, however, Penn was converted from Atheism to Christianity after hearing Thomas Loe's famous sermon: "The Sandy Foundation Shaken." Young William joined the Friends Society of Quakers, and found himself imprisoned three times for preaching the Word of God. While serving a nine-month term in the Tower of London, Penn dreamed of starting a colony in the new world, where biblical truth could be sought, free from persecution. In 1681, he arrived with his followers on board the ship "Welcome," founding shortly thereafter "Philadelphia, City of Brotherly Love." His leather-bound Bible and Psalter, which accompanied him, is in the Penn Mutual Collection, opposite Independence Hall. On the title page to his Book of Psalms, Penn had written:

> Set forth and allowed to be sung in all churches, of all the people together, before and after morning and evening prayer, and moreover in private houses for their godly solace and comfort, laying apart all ungodly songs and ballads: which tend only to the nourishing of vice and corrupting of youth.[2]

It is interesting to note that in this Latin Bible, the section which is the most underlined is the Book of Exodus, which tells about the Israelites' escape from Egypt. This is a point of significance, in view of the English Quaker exodus to Pennsylvania, likening their removal to America with that of the Israelites' deliverance from bondage and slavery. Penn's desire for freedom extended to all persons, as is shown in this letter he sent ahead to the Indians in the area. It reads:

37

My Friends:
There is one great God and Power that hath made the world and all things therein, to whom you and I and all people owe their being and well-being, and to whom you and I must one day give an account, for all that we doe in the world; This great God hath written His law in our hearts by which we are taught and commanded to love and help and doe good to one another and not to doe harm and mischief one unto another . . . I shall shortly come to you myself at which time we may more freely and largely confer and discourse of these matters. Receive those presents and tokens which I have sent to you as a testimony to my goodwill to you and my resolution to live justly, peaceably and friendly with you.
I am, your loving friend, William Penn.[3]

The world-renowned painting by Quaker Benjamin West, "Penn's Treaty With the Indians," which is on permanent exhibition at the Pennsylvania Academy of Fine Arts in Philadelphia, celebrates Penn's excellent relationship with the Indians, which was never marred by war during his reign as governor of Pennsylvania.

William Penn's father, Admiral Penn, had transferred to his son the tract of land now known as Pennsylvania (Penn's Woods) in America, which had been given to him by the Crown of England. This was in return for exemplary service to His Majesty the King.[4] William Penn's Christian caliber and integrity, however, caused him to buy the land from the Indians, rather than take it. His famed 1682 treaty with the Indians sealed the agreement. It is graphically memorialized in sculpture and in a frieze painting within the main rotunda of the U.S. Capitol, showing William Penn's biblical approach to life.

In light of the above evidence, it would seem strange that this crucial epic of America's history has been rewritten, depicting William Penn as an entrepreneur, a salesman and a shrewd advertising campaigner. Following is an example:

Penny Wise and Pound Foolish:

. . . Few salesmen in the seventeenth century could match William Penn. He persuaded the cynical and nearly bankrupt Charles II to grant him 45,000 square miles of prime American real estate; he persuaded about six hundred investors to buy

William Penn's letter to the Indians. London, August 18, 1681. The Historical Society of Pennsylvania.

Benjamin West's famed painting: "Penn's Treaty with the Indians." Courtesy of the Pennsylvania Academy of Fine Arts, Philadelphia.

William Penn's original Charter of Privileges. Courtesy of the American Philosophical Society, Philadelphia. (Continued on page 42.)

William Penn's original Charter of Privileges.

shares in this new colony; and he persuaded about four thousand people to join him in emigrating to Pennsylvania. Penn's
advertising campaign was the most effective English colonial recruitment drive since the Puritans had founded Massachusetts half a century before . . . It is also apparent that the
Quaker founder's combination of entrepreneurial resource-
fulness, recklessness, and negligence in the 1680s were long-
established traits . . . [5]

In formulating his government, the first Constitution to Penn's
Fundamental Constitutions of Pennsylvania clearly enunciates the
foundations of the colony as being Christian:

I Constitution

Considering that it is impossible that any People or Government should ever prosper, where men render not unto God,
that which is Gods, as well as to Caesar, that which is Caesars;
and also perceiveing that disorders and Mischiefs that attend
those places where force in matters of faith and worship, and
seriously reflecting upon the tenure of the new and Spirituall
Government, and that both Christ did not use force and that he
did expressly forbid it in his holy Religion, as also that the Testimony of his blessed Messengers was, that the weapons of the
Christian warfare were not Carnall but Spirituall; And further
weighing that this unpeopled Country can never be planted if
there be not due encouragement given to Sober people of all
sorts to plant, and that they will not esteem any thing a sufficient encouragement where they are not assured but that
after all the Hazards of the Sea, and the troubles of a Wilderness, the Labour of their hands and Sweet of their browes
may be made the forfeit of their Conscience, and they and their
wives and Children ruin'd because they worship god in some
different way from that which may be more generally owned.
Therefore, in reverrence to God the Father of lights and Spir-
its the Author as well as object of all divine knowledge, faith
and worship, I do hereby declare for me and myn and establish it for the first fundamental of the Government of my
Country that every Person that does or shall reside therein
shall have and enjoy the Free Possession of his or her faith and
exercise of worship towards God, in such way and manner As
every Person shall in Conscience believe is most acceptable to

God and so long as every such Person useth not this Christian liberty to Licentiousness, that is to say to speak loosely and prophainly of God Christ or Religion, or to Committ any evil in their Conversation, he or she shall be protected in the enjoyment of the aforesaid Christian liberty by the civill Magistrate (very good).

From William Penn's well-known "Frame of Government" come these words of wisdom:

That all persons . . . having children . . . shall cause such to be instructed in reading and writing, so that they may be able to read the Scriptures and to write by the time they attain to 12 years of age.

In 1701, Penn issued a *Charter of Privileges* in which he stressed the importance of Freedom of Conscience. He stated:

Almighty God being the only Lord of Conscience . . . and Author as well as object of all Divine Knowledge, faith and worship, who only doth enlighten the minds and persuade and convince the understandings of people, I do hereby grant and declare: that no person or persons, inhabiting in this province or territory who shall confess and acknowledge our Almighty God and Creator, Upholder and Ruler of the world; and profess Him or themselves obliged to live quietly under civil government, shall be in any case molested or prejudiced in his or her person or estate . . . And that all persons who also profess to believe in Jesus Christ, the Savior of the World, shall be capable to serve this government in any capacity, both legislatively or executively.[6]

William Penn's sermons are profound and stirring, lifting up hearts and kindling souls to great heights of spiritual worship. His dynamic sermon entitled, "A summons or call to Christendom—In an earnest expostulation with her to prepare for the Great and Notable Day of the Lord that is at the Door," is alive with the Holy Spirit's pleading for repentance and spiritual growth among believers:

. . . O Christendom! Thou has long sat as Queen that should never know sorrow; great have been thy pretences, and large thy profession of God, Christ, Spirit and Scriptures; come, let me expostulate with thee and thy children in the fear and presence of Him that shall bring every word and work to judgment. God is pure, and the pure in heart only see Him. Now, are you pure? Do you see Him? God is spirit, and none can worship Him aright but such as come to His spirit, and obey it. Do you so? Christ is the gift of God, have you received Him into your hearts? If not, you are not true Christians. The spirit of truth leadeth into all truth; and the children of God are born of it, and led by it. But are you led into all the holy ways of truth, born of this eternal spirit? Then you follow not the spirit of this world; nor do your own wills, but the will of God. You profess the holy Scriptures; but what do you witness and experience? What interest have you in them? Can you set to your seal they are true by the work of the same spirit in you that gave them forth in the holy ancients? What is David's roarings and praises to thee that livest in the lusts of this world? What is Paul's and Peter's experiences to thee that walkest after the flesh?

O you that are called Christians, give ear a little unto me, for I am pressed in Spirit to write to you. Read with patience and consider my words; for behold what I have to say unto you concerneth your eternal good.

God hath so loved the world that He hath sent His only begotten Son into the world that those that believe on Him should have eternal life. And this Son is Christ Jesus, the true light that lighteth everyone coming into the world; and they that abide not in Him, the light, dwell in darkness, in sin, and are under the region and shadow of death. Yea, dead in sin and see not their own states, neither perceive the sad conditions of their own souls. They are blind to the things of God's kingdom, and insensible of true and spiritual life and motion, what it is to live to God. And in that state are alienated from God without true judgment and living knowledge; and under the curse. For in Jesus Christ, the light of the world, are hid all the treasures of wisdom and knowledge; redemption and glory; they are hid from the worldly Christian, from all that are captivated by the Spirit and lusts of the world: and whoever would see them (for therein consist the things that belong to their eternal

peace) must come to Christ Jesus the true light in their consciences, bring their deeds to Him, love Him and obey Him;
whom God hath ordained a light to lighten the Gentiles, and
for His salvation to the ends of the earth . . .

This lengthy portion of William Penn's sermon "A Call to
Christendom." shows the deep faith and true spirituality of such
men of caliber and Christian virtue who formed and fashioned
the foundational bedrock upon which this unique Republic stands.

Penn was imprisoned three times in England for preaching the
gospel. He wrote "No Cross, No Crown" during his nine-month
sojourn in the Tower of London. There he dreamed of beginning a
biblical colony in America, where he and his followers could live
godly lives, away from religious persecution.

Here are some moving passages from the founder of Pennsylvania's famed writing which further illustrate his character. It is
considered one of his best, giving insight into William Penn's own
conversion account, and the basis for his longing to establish a
Christian colony in the new world. It also explains his willingness
to risk everything, leaving family and possessions behind, in order
to serve Christ. Here are some passages from this sermon, which
illustrate his character:

> . . . Christ's cross is Christ's way to Christ's crown. This is the
> subject of the following discourse, first written during my
> confinement in the Tower of London in the year 1668, now
> reprinted with great enlargement of matter and testimonies,
> that thou mayest be won to Christ, or if won already, brought
> nearer to Him. It is a path which God in his everlasting kind-
> ness guided my feet into, in the flower of my youth, when
> about two and twenty years of age. He took me by the hand
> and led me out of the pleasures, vanities and hopes of the
> world. I have tasted of Christ's judgments, and of his mercies,
> and of the world's frowns and reproaches. I rejoice in my
> experience, and dedicate it to thy service in Christ.

> Though the knowledge and obedience of the doctrine of the
> cross of Christ be of infinite moment to the souls of men,
> being the only door to true Christianity and the path which the
> ancients ever trod to blessedness, yet it is little understood,

much neglected, and bitterly contradicted, by the vanity, superstition, and intemperance of professed Christians.

The unmortified Christian and the heathen are of the same religion, and the deity they truly worship is the god of this world. What shall we eat? What shall we drink? What shall we wear? And how shall we pass away our time? Which way may we gather and perpetuate our names and families in the earth? It is a mournful reflection, but a truth which will not be denied, that these worldly lusts fill up a great part of the study, care and conversation of Christendom. The false notion that they may be children of God while in a state of disobedience to his holy commandments, and disciples of Jesus though they revolt from his cross, and members of his true church, which is without spot or wrinkle, notwithstanding their lives are full of spots and wrinkles, is of all other deceptions upon themselves the most pernicious to their eternal condition for they are at peace in sin and under a security in their transgression . [7]

In writing the above, Penn also exposed the shallowness of the Church of England which had evolved into a form of ritualism and hierarchy, devoid of the dynamic life of Christ.

Spiritual Leader at Home

One of Penn's letters to his wife and children, while away from them in England, is here excerpted to provide insight into the length, depth and breadth of this man's love and commitment to his family in keeping with the scriptural admonitions to the spiritual leader of the home:

My dear Wife and Children:

My love, which neither sea nor land nor death itself can extinguish or lessen toward you, most endearly visits you with eternal embraces, and will abide with you forever; and may the God of my life watch over you and bless you, and do you good in this world and forever! Some things are upon my spirit to leave with you in your respective capacities, as I am to the one a husband and to the rest a father, if I should never see you more in this world.

My dear wife, remember thou wast the love of my youth, and much the joy of my life; the most beloved as well as most worthy of all my earthly comforts; and the reason of that love was more thy inward than thy outward excellencies, which yet were many. God knows, and thou knowest it, I can say it was a match of Providence's making; and God's image in us both was the first thing, and the most amiable and engaging ornament in our eyes. Now I am to leave thee, and that without knowing whether I shall ever see thee more in this world; take my counsel into thy bosom and let it dwell with thee in my stead while thou livest.

First: Let the fear of the Lord and a zeal and love to his glory dwell richly in thy heart; and thou wilt watch for good over thyself and thy dear children and family, that no rude, light, or bad thing be committed; else God will be offended, and He will repent Himself of the good He intends thee and thine.

Secondly: Be diligent in meetings for worship and business; stir up thyself and others herein; it is thy duty and place; and let meetings be kept once a day in the family to wait upon the Lord who has given us much time for ourselves. And my dearest, to make thy family matters easy to thee, divide thy time and be regular; it is easy and sweet; thy retirement will afford thee to do it; as in the morning to view the business of the house and fix it as thou desirest, seeing all be in order; that by thy counsel all may move, and to thee render an account every evening. The time for work, for walking, for meals, may be certain—at least as near as may be; and grieve not thyself with careless servants; they will disorder thee; rather pay them and let them go if they will not be better by admonitions; this is best to avoid many words, which I know wound the soul and offend the Lord.

Thirdly: Cast up thy income and see what it daily amounts to; by which thou mayest be sure to have it in thy sight and power to keep within compass; and I beseech thee to live low and sparingly till my debts are paid; and then enlarge as thou seest it convenient. Remember thy mother's example when thy father's public-spiritedness had worsted his estate, which is my

case. I know thou lovest plain things, and art averse to the
pomps of the world—a nobility natural to thee. . .

Fourthly: And now, my dearest, let me recommend to thy
care my dear children; abundantly beloved of me as the Lord's
blessings, and the sweet pledges of our mutual and endeared
affection. Above all things endeavor to breed them up in the
love and virtue, and that holy plain way of it which we have
lived in, that the world in no part of it get into my family. I had
rather they were homely than finely bred as to outward behavior; yet I love sweetness mixed with gravity and cheerfulness
tempered with sobriety. Religion in the heart leads into this
true civility, teaching men and women to be mild and cour-
teous in their behavior, an accomplishment worthy indeed of
praise. . .[8]

Regardless of the firsthand evidence of William Penn's sound
Christian character and integrity, a deluge of recent biographies and
history books attribute to this godly man negative traits which he
did not have. The following is excerpted from a 1986 book entitled
The World of William Penn:

. . . William Penn was, then, a religious rebel or a rebellious
religious. In his early years as a Friend, he was persistently con-
tentious; the rebellious and religious strains continued to be
central in his personal development until at least 1678. He
engaged others of every religious stripe, from conservative
churchmen to rather mad sectarians, in religious debate. This
took a number of forms; he wrote a great many tracts for
publication, he engaged in public and private debates, he
courted arrest in order to extend the debate into the civil
sphere. In many ways, his language was sharper and more
interesting at this state of his life than at any other—he clearly relished the quarrel with authority (or with his father) at
every turn. He became powerful in the use of invective, and he
was not very polite.[9]

In 1678, before a committee of the British House of Com-
mons, Penn pleaded for tolerance to Catholics on behalf of his
"Holy Experiment," which was to become a bastion of political,
social and religious liberty in America. By Penn's Charter of Religious Privileges (Nov. 8, 1701), Liberty of Conscience was guaran-

teed to all who acknowledged One Almighty God, the Creator, Ruler and Upholder of the world. Those who professed to believe in Christ were eligible for service in any legislative or executive capacity, provided they solemnly promised allegiance to the king, fidelity to the proprietor and governor and took the religious attests established by law. (These attests provided a difficulty for Catholics.)

The Holy Experiment Tour literature, put out by the Independence National Historic Park, Department of the Interior, begins thus:

> *The Holy Experiment* was William Penn's name for the liberal government which he established in 1681. Penn's Charter of Privileges (1701) assured religious toleration as a major principle to be maintained. This key article served as the foundation for our present religious freedoms . . .

The above quotation, contrasted with the true meaning and import of Penn's "Holy Experiment" as discussed, represents an inaccurate reinterpretation of a crucial part of America's foundational history—replete with Christianity and God-given principles. Penn did not found a "liberal" government at all, in the context of today's meaning of the word "liberal"; but rather his "Holy Experiment" was the pleading of toleration for Catholics within the sphere of his government.

St. Joseph's Church

In the heart of historic Philadelphia, not far from Independence Hall, is the site of old St. Joseph's Church, the city's first Roman Catholic Church. It was originally built in the 1700s when Catholic worship was prohibited by law in Britain and America, the present structure dating to 1838. A bronze plaque on the wrought-iron gate outside old St. Joseph's Church told the following poignant story:

> When in 1733, St. Joseph's Roman Catholic Church was founded . . . it was the only place in the entire English-speaking world where public celebration of the Mass was permitted by law.

In 1734, the Provincial Council of Pennsylvania, defending the liberty of worship granted by William Penn to this colony, successfully withstood the demand of the Governor of the Province that this church be outlawed and such liberty be suppressed. Thus was established permanently in our nation the Principle of Religious Freedom which was later embodied into the Constitution of the United States of America.

The "Principle of Religious Freedom" embodied into the Constitution of the United States, or First Amendment Clause as it was called, thus stems from William Penn's "Holy Experiment" which was his successful pleading for toleration of the Catholic mode of worship in America. Thus the original intent of Penn's "Holy Experiment" extended itself only to Protestant and Catholic liberty of worship, excluding all false philosophies and cults.

The charming red brick Georgian architecture of St. Joseph's Church reflects the beauty of its message: freedom of worship under the banner of Christianity. However, that priceless bronze plaque memorializing this fact was replaced in early 1988 by the following ambiguous sign by the Independence National Historic Park authorities:

Old St. Joseph's Roman Catholic Church founded 1733 A.D. by the Jesuit Fathers National Shrine of Religious Freedom.

Circumstances of its earliest years were such as to make it today, for Americans of all faiths, the symbol of a liberty which is precious to every citizen . . . This is liberty of conscience, the religious freedom without which no man is wholly a man. Old St. Joseph's is a symbol of this freedom in a way that is unparalleled in any other place in our land. The Senate of Pennsylvania, April 4, 1956.

The first phrase of the Independence National Historic Park's 1988 marker is ambiguous and unclear to thousands, as it has no punctuation marks. Secondly, the excerpted quote used by the Independence National Historic Park dates to a recent, April 4, 1956, statement from the Senate of Pennsylvania. This statement replaces the "Principle of Religious Freedom" with "liberty of conscience for Americans of all faiths."

Above: St Joseph's Church, Philadelphia, Pennsylvania. Wrought-iron railing upon which original plaque stood until removal, Spring 1987. Below: The ambiguous replacement of original plaque, installed Spring, 1987.

Thus, once again, in conformity with the national phenomenon of rewriting America's history, we see that the true Christian historical account of the origins of the First Amendment clause has been drastically changed to suit their new version, encompassing "all faiths," which is untrue of the original event at St. Joseph's Church.

It is a discredit to every intelligent citizen that the previous plaque—so clear and succinct in its historical account—was replaced with something as evasive, lacking in historical content and integrity to the spirit of the event (Penn's toleration of all mainline Christian denominations, including the ostracized Catholics, being one of the main factors leading to the First Amendment clause granting freedom of religion under our Constitution).

It is frightening that the Independence National Historic Park authorities oversee the most historic square mile in America, historic Philadelphia! It is just another example of our Christian heritage being reduced to insignificance and irrelevance.

Loss of an American Tradition

A unique part of rewriting William Penn's history is the breaking of an unwritten, but sacredly maintained, law.

For years the unwritten law in Philadelphia had been upheld: that no structure could be built that stood taller than the William Penn statue atop City Hall, which reached 547 feet, three and one-half inches into the sky. The tradition behind it was that William Penn, with outstretched hand, looked over the city he founded.

Unfortunately, the stipulation was brushed aside and disregarded by a business tycoon, Willard Rouse, who, in 1987, built a skyscraper resembling a hypodermic syringe towering over Penn's beloved city and dwarfing the famed statue.

Of great interest to the American public is one of the many letters to the editor of the *Philadelphia Inquirer*, this one dated January 7, 1984:

Above: William Penn atop City Hall. Courtesy of the Library Company of Philadelphia. Below: City tourism brochures: Philadelphia's new skyline. Right: Rouse Building (One Liberty Place) to left replaced William Penn atop City Hall. Left: "The Clothespin" in front of City Hall. Courtesy of Convention and Visitor's Bureau, Philadelphia.

Whether to build above Billy Penn—Don't Compete

To the Editor: "One of the world's great cities thrives without a skyscraper" (or "is under its founder's hat" or "still looks up to William Penn").

Philadelphia could boast internationally with these words, and attract new businesses, trade and tourism in the process.

Our city is blessed with magnificent layout. Horizontal and vertical space complement our character. Europeans love our scale for its humanness, in contrast to New York's concrete jungle impact.

We have tens of dozens of sizable buildings of architectural significance begging to be adapted to 1980's use. More important, we have as many sizable empty lots—within minutes of City Hall—wide open for good architects to build the most imaginative buildings in the world. Space is not a Philadelphia development problem.

Yet developers and a wavering Planning Commission blithely are considering buildings higher than Billy Penn's hat. Philadelphia's integrity is threatened.

We are the nation's fourth largest city, and we earned the status. But size is not what makes Philadelphia one of the world's great cities. Reputation, character, competitiveness and caring for people make us that. Never should Philadelphia stoop to the winless battle for height. Fred A. Barfoot, Philadelphia.[10]

Further light is thrown on the subject by this excerpted article from Philadelphia's *Daily News*, dated April 5, 1984:

You give Billy Penn high Sign in Poll

. . . Readers had been asked to call one of two numbers that recorded votes electronically from 1 P.M. Tuesday to 9 last night. One number registered those in favor of the construction of buildings taller than the top of Penn's statue on City Hall—

about four stories—and the other tallied those opposed to such construction.

The newspaper set up the two automatic answering machines on city desk on Tuesday. Reporters and editors, hardened against surprise by long experience with disaster and madness, came by to stare in fascination at the gadget—tiny lights ignited by invisible forces and tape spools spinning as if by magic—as Philadelphians rushed to record their opinions.

Of course, there were no safeguards against multiple and frivolous voting, but the results were so overwhelmingly in opposition to buildings taller than Penn's hat that a few mischievous tallies couldn't have made much difference.

The question was inspired by a proposal by Rouse Associates to put up two office towers of 60 and 50 stories in Center City, contrary to a long-standing "Gentleman's Agreement" against overshadowing Penn.

One person who is not revealing his opinion on the matter is Mayor Goode. He said yesterday he is deferring to City Council, which was taking up the subject at today's meeting.
As for the Mayor's position, he said, "I'm prepared to receive comments from the Planning Commission and then through some public process understand the issues more and then make a decision on it."

Then he doesn't have a personal view right now? "I have a personal view but I am an elected official and I will not share my personal views," the mayor replied.[11]

Another article, written by George Anastasia and William W. Sutton, Jr., comes from the *Philadelphia Inquirer*, dated April 6, 1984:

Rouse unveils plans to redraw the Skyline

Developer Willard Rouse yesterday unveiled his plans for two Center City office towers that would shatter the city's traditional 491-foot height barrier and dwarf the statue of William Penn atop the City Hall tower.

The bronze statue of Penn, 548 feet in the air, has been the focal point of Center City for 90 years, and the hat on top of Penn's head has been, by tradition, the highest spot in the city.

Rouse, head of Rouse and Associates, detailed plans for a $600 million development project at a meeting of the City Planning Commission held in the auditorium of the Free Public Library. About 300 people attended the special session set up by the commission because of the controversial nature of the Rouse proposal.

Rouse, conscious of the emotional debate his proposal has touched off, called yesterday's session "the start of a wonderful forum to make our city a better place to live and work," and said his project presented a "dilemma as well as an opportunity" . . .[12]

In the midst of fierce debate over this affront to American patriotism, Rouse plunged ahead, naming his modern creation—"One Liberty Place,"—sad counterfeit of Philadelphia's real liberty, defined as "the gift of God,"[13] by Thomas Jefferson.

Of great significance to all Americans, is William Penn's magnificent *Prayer for Philadelphia*, delivered in 1684. It appears on a plaque within City Hall itself, the building upon which his magnificent statue stands with outstretched hand over the city he loved and prayed for:

And thou, Philadelphia, the Virgin settlement of this province named before thou wert born. What love, what care, what service and what travail have there been to bring thee forth and preserve thee from such as would abuse and defile thee. O that thou mayest be kept from the evil that would overwhelm thee. That faithful to the God of thy mercies, in the Life of Righteousness, thou mayest be preserved to the end. My soul prays to God for thee, that thou mayest stand in the day of trial, that thy children may be blest of the Lord and thy people saved by His Power.[14]

"George Washington at Prayer in Valley Forge." Photo by John W. Wrigley.

(iv) George Washington—Man, or Giant among Men?

George Washington was the son of Augustine Washington and his second wife, Mary Ball. He was a direct descendant of King John of England and nine of the 25 Baron Sureties of the Magna Charta. His father died in 1743 when the boy was 11 years old. Therefore, until age 16, he lived with his half brother, Augustine on the ancestral acres in Westmoreland County, 40 miles from Fredericksburg, Virginia. Much of his education took place in the home.

At the age of 15, this exceptional young man copied in meticulous handwriting the "110 Rules of Civility and Decent Behavior in Company and Conversation."[1] These maxims were so fully exemplified in George Washington's life that biographers have regarded them as formative influences in the development of his character.

Here are some of these rules. They fall into several categories, beginning with the basics of personal grooming and advancing to the inner life of a well-rounded individual.

I Personal Grooming

5) If you cough, sneeze, sigh or yawn, do it not loud but privately; and speak not in your yawning, but put your handkerchief or hand before your face and turn aside.

15) Keep your nails clean and short, also your hands and teeth clean yet without showing any great concern for them.

II Manners in Interaction with Others

6) Sleep not when others speak, sit not when others stand, speak not when others stand, speak not when you should hold your peace, walk not on when others stop.

14) Turn not your back to others especially in speaking, jog not the table or desk on which another reads or writes, lean not upon anyone.

III Consideration and Concern for Others

18) Read no letters, books, or papers in company but when there is a necessity for the doing of it you must ask leave.

19) Let your countenance be pleasant but in serious matters somewhat grave.

IV Moral behavior

22) Shew not yourself glad at the misfortune of another though he were your enemy.

109) Let your recreations be manfull not sinfull.

V Spiritual Life

108) When you speak of God, or His attributes, let it be seriously and with reverence. Honor and obey your natural parents although they be poor.

110) Labour to keep alive in your breast that little spark of celestial fire called conscience.

With such guidelines in his everyday life, Washington was considered by all who knew him as a virtuous, humble man. In manhood we see the full fruit of the character traits that nurtured his youth. Even at the very darkest hours of his life, these did not fail him. Thus, at Valley Forge, May 2, 1778, with the Continental Army suffering from cold, lack of food, clothing and equipment, Washington could issue orders with that strength of character which earned him the loyalty and respect of his volunteer army:

> While we are zealously performing the duties of good citizens and soldiers, we certainly ought not to be inattentive to the higher duties of religion. To the distinguished character of patriot, it should be our highest glory to laud the more distinguished character of Christian. The signal instances of Providential goodness which we have experienced and which have now almost crowned our labors with complete success demand from us in a peculiar manner the warmest returns of gratitude and piety to the Supreme Author of all good. [2]

Thomas Jefferson, founding father and author of the Declaration of Independence, summarizes Washington's character as follows:

> He was incapable of fear, meeting personal dangers with the calmest unconcern. Perhaps the strongest feature in his character was prudence, never acting until every circumstance, every consideration, was maturely weighed; refraining if he saw a doubt, but, when once decided, going through with his purpose, whatever obstacles opposed. His integrity was most pure, his justice the most flexible I have ever known, no motive of interest or consanguinity, or friendship or hatred, being able to bias his decision. He was in every sense of the words, a wise, a good and a great man.[3]

Washington knew that the hand of God had been strong in shaping not only his own personal life, but that of the newly formed nation. Note the following letter he wrote on August 20, 1778 to his Virginian friend, Thomas Nelson:

> The hand of Providence has been so conspicuous in all this (the course of the war) that he must be worse than an infidel that lacks faith, and more wicked that has not gratitude to acknowledge his obligations; but it will be time enough for me to turn Preacher when my present appointment ceases.

It was not in this man's destiny to become a preacher, but as president of the United States he was able to channel that sense of gratitude to Almighty God, felt by him and his countrymen, into a national tradition, continuous and unbroken to this day. On January 1, 1795, he wrote his famed *National Thanksgiving Proclamation*:

> When we review the calamities which afflict so many other nations, the present condition of the United States affords much matter of consolation and satisfaction. Our exemption hitherto from foreign war, an increasing prospect of the continuance of that exemption, the great degree of internal tranquility we have enjoyed, the recent confirmation of that tranquility by the suppression of an insurrection* which so wan-

---

The Whisky Insurrection in Western Pennsylvania

tonly threatened it, the happy course of our public affairs in general, the unexampled prosperity of all classes of our citizens, are circumstances which peculiarly mark our situation with indications of the divine beneficence toward us. In such a state of things it is in an especial manner our duty as a people, with devout reverence and affectionate gratitude, to acknowledge our many and great obligations to Almighty God, and to implore Him to continue and confirm the blessings we experienced.

Deeply penetrated with this sentiment, I, George Washington, President of the United States, do recommend to all religious societies and denominations, and to all persons whomsoever, within the United States, to set apart and observe Thursday, the 19th day of February next, as a day of public thanksgiving and prayer, and on that day to meet together and render sincere and hearty thanks to the great Ruler of nations for the manifold and signal mercies which distinguish our lot as a nation; particularly for the possession of constitutions of government which unite and, by their union, establish liberty with order; for the preservation of our peace, foreign and domestic; for the reasonable control which has been given to a spirit of disorder in the suppression of the late insurrection, and generally for the prosperous condition of our affairs, public and private, and at the same time humbly and fervently beseech the kind Author of these blessings graciously to prolong them to us; to imprint on our hearts a deep and solemn sense of our obligations to Him for them; to teach us rightly to estimate their immense value; to preserve us from the arrogance of prosperity, and from hazarding the advantages we enjoy by delusive pursuits, to dispose us to merit the continuance of His favors by not abusing them, by our gratitude for them, and by a corresponding conduct as citizens and as men to render this country more and more a safe and propitious asylum for the unfortunate of other countries; to extend among us true and useful knowledge; to diffuse and establish habits of sobriety, order, morality and piety, and finally to impart all the blessings we possess or ask for ourselves to the whole family of mankind. In testimony whereof, I have caused the seal of the United States of America to be affixed to these presents, and signed the same with my hand. Done at the city of Philadelphia the first day of January, 1795.

(signed) George Washington

Further evidence of the Washingtons having pursued a Christian way of life is found in the library at Mount Vernon, which houses the following sacred books belonging to, and constantly used by, the first First Family of America:

The Washington family Bible (wherein is recorded the birth of George Washington)

The Book of Common Prayer (bearing Martha Washington's signature)

A concordance to the Holy Scriptures (1760)

Martha Washington's personal autographed family Bible (containing the Lewis family genealogy).[4]

It is further recorded that Martha Washington would shut herself up in her bed chamber each morning from 5 to 6 a.m. reading her Bible and meditating upon its contents, in order to begin each day on the right foot.

Martha Washington's hand autographed family Bible, on exhibition in museum on grounds of Mount Vernon, home of George and Martha Washington. Permanently removed to archives, Winter 1987.

Washington owned two family pews, numbered 28 and 29. From October 25, 1762, to February 23, 1784, Washington served as vestryman of Truro Parish. One of the civil functions of the old vestries was to oversee the needs of the poor.

In the possession of Pohick Church is one of George Washington's original Bibles. The inside cover has the following inscription in the handwriting of the subscriber and donor, who was his adopted grandson.

> Presented to Truro Parish for the use of Pohick Church, July 11, 1802. With the request that should said church cease to be appropriated to Divine worship which God forbid, and for the honor of Christianity, it is hoped will never take place. In such case I desire that the vestry will preserve this Bible as a testimony of regard from the subscriber after a residence of 19 years in the Parish.
>
> George Washington Parke Custis.

Among the treasures belonging to America's posterity are Washington's hand-autographed, three-volume Bible, which is in the safekeeping of the Rare Book Collection of our national Library of Congress, together with the original *1732-1785 Vestry Book of Pohick Church*. This *Vestry Book* contains a continuous record of every vestry from its founding in 1732 to January 23, 1785, when the old colonial church came to an end.

George Washington purchased a large, leatherbound Bible and Psalter, for use by the church. It also comprises the Book of Common Prayer. At the end of the book of Malachi, this inscription is found:

> This Bible was used in Pohick Church, Fairfax County, Virginia, when in that ancient temple which is yet in use, the "father of this country" worshipped the God of his fathers.

In the Book of Common Prayer, prayers and petitions for the King of England are crossed out and replaced with prayers for the governor of the state and local magistrates.

When in Williamsburg, Washington attended Bruton Parish Church, and when residing in Pennsylvania, he attended Christ Church of Philadelphia.

Personal Life

Another dimension of George Washington was his rich, personal life. On June 24, almost 20 years after his marriage, George Washington wrote the following intimate letter to his beloved wife, Martha. His words, "there never was a moment in my life since I first knew you, in which it [my heart] did not cleave and cling to you with the warmest affection," reveal a man of deep emotion and feeling.

> My dearest Life and Love:
> You have hurt me, I know not how much, by the insinuation in your last, that my letters to you have lately been less frequent, because I have felt less concern for you. The suspicion is most unjust—may I not add, it is most unkind! Have we lived, now almost a score of years, in the closest and dearest conjugal intimacy to so little purpose that, on an appearance only of inattention to you, and which you might have accounted for in a thousand ways more natural and more probable, you should pitch upon that single motive which alone is injurious to me? I have not, I own, wrote so often to you as I wished, and as I ought. But think of my frustration and then ask your heart, if I be without excuse. We are not, my dearest, in circumstances the most favorable to our happiness; but let us not, I beseech you, idly make them worse, by indulging suspicions and apprehensions which minds in distress are but too apt to give way to. I never was, as you have often told me, even in my better and more disengaged days, so attentive to the little punctilies of friendship, as, it may be, became me: but, my heart tells me, there never was a moment in my life since I first knew you, in which it did not cleave and cling to you with the warmest affection: and it must cease to beat, ere it can cease to wish for your happiness, above anything on earth! . . . the perpetual solicitude of your poor heart about me, is certainly highly flattering to me; yet I should be happy to be able to quiet your fears . . . I beg to be affectionately remembered to all our friends and relations; and that you will continue to believe me to be your most faithful and tender Husband,
>
> G.W.[5]

How refreshing and touching to see the manly emotion of love expressed by an influential national leader. While many in powerful positions—be it politics, business or even church—fall prey to the demands of the profession at the expense of their families, Washington maintained his love for his wife and family, keeping them in proper priority throughout his life. But it is a sad commentary on modern documentary-makers who will unabashedly insinuate that Washington married the widowed Martha for her money!

The first President of the United States was sworn into office in New York on April 30, 1789. His left hand rested upon the Bible, which had been opened between the 49th and 50th chapters of Genesis. He then kissed the Bible and reverently said: "So - help - me - God."

By this means, our first president set a precedence for succeeding inaugurations of U.S. presidents by which each president selects a Scripture of personal significance to him, and repeats "So help me God" after swearing allegiance to the Constitution.

George Washington took his second oath of office in Congress Hall in Philadelphia and in 1796 delivered his famous "Farewell Address" praying for the nation as follows:

> . . . May Heaven continue to you the choicest tokens of its beneficence: that your union and brotherly affection may be perpetual; . . . that the free Constitution, which is the work of your hands, may be sacredly maintained; that its administration in every department may be stamped with wisdom and virtue; that in fine, the happiness of the people of these states, under the auspices of liberty may be made complete by so careful a preservation and so prudent a use of this blessing as will acquire to them the glory of recommending it to the applause, the affection and adoption of every nation which is yet a stranger to it. . . . It is of infinite moment that you should properly estimate the immense value of your national union to your collective and individual happiness. The name American, which belongs to you in your national capacity, must always exult the just pride of patriotism more than any appellation derived from local discriminations. . . .

On December 14, 1799, the instrument chosen by Almighty God to found and fashion *this nation under God*, relinquished his soul into the hands of his Maker, and passed on to eternal life.

The president of William and Mary College, Bishop James Madison, delivered a famous discourse on the death of General Washington on February 22, 1800, in Bruton Parish Church, Williamsburg, Virginia. He quoted Second Timothy 4:7, "I have fought a good fight, I have finished my course, I have kept the faith."

Madison further stated:

> With the life of Washington is connected a new arena in this history of man. He seems to have been called forth by Heaven, as the instrument of establishing principles fundamental in social happiness, and which *must*, and *will* pervade the civilized world . . . David, when a youth, fought out the lion and the bear as subjects for his valour, and voluntarily joined himself to the armies of Israel, to be instructed in the arts of war. Washington fought out the warrior of the wilderness, and, at an early age, provoked his courage and his stratagems.[6]

As a legacy to all Americans, George Washington left this magnificent and moving prayer to Almighty God for his country. A framed, calligraphied copy can be found within the Washington Memorial Chapel in Valley Forge:

> Almighty God; we make our earnest prayer that Thou wilt keep the United States in Thy holy protection; that Thou wilt incline the hearts of the citizens to cultivate a spirit of subordination and obedience to government; and entertain a brotherly affection and love for one another and for their fellow citizens of the United States at large. And finally that Thou wilt most graciously be pleased to dispose us all to do justice, to love mercy, and to demean ourselves with that charity, humility and pacific temper of mind which were the characteristics of the Divine author of our blessed religion, and without a humble imitation of whose example in these things we can never hope to be a happy nation. Grant our supplication, we beseech Thee, through Jesus Christ our Lord. Amen.[7]

A letter written to Joseph Rakestraw, dated July 20, 1787, by George Washington, gives firsthand information concerning the Christian symbol crowning his beloved plantation home, Mount Vernon. He wrote ". . . I should like to have a bird (in place of the vane) with an olive branch in its mouth. . . ."[8] It is interesting that Washington selected a theme from Genesis 8 (that of Noah and the dove carrying an olive branch in its beak, signifying that the flood waters had subsided). The symbol bears the name "Dove of Peace."

Washington Memorial Chapel at Valley Forge

In 1909, Reverend W. Herbert Burk, while formulating plans for the Washington Memorial Chapel and Carillon at Valley Forge, Pennsylvania, bought from the Smithsonian Institution the tent in which Washington slept and worked at Valley Forge during the bitterly cold 1777-1778 winter. Mary Custis Lee, daughter of Robert E. Lee, loaned him $500 for the purchase. This was used as a downpayment and the rest was paid by the American people who paid 10 cents to view it on exhibition. By strange coincidence, the bankers' names were Burke and Herbert. Dr. Burk would often say laughingly, yet half ruefully too, that in the years to come people might say he cleverly paid the money to himself from the similarity of names, his name being W. Herbert Burk.

The Washington Memorial Chapel and Carillon, Valley Forge, Pennsylvania. Inside this chapel: The George Washington stained-glass window and the Martha Washington stained-glass window depicting their godly lives. Illustration: Helen Weir.

Reverend Burk spoke of Valley Forge as hallowed ground for each American:

> Surely there is no place like this for the Commemoration of the adoption of the Declaration of Independence and happy indeed is that American who can keep the Nation's Holy Day upon the hills at Valley Forge. Here, the heart must well with grateful praise. Here, Washington-like, the soul must commune with God in new and higher consecration, and make a more earnest intercession for the richest blessings upon our country, its rulers and its people.[9]

The ceiling of this moving chapel is called the *Roof of the Republic* and bears the hand-carved state seals of all the states, placed in order in which they came into the Union, starting with Delaware, overhead to the left as one enters the chapel. Keys to these seals are found in the bronze plaques embedded in the floor of the central aisle. The ceiling is supported by hand-carved angels to represent God's providence, and hand-carved pelicans in the choir to represent man's sacrifice. Dr. Burk always said that it was only through God's providence and man's sacrifice that the Republic can exist.[10]

Reverend William Herbert Burk's sermon text, delivered at the Washington Memorial Chapel, Valley Forge, Sunday July 5, 1931, was most appropriately taken from Leviticus 25:10: ". . . Proclaim liberty throughout the land unto all the inhabitants thereof."

An exact replica of the famed Liberty Bell, symbol of American independence, is to be found on the grounds of this beautiful chapel. Inscribed upon it are the words: "Justice Bell—Symbol of U.S. Constitution—Secure the Blessings of Liberty."

Stained-glass Windows

Dr. Burk's love of God and country further led him to create the magnificent stained-glass multiple lancet windows within the Washington Memorial Chapel at Valley Forge, a number of which narrate George Washington's exemplary life as a Christian. The entire wall over the main entranceway to this inspiring chapel is covered by the George Washington Window. This window consists of 36 scenes in the life of Washington, beginning in the upper left hand medallion with his baptism and ending with him reading his Bible at the close of the day at Mount Vernon. *Washington in prayer at Valley Forge* is seen in the central opening over the door, the second on the left. This window was given by the Pennsylvania State Society, Daughters of the American Revolution, as a memorial to Washington.[11] Of the window, *Peace at Eventide*, Dr. Burk writes:

> To many people Washington's Prayer at Valley Forge is the only one of which they know. They do not know that he was a man of prayer, that prayer was woven into the web and woof of the fabric of his life, that it is written in his private letters and public documents. Here in the Washington Memorial Chapel one must catch the large vision of his worship, and see him in camp and city, at church and at home, in prayer. Robert Lewis, Washington's nephew and private secretary, in 1827 told Mr. Sparks that he had accidentally witnessed his private devotions in his library, both morning and evening; that on these occasions he had seen him in a kneeling posture with a Bible open before him, and that he believed such to have been his daily practice! That must be our picture of him, the man in his closet, communing with his God. It was in that worship that he found peace at eventide, and that must be our last vision of him, kneeling in his library, the Bible spread out on the chair before him, and his hands clasped in prayer.[12]

The following account, written by the adopted grandson of General Washington, inspired Dr. Burk to design and create the stained-glass window, "Washington and his mother celebrate the Victory":

> The foreign officers were anxious to see the mother of their Chief. They had heard indistinct rumors touching her remarkable life and character, but forming their judgments from European examples, they were prepared to expect in the mother, that glitter and show which would have been attached to the parents of the old world. How were they surprised, when, leaning on the arm of her son, she entered the room, dressed in the very plain, yet becoming garb, worn by the Virginia lady of the old time. Her address always dignified and imposing, was courteous, though reserved. She received the

complimentary attentions which were paid to her without evincing the slightest elevation, and at an early hour, wishing the company much enjoyment of their pleasure, observed that it was high time for old folks to be in bed and retired leaning as before on the arm of her son.[13]

Another of these remarkable evidences of Washington's Christian conduct is recorded for posterity in the stained-glass window entitled: "Washington receives his mother's Blessing."

On Tuesday, April 14, 1789, Washington was officially notified of his election as President of the United States of America. One of his most important duties before leaving for New York was to visit his mother, who was fast coming to the close of her life. He spent the first Sunday in March with her, never to see her again. George Washington Parke Custis, George Washington's adopted grandson, wrote the following account of that last interview:

> . . . an affected scene ensued. The son feelingly remarked the ravages which a torturing disease (cancer) had made upon the aged frame of the mother, and addressed her with these words:

>> "The people, madam, have been pleased, with the most flattering unanimity, to elect me to the Chief magistracy of these United States, but before I can assume the functions of my office, I have come to bid you an affectionate farewell. So soon as the weight of public business, which must necessarily attend the outset of a new government, can be disposed of, I shall hasten to Virginia, and," (here the matron interrupted with—) "and you will see me no more; my great age, and the disease which is fast approaching my vitals, warn me that I shall not be long in this world; I trust in God that I may be somewhat prepared for the better. But go, George, fulfill the high destinies which Heaven appears to have intended for you; go, my son, and may that Heaven's and a mother's blessing be with you always."[14]

Mrs. Mary Washington died on August 5, at 82 years of age, happy in the achievements of her son and in the universal honor bestowed upon him.

Another fascinating stained-glass window created by Reverend Burk for the Washington Memorial Chapel at Valley Forge is entitled: "Washington, the Church Builder".

He describes the scene as follows:

> In 1769 the plans for Pohick Church, Truro Parish, were drawn, probably by George Washington, who was a member of the vestry and had selected the site by his own surveys. The Building Committee consisted of George Washington, William Fairfax, George Mason, Daniel McCarty and Edward Payne. The contract was given to Daniel French, Gentleman, for 877 English pounds. That the work was well done is evidenced by the endurance of the building, which for 150 years has withstood the fierce attacks of the elements, the desecration of the Civil War, and the destructiveness of indifference and neglect. George Washington superintended the building of the famous old church which ought to be dear to the heart of every loyal American. He and Lord Fairfax gave the gold leaf to enrich the interior of the sanctuary when the contract called for the lettering of the Apostles' Creed, the Ten Commandments and the Lord's Prayer in black. Washington's was the pew nearest to the communion table.[15]

A stained-glass window depicts "Washington Resigning his Commission as Commander-in-Chief of the Continental Army." This takes place in the Maryland Capitol at Annapolis. Before this event, on the morning of December 23, 1783, Washington wrote to Baron Steuben:

> This is the last letter I shall write while I continue in the service of my country. The hour of my resignation is fixed at 12 today, after which I shall become a private citizen on the banks of the Potomac . . . I consider it an indispensable duty to close this last act to my official life by commending the interest of our dearest country to the protection of Almighty God, and those who have the super-intendence of them to his holy keeping.[16]

Another poignant message is conveyed in the Washington Memorial Chapel Window entitled "Washington keeps the Fast Day." This day (June 1, 1774) was a day of fasting and prayer where the colonies appealed to God to maintain peace between Great Britain and the American Colonies, if it be His will. The window commemorates the date set for the closing of the port of Boston in order to starve that turbulent town into good behavior. On that day Washington was in Williamsburg, and he wrote in his diary, "Went to church and fasted all day." This is inscribed on the lectern of the Washington Memorial Chapel, a replica of his own handwritten notation in his diary.

The world-renowned window entitled "Washington's Prayer at Valley Forge," is the visualization of Isaac Potts' description of the great commander at prayer in the woods. It is a familiar story, and one which Ruth Anna Potts has left the following account of:

> In 1777 while the American army lay at Valley Forge, a good old Quaker by the name of Potts had occasion to pass through a thick woods near headquarters. As he traversed the dark brown forest, he heard, at a distance before him, a voice which as he advanced became more fervid and interested. Approaching with slowness and circumspection, whom should he behold in a dark bower, apparently formed for the purpose, but the Commander-in-Chief of the armies of the United Colonies on his knees in the act of devotion to the Ruler of the Universe! At the moment when Friend Potts, concealed by the trees, came up, Washington was interceding for his beloved country. With tones of gratitude that labored for adequate expression he adored that exuberant goodness which, from the depth of obscurity, had exalted him to the head of a great nation, and that nation fighting at fearful odds for all the world holds dear . . . Soon as the General had finished his devotions and had retired, Friend Potts returned to his house, and threw himself into a chair by the side of his wife. "Heigh! Isaac!" said she with tenderness, "thee seems agitated; what's the matter?" "Indeed, my dear" quoth he, "if I appear agitated 'tis no more than what I am. I have seen this day what I shall never forget. Till now I have thought that a Christian and a soldier were characters incompatible; but if George Washington be not a man of God, I am mistaken, and still more shall

I be disappointed if God do not through him perform some
great thing for this country."[17]

Today, many so-called historians are trying to discredit
George Washington's life, attacking his character, his devotion to
God, his intelligence and his moral excellence. For example, the Valley Forge Historical Society Museum, which was founded by the
godly Dr. W. Herbert Burk, its first president, now has on display
the following questionable plaque. It is located in the center of a permanent exhibit of *George Washington kneeling in Prayer:*

> Those who have studied Washington declare he did not kneel
> in prayer when he attended church services and he never
> made an emotional display of his religious beliefs, that in
> fact he kept those beliefs so subdued that no one now knows
> what they were. All the old accounts say it was (old) Isaac
> Potts. . . . But Isaac Potts was born in 1750, and hence was 27
> years old. . . . There is no evidence that Isaac Potts lived at Val-
> ley Forge in the winter of 1777-8. When Potts went home
> Weems (in whose book the legend first found wide circulation)
> says he addressed his wife thus: "Sarah, my dear Sarah; all's
> well, George Washington will yet prevail." However, Isaac
> Potts' wife was named Martha.
>
> Norristown *Times Herald,* November 4, 1932.

Traditional Philadelphians, such as Dr. and Mrs. Eugene
Jaeger, have been outraged at the above fallacy, resuscitated from
a newspaper column entitled "Up and down Montgomery County"
in a local newspaper, written 58 years ago, and cited as an authority in the *George Washington Kneeling in Prayer* exhibit at Valley
Forge.

Another fallacious plaque, exemplifying the rewriting of
America's history, is to be found to the left of this central commentary. It reads thus:

Valley Forge as a Legend

> By the mid-19th century the story of Valley Forge was a fully
> formed and popular symbol in the American popular con-
> sciousness: a symbol of perseverance, courage and patrio-
> tism. The historical reality of the Valley Forge encampment

was much more complex than this. But the symbol was some-how more majestic than fact. It was the symbol that endured. Legends supported this symbol; legends of bloody footprints in the snow; of Washington kneeling in prayer in the woods; of freezing, starving patriots enduring unprecedented hardships; of a shattered army arising transformed, its ultimate triumph assured.

Original historical accounts bear out the fact that the story of George Washington and the tattered and torn American troops' encampment at Valley Forge during the 1777–8 bitterly cold winter, was neither "a legend" nor "a popular symbol in the American popular consciousness," to quote the above plaque. It was a stark reality, its victory being wrought through George Washington's fervent prayers to Almighty God to save his countrymen from annihilation. It was for this that he labored in prayer early in the morning in the forests of Valley Forge, following the example of his Savior and Lord, Jesus Christ.

May we, as Americans, revere this memory of our first president humbly kneeling in prayer to his God and Father, to save this newly-declared independent nation from near destruction by His miraculous intervention. May we teach it to our children and our children's children, for posterity.

Rewritten History

A recent commentary on George Washington's character traits and purpose in life is here excerpted from a 1966 work entitled *Washington and Lee—A Study in the Will to Win*, by Holmes M. Alexander, as follows:

> The ruling passion of Washington's character was for accomplishment. In civil life, this passion was expressed in a myriad of business enterprises, all of which were activated for the purpose of making money—lots of money—and he prosecuted this single purpose with all the energy of his strenuous nature. In military life, the urge for accomplishment—this will to succeed—expressed itself in a hot, panting, unflagging desire for two things: promotion and victory. For him there was no such thing as second best. He demanded the ulti-

mate, the topmost, the uncompromised facts of superiority. This feeling gave him an outspoken scorn for undeserving superiors and a sulphurous temper toward insubordinate juniors. His competitive spirit caused him to dislike his business rivals and military allies, and to hate whatever enemy he happened to be fighting. Any sort of frustration was a fire that brought him to a boil, but instead of boiling over he habitually released the stored-up energy into a rectifying action. Military defeat—the greatest frustration of all—he loathed to the depth of his soul. It filled him with power to do the seemingly impossible. In the parlance of the sporting world, he was a "bad loser". He was never more dangerous in battle than after he had taken a beating. George Washington's mother was a vulgar, selfish, unlovable fool. . . .[18]

However, this is what his colleague, John Adams, said about him in his June 17, 1775, letter to his wife, Abigail, written from Philadelphia:

I can now inform you that the Congress have made choice of the modest and virtuous, the amiable, generous and brave George Washington, Esquire, to be General of the American army, and that he is to repair, as soon as possible, to the camp before Boston. This appointment will have a great effect in cementing and securing the union of these colonies. The continent is really in earnest, in defending the country. . . . [19]

Thus we see just another example of the restructuring and reinterpretation of America's founding period history—to fit a mold totally alien to the founder, the father of our nation and to our true cultural heritage.

(v) John Adams

Words cannot express the depth of emotion experienced by these colonists who struggled and sought God's direction for the young nation. The Declaration of Independence, once written, sealed their destiny. They chose the higher, nobler course. The following is excerpted from John Adams' famous speech given to Congress on July 2, 1776:

> The second day of July, 1776, will be the most memorable epoch in the history of America, to be celebrated by succeeding generations as the great anniversary festival, commemorated as the day of deliverance by solemn acts of devotion to God Almighty from one end of the Continent to the other, from this time forward forevermore. You will think me transported with enthusiasm, but I am not. I am well aware of the toil, the blood, and treasure that it will cost us to maintain this Declaration and support and defend these states; yet, through all the gloom, I can see the rays of light and glory; that the end is worth all the means; that posterity will triumph in that day's transaction, even though we shall rue it, which I trust in God we shall not.

Notice founding father John Adams' emphasis upon devotion to Jehovah God, on Independence Day celebrations* for all succeeding generations of Americans: " . . . commemorated as the day of deliverance by solemn acts of devotion to God Almighty from one end of the Continent to the other, from this day forward forevermore . . ." Take note also of his triumphal ending . . . "even though we shall rue it, which I trust in God we shall not."

The first session of Congress convened under the Articles of Confederation in Carpenters' Hall, Philadelphia, September 7, 1774. Jacob Duché, first rector of Christ Church, opened the session in prayer, reading Psalm 35 in its entirety. Of it, John Adams wrote: "I have never heard a better prayer . . . it stirred the bosom of every man present." This event is recorded in the Journals of Congress. These same Journals, meticulously kept by Secretary of Congress, Charles Thomson, enumerate grievances against the ruling power. The 10th article reads thus:

*The Declaration of Independence was proclaimed on July 2, 1776, but actually signed on July 4, 1776.

10. That the late Act of Parliament for establishing the Roman Catholic Religion and the French Laws in that extensive country now called Quebec, is dangerous in an extreme degree to the Protestant Religion and to the civil rights and liberties of all America; and therefore as men and protestant Christians, we are indispensably obliged to take all proper measures for our security.

The above grievance enunciated by our founding fathers at the birth of our nation, shows how strongly they felt they needed to protect themselves against a state-controlled church. It once again validates the true meaning of the Establishment Clause: Separation of Church from Interference by the State. It also confirms the true identity of our first Congress whose members proudly proclaimed that they were Protestant Christians, insisting upon maintaining their freedom of religion.

John Adams, second U.S. president, was the first president to inhabit the White House. The night after his arrival, in November, 1800, he wrote to his wife, Abigail, incorporating a beautiful prayer to Almighty God, as follows:

I Pray Heaven to bestow THE BEST OF BLESSINGS ON This House and All that shall hereafter Inhabit it, May none but Honest and Wise Men ever rule under This Roof.

This prayer is engraved upon the mantel of the state dining room for all to see.

John Adams carried on a long-term correspondence with his friend, Thomas Jefferson. Their lively letters covered a range of topics from personal tragedy to spiritual matters; government and history. It continued up until the time of their death, both men having died on July 4, 1826:

September 2, 1813:
. . .You suppose a difference of opinion between you and me on the subject of Aristocracy. I can find none. I dislike and detest hereditary honours, office, emoluments established by law. So do you. I am for excluding legal hereditary distinctions from the U.S. as long as possible. So are you. I only say that mankind has not yet discovered any remedy against irre-

Above: "John Adams' Prayer" engraved upon the mantel, state dining room, the White House. White House Collection. Below: John Adams—a portrait of the founding father by Charles Willson Peale. Independence National Historical Park Collection.

sistible Corruption in elections to offices of great Power and Profit by making them hereditary . . . [1]

April 19, 1817:
. . . Without religion, this world would be something not fit to be mentioned in polite company . . . The most abandoned scoundrel that ever existed, never yet wholly extinguished his Conscience and while Conscience remains, there is some religion . . . The vast prospect of Mankind, which these books have passed in review before me . . . has sickened my very soul . . . Yet I can never be a misanthrope. Homo sum—"I am a man." I must hate myself before I can hate my fellow men; and that I cannot and will not do . . . [2]

October 7, 1818:
My dear Friend:
. . . Now, sir, for my griefs! The dear partner of my life for 54 years as a wife and for many years more as a lover, now lies in extremis, forbidden to speak or to be spoken to . . . If human life is a bubble, no matter how soon it breaks, if it is, as I firmly believe, an immortal existence, we ought patiently to wait the instructions of the great Teacher.
I am, Sir, your deeply afflicted friend,

John Adams [3]

. . . Your letter of November 13 gave me great delight not only by the divine consolation it afforded me . . . but as it gave me full proof of your restoration to health. While you live, I seem to have a Bank at Monticello in which I can draw for a letter of friendship and entertainment when I please . . . [4]

. . . Have you ever found in history, one single example of a Nation thoroughly corrupted that was afterwards restored to virtue? . . . And without virtue, there can be no political liberty . . . Will you tell me how to prevent riches from becoming the effects of temperance and industry? Will you tell me how to prevent luxury from producing effeminacy, intoxication, extravagance, vice and folly? When you will answer me these questions, I hope I may venture to answer yours. Yet all these ought not to discourage us from exertion, for . . . I believe no effort in favour of virtue is lost, and all good men ought to struggle both by their council and example . . . To return to the Romans, I never could discover that they possessed much virtue, or real liberty there. Patricians were in general gripping usurers and tyrannical creditors in all ages. Pride, strength and courage were all the virtues that composed their National characters. A few of their nobles, affecting simplicity, frugality and piety, perhaps really possessing them, acquired popularity among the Plebeians and extended the power and dominions of the Republic and advanced in glory till riches and luxury came in, sat like an incubus on the Republic and "took vengeance on an overwhelmed people . . ."

John Adams [5]

Rewritten History

Regardless and in spite of the above original correspondence between two great friends, Adams and Jefferson, both of whom "disliked and detested hereditary honours, office, emoluments established by law . . ." and ". . . corruption in election to offices of great power and profit by making them hereditary . . . ," recent biographies and teenage history books give a different story of Adams:

Blunders in Print
. . . The first of Adams' blunders came to be called his "titles campaign" . . . Adams had said that no nation could survive without some recognition of its wealthy, capable and well-born citizens. This and other statements were taken to mean that Adams believed in titles, aristocrats, possibly even kings. And Americans in general felt that such things were contrary to the Republican spirit of their nation. (There had been some talk about making Washington a king, but no one took it seriously.) So when the new Vice President suggested that America needed aristocratic titles, he created an uproar. Adams was not the only one to feel that the new republic needed an element of stately showiness. In fact, one of the first debates in the Senate was over the way in which Washington should be addressed. One group suggested "Your Most Highness" (Adams agreed with this group), but straight-forward "Mr. President" won out—and that is how the President of the United States is always addressed. Adams, however, predicted that unless given the title "Your Majesty," Washington would be made fun of by European heads of state. He also said

that the United States government should grant hereditary titles, like those of England, to people who performed great deeds for it; he claimed that this would be a good way of attracting competent men to public service . . . Hamilton and others suggested that Adams really wanted a title for himself, and they gave him absurd nicknames, such as the "Duke of Braintree" . . . [6]

And again, falsifying America's true historical records on the unbroken Adams/Jefferson friendship and the mutual respect and admiration shared between these two men, right up until their death on the same day—July 4th, 1826, we read:

Quarrel with Jefferson:
The *Davila* essays were the indirect cause of a falling-out between Adams and Thomas Jefferson. Adams and Jefferson had been friends during the American Revolution and the Continental Congresses. Then in the early 1780's in Europe, Adams had cooled toward Jefferson because the Virginian seemed to side with Franklin during the treaty negotiations with England. Now, after the Davila essays appeared, Jefferson wrote an introduction to a new edition of Tom Paine's book *The Rights of Man.*

In his introduction, Jefferson recommended the book as a good antidote to certain recent 'heresies' (statements that disagree with popular belief). Although Jefferson did not mention Adams by name, everyone knew he meant the essays. . . . Adams and Jefferson quarreled over the matter of the introduction and the letters. They remained enemies for many years—although the traditional image of America's Founding Fathers tends not to show their very human squabbles, disagreements, and bad habits . . . [7]

The above is just another unscrupulous attempt to debase and malign the founding fathers, in particular John Adams, whose exemplary Christian life in both the political arena and homefront is a worthy testimony to the biblical foundations of America.

Two of Adams' letters written on June 20, 1815, and November 4, 1816, respectively, are here excerpted. They shed further light upon his adherence to the Christian religion:

. . . The question before the human race is, whether the God of nature shall govern the world by His own laws, or whether priests and kings shall rule it by fictitious miracles? . . . [8]

. . . The Ten Commandments and the Sermon on the Mount contain my religion . . . [9]

John Adams and his wife Abigail had a strong marriage and family life. Due to obligations to country, John Adams frequently had to be away from home, but they were careful to nurture their relationship through frequent letters.

Patten's at Arundel, 4 July 1774:
We went to meeting at Wells and had the pleasure of hearing my friend upon "Be not partakers in other men's sins. Keep yourselves pure." Mr. Hemmenway came and kindly invited us to dine, but we had engaged a dinner at Littlefield's, so we returned there, dined, and took our horses to meeting in the afternoon and heard the minister again upon "Seek first the kingdom of God and his righteousness, and all these things shall be added unto you." There is a great pleasure in hearing sermons so serious, so clear, so sensible and instructive as these . . . [10]

Philadelphia, 16 September, 1774:
Having a leisure moment, while the Congress is assembling. I gladly embrace it to write you a line.

When the Congress first met, Mr. Cushing made a motion that it should be opened with prayer. It was opposed by Mr. Jay, of New York, and Mr. Rutledge of South Carolina, because we were so divided in religious sentiments, some Episcopalians, some Quakers, some Anabaptists, some Presbyterians, and some Congregationalists, that we could not join in the same act of worship. Mr. Samuel Adams arose and said he was no bigot, and could hear a prayer from a gentleman of piety and virtue, who was at the same time a friend to his country. He was a stranger in Philadelphia, but had heard that Mr. Duché (Dushay they pronounce it) deserved that character, and therefore he moved that Mr. Duché, an Episcopal clergyman, might be desired to read prayers to the Congress, tomorrow morning. The motion was seconded and passed in the affirmative. Mr. Randolph, our president, waited on Mr. Duché, and received for an answer that if his health would permit he certainly would. Accordingly, next morning he appeared with his clerk and in his pontificals, and read several prayers in the established form; and then read the Collect for the seventh day of September, which was the thirty-fifth Psalm. You must remember this was the next morning after we heard the horrible rumor of the cannonade of Boston. I never saw a greater effect upon an audience. It seemed as if Heaven had ordained that Psalm to be read on that morning.

After this Mr. Duché, unexpected to everybody, struck out into an extemporary prayer, which filled the bosom of every man present. I must confess I never heard a better prayer, or one so well pronounced. Episcopalian as he is, Dr. Cooper himself (Dr. Samuel Cooper, well known as a zealous patriot and pastor of the church in Brattle Square, Boston) never prayed with such fervor, such earnestness and pathos, and in language so elegant and sublime—for America, for the Congress, for the Province of Massachusetts Bay, and especially the town of Boston. It has had an excellent effect upon everybody here. I must beg you to read that Psalm. If there was any faith in the Sortes Biblicae, it would be thought providential.

It will amuse your friends to read this letter and the thirty-fifth Psalm to them. Read it to your father and Mr. Wibird. I wonder what our Braintree Churchmen will think of this! Mr. Duché is one of the most ingenious men, and best characters, and greatest orators in the Episcopal order, upon this continent. Yet a zealous friend of Liberty and his country.

I long to see my dear family. God bless, preserve and prosper it. Adieu.

John Adams.[11]

Philadelphia, October 9, 1774:
This day I went to Dr. Allison's meeting in the forenoon, and heard the Dr. Francis Allison, D.D., (pastor of the First Presbyterian Church in Philadelphia, as well as Vice Provost and Professor of Moral Philosophy in the college then established in that city) give a good discourse upon the Lord's Supper. This is a Presbyterian meeting. I confess I am not fond of the

wind and directs the storm, I will cheerfully leave the ordering of my lot and whether adverse or prosperous days should be my future portion, I will trust in His right Hand to lead me safely through, and after a short rotation of events, fix me in a state immutable and happy . . . Adieu! I need not say how sincerely I am your affectionate

Abigail Adams.[14]

And at the time of her husband's election as second president of the United States, she writes:

John Adams' Election as president

Quincy, 8 February, 1797:

"The sun is dressed in brightest beams, to give thy honors to the day."

And may it prove an auspicious prelude to each ensuing season. You have this day to declare yourself head of a nation. "And now, O Lord, my God, Thou hast made thy servant ruler over the people. Give unto him an understanding heart, that he may know how to go out and come in before this great people; that he may discern between good and bad. For who is able to judge this thy so great a people?" were the words of a royal Sovereign; and not less applicable to him who is invested with the Chief Magistracy of a nation, though he wear not a crown, nor the robes of royalty.

My thought and meditations are with you, though personally absent; and my petitions to Heaven are that "the things which make for peace may not be hidden from your eyes." My feelings are not those of pride or ostentation upon the occasion. They are solemnized by a sense of obligations, the important trusts, and numerous duties connected with it. That you may be enabled to discharge them with honor to yourself, with justice and impartiality to your country, and with satisfaction to this great people, shall be the daily prayer of your

Abigail Adams.[15]

The following two letters were written by John Quincy Adams to his father at ages 7 and 10 respectively. They demonstrate a well disciplined, respectful child who loves and honors his parents:

Presbyterian meetings in this town. I had rather go to Church. We have better sermons, better prayers, better speakers, softer, sweeter music, and genteeler company. And I must confess that the Episcopal church is quite as agreeable to my taste as the Presbyterian. They are both slaves to the domination of the priesthood. I like the Congregational way best, next to that the Independent . . .

John Adams.[12]

The letters of Abigail Adams to her husband and cheri friend give us a glimpse into their character and virtue. T include her encouragement to him in fulfilling duty to nati spite of personal cost; grief at the loss of a cherished friend war effort; her handling of perilous times and her humble pray her husband upon being elected president of the nation:

Will there be war?
> Braintree, 16 October, 1774:
> My much loved friend:
> I dare not express to you, at three hundred miles distance, how ardently I long for your return . . . And whether the end will be tragical, Heaven only knows. You cannot be, I know, nor do wish to see you, an inactive spectator; but if the sword b drawn, I bid adieu to all domestic felicity, and look forward t that country where there are neither wars nor rumours war, in a firm belief that through the mercy of its King we sha both rejoice there together . . . Your mother sends her love t you, and all your family, too numerous to name, desire to b remembered. You will receive letters from two who are a earnest to write to papa as if the welfare of a kingdom depend ed upon it.

Your most affectionat
Abigail Adams

Trust in God
> Braintree, Sunday, 16 September, 1775:
> I set myself down to write with a heart depressed with tl melancholy scenes around me. My letter will be only a bill mortality; though thanks be to that Being who restraineth t pestilence, that it has not yet proved mortal to any of our far ily, though we live in daily expectation that Patty will not co tinue many hours . . . And unto Him who mounts the whi

Age 7

October 13, 1774:

Sir,

I have been trying ever since you went away to learn to write you a letter. I shall make poor work of it; but sir, Mamma says you will accept my endeavors, and that my duty to you may be expressed in poor writing as well as good. I hope I grow a better boy, and that you will have no occasion to be ashamed of me when you return. Mr. Thaxter says I learn my books well. He is a very good master. I read my books to Mamma. We all long to see you. I am Sir, your dutiful son,

John Quincy Adams.[16]

The second moving letter addressed to his father shows the respect for parental authority and guidance — American Christian values which John Quincy Adams demonstrated early in life:

Age 10

Dear Sir,

I love to receive letters very well; much better than I love to write them. I make but a poor figure at composition, my head is fickle, my thoughts are running after birds eggs, play and trifles, till I get vexed with myself. Mamma has a troublesome task to keep me steady and I own I am ashamed of myself. I have just entered the third volume of Smollett, 'tho I had designed to have got it half through by this time. I have determined this week to be more diligent as Mr. Thaxter will be absent at court, and I cannot pursue my other studies. I have set myself a stent and determine to read the third volume half out. If I can but keep my resolution, I will write again at the end of the week and give a better account of myself. I wish, Sir, you would give me some instructions, with regard to my time, and advise me how to proportion my studies and my play, in writing, and I will keep them by me, and endeavor to follow them. I am, dear Sir, with a present determination of growing better, yours.

P. S. Sir, if you will be so good as to favor me with a Blank Book, I will transcribe the most favorable occurrences I meet with in my reading, which will serve to fix them upon my mind.

John Quincy Adams[17]

Further insights into the godliness and patriotism exemplified by the Adams family are gleaned in Abigail Adams' letter to her husband, dated Sunday, 18 June, 1775:

In the midst of war

> THE day—perhaps the decisive day—is come, on which that fate of America depends. My bursting heart must find vent at my pen. I have just heard that our dear friend, Dr. Warren, is no more, but fell gloriously fighting for country; saying, Better to die honorably in the field, than ignominiously hang upon the gallows. Great is our loss. He has distinguished himself in every engagement, by his courage and fortitude, by animating the soldiers, and leading them on by his own example. A particular example of these dreadful, but I hope glorious days, will be transmitted you, no doubt, in the exactest manner.

> > "The race is not to the swift, nor the battle to the strong; but the God of Israel is He That giveth strength and power unto His people. Trust in Him at all times, ye people, pour out your hearts before Him; God is a refuge for us."

> Charlestown is laid in ashes. The battle began upon our entrenchments upon Bunker's Hill, Saturday morning about 3 o' clock, and has not ceased yet, and it is now three o'clock Sabbath afternoon. It is expected they will come out over the Neck tonight, and a dreadful battle must ensue. Almighty God, cover the heads of our countrymen, and be a shield to our dear friends. How many have fallen, we know not. The constant roar of the cannon is so distressing that we cannot eat, drink or sleep. May we be supported and sustained in the dreadful conflict. I shall tarry here till it is thought unsafe by my friends, and then I have secured myself a retreat at your brother's who has kindly offered me part of his house. I cannot compose myself to write any further at present. I will add more as I hear further.

> > Abigail Adams.[18]

From what we have seen in John Adams' correspondence and writings, the rewritten, derogatory accounts quoted above contradict his character, values and approach to life which was an exemplary one, devoid of petty jealousy, unforgiveness and revenge. This is amply demonstrated by his political speeches and personal correspondence, some of which have been excerpted above, for the reader to peruse and evaluate.

Thomas Jefferson—a portrait of the founding father by Charles Willson Peale. Independence National Historical Park Collection.

(vi) Thomas Jefferson—Champion of Religious Freedom

We hold these truths to be self-evident, that all men are created equal. That they are endowed by their Creator with certain inalienable rights. Among these are life, liberty, and the pursuit of happiness, that to secure these rights governments are instituted among men. . . .

Thomas Jefferson penned these words of the Declaration of Independence in Philadelphia, in 1776. These truths which underlie our United States Constitution were well-known and widely accepted throughout the American colonies at the time. The Declaration was a summarization of the opinions and feelings held by many of the colonists of the day. Discussing his authorship of it, Jefferson wrote these words to James Madison in 1823: "I know only that I turned to neither book nor pamphlet while writing it. I did not consider it as any part of my charge to invent new ideas altogether and to offer no sentiments which have never been expressed before."

Thomas Jefferson has been called numerous things, including atheist, deist, devil and/or agnostic. None of these titles is accurate, according to original writings and to his own description of himself and what he stood for.

According to Noah Webster's definition in his original 1854 Dictionary, a "deist" was:

One who believes in the existence of a God, but denies revealed religion; one who professes no form of religion, but follows the light of nature and reason, as his only guides in doctrine and practice; a free-thinker.[1]

However, the following quotations from Jefferson's own writings belie the fact. Few people are aware of Jefferson's *Prayer for Peace*, as it is called. Excerpted from his Second Inaugural Address, it was delivered on March 4, 1805, as follows:

I shall now enter on the duties to which my fellow-citizens have again called me, and shall proceed in the spirit of those principles which they have approved. . . . I shall need, therefore, all the indulgence I have heretofore experienced . . . I shall need, too, the favor of that Being in whose hands we are, who led our forefathers, as Israel of old, from their native land and planted them in a country flowing with all the necessities and comforts of life, who has covered our infancy with His Providence and our riper years with His wisdom and power, and to whose goodness I ask you to join with me in supplications that He will so enlighten the minds of your servants, guide their councils and prosper their measures, that whatever they do shall result in your good, and shall secure to you the peace, friendship and approbation of all nations.[2]

In a letter to Dr. Benjamin Rush, dated April 21, 1803, Jefferson voices his opinion on religion:

My views . . . are the result of a life of inquiry and reflection, and very different from the anti-Christian system imputed to me by those who know nothing of my opinions. To the corruptions of Christianity I am indeed opposed, but not the genuine precepts of Jesus himself. I am a Christian in the only sense in which he wished anyone to be, sincerely attached to his doctrines in preference to all others. . . . [3]

Elaborating on the excesses inherent within the hierarchal state-controlled church, Jefferson writes to Moses Robinson on March 23, 1801, from Washington, D.C.:

. . . the Christian Religion, when divested of the rags in which they (the clergy) have enveloped it, and brought to the original purity and simplicity of its benevolent institutor, is a religion of all others most friendly to liberty, science, and the freest expansion of the human mind.[4]

In another letter, this time to Levi Lincoln, and written from his Virginian home, Monticello, on August 26, 1801, Jefferson gives his views on the New England clergy:

. . . From the clergy I expect no mercy. They crucified their saviour who preached that their kingdom was not of this world: and all who practice on that precept must expect the extreme of their wrath. The laws of the present day withhold their hands from blood; but lies and slander still remain to them . . .[5]

As the above letters demonstrate, an open conflict existed between Jefferson and some of the religious leaders of his day. There were, however, specific circumstances underlying this conflict. Jefferson was the author and key proponent of a bill to which some of the clergy of that day widely and vehemently disapproved. This was the Virginia Statute for Religious Freedom, a forerunner to the establishment of religious freedom in the United States, and today widely acclaimed by Christendom. In Virginia, the example of the mother country had been followed with the Anglican Church being the established state church. As we saw in Chapter I *(ii) William Bradford, the Pilgrims and the Mayflower Compact*, it was the established church of England which had persecuted the Pilgrims who were forced to flee to Holland and later come to America. This they did in order to obtain the freedom to worship God according to biblical truth.

Jefferson, like James Madison, was a man ahead of his times, one able to learn from the mistakes of history, even though such action made him unpopular with the ecclesiastical order of religious leaders who were part of the established church.

The Statute for Religious Freedom, which Jefferson considered one of his greatest contributions to the nation, was a bill written in reaction to one proposed in 1785, the establishment of Religion by Law. Had this bill been passed, all citizens of Virginia would have been taxed to support the clergy. As Jefferson wrote in his autobiography, we see that the issue was hotly debated for five years. From Jefferson's autobiography we read his own description of the disestablishment of the Anglican Church in Virginia:

> But our opponents carried, in the General Resolutions of the Committee of November 19, a declaration that Religious assemblies ought to be regulated and that provision ought to be made for continuing the succession of the clergy and superintending their conduct. And in the bill now passed was inserted an express reservation of the question whether a general assessment should not be established by law on everyone to the support of the pastor of his choice; or whether all should be left to voluntary contributions; and on this question, debated at every session from '76 to '79 (some of our dissenting allies, having now secured their particular object, going over to the advocates of a general assessment), we could only

obtain a suspension from session to session until '79 when the question against a general assessment was finally carried and the establishment of the Anglican Church entirely put down.[6]

However, in the Introduction to the Companion Guide Book of the 1989 PBS television documentary, *The Supreme Court's Holy Battles,* hosted by Roger Mudd, we read a different version from Jefferson's own documentary account of this historic event, as follows:

> In 1779, Thomas Jefferson first introduced a piece of legislation to the Virginia General Assembly so revolutionary that it set off a political battle that is still with us. His radical idea?—that religion is a purely personal, private matter between the individual and God, and that government has no right to intrude. To that end, Jefferson proposed to sever the relationship between the established Anglican church and the state of Virginia . . .

Compare the true Jeffersonian account with the recent PBS version, and you will see that the modern, coined version of "Separation of Church and State" does not fit the actual historic documentation left by our founding father himself.

Was He a Deist?

Today, many who label Jefferson a deist, and/or anti-Christian, have likely based their conclusions upon a faulty understanding of this controversial issue of that time, which directly concerned the church. He was misrepresented and maligned by the clergy of his day, who were not able to grasp the long-range effects of the bill they favored. Jefferson understood, and history has proved him right, that true Christianity would prosper without the aid of the civil government. He stood for what he believed, in spite of severe opposition and misunderstanding of his own character. James Madison's arduous efforts worked hand-in-hand with Jefferson's towards the attainment of religious freedom. (See Madison's *Memorial and Remonstrance* in the Addendum.)

Jefferson's comments on this in a letter to Mrs. Harrison Smith, dated August 6, 1816:

... I recognize the same motives of goodness in the solicitude
you express on the rumor supposed to proceed from a letter
of mine to Charles Thomson, on the subject of the Christian
religion. It is true that, in writing to the translator of the
Bible and Testament, that subject was mentioned; but equally so that no adherence to any particular mode of Christianity was there expressed, nor any change of opinions suggested. A change from what? That priests indeed have heretofore
thought proper to ascribe to me religious, or rather anti-religious sentiments, of their own fabric, but such as soothed their
resentments against the Act of Virginia for establishing religious freedom. They wished him to be thought atheist, deist,
or devil, who could advocate freedom from their religious dic-
tations. But I have ever thought religion a concern purely
between our God and our consciences, for which we were
accountable to him, and not to the priests . . . I have ever
judged of the religion of others by their lives and by this test
my dear Madam, I have been satisfied yours must be an
excellent one to have produced a life of such exemplary
virtue and correctness. For it is in our lives, and not from our
words, that our religion must be read. . . .[7]

In the above letter to Mrs. Harrison Smith, Jefferson makes
mention of Secretary of the Congress, Charles Thomson's translation
of the Bible, which he ordered for his own library. Jefferson clearly
points out that he does not choose any particular mode of mainline
Christian worship above another. He denounces the hierarchal
Anglican priestly orders as having labeled him "anti-religious," stating that this was of their own invention, in order to soothe their
resentment against his authorship of the Statute of Virginia for
Religious Freedom. This disestablished their state-church in Virginia, granting equal footing and freedom of worship to other
mainline Christian churches. Jefferson himself exposes their revenge
against his success, calling him atheist, deist or devil, for freeing
other Christians from the Anglican state-church dictatorship. He
once again denounces the tyranny of ecclesiastical-civil priesthood
over the lives and consciences of other Christian believers, "for
there is one God, and one mediator also between God and men, the
man Christ Jesus" (1 Timothy 2:5).

Jefferson concluded his letter by commending Mrs. Smith for the results of her church life, producing exemplary virtue and righteousness as an outworking of her faith.

> To Jared Sparks, November 4, 1820:
> I hold the precepts of Jesus as delivered by Himself, to be the most pure, benevolent and sublime which have ever been preached to man. . . .[8]

From the above words, we can see that Jesus Christ's doctrines and precepts were Jefferson's highest standard—being untainted, of a good reputation and heavenly in nature. It must thus be concluded that the words of Jesus Christ were taken very seriously by this founding father, which precludes his being stigmatized a "deist."

The disestablishment of the Anglican Church as a state-controlled entity was clearly the intent of Jefferson's Statute of Virginia for Religious Freedom.

Just as Thomas Jefferson was ahead of his time in the question of religious freedom, he was also ahead of his time on the issue of slavery. He had the insight to see that its continuation would ultimately result in devastation to the nation, yet he understood that the time for addressing this volatile issue could only be successfully tackled after the adoption of a national constitution, which in itself was a momentous task for the fledgling nation. The following narrative from his autobiography gives us further insights into the character and stature of this founding father:

> The bill on the subject of slaves was a mere digest of the existing laws respecting them, without any intimation of a plan for a future and general emancipation. It was thought better that this should be kept back, and attempted only by way of amendment, however the bill should be brought on. The principles of the amendment however were agreed on, that is to say, the freedom of all born after a certain day, and deportation at a proper age. But it was found that the public mind would not yet bear the proposition, nor will it bear it even at this day. Yet the day is not distant when it must bear and adopt it, or worse will follow. Nothing is more certainly written in the book of fate than that these people are to be free, nor is it

less certain that the two races, equally free, cannot live in the same government. Nature, habits, opinion has drawn indelible lines of distinction between them. It is still in our power to direct the process of emancipation and deportation peaceably and in such slow degree as that the evil will wear off insensibly and their place be pari passu filled up with free white laborers. If on the contrary it is left to force itself on, human nature must shudder at the prospect held up. . . .[9]

The Jefferson Bible Myth

Most Americans have been sold the widely-accepted myth that Thomas Jefferson wrote his own Bible. This is what I had been told, and having neither seen the Bible, nor anything to the contrary, was unable to form an opinion based upon fact. In 1987 I set about tracking down this elusive book. It is in the Smithsonian Institution and I was not only able to scrutinize it, but also able to make photocopies of the Title page and Table of Contents, both written in Jefferson's own handwriting. The book is entitled *The Life and Morals of Jesus of Nazareth, extracted textually from the Gospels in Greek, Latin, French and English.* The Table of Contents reads: "A Table of the Texts from the Evangelists employed in this Narrative and the order of their arrangement." (See reprint of original)

There is only one copy, the original of this personal exercise of Jefferson. It was never published by this founding father, nor was it part of his extensive 6,000 plus volume library which he sold to the Library of Congress. Jefferson's "Life and Morals of Jesus of Nazareth, extracted textually from the Gospels" is now a museum piece in the custody of the Smithsonian Institution.

In 1904, 78 years after Jefferson's death, the United States Congress ordered the printing of 9,000 copies of Jefferson's "Life and Morals . . ." but they did so under the erroneous title of: "The Jefferson Bible." This was executed as a government document by the 57th Congress, first session, as follows:[10]

> That there be printed and bound, by photolithographic process, with an introduction of not to exceed twenty-five pages, to be prepared by Dr. Cyrus Adler, Librarian of the Smithsonian Institution, for the use of Congress, 9,000 copies of Thomas Jefferson's Morals of Jesus of Nazareth, as the same appears in

A photocopy of the title page (above) and first page of the table of contents (below) of "The Life and Morals of Jesus of Nazareth, extracted textually from the Gospels in Greek, Latin, French and English," in Thomas Jefferson's handwriting.

the National Museum; 3,000 copies for the use of the Senate
and 6,000 copies for the use of the House.
Cyrus Adler.[11]

It is unfortunate that the title given by Jefferson was not utilized, but instead it was entitled: "The Jefferson Bible." In addition,
Jefferson's format of chapter and verse, followed by word for word
Scripture verses, on the doctrinal teachings of Christ was also
changed. The Bible chapters and verses were removed, and the text
was written in narrative form. In Jefferson's original, not one word
of commentary or opinion by him was included. The rewritten
version of 1904 is misleading at best, giving the false impression that
Thomas Jefferson "wrote his own Bible." Further, this work was a
pure exercise for Thomas Jefferson. Similar harmonies of the Word
of God have been produced in recent years as Bible study aids. (See
reprint.)

Jefferson was a seeker of truth and in order to find truth, he
went to the source, rather than relying on the interpretations of man.
His excerpted letter dated June 17, 1804, to Henry Fry shows his
motivation:

> . . . I consider the doctrines of Jesus as delivered by himself to
> contain the outlines of the sublimest system of morality that
> has ever been taught but I hold in the most profound detes-
> tation and execration the corruptions of it which have been
> invented by priestcraft and established by kingcraft consti-
> tuting a conspiracy of church and state against the civil and
> religious liberties of mankind. . . .[12]

From the above correspondence, it seems clear that Jefferson
had no intention whatever, nor did he ever attempt to "write his
own Bible." A brilliant intellect had been one of his gifts from
Almighty God—and he used it in many creative avenues, including
a compilation of the genuine moral teachings of Jesus of Nazareth.

Thomas Jefferson's Library

Thomas Jefferson's library included many volumes on religion. This is now part of the Library of Congress Rare Book Collection and is listed under the title *Jefferson Collection.* There are 190

entries under the title "Religion," 187 of these pertaining to Christianity, while the remaining three are as follows:

> An Historical Account of the Heathen gods and heroes necessary for understanding of the ancient poets. 1722.
> Boyse's Pantheon History of Heathen gods, for those who would understand History, Poetry, Painting, Statuary, Medals, coins, etc. 1753. And one copy of Sale's Koran, 1764.[13]

On the title page of this catalog, Jefferson's famous words are quoted: ". . . I am for freedom of Religion, and against all maneuvers to bring about a legal ascendancy of one sect over another. . . ."[14]

From these words we see Jefferson's abhorrence of a legally established state church, dictating to, and controlling other Christian denominations at will. This he denounces and calls "priestcraft."

Among Jefferson's entries on religion are innumerable Bibles—Greek, Latin, French and English versions; the *Septuagint* (Greek Old Testament); the Apocrypha; The Holy Bible—Old and New Testaments, translated out of the original tongues, and with the former translations diligently compared and revised, 1804.

Jefferson's well-worn, beautifully leatherbound, four-volume personal Bible holds preeminence in this collection. Its Jefferson Collection Rare Book card catalog entry (BS.195.T55) describes Jefferson's Bible as:

> Bible. English. 1808.
> Thomson
> The Holy Bible containing the Old and New Covenant, commonly called the Old and New Testament
> Translated from the Greek by Charles Thomson, late Secretary to the Congress of the United States.
> Philadelphia. Printed by J. Aitken, 1808. The Bible on which Dr. Daniel Boorstin took the oath of office as the 12th Librarian of Congress, November 12, 1975.

Other entries in the collection include:

> Old and New Testament and Apocrypha 1798
>
> Greek New Testament 1583

Greek and Latin New Testament 1578

Latin New Testament 1735

Bible—New Testament Greek 1800

Hammond's New Testament—A Paraphrase and Annotation upon all the Books of the New Testament, briefly explaining all the difficult places therein.

The New Testament of our Lord and Saviour Jesus Christ, translated out of the original Greek, 1802.

The History of Jesus by Thompson and Price, 1805.

The History of our Blessed Lord and Saviour Jesus Christ: with the Lives of the Holy Apostles, and their successors for three hundred years after the crucifixion.

Newman's Concordance to the Bible, 1650.

Cruden's Concordance, 1738.

Clarke's Concordance to the Holy Bible, 1696.

Brown's Dictionary of the Holy Bible.

The Truth of the Christian Religion by Hugo Grotius in six books, written in Latin by Grotius, and now translated into English, with an addition of a seventh book against the present Roman Church, 1694. (Hugo Grotius was the father of International Law).

Evidences of Christianity, a view of the evidences of Christianity in three parts. Part I: Of the direct Historical Evidence of Christianity, and wherein it is distinguished from the evidence alleged for other miracles. Part II: Of the Auxiliary Evidence of Christianity. Part III: A brief Consideration of some popular objections, 1795.

Barclay's Minute Philosopher, in seven dialogues, containing an apology for the Christian Religion, against those who are called Freethinkers, 1732.

The works of Reverend John Witherspoon, D.D., LL.D., late President of the College, at Princeton, New Jersey. To which is prefixed an account of the author's life, in a sermon occasioned by his death, by the Reverend Dr. John Rodgers of New York. In three volumes. (Dr Witherspoon was the only preacher-signer of the Declaration of Independence). It was Witherspoon, in 1781, noting the differences in the English language as spoken in America, who coined the word "Americanism."

Primitive Christianity Revived, by William Whiston, Volume I: Epistles of Ignatius; Volume II: The Apostolical Constitutions in Greek and English; Volume III; An Essay on those Apostolical Constitutions; Volume IV: An Account of the Primitive faith, concerning the Trinity and Incarnation.

A Scriptural Account of the Millenium: being a Selection from the Prophecies concerning Christ's Second Coming, and personal glorious reign on earth a thousand years. To which are added a number of arguments to shew that this event has not yet taken place. Also, some observations, calculated to stimulate man to an enquiry into the matter to make the necessary preparation for that all important event. By Benjamin Gorton, 1802.

The Christian's Duty from the Sacred Scriptures, containing all that is necessary to be believed and practiced in order to our Eternal Salvation. Collected out of the Old and New Testament, and the books of Wisdom and Ecclesiasticus, etc. (Initialled by Jefferson).

Tracts in Religion: The Blessings of America. A sermon preached in the Middle Dutch Church, on the 4th July, 1791, being the Anniversary of the Independence of America. By William Linn.

Principles of Civil Union and Happiness considered and Recommended. A sermon by Elizur Goodrich.

The Inquirer: Being An examination of the Question lately agitated, respecting the legitimate Powers of Government, whether they extend to the Care of Religion, and warrant making and enforcing Laws for the Purpose of establishing, supporting or encouraging the Christian Religion. 1801.

Prideaux' Connections. 2 vol. fol. The Old and New Testament connected in the History of the Jews and neighboring Nations, from the Declension of the Kingdoms of Israel and Judah to the Time of Christ, by Humphrey Prideaux, 1719.

The above list of books on the subject of religion in Jefferson's library represents but a small fraction of his collection on Christianity. It is reminiscent of a well-equipped and balanced library of Bibles and Christian works of the highest caliber. It also shows Thomas Jefferson's extensive personal collection of Old and New Testaments, intact. These hold preeminence in his library of books entitled, "Religion." This precludes "deism," "atheism" and alien false religions which are non-existent in this founding father's extensive collection. Biblical sermons, such as "The Blessings on America" also show the inseparable link between Christianity and our government. It would seem questionable whether one would collect such an extensive library on Bibles and Bible-related materials if the Word of God was not an integral part of one's life.

During a recent visit to Monticello, Jefferson's gracious southern home in Charlottesville, Virginia, I was shown a number of Christian paintings in the hall, parlour and dining room of that handsome estate. I subsequently received a catalog made up by Jefferson himself, on his paintings and *objets d'art* at Monticello. Having studied this great founding father and having reached the conclusion that his foremost adherence was to the teachings of the Bible, it did not surprise me at all to find that no less than 25 works of the great masters belonging to Jefferson reflected the Old and New Testament narrative. In perusing this hand-written catalog by Jefferson, one is struck by this founding father's knowledge, love, awe and respect for the Scriptures, both Old and New Testaments. Jefferson relates vividly in his own words, events in Jesus Christ's life, taking you to chapter and verse of Scripture. He also describes Joseph "in the act of fervent prayer"; the sacrifice of Isaac and God's miraculous intervention, from Genesis 22; Jesus' parable of the Prodigal Son returning home; the Transfiguration; Jesus before Pilate, from Mark 15 and Matthew 27; the crucifixion from Luke 23:44–45 "when the sun is darkened, the temple rent, the atmosphere kindled with lightning, the tombs open and yield their dead;" the Descent from the Cross and other cataclysmic gospel events. They are cataloged chronologically by Jefferson, as follows:

Catalogue of Paintings &c. at Monticello.
Hall.
1. An Ecce homo. a bust of Jesus of about ⅔ the natural scale on canvas. he is clothed with a robe of purple and a crown of thorns on his head. Copied from Guido.
2. A bust of St. Jerom in meditation, his head reclined on his right hand, and a book in his left. Of full size, on Canvas. Copied from Goltzius.
3. Jesus driving the money changers out of the temple. Seven figures of full length and about half the natural module, the subject Matthew 21:12 on Canvas. Copied from Valentin.
4. St Peter weeping. his hands are pressed together, and near him the cock shews it was in the moment of Matthew 26.75 "and Peter remembered the words of Jesus, which said unto him before the cock crows thous shalt deny me thrice. and he went out and wept bitterly " a half length figure of full size, on Canvas, copied from Carlo Lotti. purchased from St. Severin's collection. Catalogue No. 36.
5. John Baptist, a bust of the natural size. the right hand pointing to heaven, the left, deeply shaded, is scarcely seen pressing his breast, which is covered by his hair flowing thickly over it. it is seen almost in full face. on canvas. Copied from Leonardo da Vinci.
6. Jesus among the Doctors, and disputing with them. The subject Luke 2:46. his right hand pointing to heaven, the left pressing his breast, the drapery blue and purple, the hair flowing loose. a half length figure of full size, seen in profile, on Canvas.
7. St. Joseph the husband of Mary the mother of Jesus. A ¾ length of full size on Canvas. a book is laying open before him. (Page 2) hands interlocked with energy, his head and eyes turned up to heaven, and his mouth open, as in the act of fervent prayer.

8. Jesus in the Praetorium, stripped of the purple, as yet naked and with the crown of thorns on his head. he is sitting. a whole length figure of about 4 feet. the persons present seem to be one of his revilers, one of his followers, and the superintendent of the execution. the subject from Mark 15.16–20. An original on wood by Malbodius.

9. David with the head of Goliah, copied on canvas from Guido, who has given his own picture in the person of David, a whole length of 2.f.6.I.

10. The sacrifice of Isaac. he is placed on the pile, on his knees, his wrists bound. Abraham with his left hand grasping the back of his neck, a naked sword (sic) in his right uplifted and ready to strike the fatal stroke. in that instant an Angel hovering above him, stays his hand, and Abraham looks up with distraction to see by what power his (sic) hand is withheld. in a bush on the right hand is seen the ram. the figures are whole length: that of Abraham on scale of not quite half the natural size. On canvas, an original. The subject Gen. 22.

11. Jesus before Pilate. the subject Matthew 27 on canvas, copied from Pordononi.

(page 3)

Parlour. upper tier.

22. Herodiade bearing the head of St. John in a platter. A ¾ length of full size on canvas, copied from Simon Vouett, purchased from St. Severin's collection, Catal. No. 248. the subject Matthew 14.11. Mark. 6.28.

34. the Prodigal son. he is in rags kneeling at the feet of his father, who extends his hands to raise him. the mother and sister appear shocked at his condition, but the elder son views him with indignation. the figures of full size on Canvas purchased from St. Severin's collection. Catal. 306. an Original.

(page 4)

35. A Magdalen penitent, sitting, her hair dishevelled, her eyes looking up to heaven, a book in her right hand, and the left resting on a skull. a ¾ length of full size on Canvas, copied from Joseph de Ribera, called Espagnolet, purchased from St. Severin's collection. Catal. No. 59.

Middle tier.

36. a transfiguration. copied from Raphael. Whole length figures of 6.I on Canvas. the subject Matthew 17. 1–8. see 4. Manuel du Museum. PL. I

37. the Baptism of Jesus by John. figures whole length of 10.I on wood from Devois. the subject Luke 3.21.22.

38. a crucifixion. whole length figure on wood. an Original by Gerard Seggers. The moment is that of Luke 23.44–45. (page 5)

41. Susanna and the elders. three figures of about an eighth of the natural module. on Canvas. copied from Coypel.

49. Jephtha leading his daughter Seila to be sacrificed. on one side is the altar and the high-priest with the implements of sacrifice: on the other the mother, sisters, and by-standers weeping and holding the victim by one hand, while Jephtha pulls her towards the altar by the other. there are 17 figures, the principal of which is 16½ I. on Canvas. copied from Coypel. the subject from Judges 11 (cf. Appendix B, no. 16)

Lower Tier.

50. the Prodigal son from West. done on Canvas in the manner called Polyplasiasmos, or the Polygraphic art.

51. a Descent on Copper. the Christ is of about 10.I behind him is the virgin weeping. on each side angels. it is copied from Vandyke by Dispenbec. see Rubens' management of the same subject. 3. Manuel du Museum 483.

52. a Descent from the cross on wood. a group of 5 figures. the body of Jesus is reclined on the ground, the head and shoulders supported in the lap of his mother, who with four others, women from Galilee, are weeping over him. the figures are whole lengths; the principal one 13.I. it is an original by Francis Floris.

(Page 8)

73. the holy family copied from Raphael on Canvas. the figures are whole lengths. the Virgin and infant Jesus, Joseph, Elizabeth and the infant John and two angels. see the 4. Manuel du Museum Pl.3.

74. A crucifixion. the instant seized is that of the expiration, when the sun is darkened, the temple rent, the atmosphere kindled with lightning, the tombs open and yield their dead. on one side is the Centurion, struck with awe, and seeming to say "verily, this was a righteous man." on the other the two Marys, one of them her hair bristled with fear, the other in adoration. the subject is taken from Matt. 27.51,52 and Luke 23.45. The figures are whole lengths, the largest of 16.I copied on canvas from Vandyke.

75. A Flagellation of Christ, a groupe of 10 figures, the principal of which is 21.I. he is bound to a post, two soldiers whipping him with bundles of rods, and third binding up another bundle. on the right are the Superintendents and Spectators.

the subject Matt. 27.26. it is copied on wood from Devoes.
see the same subject treated very similarly by Rubens. 3
Manuel du Musee. 501

Again, as with this founding father's library on Christianity,
it would be preposterous for him to take the time and care to
describe each event portrayed in these works of art in detail from
Scripture if they contradicted his beliefs.

The following excerpts from Jefferson's letters give added
insights into his religious beliefs.

In a letter written to William Canby dated September 18,
1813, Jefferson expresses himself thus:

> An eloquent preacher of your religious society, Richard Motte,
> in a discourse of much emotion and pathos, is said to have
> exclaimed aloud to his congregation that he did not believe
> there was a Quaker, Presbyterian, Methodist, or Baptist in
> heaven, having paused to give his hearers time to stare and to
> wonder. He added, that in Heaven, God knew no distinc-
> tions, but considered all good men as His children, and as
> brethren of the same family. . . . .[15]

The above words denote Jefferson's belief that one could
attain eternal life whether Quaker, Presbyterian, Methodist or Baptist, referring to members of these Christian congregations as "all
good men." The distinction not made by Jefferson, however, was
that one still had to be "born again" into the family of God through
faith in Jesus Christ, regardless of church attendance. (In Christ's
own words—John 3:3; 13–16.)

> To Miles King, September 26, 1814:
> . . . Nay, we have heard it said that there is not a Quaker or a
> Baptist, a Presbyterian or an Episcopalian, a Catholic or a
> Protestant in heaven; that on entering that gate, we leave
> those badges of schism behind, and find ourselves united in
> those principles only in which God has united us all. Let us not
> be uneasy about the different roads we may pursue, as believ-
> ing them the shortest, to that our last abode; but, following the
> guidance of a good conscience, let us be happy in the hope that
> by these different paths we shall all meet in the end. And
> that you and I may there meet and embrace, is my earnest

prayer. And with this assurance I salute you with brotherly esteem and respect.[16]

Although some would hold that any belief in a god is what Jefferson was speaking about, the above writings clearly disclose that Jefferson stated Christianity alone, regardless of denominational preference, was the road to heaven. The issue which was at that time the bone of contention was separation from the control of the Anglican state church to freedom of worship through other mainline Christian denominations, namely Presbyterians, Quakers, Baptists, Episcopalians and Catholics. To Jefferson, the narrow path was through Christianity and Christianity alone (Protestants and Catholics), excluding Eastern religions, false, heathen gods and alien philosophies.

However one wishes to interpret Jefferson's religious beliefs, the above documentation authenticates the fact that he himself believed he was a Christian and history bears out that Jefferson had a great interest in the Bible and Christianity.

Furthermore, his belief in God is immortalized within the Jefferson Memorial in Washington, D.C. Three out of the four inscriptions chosen to represent his mind and outlook acknowledge Almighty God as a personal God, interested and involved in the lives of His creation. These include quotations from The Declaration of Independence, the Statute of Virginia for Religious Freedom and his autobiography. They give God the glory for being the benefactor of all our gifts and freedoms as a nation, attest to God creating the mind free and man equal and assert that without His blessings and His hand upon our nation, we would be insecure. I quote:

> Can the liberties of a nation be secure when we have removed the conviction that these liberties are the gift of God? I tremble for my country when I reflect that God is just, and that His justice cannot sleep forever.

The above, coming from Jefferson, negates the notion that he was a deist.

Jefferson attended Christ Church in Philadelphia and Bruton Parish Church (Episcopalian) in Williamsburg, Virginia. Both were also attended by George and Martha Washington and many other founding fathers who professed themselves to be Christian. Jefferson never intended to publish his *Life and Morals of Jesus of Nazareth*, but called it "a wee book," exerting no influence upon the public whatever.

It has been my intent to expose the myths on Thomas Jefferson's religious precepts, morality and character, spotlighting the truth from original sources. Even many modern evangelical Christian historians and writers have fallen into the trap of labeling Jefferson a "deist" and/or "anti-Christian." Apparently, they relied upon secondary sources of information, and not on his own words or original documentation.

Although there is no evidence of his having had a personal relationship with Jesus Christ, Son of God and Son of Man, the long-awaited Messiah and Savior of the world for all who would put their trust in Him, Jefferson had a Christian value-system and world view, based upon principles taken from the Word of God itself. This precludes atheism, agnosticism, deism or humanism, the last of which has permeated America's godly foundations to their very core, creating the crisis situation in which we find ourselves today.

In stark contrast to the un-American, modern-day view that man created himself and is in total control of his own destiny, Jefferson, in his Declaration of Independence, gives all glory to Almighty God. He affirms that God created each man and woman equal, endowing or blessing them with the gift of life, liberty and the freedom to pursue a course of happiness during their time on earth. This incredible document forms the basis for our United States Constitution and makes some assertive claims for each American in this blessed land, as to our God-given freedoms and equality.

James Madison—a portrait of the founding father by Charles Willson Peale. Independence National Historical Park Collection.

(vii) James Madison—Father of the U.S. Constitution

James Madison, who later became the fourth president of the United States, was acclaimed for his work entitled: *Memorial and Remonstrance*, presenting it to the General Assembly of the State of Virginia at the session in 1785. This was in opposition to the introduction of a bill in the assembly for the Establishment of Religion by Law. Both Madison and Jefferson, called the "Champions of Religious Freedom," stood against legislation that would require citizens to be taxed for the support of something which they may be opposed to in conscience. In this case, it was the support of the teachers of the Christian religion of one sect, selected by the government. Madison was outraged at this affront to Christianity. He was apparently in the minority. As he states here in his *Memorial and Remonstrance*, it appears only the Quakers and Mennonites as a whole could foresee the error of passing such a law:

> . . . Who does not see that the same authority, which can establish Christianity in exclusion of all other religions, may establish with the same ease, any particular sect of Christians, in exclusion of all other sects; that the same authority, which can force a citizen to contribute threepence only of his property, for the support of any one establishment, may force him to conform to any other establishment, in all cases whatsoever. . . . Are the Quakers and Mennonites the only sects who think a compulsive support of their religions unnecessary and unwarrantable? Can their piety alone be intrusted with the care of publick worship? Ought their religions to be endowed, above all others, with extraordinary privileges, by which proselytes may be enticed from all others. . . .[1]

Not only was the bill not beneficial to Christianity, but the passage of such a bill was based upon ignorance, rather than faith in God. As he clearly shows, Christianity not only does not need the help of the State for support, but such help would result in a weakening of the church:

> . . . Because the establishment proposed by the bill is not requisite for the support of the Christian Religion. To say that it is, is a contradiction to the Christian Religion itself; for every page of it disavows a dependence on the power of this world; it is a contradiction to fact, for it is known that this religion both

existed and flourished, not only without the support of human laws, but in spite of every opposition from them; and not only during the period of miraculous aid, but long after it had been left to its own evidence and the ordinary care of Providence: nay, it is a contradiction in terms; for any religion, not invented by human policy must have pre-existed and been supported, before it was established by human policy; it is, moreover, to weaken in those, who profess this religion, a pious confidence in its innate excellence, and the patronage of its Author; and to foster in those, who still reject it, a suspicion that its friends are too conscious of its fallacies, to trust it to its own merits. . . .[2]

Madison then goes on to explain that this has been proven repeatedly through the 15 centuries of Christianity. What have been its fruits, asks Madison?

. . . pride and indolence in the clergy; ignorance and servility in the laity: in both, superstition, bigotry and persecution. Inquire of the teachers of Christianity for the ages in which it appeared in its greatest lustre; those of every sect point out the ages prior to its incorporation with civil policy . . . what influence, in fact, have ecclesiastical establishments had on civil society? In some instances, they have been seen to erect a spiritual tyranny on the ruins of the civil authority; in more instances, have they been seen upholding the thrones of political tyranny; in no instance have they been seen the guardians of the liberties of the people. . . .[3]

The adverse effects of this law in the future could be seen by Madison, even in the initial discord it currently brought to the Christian church, as he writes:

. . . The very appearance of the bill has transformed that "Christian forbearance, love and charity," which of late mutually prevailed, into animosities and jealousies, which may not soon be appeased. What mischiefs may not be dreaded, should this enemy to the publick quiet be armed with the force of law? . . . Because the policy of the bill is adverse to the diffusion of the light of Christianity. The first wish of those, who ought to enjoy this precious gift, ought to be, that it may be imparted to the whole race of mankind. Compare the num-

ber of those who have as yet received it, with the number
still remaining under the dominions of false religions, and
how small is the former! Does the policy of the bill tend to lesson the disproportion? No; it at once discourages those who
are strangers to the light of truth, from coming into the regions
of it; and countenances, by example, the nations who continue
in darkness in shutting out those who might convey it to
them. . . .[4]

History Rewritten

James Madison's *Memorial and Remonstrance* has been quoted
at length because of the recent anti-Christian onslaught upon our
society with the now popular phrase: "Separation of Church and
State." In the past score of years in America, the coined phrase:
"Separation of Church and State" has been proclaimed and her-
alded by the media. The interpretation given is that the state or government of our nation and the Christian religion are two separate
and distinct entities, totally disconnected and disassociated one
from the other. Armed with this reasoning, the State has encroached
more and more upon the education of America's youth, thus gaining control of their minds. Examples are given, such as removing
prayer and the Ten Commandments from the public school classrooms. The Christian church has now been targeted, new laws
dictating more and more as to what it can and cannot do. The
term "Separation of Church and State," however, was never used by
Madison, the father of the U.S. Constitution. Neither was it ever
employed by George Washington or John Adams; but only once
used in a letter written by Thomas Jefferson to a Baptist group,
never in any public or political writing.

The truth of the matter is that Madison's famous document
extols the values of Christianity and the light of the gospel. It has
been singled out as the great document which undergirds the
"Religious Freedom Clause" in our United States Constitution.
The message is crystal clear, as with Thomas Jefferson's statute
for Religious Freedom in Virginia: *Freedom of worship under the
banner of Christianity*. Both of these founding fathers spoke about the
Christian religion when dealing with freedom of religion. They
were referring to the different and varying types of Christian wor-

ship: Quakers, Mennonites, Baptists, Episcopalians, Methodists and so forth—and not to anything outside mainline Christianity. This is apparent in all their writings. The founding fathers were indisputably Christian and biblical in their thinking and approach to drafting a unique form of government.

Madison's writings, as also those of Jefferson, clearly outline what the issue, which led to our first Amendment Clause, really was: Separation of Church from interference by the State in its mission, goals and outreach for Christ. In other words, it is the guaranteeing of liberty of worship of different denominational groups within the Christian community outside the civil jurisdiction and interference of the State.

However, in the Companion Guide Book to the 1989 PBS film Odyssey Production, entitled *The Supreme Court's Holy Battles*, with correspondent Roger Mudd, under the subtitle "JAMES MADISON '... THAT DIABOLICAL HELL-CONCEIVED PRINCIPLE,' " the following inaccurate statement regarding his *Memorial and Remonstrance* is made:

> ... Madison further outlined his views on matters of religion in the Memorial and Remonstrance Against Religious Assessments which he wrote in 1785 ...[5]

The title of James Madison's great document is "*A Memorial and Remonstrance,* presented to the General Assembly, of the State of Virginia, at their session in 1785, in consequence of a Bill brought into that Assembly for the Establishment of Religion by Law." It is not "Memorial and Remonstrance against Religious Assessments," the latter three words having been added by the authors of this Companion Guide Book. Madison's document, together with its title page, has been reprinted in the addendum for the reader to assess its original intent and meaning.

Further to the above, recent biographers impute negative character traits to this great founding father, weaving a narrative web that portrays the brilliant, restrained and self-contained Madison as "furious, scolding, abusing and ridiculizing!" These unchristian traits were never evidenced in Madison's comportment and writings:

... Nothing made James angrier than to see men punished for their religious views. . . Furious, James wrote to a college friend: "I have squabbled and scolded, abused and ridiculed so long about it. . . I am without common patience." . . .[6]

And:

... Most young men in Virginia attended the nearby College of William and Mary, but that wouldn't do for James. Too much drinking and partying at that school . . .[7]
(see Chapter III (viii) for original Charter and Seminary student life of William and Mary Divinity School at this epoch.)

And again:

... Because James was ahead of the freshman class in his studies, he entered as a sophomore and perhaps this was the happiest year of his college life. He made close friends, devoured books as if he couldn't get enough of them, and joined in student fun—putting greasy feathers on the floor where fellow students would slip on them, setting off fire-crackers in new-comers' rooms, and eyeing girls through tele-scopes . . .[8]

Aptly is Madison called the Father of the U.S. Constitution and a great Christian founding father.

John Quincy Adams, seventh president of the United States in his "Eulogy on the Life and Character of James Madison," delivered at the request of the Mayor, Alderman and Common Council of the City of Boston, September 27, 1836, throws further light on his stance against government interference in the mode of worship of all mainline Christian denominations:

... After the close of the War, in the year 1784, Mr. Jefferson introduced into the Legislature a Bill for the establishment of Religious Freedom. The principle of the Bill was the abolition of all taxation for the support of Religion, or of its Ministers, and to place the freedom of all religious opinions wholly beyond the control of the Legislature.[9]

Benjamin Franklin—a portrait of the founding father by Charles Willson Peale. Independence National Historical Park Collection.

(viii) Benjamin Franklin

Of all the founding fathers, Benjamin Franklin was perhaps the most versatile in his accomplishments. He achieved great heights in the fields of philosophy, diplomacy, government, invention, science and printing. He served in the Continental Congress, the Constitutional Convention and as president of Pennsylvania. This great statesman and inventor arrived in Philadelphia at age 17 as a poor Bostonian. The site of the house in which he lived with his wife, Deborah, and family, together with his original print shop facing Market Street in Philadelphia, is open to inspection by the public.

His contributions to charitable causes are many, including the founding of Pennsylvania Hospital in 1751, for which he composed the inscription for the cornerstone. It reads:

> In the year of Christ, 1755: George the second happily reigning, (for he sought the happiness of the people); Philadelphia flourishing, for its inhabitants were publick-spirited. This building, by the bounty of the Government and of many private persons, was piously founded, for the relief of the sick and miserable. May the God of mercies bless the undertaking!

A short time after the establishment of the hospital, Franklin wrote an account of the undertaking. It is called *Some Account of the Pennsylvania Hospital from its first rise, to the beginning of the fifth month, called May 1754*, and it was printed in Philadelphia by B. Franklin and D. Hall. It is now housed in the Rare Book Collection of the Library of Congress. Franklin concludes his account of this charitable institution with a sermon on the subject of charity, preached by Thomas Hartley, in Northhampton, Great Britain, in 1750. The sermon clearly illustrates the biblical foundations on which the hospital was built, and the implementing of Scriptural principles, to include: "But prove yourselves doers of the Word and not merely hearers who delude themselves" (James 1:22).

> The Experience of the above nine years, has given undeniable Proofs of the necessity and usefulness of this laudable institution, and, it is hoped, the perusal of the foregoing account, with what has been heretofore published, will afford pleasing Reflections to the beneficent Contributors, by whose generous

117

In the Year of Christ,
        1755;
George the second happily reigning;
(For he sought the Happiness of his People)
        Philadelphia flourishing,
(For its Inhabitants were publick-spirited)
        This Building,
By the Bounty of the Government,
And of many private Persons,
        Was piously founded,
For the Relief of the Sick and Miserable;
May the God of Mercies
        Bless the Undertaking!

Benjamin Franklin's handwritten cornerstone inscription for Pennsylvania Hospital which he founded in 1755. Outside Facade, Pennsylvania Hospital, Philadelphia. Photo by John W. Wrigley.

Assistance and Encouragement it has gradually arrived to its present situation, capable of extending relief to the distresses of many miserable objects, depressed by Poverty and Disease.

It would be a neglect of that justice which is due to the physicians and surgeons of this hospital, not to acknowledge, that their care and skill, and their punctual and regular attendance, under the Divine Blessing, has been a principal means of advancing this charity to the flourishing state in which we have now the pleasure to view it.

Relying on the continuance of the Favour of Heaven, upon the future endeavors of all who may be concerned in the management of the institution, for its further advancement, we close this account with the abstract of a sermon, preached before the Governors and Subscribers to the Infirmary of Northhampton, in Great Britain on the 24th of September 1750, by Thomas Hartley, Rector of Wenwick, Etc., viz.

I come thirdly, to speak of Charity, under view of Beneficence to the poor; and in this light we behold it in its fruits, as the Principle called forth into act, and which may therefore properly be styled the expression or evidence of our Charity, as it respects the temporal wants of our needy brethren. And here let it be observed, that as true Charity always produces this effect to the extent of our power, so it is this inward disposition that dignifies and consecrates the outward act. For as there may be mistaken zeal for Religion, even to the giving our bodies to be burnt for what we may call such, and yet without any true Love for God in our Hearts; so likewise the same Apostle tells us, that we may bestow all our goods to feed the poor, and yet, notwithstanding such a distribution, be void of the Spirit of real Charity. But I am now speaking of, and recommending that kind of Beneficence which is the fruit of Christian Benevolence; and among the various occasions which we offer for the exercise of it, the relief of the sick and lame poor, under the provision of a publick Infirmary, is that which lays claim to our present attention . . .

We read, that Almighty God, upon taking a Survey of the six days work of Creation, pronounced of everything which he

had made, that it was very good: How beautiful and perfect
then must he have been in his better part, for whose sake all
things were created! How excellent that Creature, who was
made in the image, and after the likeness of his Creator! But he
lusted after the vanity of Time, and so lost the riches of Eter-
nity; together with his Innocence, his Divine Light and Love,
and Purity departed from him—God made Man upright, but
he sought out many inventions, Eccls. VII.29. He sought to be
happy independently of God, and so lost his happiness in
him: Hence by nature our sad alienation from the Life of God;
instead of heavenly Wisdom, a serpentine craft; instead of
Divine Love, gross and corrupt affections; and in the room of
that perfect harmony in all its powers and faculties, which
tuned the soul to peace, all the discord and rage of conflicting
passions—behold, O Man! In this thy aggravated misery of a
distempered soul and body, the greatness of thy fall, and sad
apostasy! But behold also the greatness of Redeeming Love,
the infinite compassion of thy so much neglected Saviour!
Who, when thou wast cast out in the open field to the loathing
of thy person, passed by thee, and when he saw thee polluted
in thine own blood, said unto thee,—Live. I passed by thee,
and looked upon thee; and I spread my skirt over thee, and
covered thy nakedness; yea, I sware unto thee, and entered
into a Covenant with thee; saith the Lord God, and thou
becamest mine, Ezek. XVI. 5,6,8.

This application to you all, of every degree, on the subject
before us, comes backed with a notice of undeniable force, viz.
That our blessed Lord has declared his Acceptance of this
Relief which you afford to your afflicted Christian Brethren
from a Spirit of Charity, as done to Himself; For such as
appointed his substitutes for the receipt of it; I call upon you
then, for Christ's sake, that you be ready to distribute, willing
to communicate, I Tim. VI.18 or if this argument fails, there
remains at least one, which if rightly laid to heart, I am sure
must prevail, which is that we all stand in need of Mercy,
and therefore ought to shew it: I call upon you therefore, for
your own sakes, by the Love you bear to your immortal souls,
that you come not short of the promise of Him who hath
said, Blessed are the Merciful, for they shall obtain Mercy,
Matt. V.7.

And now having pointed out that most excellent Way of Charity, or Love to God, and our Neighbor, that Gospel Way of Pleasantness, that sure Path of Peace leading on to Glory, what remains but that we walk therein. We are called Christians, professing one Faith, one Lord, one Baptism: Let us shew ourselves to be such, not in Word only, but in Deed and in Truth; whilst our Faith worketh by Love, and our Love by shewing Mercy to the Poor.[1]

In comparison to Franklin's and Hartley's accounts of the hospital, the information put out by the Independence National Historic Park, Department of the Interior, is dry, sterile and incomplete. For example, their cultural tour literature reads that the Pennsylvania Hospital was conceived by Thomas Bond, the East Wing opening its doors in 1756 "for the relief of the sick, poor and for the reception and care of lunatics." They fail to even mention the actual founding of the hospital in 1751 by Benjamin Franklin—not even his cornerstone inscription for this hospital which reads that it " . . . was piously founded for the relief of the sick and miserable. May the God of Mercies bless this undertaking"!

There is no excuse for such an inane description, when Franklin's very own words are readily accessible to them. Visitors would much prefer to hear of the founding fathers' accounts of history rather than bland, secular, rewritten accounts by modern-day curators, who are deliberately misleading avid history-lovers by falsifying the truth. The beauty of founding period history, such as that of the Pennsylvania Hospital, is that Christianity and Christian principles were at the core of its inception.

Half a dozen organizations funded by Franklin still flourish today. Some of Franklin's money is still held in trust under his will for the benefit of the city of Philadelphia. Franklin cared for Philadelphia; his great mind, talents, and money benefited its citizens, from poor to rich alike.

Franklin was committed to a life of personal betterment, so much so that he carried on his person a small book with a list of 13 virtues he had selected as lifetime goals. Each day he would concentrate on cultivating one of the virtues. Following is this list from his autobiography.

1) Temperance:
Eat not to dullness; drink not to elevation.
2) Silence
Speak not but what may benefit others or yourself; avoid trifling conversation.
3) Order
Let all your things have their places; let each part of your
business have its time.
4) Resolution
Resolve to perform what you ought; perform without fail
what you resolve.
5) Frugality
Make no expense but to do good to others or yourself; i.e.
waste nothing.
6) Industry
Lose no time; be always employ'd in something useful; cut off
all unnecessary actions.
7) Sincerity
Use no hurtful deceit; think innocently and justly; and if you
speak, speak accordingly.
8) Justice
Wrong none by doing injuries, or omitting the benefits that are
your duty.
9) Moderation
Avoid extremes; forbear resenting injuries so much as you
think they deserve.
10) Cleanliness
Tolerate no uncleanliness in body, cloaths, or habitations.
11) Tranquility
Be not disturbed at trifles, or at accidents common or inavoid-
able.
12) Chastity
Rarely use venery but for health or offspring, never to dullness,
weakness, or the injury of your own or another's peace or
reputation.
13) Humility
Imitate Jesus . . .[2]

Franklin continues to explain his methodology: "My intention
being to acquire the habitude of all these virtues, I judg'd it would
be well not to distract my attention by attempting the whole at once,
but to fix it on one of them at a time; and, when I should be master

of that, then proceed to another, and so on till I had gone thro' the thirteen . . ."[3]

The little book included Scripture verses and prayers. Franklin had jotted down Proverbs 3:16 and 17, which speaks about the wisdom of God. "Length of days is in her right hand and in her left hand riches and honor. Her ways are ways of pleasantness, and her paths are peace."

Franklin wrote that he began each day with this prayer:

O powerful goodness! Bountiful Father! Merciful Guide! Increase in me that wisdom which discovers my truest interest. Strengthen my resolution to perform what that wisdom dictates. Accept my kind offices to thy other children as the only return in my power for thy continual favours to me.[4]

Benjamin Franklin's *Maxims and Morals* contain great and deep lessons for all. Among these are some worth remembering and learning:

But dost thou love life? Then do not squander time, for that is the stuff life is made of.
Search others for their virtues, thyself for thy vices.
Learn to be quiet and respect each other's rights.
Keep your eyes open before marriage, half shut afterwards.
Hast thou virtue? Acquire also the graces and beauties of virtue.
My father convinced me that nothing was useful which was not honest.
Freedom is not a gift bestowed upon us by other men, but a right that belongs to us by the laws of God and nature.
Virtue alone is sufficient to make a man great, glorious and happy.
Let the fair sex be assured that I shall always treat them and their affairs with the utmost decency and respect.
Self-denial is really the highest self-gratification.
Beware of little expenses.
Happiness in this life depends rather upon internals than externals.
Remember Job suffered and was afterwards prosperous.
I never doubted the existence of the Deity, that he made the world, and governed it by His Providence.

The event God only knows.

Good wives and good plantations are made by good husbands.

Hope and faith may be more firmly grounded upon Charity, than Charity upon hope and faith.

Virtue is not secure until its practice has become a habitude.

How much more profitable it is prudently to remove, than to resent, return and continue mimical proceedings!

Pride breakfasted with Plenty, dined with Poverty, and supped with Infamy.

Disputing, contradicting and confuting people are generally unfortunate in their affairs.

Without virtue man can have no happiness.

Here comes the orator with his flood of words and his drop of reason.

The pleasures of this world are rather from God's goodness than our own merit.

Increase in me that Wisdom which discovers my truest interest.

Contrary habits must be broken, and good ones acquired and established, before we can have any dependence on a steady, uniform rectitude of conduct.

Now I have a sheep and a cow everybody bids me good-morrow.

I was surprised to find myself so much fuller of faults than I had imagined.

Let no pleasures tempt thee, no profit allure thee, no ambition corrupt thee, no example sway thee, no persuasion move thee to do anything which thou knowest to be evil; so thou shalt live jollily, for a good conscience is a continual Christmas.

No qualities are so likely to make a poor man's fortune as those of probity and integrity.

Nothing is so likely to make a man's fortune as virtue.[5]

How important are these morals and maxims to be taught to our children today! Franklin also discusses how the necessity of industry preserved the youth of his day from many vices that arise from idleness. This was written in his remarkable work, *Information on those who would Remove to America*, published in 1794, in which Franklin also extolled the degree to which the Christian religion was esteemed and practiced in America. According to him, this was so much the case that atheism was virtually nonexistent, unfaithfulness rare and secret:

> . . . The almost general mediocrity of fortune that prevails in America obliging its people to follow some business for subsistence, those vices that arise usually from idleness are in a great measure prevented. Industry and constant employment are great preservatives of the morals and virtue of a nation. Hence bad examples to youth are more rare in America; which must be a comfortable consideration to parents. To this may be truly added, that serious religion, under its various denominations, is not only tolerated, but respected and practiced. Atheism is unknown there, infidelity rare and secret; so that persons may live to a great age in that country without having their piety shocked by meeting with either an atheist or an infidel. And the Divine Being seems to have manifested his approbation of the mutual forbearance and kindness with which the different sects treat each other, by the remarkable prosperity with which He has been pleased to favour the whole country.[6]

History Rewritten

Benjamin Franklin founded the Library Company of Philadelphia in 1731 "for the Advancement of Knowledge and Literature." It is the oldest private library in America, and the nation's major Colonial library which has survived intact. It served as America's first "Library of Congress" from 1774 until Congress established our present-day Library of Congress in 1800. It was a key intellectual resource for those who formed the Continental Congress, members of the Constitutional Convention and senators and representatives of Congress of the United States. The Library Company's informative literature describes its importance:

> If America had a national library before 1800, it was the Library Company. It served as "the Library of Congress" from 1774-1800, providing intellectual resources for the Continental Congress, members of the Constitutional Convention and Senators and Representatives of Congress of the United States. Chartered in 1731, the Library Company is a tax free, publically supported Charity.

As such, the Library Company is one of America's oldest and most valuable educational institutions. However, in recent years, the overseers of the Library Company have chosen to provide frivolous topics unrelated to Franklin's life and his library. The primary displays and exhibits of this library should focus on the great issues and subjects for which Franklin stood, ranging from his original works to the founding of the nation, education, knowledge, printing, inventions, writing, fine literature, scholarship and charitable endeavors. It should include excerpts from his original writings and create an atmosphere that appeals to the intellect and nurtures the soul.

Unfortunately, that is not the case. For instance, consider the following exhibit which ran from November, 1986, through April, 1987, entitled: "The Larder Invaded—Three Centuries of Philadelphia Food." Lectures were made available to the public with such topics as: Pennsylvania Wine and Cheese; Scrapple or Philadelphia Paté History Demonstration and Tasting; History of Coffee and Special Brewing Techniques; Cheers!! Philadelphia Brewing today brief History and Lecture by Philadelphia's newest entrepreneur of

The Library Company of Philadelphia Exhibit "The Larder Invaded." The famed old statue of founding father Benjamin Franklin, erudite scholar and founder of the Library Company, the oldest private library in the United states, dressed in a coarse kitchen apron.

Dock St. Brewery. While there is a place for such a thing, it belongs in a restaurant, tavern or inn, but not in Franklin's Library Company.

Upon entering Benjamin Franklin's Library, the author was struck by the traditional, old statue of Ben Franklin—founding father, inventor, philosopher and statesman, dressed in a coarse kitchen apron (see photograph). In addition, the exhibit intermingled religious and secular terminology. For example, prominent library exhibits bore titles such as: "Saints and Sinners;" "Holy Food;" and "Wholey, Good Food." Other titles used were: "Can you Guess, Enforce the 18th Amendment;" and "If you wish perfect health, use National Bitters." Religious material was interspersed with old recipe books, confusing the issue as to whether they were open Bibles, hymnals or cooking recipes.

Furthermore, to mix in Bible-related books and title pages bearing the word "Bible" upon them with FOOD, gives the clear implication, especially to children, that the *Bible*, containing *Spiritual Holiness and Wholeness* is equated with, and watered down to the level of plain, edible FOOD. Thus food for the soul, mind and spirit, our American Christian value system, (and the nurturing of the mind for which the Library Company was chartered), has been eliminated and replaced with FOOD AND DRINK (both alcoholic and non-alcoholic) for the body. This is another subtle example of rewritten history.

Another irregularity that struck the visitor to the Library Company's exhibit, was a white marble statue of Hester Prynn, the unwed mother and heroine of Nathaniel Hawthorne's *Scarlet Letter*, who was forced to wear a large, capital letter "A" upon her bosom in punishment for adultery. The statue stood in a place of prominence. At first glance it appeared to be that of Mary and her infant son , Jesus Christ. But a closer look revealed the caption disclosing her true identity as Hester Prynn who bore a child out of wedlock. What is the purpose of having such a statue in Benjamin Franklin's Library Company? The statue represents a character from a time period a century prior, an entirely different habitat and a different subject matter. Is it perhaps an attempt to debase Franklin's character via association? Once again, another great American founding father has been lowered and degenerated to the level of a cook within his own magnificent collection of fine literature, and this erudite library has been turned into "Food and Drink History." And this is considered part of the Educational Department of the Historical Society of Pennsylvania.

Another attempt to degrade this founding father is the popular belief that Franklin was a philanderer and an adulterer. This myth has caused many to think that Franklin wasn't married or a devoted husband. But in fact, while he may have had a winning and versatile personality, there is no proof that he was ever unfaithful to his wife.

Such greatly embellished stories could be said to stem from accounts of Franklin's years in the Corps Diplomatique in France. In a recent biography under the chapter title: "I Love the Ladies," we read:

> His success as a diplomat Franklin matched with his success in the salons. To the ladies of Paris he was "mon cher Papa" (my dear father). Even while raising arms and funds for his country, he found time to court the ladies. French society permitted the paying of frank compliments, and Franklin's wit found full play in conversation and correspondence. . . . There are stories of half a dozen women with whom he had affectionate relationships during his years in France. One of the younger was Anne-Louise Brillon de Jouy. Thirty-six when she met him, she was a beautiful and intelligent woman married to a man twenty years her senior. He was a government official who acted as intermediary for French Merchants selling weapons to the Americans. Franklin, of course, was almost forty years older than Madame Brillon, but she found age no barrier to the enjoyment of his company. An excellent musician, she and her daughters entertained Franklin "with little concerts, a cup of tea and a game of chess. . ." He wrote his famous Bagatelles for her and other intimate friends, printing them on his private press in his house at Passy. These are short essays, charming and whimsical. . .[7]

The above only validates my conclusion that Benjamin Franklin was a highly polished, versatile and charming diplomat, whose presence was sought at social gatherings. Far removed from such accounts is the myth that Franklin was "a philanderer and an adulterer!" Being of French descent, and familiar with the society salon receptions of Paris, I can with authority say that nothing of a derogatory nature could possibly be construed from the above description of well-bred French customs in entertaining.

Toward the end of his life Benjamin Franklin wrote the following letter to Robert R. Livingston, which reveals a strong faith in God.

> I am now entering on my 78th year; I wish now to be, for the little time I have left, my own master. If I live to see this peace concluded, I shall beg leave to remind the Congress of their promise, then to dismiss me. I shall be happy to sing with old Simeon, "Now lettest thou thy servant depart in peace, for mine eyes have seen thy salvation."[8]

In 1790, after a full, long and useful life, Franklin's mortal remains were laid to rest in the burial grounds of Christ Church, Philadelphia, later dubbed "the Nation's Church" because of the pivotal role played by members of this church leading to the birth of the nation. His wife and life-long companion, Deborah, is buried by his side.

Seven other signers of the Declaration of Independence are buried here. The eulogy, verbalized by Washington, and inscribed on a bronze plaque adjacent to the tomb, reads as follows:

> Venerated for benevolence, admired for talents; esteemed for patriotism; beloved for philanthropy.

A plaque on Franklin's family pew in Christ Church honors this great American patriot as well.

> Here worshipped Benjamin Franklin, philosopher and patriot. Member of the Committee which drafted the Declaration of Independence. Negotiator of the French Alliance of the Revolutionary War. Negotiator of the Treaty of Peace by which George III recognized the Independence of America. Member of the Convention which framed the Constitution of the United States. Member of the Committee which erected the Spire of this Church. Interred according to the terms of his will in this churchyard.

The state of Benjamin Franklin's soul is not for me to judge. Many historians express doubt that Franklin, at least publicly, ever acknowledged Christ as his personal Lord and Savior. However, there can be no debate that Franklin's life was deeply influenced by Christianity, and, as he points out, so was the well-being of the nation—as his maxims and morals, his letters and political writings exude. Of equal importance, his actions and selfless giving of his talents for the good of the new nation, attest to a Christian value system and world view.

Patrick Henry—a portrait of the founding father by Thomas Sully. Independence National Historical Park Collection.

(ix) Patrick Henry

> An Appeal to arms and to the God of Hosts is all that is left us!
> . . . There is a just God who presides over the destinies of
> nations; and who will raise up friends to fight our battles for
> us. The battle, sir, is not to the strong alone; it is to the vigilant,
> the active, the brave. Is life so dear, or peace so sweet, as to be
> purchased at the price of chains and slavery? . . . Forbid it,
> Almighty God! I know not what course others may take but as
> for me, give me Liberty, or give me death!
>
> Patrick Henry
> (Oration given at St. John's Church,
> Richmond, Virginia, March 23, 1775.)

Of all the great leaders of our nation's Revolutionary Period,
Patrick Henry strikes the most dashing and eloquent figure. When-
ever his name is mentioned, people invariably cite his famed
words: "Give me liberty, or give me death!" Henry was known for
his fiery oratory and eloquence of speech.

St. John's Episcopal Church in Henrico Parish, Richmond,
Virginia, was where Patrick Henry's famous speech was made. It
was founded in 1611 in Jamestown, Virginia, by the first English settlers who disembarked in 1607; the parish subsequently moved to
Richmond. In 1741 the present church was built. It stands upon a
hill, on a street called "Grace Street," depicting God's unlimited
grace to His people, and is surrounded by a quaint old historic
graveyard. Its beautiful wooden church steeple glorifies God with
the cross of our Lord and Savior Jesus Christ, soaring into the sky.

The original communion area within the church shows forth
the Ten Commandments, the Lord's Prayer and the Apostles'
Creed, upon a wall, in handsome calligraphy. Of great interest to
history-loving Americans, too, is the original 1607 baptismal font
which accompanied the first settlers to Jamestown.

It was here that the Second Virginia Convention convened
after having been removed from the House of Burgesses by the governor, and where, on March 23, 1775, Patrick Henry gave his "Liberty or Death" speech. Amazingly enough, Henry's formal education only reached third grade.

Not far from the pulpit, an enclosed desk was provided from
which Patrick Henry opened the convention with his magnificent
oratory. The desk is still there for all to see. A bronze plaque on the

wall directly behind Patrick Henry's desk, where he presided over this strategic meeting of America's founding period patriots, reads:

> Give me Liberty or give me Death.
>
> To the glory of God and as a grateful tribute to the memory of her illustrious son and first Governor Patrick Henry
>
> Patriot - Orator - Statesman
>
> The commonwealth of Virginia has caused this tablet to be erected in the Virginia Convention assembled in this church March 23, 1775. By his immortal eloquence he inspired in his countrymen the clear vision of truth and duty and roused them to consecrate themselves to the defence of Liberty. May 29, 1736—June 6, 1799.

On the cover of a brochure put out by St. John's Episcopal Church we read the following:

> St. John's Church, Richmond Virginia. A Registered National Landmark erected 1741.

In this church, on March 23, 1775, in the presence of Washington, Jefferson and the other members of the Second Virginia Convention, the torch of Liberty was kindled by the inspired words of Patrick Henry:

> "Give me Liberty . . . or give me death!"

Unbeknownst to most Americans, Patrick Henry's "Liberty" speech also contained great appeals and supplications to Almighty God for his beloved America and for the breaking of the yoke of tyranny from around her neck. In order to fully comprehend the import and meaning of his eloquent and galvanizing speech, it is here reproduced in its entirety.

> Mr. President: no man thinks more highly than I do of the patriotism, as well as abilities, of the very worthy gentlemen who have just addressed the House. But different men often see the same subject in different lights; and, therefore, I hope

that it will not be thought disrespectful to those gentlemen, if entertaining as I do, opinions of a character very opposite to theirs, I shall speak forth my sentiments freely and without reserve. This is no time for ceremony. The question before the House is one of awful moment to this country. For my own part I consider it as nothing less than a question of freedom or slavery; and in proportion to the magnitude of the subject ought to be the freedom of the debate. It is only in this way that we can hope to arrive at truth, and fulfill the great responsibility which we hold to God and our country. Should I keep back my opinions at such a time, through fear of giving offense, I should consider myself as guilty of treason toward my country, and of an act of disloyalty toward the majesty of heaven, which I revere above all earthly kings.

Mr. President, it is natural to man to indulge in the illusions of hope. We are apt to shut our eyes against a painful truth, and listen to the song of that siren, till she transforms us into beasts. Is this the part of wise men, engaged in a great and arduous struggle for liberty? Are we disposed to be of the number of those who, having eyes, see not, and having ears, hear not, the things which so nearly concern their temporal salvation? For my part, whatever anguish of spirit it may cost, I am willing to know the whole truth; to know the worst and provide for it.

I have but one lamp by which my feet are guided; and that is the lamp of experience. I know of no way of judging of the future but by the past. And judging by the past I wish to know what there has been in the conduct of the British ministry for the last ten years to justify those hopes with which gentlemen have been pleased to solace themselves and the House? Is it that insidious smile with which our petition has been lately received? Trust it not, sir; it will prove a snare to your feet. Suffer not yourselves to be betrayed with a kiss. Ask yourselves how this gracious reception of our petition comports with these warlike preparations which cover our waters and darken our land. Are fleets and armies necessary to a work of love and reconciliation? Have we shown ourselves so unwilling to be reconciled, that force must be called in to win back our love? Let us not deceive ourselves, sir. These are the implements of war and subjugation; the last arguments to which kings resort. I ask gentlemen, sir, what means this martial array, if its purpose be not to force us to submission? Can gentlemen assign any other possible motives for it? Has Great Britain any enemy, in this quarter of the world, to call for all this accumulation of navies and armies? No, sir, she has none. They are meant for us; they can be meant for no other. They are sent over to bind and rivet upon us those chains which the British ministry have been so long forging. And what have we to oppose them? Shall we try argument? Sir, we have been trying that for the last ten years. Have we anything new to offer on the subject? Nothing. We have held the subject up in every light of which it is capable; but it has been all in vain. Shall we resort to entreaty and humble supplication? What terms shall we find which have not been already exhausted? Let us not, I beseech you, sir, deceive ourselves longer. Sir, we have done everything that could be done to avert the storm which is now coming on. We have petitioned; we have remonstrated; we have supplicated; we have prostrated ourselves before the throne, and have implored its interposition to arrest the tyrannical hands of the ministry and parliament. Our petitions have been slighted; our remonstrances have produced additional violence and insult; our supplications have been disregarded; and we have been spurned, with contempt, from the foot of the throne. In vain, after these things, may we indulge the fond hope of peace and reconciliation. There is no longer any room for hope. If we wish to be free—if we mean to preserve inviolate those inestimable privileges for which we have been so long contending—if we mean not basely to abandon the noble struggle in which we have been so long engaged, and which we have pledged ourselves never to abandon until the glorious object of our contest shall be obtained, we must fight! I repeat it, sir, we must fight! An appeal to arms and to the God of Hosts is all that is left us!

They tell us, sir, that we are weak; unable to cope with so formidable an adversary. But when shall we be stronger? Will it be the next week, or the next year? Will it be when we are totally disarmed, and when a British guard shall be stationed in every house? Shall we gather strength by irresolution and inaction? Shall we acquire the means of effectual resistance by lying supinely on our backs, and hugging the delusive phantom of hope, until our enemies shall have bound us hand and foot? Sir, we are not weak, if we make a proper use of the means which the God of nature hath placed in our power. Three millions of people, armed in the Holy cause of Liberty, and in such a country as that which we possess, are invincible by any force which our enemy can send against us. Besides, sir, we shall not fight our battles alone. There is a just God who presides over the destinies of nations; and who will raise up friends to fight our battles for us. The battle, sir, is not to the strong alone; it is to the vigilant, the active, the brave. Besides, sir, we have no election. If we were base enough to desire it, it is now too late to retire from the contest. There is no retreat but in submission and slavery! Our chains are forged! Their clanking may be heard on the plains of Boston! The war is inevitable—and let it come! I repeat it, sir, let it come!

It is in vain, sir, to extenuate the matter. Gentlemen may cry peace, peace—but there is no peace. The war is actually begun! The next gale that sweeps from the North will bring to our ears the clash of resounding arms! Our brethren are already in the field! Why stand we here idle? What is it that gentlemen wish? What would they have? Is life so dear, or peace so sweet, as to be purchased at the price of chains and slavery? Forbid it, Almighty God! I know not what course others may take; but as for me, give me liberty or give me death!

Once again, we see a great American hero whose accomplishments were directly dependent upon his faith in God. So interwoven is this dependence within the speech, that one cannot separate Patrick Henry's Christian faith from his life, work and duty to his country.

A recent calligraphied print sold at a well-known store on the Duke of Gloucester Street in Williamsburg, Virginia, features a sketch of Patrick Henry with the capitalized inscription: "Give me Liberty or Give me Death."

The author of this excerpted piece taken from Patrick Henry's above-quoted speech saw fit to quote only the last portion of the oration, beginning with: ". . . The battle, sir, is not to the strong alone; it is to the vigilant, the active, the brave. . . ." and continuing on to its conclusion, ". . . but as for me, give me liberty or give me death! (signed) P. Henry."

The publisher, however, left out the most important and salient lines preceding Henry's concluding words. While he admits that "the battle is not to the strong alone," Henry's preceding lines preface this statement with, "there is a just God who will raise up friends to fight our battle for us." These words denote our weakness as a fledgling nation and our total dependence upon the miracle-working power of Almighty God:

> ... Sir, we are not weak, if we make proper use of the means which the God of nature hath placed in our power. Three millions of people, armed in the Holy cause of Liberty, and in such a country as that which we possess, are invincible by any force which our enemy can send against us. Besides, sir, we shall not fight our battles alone. There is a just God who presides over the destinies of nations; and who will raise up friends to fight our battles for us. . . .

Patrick Henry's above-quoted words denote: his dependence upon God's Omnipotence; his belief in God's miraculous intervention, due to our battle being a Holy cause of Liberty (or biblical freedom from a tyrannical power); the immutable Justice of God; God's supremacy and control over the destinies of nations; his reliance upon Almighty God to raise up allies and supporters to fight the war for us.

In short, Patrick Henry's total dependence was upon the God and Father of America, whom he believed would sovereignly intervene in the holy cause of liberty.

This omission is in accordance with the modern-day trend in public schools, government, museums and other institutions to eliminate the crucial role of Christianity from our foundations, thus eliminating it from present-day America. Unfortunately, the average citizen will only see this excerpt and will not go to the original to find out what has been left unsaid.

At the foot of this handsome print, the following lines are gleaned, in minuscule lettering:

> Excerpt from Patrick Henry's famous speech which was delivered on March 23, 1775 before the Virginia Assembly in St. John's Church in Richmond, Virginia. Patrick Henry never left a copy of his famous speech. The contents are the testimony and recollection of St. George Tucker, a lawyer and a judge, who was present and retained the essence of the speech.
> Copyright Walter H. Miller & Co., Inc.

This, however, is untrue, as the Second Virginia Convention had invited Patrick Henry to its official meeting. Moderated by Peyton Randolph, Patrick Henry's entire speech is recorded for us intact, within the proceedings of the March 23, 1775, Virginia Convention. It has thus become a valuable part of America's founding period history, proving God's intricate involvement and guidance in our nation's independence and liberty.

Once again, the rewriters of America's history have given out false information pertaining to a foundational document which sparked the entire American Revolution!

Thomas Jefferson's autobiography contains mention of Patrick Henry's eloquence as an orator for the cause of American Independence:

> I attended the debate at the door of the lobby of the House of Burgesses, and heard the splendid display of Mr. Henry's talents as a popular orator. They were great indeed; such as I have never heard from any other man. He appeared to speak as Homer wrote.

However, recent biographers have painted Patrick Henry in a derogatory light, alien to his true Christian identity and comportment:

> ... When he wasn't talking, Mr. Henry looked down his long nose at the other delegates as if they were common dirt. . . .[1]

And:

> ... Patrick Henry might be able to send his voice to the rafters, but he disliked descending to a desk and dealing with pen and paper. So he gave James the job of writing up state papers. . . . They both (James Madison and Thomas Jefferson) liked the same things: reading and collecting books, planting trees, experimenting with science, talking about history. And they agreed on what they didn't like: Great Britain, slavery, the lopsided Virginia constitution, and Patrick Henry. Neither man could stand Patrick Henry. "What shall we do with him?" James asked once when Patrick was being obstructive in his usual eloquent way. "What we have to do, I think," Jefferson replied, "is devoutly pray for his death. . . .[2]

The above narrative on Patrick Henry has no bibliographical source material attached to it whatever. In light of the lack of supportive evidence, it should be discarded as false.

The truth of the matter is that Patrick Henry and Thomas Jefferson worked together so well, that they drafted a resolution for a national day of prayer and fasting, which took place on June 1, 1774. The entire House of Burgesses in Williamsburg adjourned, going in processional to Bruton Parish Church to hear a biblical sermon.

Patrick Henry, the second of nine children, was born on May 29, 1736, to Colonel and Mrs. John Henry in Studley, Hanover County, Virginia. His father emigrated from Aberdeen, Scotland, to Virginia in 1730. Mrs. Henry's brother, William Winston, is said to have been endued with the great eloquence of speech which young Patrick seems to have inherited at birth.

At age 18, Henry fell in love and was married, his life beginning to take direction and bear fruit, with the loving support of an excellent wife. He applied to the Wythe School of Law at the College of William and Mary, and was, surprisingly, accepted. His career as a lawyer was thus begun, and eloquence in speech and oratory became his hallmarks.

When Thomas Jefferson, at age 26, was elected to the House of Burgesses in Williamsburg, Virginia, in 1768, Patrick Henry was the popular leader of this House. The two men worked together, Henry calling upon Jefferson in 1774, after the British Parliamentary Act closing the port of Boston; they drafted a resolution for a national day of prayer, humiliation and fasting.

George Washington wrote in his diary for that day, June 1, 1774: "Went to church and fasted all day." Shortly thereafter, Henry's resounding "Liberty" speech was heard around the world.

The House of Burgesses was instrumental in passing resolves in speaking out against taxation without representation as early as 1765. It was these resolves which appeared both in Virginia and Boston papers of that same year.

On the back of the resolves passed in the House of Burgesses in May, 1765, Henry wrote his summary of his pivotal point of history. He quotes a portion of Proverbs 14:34: "Righteousness alone can exalt a nation, but sin is a disgrace to any people," which summarizes his beliefs that Americans must be willing to stand for righteousness, whatever the cost.

> The within resolutions passed the House of Burgesses in May, 1765. They formed the first opposition to the Stamp Act and the scheme of taxing America by the British Parliament. All the colonies, either through fear, or want of opportunity to form an opposition or form influence of some kind or other, had remained silent. I had been for the first time elected a Burgess a few days before, was young, inexperienced, unacquainted with the forms of the House and the members that composed it. Finding the men of weight averse to opposition, and the commencement of the tax at hand, and that no person was likely to step forth, I determined to venture, and alone, unadvised, and unassisted, on a blank leaf of an old law book, wrote the within. Upon offering them to the House, violent threats were uttered, and much abuse cast on me by the party for submission. After a long and warm contest, the resolutions passed by a very small majority, perhaps of one or two only. The alarm spread throughout America with astonishing quickness, and the ministerial party was overwhelmed. The great point of resistance to British taxation was universally established in the colonies. This brought on the war which finally separated the two countries and gave independence to ours. Whether this will prove a blessing or a curse, will depend upon the use our people make of the blessing, which a gracious God hath bestowed on us. If they are wise, they will be great and happy. If they are of contrary character, they will be miserable. Righteousness alone can exalt them as a nation. Reader! Whoever thou art, remember this, and in thy sphere practice virtue thyself, and encourage it in others.
>
> (signed) P. Henry.[3]

Of further interest to those who would delve into the inner character and contributions of this American patriot is the famous oration on the Life and Character of Patrick Henry, delivered before the Patrick Henry Society of William and Mary College, on 29 May, 1840, by William R. Drinkard of Petersburg.

> . . . The glory which encircles the past history of our country, is undying and eternal; and we never recur to it but with feelings of mingled pride and joy. It is, to us, a many leaved

volume, unfolding on every page a new pleasure and an additional charm. It displays to our view, man in an altogether new aspect: it disrobes him of the gloom which the superstition and bigotry of darker ages had thrown around him—it dissipates the mystic cloud that had obscured him,— it severs the chains which had bound him to the dust; and places him upon an eminence high above the rest of his fellows,—a model that true dignity and greatness befitting only man—in the perfect and full enjoyment of all the choicest blessings that Heaven can bestow. The angel of darkness once hovered o'er our land, and deep was the midnight gloom which succeeded its advent. . . . the Christian could but weep at the desecration of those altars which had been dedicated to the service of his God. All around was cheerless gloom and hopeless despondency. Distant nations were appalled at the scene, and the red-eyed monster was about to leap upon his prey, when suddenly many stars of great magnitude appeared in our firmament, and dissipated the clouds which threatened our destruction. Among the first and brightest of this distinguished galaxy was he whom we have met this day and honor. Born and reared among those who were most sensibly affected by misrule and oppression, he was the better prepared to appreciate their feelings and uphold their rights. Blessed with poverty, an honest heart, and a sound judgment, he was insensible alike to the smiles and frowns of courtiers and of princes. . . . The advantages of an academic education were denied him, and the limited means which he possessed were but indifferently employed. . . . In the midst of his embarrassments, and in the depth of his poverty . . . he commenced the study; and soon thereafter the practice of law. Here was opened to him a new field for the exercise of those varied and transcendent powers, which had been dormant for so long a time, and which none ever supposed him to possess. The sleeping energies of his mind were aroused; as it were in the twinkling of an eye a mighty genius was called into existence. The cries of his suffering countrymen pierced his heart, and he nobly resolved to hazard all in their defence. Prostrating himself before the altar of his country, he placed upon it the rich oblation of an honest heart. . . . We might enquire, if the meekness of the Christian, and the fire of the patriot had not been so happily blended in him, what would have been the result of the union of vice with the untamed majesty of his spirit-stirring eloquence? Such is the beauty and the force of virtue. Without it, the most splendid and embellished intellect is but the unguarded and deadly instrument of dire destruction . . . The monuments of our own glory must pass away; the unequalled fame of our dear America may be retained only upon the molded leaf of some forgotten record; but the name and the deeds of Patrick Henry will ever be remembered while there is life in history, or in song . . . our people are a mighty people, and our government is a splendid government . . . It is particularly incumbent upon us, who are about to go into the world, and to perform our respective parts in the various scenes through which we shall pass, to study well the great principles upon which our government is based, and to consult the best oracles of wisdom and virtue that we may be happy, and that "our days may be long in the land which the Lord our God hath given us . . ." Let us go forth clad in the armor of truth and justice and righteousness, determined to perform our duty in defiance of the combined "powers of darkness and the wicked one;" and all may yet be well. But if, unhappily, the distressing calamities, of which I have spoken, should fall upon our devoted land, I humbly pray that Heaven may, once more, smile upon our bleeding cause. And when the hour of trial and of danger shall come, possibly there may be found among those whom I now address, another Washington who shall lead our armies to glory and to triumph, another Franklin who shall guide the awakened energies of our people, and another Henry who shall "ride upon the whirlwind and direct the storm." Finis.[4]

The above famous oration on the inner life and character of Patrick Henry points to his "meekness as a Christian" and his "zeal as an American patriot"; his spirit-stirring eloquence making him the great Revolutionary War hero that he has become.

At the end of the Revolutionary War, George Mason wrote to Patrick Henry, a letter which gives further insight into the pivotal role Henry played both prior to, and following Independence:

I congratulate you most sincerely, on the accomplishment of what I know was the warmest wish of your heart, the establishment of American independence and the liberty of our country. We are now to rank among the nations of the world; but whether our independence will prove a blessing or a curse, must depend upon our own wisdom or folly, virtue or wickedness. Judging of the future from the past, the prospect is not promising. Justice and virtue are the vital principles of Republican Government; but among us a depravity of manners and morals, prevails, to the destruction of all confidence between man and man. It greatly behooves the Assembly to revise several of our laws, and to abolish all such as are contrary to the fundamental principles of justice. . . It is in your power my dear sir, to do more good and prevent more mischief than any man in this State; and I doubt not that you will exert the great talents with which God has blessed you, in promoting the public happiness and prosperity.[5]

(x) George Mason

George Mason (1725–1792) was the author of the Virginia Declaration of Rights, which formed the basis for our Bill of Rights. He was a significant figure during the American Revolutionary years, and much has been written concerning him. Among those who admired his multifaceted personality was General Fitzhugh Lee, who said of him:

> He was indeed the people's man in a people's government. The tent of his faith was pitched upon the bedrock of the freedom of the citizen. Great was his belief in the security of a purely Republican form of government. Sublime was his reliance in the power of the people. This life of George Mason is proper and opportune. A period in our history has been selected to which we should more frequently recur, by calling attention to the service of a man with whose career we should become more familiar. "The people should control the government, not the government the people," was his war cry.[1]

As the wealthiest man in Virginia, George Mason owned 15,000 acres of land around his baronial estate, about 80,000 acres of land in Kentucky and a large estate in Ohio. He also owned or chartered a number of ships sailing from ports in Virginia and Maryland and engaged in the carrying trade of the colonies with England, France and the West Indies, and therefore may be said to have been the founder of our Merchant Marine.

This American son was member of the Board of Trustees of Alexandria, represented Fairfax County in the Virginia Assembly and was one of the presiding judges of the county.

George Mason, along with George Washington, served on the building committee and was a vestryman of Truro Parish, which consisted of three churches. Mason's term as vestryman lasted 35 years. In the historic records of Pohick Church, kept for posterity, we read that: "The Civil functions of the old vestries devolved by law on the overseers of the poor." Records show Mason and Washington disagreed on the selection of a suitable site for rebuilding Pohick Church, Mason preferring that the new church be built on the old site, while Washington urged for a new site, more conveniently located for the parishioners. Washington prevailed.

George Mason by John Hesselius (c. 1760). Oil on canvas Acc. no. 70950. Virginia State Library and Archives.

It was completed in 1774, and still stands near Mount Vernon. The beautiful interior of this church includes calligraphy-inscribed wall panels that face the congregation. Inscriptions comprise the Ten Commandments from Exodus 20, the Lord's Prayer from Matthew 6, and the Apostles' Creed. It's interesting to note the similarity of design in the ornamental woodwork of Pohick Church and George Mason's own Virginia plantation home, Gunston Hall.

A noted historian says the following about this American patriot:

> George Mason was the first man in the history of the world to formulate the principles of liberty and justice in a great state paper. His Virginia Constitution was the forerunner and pattern of all the Constitutions subsequently made. The first ten amendments of the Constitution of the United States are practically his and may be found expressed in the Virginia Bill of Rights. The influence of his work is worldwide. His ideals of Liberty, Freedom and Equality constitute the essence of all modern thought on this subject.
>
> His ideals have become a safeguard to human rights all the world over. . . . He was probably the wisest and most disinterested man to whom so great a task has ever been allotted by Divine Providence. He must be considered one of the greatest benefactors of our race.[2]

The last of the 16 articles in the Virginia Bill of Rights, authored by George Mason, and forerunner to the United States Bill of Rights, reads:

> That Religion, or the Duty which we owe to our Creator, and the Manner of discharging it, can be directed only by Reason and Conviction, not by Force or Violence; and therefore, all Men are equally entitled to the free exercise of Religion, according to the Dictates of Conscience; and that it is the mutual Duty of all to practice Christian Forbearance, Love, and Charity, towards each other.
>
> Article XVI
> The Virginia Declaration of Rights

(Drawn originally by George Mason and adopted unanimously by the Convention of Delegates at the Capitol in Williamsburg on June 12, 1776).

Once again, as with James Madison, we see the recurring theme among our founding fathers of *freedom of religion under the banner of Christianity*.

However, in the Companion Guide Book to the 1989 PBS production entitled *The Supreme Court's Holy Battles*, with correspondent Roger Mudd (available on videocassette for educational agencies, libraries, organizations and corporations), I was appalled to find that, in quoting the 16th and final article of the Virginia Bill of Rights, the authors had omitted the last sentence:[3] "and that it is the mutual Duty of all to practice Christian Forbearance, Love, and Charity, towards each other."

This is, of course, the key sentence on Christianity, thus giving the meaning that religion at the birth of our nation was left entirely to the dictates of conscience, without the need to practice Christian forbearance, love and charity towards each other.

The authors of *The Supreme Court's Holy Battles* fail to denote that information has been deleted from this foundational legal document of America's history.

The Introduction to the *Companion Guide Book of The Supreme Court's Holy Battles* states that this documentary:

> . . . was developed from current scholarship and archival research and from filmed interviews with these leading historians and Constitutional Experts:
>
> Richard R. Beeman, Professor of History, University of Pennsylvania
>
> Thomas E. Buckley, S.J., Professor of History, Loyola Marymount University
>
> A.E. Dick Howard, White Burkett Miller Professor of Law and Public Affairs, University of Virginia
>
> Rhys Isaac, Professor of History, LaTrobe University, Australia

Rex E. Lee, President, Brigham Young University, and former Solicitor General of the United States

Leonard W. Levy, Andrew W. Mellon All Claremont Professor of Humanities, Claremont Graduate School

Martin E. Marty, Fairfax Cone Distinguished Service Professor of the History of Modern Christianity, University of Chicago

Merrill D. Peterson, Thomas Jefferson Foundation Professor of History, Emeritus, University of Virginia.

and that:

This publication amplifies the historical information presented in *The Supreme Court's Holy Battles;* it also includes background essays on the meaning of the religion clauses.[4]

It is an impropriety on the part of professors of American history, law and public affairs, to rewrite America's history, leaving out the true importance and meaning of George Mason's own document, which concludes on a Christian note.

The above seriously puts in question the credibility of these modern-day historians who would rewrite the Virginia Declaration of Rights to fit a mold of their own invention and preference, in order to eliminate all mention of Christianity from this great document of our nation's governmental history. This very Christianity was not only the bedrock of George Mason's faith, but also that of our founding fathers. Whether these professors of U.S. Constitutional history and law agree with it or not, it is not their prerogative to eliminate or change one word from this legal document penned by George Mason in 1776. The Virginia Declaration of Rights forms an integral part of America's Christian heritage.

Evidence of George Mason's Faith

In his own handwriting, Mason wrote the following in his family 1759 Bible (unclassified) now in the possession of Gunston Hall Plantation, property of the Commonwealth of Virginia. This he wrote on the event of his beloved wife's death on March 19, 1773:

On Tuesday, the 9th of March, 1773, about three o'clock in the morning, died at Gunston-Hall, of a slow fever, Mrs. Ann Mason, in the thirty-ninth year of her age; after a painful and tedious illness of more than nine months, which she bore with truly Christian Patience and resignation, in faithful hope of eternal Happiness in the world to come. She, it may be truthfully said, led a blameless and exemplary life. She retained unimpaired her mental faculties to the last; and spending her latest moments in prayer for those around her, seem'd to expire without the usual pangs of dissolution. During the whole course of her illness, she was never heard to utter one peevish or fretful complaint, and constantly, regardless of her own pain and danger, endeavoured to administer hope and comfort to her friends, or inspire them with resignation like her own. For many days before her death she had lost all hopes of recovery, and endeavour'd to wean herself from the affections of this life, saying that tho' it must cost her a hard struggle to reconcile herself to the hopes of parting with her husband and children, she hoped God would enable her to accomplish it; and after this, tho' she had always been the tenderest parent, she took little notice of her children, but still retain'd her usual serenity of mind. She was buried in the new Family-burying-ground at Gunston-Hall; but (at her own request) without the common parade and ceremony of a grand Funeral.

Her funeral sermon was preached in Pohick Church by the Reverend Mr. James Scott, Rector of Dettingen Parish in the County of Prince William, upon a text taken from the 23rd, 24th, and 25th verses of the 73rd Psalm: "Nevertheless, I am continually with Thee; Thou hast taken hold of my right hand. With Thy counsel Thou wilt guide me, And afterward receive me to glory. Whom have I in heaven but Thee? And besides Thee I desire nothing on earth."

In the beauty of her person and the sweetness of her disposition she was equalled by few and excelled by none of her sex. She was something taller than the middle size and elegantly shaped. Her eyes were black, tender and lively; her features regular and delicate; her complexion remarkably fair and fresh. Lilies and roses (almost without a metaphor) were blended there, and a certain inexpressible air of cheerfulness

and health. Innocence and sensibility diffused over her countenance formed a face the very reverse of what is generally
called masculine. This is not an ideal but a real picture drawn
from the life, nor was this beautiful outward form disgraced by
an unworthy inhabitant. "Free from her sex's smallest faults,
and fair as womankind can be."

She was blessed with a clear and sound judgement, a gentle
and benevolent heart, a sincere and an humble mind, with an
even, calm and cheerful temper to a very unusual degree;
affable to all, but intimate with few. Her modest virtues
shunned the public eye; superior to the turbulent passions of
pride and envy, a stranger to altercation of any kind, and
content with the blessings of a private station, she placed all
her happiness here, where only it is to be found, in her own
family. Though she despised dress she was always neat; cheerful but not gay; serious but not melancholy. She never met me
without a smile! Though an only child she was a remarkably
dutiful one. An easy and agreeable companion, a kind neighbor, a steadfast friend, a humane mistress, a prudent and tender mother, a faithful, affectionate and most obliging wife;
charitable to the poor and pious to her Maker, her virtue and
religion were unmixed with hypocrisy or ostentation. She was
formed for domestic happiness, without one jarring atom in her
frame! Her irreparable departure I do ever shall deplore, and
though time, I hope, will soften my sad impressions and restore
me greater serenity of mind than I have lately enjoyed, I shall
ever retain the most tender and melancholy remembrance of
one so justly dear. [5]

The above gives a little-known inside view of Mason's Christian value system, as he extols his wife's inner beauty and character.

On the reverse side of the eulogy on his beloved wife, are
found the following lines written shortly after his death by a family member. It gives an accurate account of the founding father's
stature and caliber as a patriot.

George Mason of Gunston died at the Seat of Gunston Hall in
Fairfax County, Virginia, on the afternoon of Sunday, the seventh day of October, 1792 in the 67th year of his age, and
was buried on the family ground at that place. A profound

statesman and a pure patriot, he was a man of the first order, among those who acted on the theatre of the Revolution. He was active, earnest and influential in the counsels of Virginia, steering the struggle with Great Britain and took a zealous part, as a member of the Federal Convention in 1787, giving strong reasons, why the proposed Constitution, as it then stood, should not be adopted, and finally refused to sign it; for which he published to the world his reasons. The Virginia Convention of 1788 called to pass on that Constitution, he then opposed its adoption, and advocated another General Convention to revise it.

Contrary to the firsthand detailed evidence of the Masons' biblical way of life and their dependence upon Almighty God in prayer, a prominent article entitled, "George Mason: The Squire of Gunston Hall," published in the Spring 1991 edition of the Colonial Williamsburg Foundation's Journal, *Colonial Williamsburg*, states that:

> . . . Astonishingly, John Mason's (George Mason's second youngest son) disorganized recollections remain the chief source for what little we know of the private life of this statesman who helped shape our government. The same haze surrounds all the great figures of our colonial past, for early America managed to make history without benefit of Dan Rather, "Good Morning America," and *Time*. Communication was so threadbare that our leaders were usually granted privacy whether or not they wanted it. George Mason wanted it . . .[6]

Had the author of the above literary piece consulted George Mason's hand-written entries within his own 1759 original family Bible, housed at Gunston Hall, in the very building where his article appeared in the Spring 1991 edition of the *Colonial Williamsburg* journal, he would have assuredly found a wealth of inside facts about this founding father's Christian comportment and way of life.

Another excellent source available to him is the original *Vestry Records of Pohick Church, Truro Parish,* County of Fairfax, Virginia (now housed in the Library of Congress Rare Book Collection). This founding father served on the vestry of Pohick Church for 35 years. As the care and concern for the poor and needy of the

community-at-large developed around the vestry, Mason's intimate life is reflected in his duties as a vestryman.

Quite in keeping with the above excerpted quotation from the
article, "George Mason: The Squire of Gunston Hall," we read the
author's portrayal of Ann Mason:

> . . . His wife, physically devastated by bearing 12 children
> and rearing the nine who survived, died in 1773. She was
> only 39. Her husband remembered her eyes, "black, tender and
> lively; her features regular and delicate; her complexion
> remarkably fair and fresh . . ."[7]

I submit that this is a deliberate falsification of the cause of
Ann Mason's death, as George Mason attributes her departure
from this world to "a slow fever after a painful and tedious illness
of more than nine months." The above-excerpted article also deni-
grates her excellent role as a Christian wife and exemplary mother
of nine. Mason's own glowing account of his wife's "Christian
patience and resignation, . . . her blameless and exemplary life . . .
spending her last moments in prayer for those around her . . . saying that tho' it must cost her a hard struggle to reconcile herself to
the thoughts of parting with her husband and children, she hoped
God would enable her to accomplish it"; . . . and that "she had
always been the tenderest parent . . . a prudent and tender mother
. . ." exposes the above as rewritten history.

In his lengthy eulogy, Mason did not only remember his
wife by her eyes, which he prefaced by "In the beauty of her person
and the sweetness of her disposition she was equaled by few and
excelled by none of her sex, . . ." but he remembered her Christian
beauty as well, which, he stated, "diffused her countenance . . . nor
was this beautiful outward form disgraced by an unworthy inhabitant . . . "

After Mason's departure from this life, these lines were
retrieved from his pocketbook by his daughter Sarah:

> Alas! What can the honors of the world impart
> To soothe the anguish of a bleeding heart.[8]

George Mason's last Will and Testament shows forth his love
and adherence to the Lord Jesus Christ, during his sojourn upon
earth:

I, George Mason, of "Gunston Hall," in the parish of Truro and county of Fairfax, being of perfect and sound mind and memory and in good health, but mindful of the uncertainty of human life and the imprudence of man's leaving his affairs to be settled upon a deathbed, do make and appoint this my last Will and Testament. My soul, I resign into the hands of my Almighty Creator, whose tender mercies are over all His works, who hateth nothing that He hath made and to the Justice and Wisdom of whose dispensation I willingly and cheerfully submit, humbly hoping from His unbounded mercy and benevolence, through the merits of my blessed Savior, a remission of my sins." [9]

(xi) Noah Webster

Noah Webster was born in Hartford, Connecticut, on October 16, 1758. His father was a respectable farmer and Justice of the Peace. Webster was a fourth generation descendant of John Webster, one of the first settlers of Hartford. His mother was a descendant of William Bradford, second governor of Plymouth Colony.

Mr. Webster commenced the study of the classics in the year 1772, under the instruction of the clergyman of the parish, the Reverend Nathan Perkins, D.D., and in 1774 was admitted as a member of Yale College.

Not having the means to obtain a regular education for the bar, Webster pursued the study of law during intervals of his regular employment, without the aid of an instructor. He was admitted to the bar in 1781. In 1783, Webster published "First part of a Grammatical Institute of the English Language," the second and third parts being published shortly thereafter.

During the summer of 1785, Webster worked on a series of lectures on the English language, which were delivered in principal East Coast cities in 1786, and were subsequently published in 1789 under the title: "Dissertations on the English Language."

Webster became superintendent of an Episcopal Academy in Philadelphia in 1787. The Constitutional Convention solicited his eloquent pen to recommend the new system of government to the people. This resulted in a pamphlet entitled: "Examination of the Leading Principles of the Federal Constitution."

In 1789, Webster published a New York periodical entitled: the *American Magazine*. After the adoption of the new constitution in 1798, Webster settled in Hartford, where he practiced law.

In 1807, he published *A Philosophical and Practical Grammar of the English Language*—a unique work and the result of many years' research and study.

The results of his inquiries into the origin and filiation of languages were embodied in a work about half the size of the American Dictionary, entitled: *A Synopsis of Words in Twenty Languages*.

During these labors, Mr. Webster found his resources inadequate to support his family at New Haven. He thus moved, in 1812, to Amherst, a country town eight miles from Northampton, Massachusetts. In 1824, after spending two months in Paris consulting rare books at La Bibliotéque du Roi, and a subsequent eight months at Cambridge University in England; his most famous work, *The American Dictionary*, was finally completed in May of 1825.[1]

Webster expressed his entire resignation to the will of God, and his unshaken trust in the atoning blood of his Redeemer, the Lord Jesus Christ.[2]

In his "Memoir of the Author" the Editor concludes:

> It may be said that the name Noah Webster, from the wide circulation of some of his works, is known familiarly to a greater number of the inhabitants of the United States, than the name, probably, of any other individual except the father of the Country. Whatever influence he thus acquired was used at all times to promote the best interests of his fellowmen. His books, though read by millions, have made no man worse. To multitudes they have been of lasting benefit not by the course of early training they have furnished, but by those precepts of wisdom and virtue with which almost every page is stored. August, 1847.[3]

The preface to Webster's greatest work, *An American Dictionary of the English Language—with pronouncing vocabularies of Scripture, classical and geographical names*, finishes with the following thanksgiving and praise to Almighty God:

> To that great and benevolent Being, who, during the preparation of this work, has sustained a feeble constitution amidst obstacles and toils, disappointments, infirmities and depression; who has borne me and my manuscripts in safety across the Atlantic, and given me strength and resolution to bring the work to a close, I would present the tribute of my most grateful acknowledgements. And if the talent which He entrusted to my care, has not been put to the most profitable use in his service, I hope it has not been "kept laid up in a napkin" and that any misapplication of it may be graciously forgiven.
>
> New Haven.
Noah Webster.

Webster's academic and professional credentials are quite extensive, ranging from: Member of the American Philosophical

Society in Philadelphia; Fellow of the American Academy of Arts and Sciences in Massachusetts; Member of the Connecticut Academy of Arts and Sciences; Fellow of the Royal Society of Northern Antiquaries in Copenhagen; Member of the Connecticut Historical Society; Corresponding Member of the Historical Societies in Massachusetts, New York and Georgia; of the Academy of Medicine in Philadelphia; and of the Columbian Institute in Washington; and Honorary Member of the Michigan Historical Society.

Yet, with all these academic honors, Noah Webster knew and loved the Word of God with such intensity, being thoroughly convinced of its eternal and inerrant value, that he used Scripture verses throughout his dictionary, describing and explaining the meanings and import of much vocabulary and syntax. The title page of his original dictionaries bears this out with the wording: " . . . with pronouncing vocabularies of Scripture, Classical, and Geographical Names." For example, his descriptions for the verb "to follow," include:

> To pursue as an object of desire; to endeavor to obtain. "Follow peace with all men." Hebrews 12

> To adhere to; to side with. "The House of Judah followed David." II Samuel 2.

> To adhere to; to honor; to worship; to serve. "If the Lord be God, follow Him." I Kings 18.

> To be led or guided by. "Woe to the foolish prophets who follow their own spirit and have seen nothing." Ezekiel 13.

And then, the noun "country," is described in the following manner:

> The kingdom, state or territory, in which one is born; the land of nativity; or the particular district indefinitely in which one is born. America is my country, or England is my country. "Laban said, it must not be so done in our country." Genesis 29.

The region in which one resides. "He sojourned in the land of promise, as in a foreign country." Hebrews 11.

Land, as opposed to water; or inhabited territory. "The ship-men deemed that they drew near to some country." Acts 27. The inhabitants of a region. "All the country wept with a loud voice." 2 Samuel 15.

A place of residence; a region of permanent habitation. "They declare plainly that they seek a country." "They desire a better country, that is a heavenly one." Hebrews ll.

The above illustrations were taken from Webster's 1848 Dictionary. The author prefaces his work with explanations and reasons for the undertaking of this monumental task, as unto the Lord:

In the year 1783, just at the close of the Revolution, I published an elementary book for facilitating the acquisition of our ver-nacular tongue, and for correcting a vicious pronunciation, which prevailed extensively among the common people of this country. Soon after the publication of that work, I believe in the following year, that learned and respectable scholar the Rev. Dr. Goodrich of Durham, one of the trustees of Yale College, suggested to me the propriety and expediency of my compil-ing a dictionary, which would complete a system for the instruction of the citizens of this country in the language . . . About 35 years ago, I began to think of attempting the com-pilation of a dictionary. . . . I published my compendious dic-tionary in 1806; and soon after made preparation for under-taking a larger work. . . . It is not only important, but in a degree necessary, that the people of the country should have an "American Dictionary of the English Language;" for, although the body of the language is the same as in England, and it is desirable to perpetuate that sameness, yet some dif-ferences must exist. Language is the expression of ideas; and if the people of one country cannot preserve an identity of ideas, they cannot retain an identity of language. Now, an identity of ideas depends materially upon a sameness of things or objects with which the people of the two countries are conversant. But in no two portions of the earth, remote from each other, can such identity be found. Even physical objects must be different. But the principal differences between the people of this country and of all others, arise from different forms of government, different laws, institutions and customs . . . If the language can be improved in regularity, so as to be more easily acquired by our own citizens and by foreigners, and thus be rendered a more useful instrument for the propagation of science, arts, civilization and Christianity . . . and if, in short, our vernacular language can be redeemed from corruptions and our philology and literature from degradation; it would be a source of great satisfaction to me to be one among the instruments of promoting these valuable objects. . . .

It was thus that Noah Webster used his God-given talents to the glory of Almighty God, without a doubt refusing to be counted among those unworthy stewards of Christ's bounty, who were reprimanded and cast into utter darkness for having "kept their talents laid up in a napkin" (at the last judgment).

Upon near completion of his great dictionary, Webster penned these moving lines:

I was seized with trembling, which made it somewhat difficult to hold my pen steady for writing. The cause seems to have been the thought that I might not then live to finish the work . . . But I summoned strength to finish the last work, then, walking about the room a few minutes, I recovered.

An 1828 newspaper clipping announced the completion of Webster's famous dictionary, in these terms, showing forth his sacrifice, and the good stewardship of his God-given talents and abilities:

Noah Webster, Esq., author of the Spelling Book, has given notice in the Eastern newspapers, that he has completed a Dictionary of our language, "at the expense of 20 years of labor, and thirty thousand dollars in money." He mentions that he made a visit to England, partly with a view to ascertain the real state of the language, and there discovered that no book whatever was considered a rule in that country as a standard of orthoepy. He observes, incidentally, that not less than 7 millions of copies of his Spelling Book have been sold. He thinks that the English dictionaries, are all, half a century behind the state of science, and hopes that his fellow citizens will be furnished with something better in the one which he is about to publish.

In the year 1790, Noah Webster published his *American Spelling Book—Containing an easy Standard of Pronunciation. Being the first part of a Grammatical Institute of the English Language.*

The second page of this magnificent teaching tool for America's youth (and adults) is dedicated to the Reverend Ezra Stiles, S.T.D., President of Yale College, and professor of Ecclesiastical History. Webster states:

> This first part of a Grammatical Institute of the English Language, is, with permission, most humbly inscribed, as a testimony of my veneration, for the superior talents, piety and patriotism, which enable him to preside over that seat of literature, with distinguished reputation, which render him an ornament to the Christian Profession, and give him an eminent rank among the illustrious characters that adorn the Revolution.

Webster's *Fourth Rule for Reading and Speaking* articulates tones, looks and gestures as here quoted:

> If a person is rehearsing the words of an angry man, he should assume the same furious looks, his eyes should flash with rage, his gestures should be violent, and the tone of his voice threatening. If kindness is to be expected, the countenance should be calm and placid, and wear a smile—the tone should be mild, and the motion of the hand inviting. An example of the first, we have in the words, "Depart from Me, ye cursed, into everlasting fire prepared for the devil and his angels." Of the last, in these words, "Come ye blessed of my Father, inherit the Kingdom prepared for you from the foundation of the world." A man who should repeat these different passages with the same looks, tones and gestures would pass with his hearers for a very injudicious speaker. . . .

Webster's Speller, Table VI, consists of three syllable words: the full accent being on the first, and a weaker accent on the third. The first example given is the word: "Cru-ci-fix." (The cross upon which our Lord and Savior Jesus Christ died to save the souls of all who would believe in Him.) Another word is: "chast-i-ty;" and yet another is "pu-ri-ty."

An illustration of "Merit's Prize" vouchers, printed and distributed by G.C. Merriam Company, shows how good behavior and diligent attention at school were rewarded.

Webster was not only a schoolmaster, lecturer, pamphleteer and publisher of schoolbooks, but he was also the author of a pamphlet entitled: "Sketches of American Policy." The following initialed notation in Webster's handwriting shows his intricate involvement with founding fathers George Washington and James Madison in establishing a unique form of government. All three men were American Christian statesmen of the highest caliber:

> The following sketches were written in the month of February, 1785, before any proposal had even been made to remodel the government of the States. In May, I carried one copy of them to Virginia and presented it to General Washington. Mr. Madison saw and read it at the General's soon after, and in November the same year, he, in conversation with me, expressed a warm approbation of the sentiments it contains. At the next session of the Legislature, which indeed began the same month, a proposition was made in the Assembly, for appointing the commissioners, who afterward met at Annapolis and whose recommendations originated the convention at Philadelphia in 1787.

By 1947, the year during which Webster's publishers, the G. & C. Merriam Company, celebrated a centennial of Webster's magnificent dictionary, Noah Webster's famous *Blue-Back Speller* published in 1783, had sold more than 70,000,000 copies.

Among the greatest American best sellers, after the Bible, are: *Webster's Dictionary of the English Language, Webster's Biographical Dictionary* and *Webster's Dictionary of Synonyms.*

Webster's 1886 *Unabridged Dictionary,* with Scripture quotations throughout, was "warmly recommended by State Superintendents of Public Schools of Maine, New Hampshire, Vermont, Massachusetts, Rhode Island, Connecticut, New York, Pennsylvania, New Jersey, Delaware, Ohio, Virginia, Indiana, Illinois, Wisconsin, Minnesota, Kansas, Nebraska, Arkansas, Texas, Mississippi, Kentucky, California, Colorado, West Virginia, Oregon and ten other States of the Union."[4]

Further to this, an early advertisement for the 1890 edition of *Webster's International Dictionary*, describes this great book as being invaluable in office, school and home, standard of the United States Government Printing Office, the Supreme Court and of nearly all the schoolbooks; warmly recommended by educators almost without number, The One Great Standard Authority.[5] Hon. D. J. Brewer, Justice of the U. S. Supreme Court, writes: "The International Dictionary is the perfection of dictionaries. I commend it to all as the one great standard authority."[6] In the Preface to his Common Version translation of *The Holy Bible, containing the Old and New Testaments, with Amendments of the Language,* Webster states:

> The English version of the sacred Scriptures, now in general use, was first published in the year 1611, in the reign of James I. Although the translators made many alterations in the language of the former versions, yet no small part of the language is the same, as that of the versions made in the reign of Queen Elizabeth. . . . The Bible is the Chief moral cause of all that is good, and the best corrector of all that is evil, in human society; the best book for regulating the temporal concerns of men, and the only book that can serve as an infallible guide to future felicity. With this estimate of its value, I have attempted to render the English version more useful, by correcting a few obvious errors and removing some obscurities with objectionable words and phrases; and my earnest prayer is that my labors may not be wholly unsuccessful.
>
> Noah Webster
New Haven. 1833.[7]

It was thus that Noah Webster used his God-given talents fruitfully and diligently during his span of life upon earth, distinguishing himself in the production of two of the greatest masterpieces of our national Christian heritage: *Webster's original Dictionary of the English language—replete with Scripture verses;* and *The Holy Bible containing the Old and New Testaments, in the Common Version, with Amendments of the Language, 1833.*

How is it then, that Scripture, prayer and Christian values, which were all so prevalent in America's foremost textbooks and dictionaries, have been in recent years expunged from all of Webster's original works—and "banned" from the public school domain? One of the multiple examples of Scripture having been expunged from Webster's original Dictionaries, is as follows:

Webster's 1854 Dictionary described the word "Generation," n., as:

1. The act of begetting, procreation, as of animals.
2. Production, formation; as, the generation of sounds, or of curves or equations.
3. A single succession of natural descent, as the children of the same parents; hence, an age. Thus we say, the 3rd, the 4th or the 10th generation.
Genesis XV:16.
4. The people of the same period or living at the same time.
O faithless and perverse generation!
Luke IX.
5. Genealogy; a series of children or descendants from the same stock.
This is the book of the generation of Adam.
Genesis V.

Webster's New 20th Century Dictionary, Unabridged, Second Edition, describes the same word as:

1. The act of begetting; reproduction; procreation.
2. Production; creation; origination; as the generation of sounds.
3. A single stage or degree in the succession of natural descent; as, father, son, and grandson are three generations.
4. The period of time (about thirty years) between the birth of one generation and that of another.
5. All people born at about the same time or living in the same period of time.

The above is a remarkable and astounding phenomenon, and one which baffles me and befuddles the most astute foreigner and inquirer into the customs and traditions of the United States. Why did editors feel it necessary to make these deletions and changes? Is it a part of a deliberate, well-organized and well-thought out master plan over a period of half a century or more, operating within the ranks of our country's government and culture dedicated to the deletion and eradication of all traces of Christianity from *this Nation under God*. This could be equated with "robbery in the burnt offering to Almighty God," as the first-fruits of the nation, i.e. our children, belong to Him, and should continue to be nurtured in His truths.

Chapter II

19TH-CENTURY HEROES
WHO BUILT UPON THE FOUNDATION

"The Abraham Lincoln Prayer Window"—showing Lincoln in his family pew in prayer, New York Avenue Presbyterian Church, two blocks from the White House.

(i) Abraham Lincoln

Abraham Lincoln, the 16th president of the United States, came from humble origins. He was born in Hardin County, Kentucky in 1809, and then moved with his family to Gentryville, Indiana. He lived in a plain cabin with a dirt floor, beds made of dried leaves and stools and table formed of logs.

His mother's only book was a Bible, from which Lincoln was taught and nurtured each day. She taught him to base his entire life upon the contents of that book. At his mother's untimely death when the boy was 10 years old, Lincoln knew much of the Word of God almost by heart. Many years later, as president of the United States, Lincoln is quoted as having said: "All that I am or hope to be, I owe to my angel mother. Blessings on her memory!" The second book Lincoln read was Weem's *Life of Washington*, followed by *The Life of Benjamin Franklin*. Lincoln, being thirsty for knowledge, walked six miles in order to obtain a grammar book. At night, he would study diligently by the light given out through the burning of shavings, candles being too expensive for his meager wages.

A hard-working lad, Lincoln was not always paid in money for his work. It is remembered that once, for a certain Mrs. Miller, he split 400 rails for every yard of brown jeans, dyed with white walnut bark, necessary to make a pair of trousers. Honesty, hard work and integrity became his hallmarks.

Six feet, four inches tall, Lincoln was known to have had a big heart and thus his nickname: "Honest Abe." This name was acquired because of his scrupulous honesty, as attested to by the example: While managing a mill and store at New Salem, Lincoln overcharged a woman 6 ¼ cents. When the error came to his attention, night had fallen. This did not deter Lincoln, who walked several miles to return her money to her. Another woman bought a half pound of tea. Afterwards, to his dismay, he found that he had used a four-ounce weight on the scales and thus walked a long way to return the funds to her.

His mother's life and example ever being before his eyes, he insisted on politeness in front of women. One day, a boorish man used profane speech in front of two ladies. Lincoln asked him to desist. The man subsequently became angered, so young Abraham announced: "Well, if you must be whipped, I suppose I may as well whip you as any other man," and he gave him a severe punishing. The man became a polite individual, and Lincoln's friend for life.

Upon witnessing the auction of slaves, Lincoln is reported to have said: "By the grace of God I'll make the ground of this country too hot for the feet of slaves."[1]

A quaint story is passed down about an old black woman coming to the door of the White House to meet the president as he left. She asked to see "Abraham the Second." "And who was Abraham the First?" asked Lincoln. "Why, Lor' bless you, we read about Abraham de First in de Bible, and Abraham de Second is de President." "Here he is," said Lincoln, overcome with emotion.

Lincoln's magnificent Gettysburg Address, delivered at Gettysburg, Pennsylvania, on November 19, 1863, was the shortest speech any United States president ever gave, being two minutes in length. Lincoln was wrong when he said: "The world will little note, nor long remember, what we say here . . ." Inscribed within the Lincoln Memorial* in our nation's capital, his words are memorialized for millions of American schoolchildren. They continue to touch the hearts of all who read these simple, but deeply moving words, and to challenge the citizens of every generation to assume responsibility for their nation and its unique problems in history. Here is the address in its entirety:

> Fourscore and seven years ago our fathers brought forth on this continent a new nation, conceived in liberty, and dedicated to the proposition that all men are created equal. Now we are engaged in a great civil war, testing whether that nation, or any nation so conceived and so dedicated can long endure. We are met on a great battlefield of that war. We have come to dedicate a portion of that field as a final resting-place for those who here gave their lives that that nation might live. It is altogether fitting and proper that we should do this. But in a larger sense, we cannot dedicate, we cannot consecrate, we cannot hallow this ground. The brave men, living and dead, who struggled here, have consecrated it far above our poor power to add or detract. The world will little note, nor long remember, what we say here, but it can never forget what they did here. It is for us, the living, rather to be dedicated here to the

*See Addendum for the "Invocation at the Dedication of the Lincoln Memorial."

unfinished work which they who fought here have thus far so nobly advanced. It is rather for us to be here dedicated to the great task remaining before us, that from these honored dead we take increased devotion to that cause for which they gave the last full measure of devotion; that we here highly resolve that these dead shall not have died in vain; that this nation, under God, shall have a new birth of freedom, and that this government of the people, by the people, for the people shall not perish from the earth.

Lincoln was the first United States president to use the term: "This nation under God" in reference to our country. After his death, in 1865, on each succeeding February 12, a "Lincoln Day Observance Service" is held at the New York Avenue Presbyterian Church, his parish church, situated just two blocks from the White House. In 1954, Dwight Eisenhower was in attendance with his wife at this service. He was so moved by George Docherty's sermon entitled "Under God," taken from Lincoln's words, that he initiated action in Congress to have it permanently made a part of the Pledge of Allegiance: "I pledge allegiance to the Flag of the United States of America and to the Republic for which it stands, *One Nation Under God*, indivisible, with liberty and justice for all."

Among the treasures in the safekeeping of the Rare Book Collection of the Library of Congress, is Abraham Lincoln's 1847 Family Bible (unclassified), with his family records inscribed within; Mrs. Abraham Lincoln's 1854 Bible, with her own hand-written words therein as follows:

This Holy Bible is presented
to my dear son's eldest daughter, by her affectionate Grandmother,
Mary Lincoln
October 16, 1872;

and Abraham Lincoln's Presidential Inaugural Bible, upon which he took his oath of office, his left hand resting upon its contents.

William J. Wolf in his book entitled *The Religion of Abraham Lincoln* wrote:

No president has ever had the detailed knowledge of the Bible that Lincoln had. No president has ever woven its thoughts and its rhythms into the warp and woof of his state papers as he did.[2]

This is evidenced in his "Second Inaugural Address," where Lincoln incorporated three magnificent Scriptures—Matthew 7:1, 18:7 and Revelation 16:7—into his speech. He also spoke quite openly about the Bible, the Word of God and prayer in this discourse referring to Almighty God seven times.

While Abraham Lincoln was a man of few words, his words bore great weight. In characteristic fashion, he opened his "Second Inaugural Address" by stating that an extended address was not needed since this was a continuation of his first term as president. Aptly, a major portion of the address is given to the Civil War. It is fitting to view the words of this great president and statesman, for they bear in them the wisdom of the Word of God, and his concern to foster healing and restoration for the entire nation. Inscribed upon the North Wall of the Lincoln Memorial in our nation's capital, they are here reprinted for all to read:[3]

At this second appearing to take the oath of the Presidential office there is less occasion for an extended address than there was at the first. Then a statement somewhat in detail of a course to be pursued seemed fitting and proper. Now, at the expiration of four years, during which public declarations have been constantly called forth on every point and phase of the great contest which still absorbs the attention and engrosses the energies of the nation, little that is new could be presented. The progress of our arms, upon which all else chiefly depends, is as well known to the public as to myself, and it is, I trust, reasonably satisfactory and encouraging to all. With high hope for the future, no prediction in regard to it is ventured.

On the occasion corresponding to this four years ago all thoughts were anxiously directed to an impending civil war. All dreaded it, all sought to avert it. While the inaugural address was being delivered from this place, devoted altogether to saving the Union without war, insurgent agents were in the city seeking to destroy it without war—seeking to dissolve the Union and divide effects by negotiation. Both parties deprecated war, but one of them would make war rather than let the nation survive, and the other would accept war rather than let it perish, and the war came.

One-eighth of the whole population were colored slaves, not distributed generally over the Union, but localized in the southern part of it. These slaves constituted a peculiar and powerful interest. All knew that this interest was somehow the cause of the war. To strengthen, perpetuate, and extend this interest was the object for which the insurgents would rend the Union, even by war; while the Government claimed no right to do more than to restrict the territorial enlargement of it. Neither party expected for the war the magnitude or the duration which it has already attained. Neither anticipated that the cause of the conflict might cease with, or even before, the conflict itself should cease. Each looked for an easier triumph, and a result less fundamental and astounding. Both read the same Bible and pray to the same God, and each invokes His aid against the other. It may seem strange that any men should dare to ask a just God's assistance in wringing their bread from the sweat of other men's faces, but let us judge not, that we be not judged.[4] The prayers of both could not be answered. That of neither has been answered fully. The Almighty has His own purposes. "Woe unto the world because of offenses; for it must needs be that offenses come, but woe to that man by whom the offense cometh."[5] If we shall suppose that American slavery is one of those offenses which, in the providence of God, must needs come, but which, having continued through His appointed time, He now wills to remove, and that He gives to both North and South this terrible war as the woe due to those by whom the offense came, shall we discern therein any departure from those divine attributes which the believers in a living God always ascribe to Him? Fondly do we hope, fervently do we pray, that this mighty scourge of war may speedily pass away. Yet, if God wills that it continue until all the wealth piled by the bondsmen's two hundred and fifty years of unrequited toil shall be sunk, and until every drop of blood drawn with the lash shall be paid by another drawn with the sword, as was said three thousand years ago, so still it must be said "the judgments of the Lord are true and righteous altogether."[6]

with malice toward none, with charity for all, with firmness in the right as God gives us to see the right, let us strive on to finish the work we are in, to bind up the nation's wounds, to care for him who shall have borne the battle and for his widow and his orphan—to do all which may achieve and cherish a just and lasting peace among ourselves and with all nations.

Regardless of the above evidence of Abraham Lincoln's Christian qualities and detailed knowledge of the Bible, the shrine in our nation's capital, site of Lincoln's death, has a different story to tell.

Ford's Theatre, National Historic Shrine

Ford's Theatre, constructed in 1861, is a gem of old classic architecture and loveliness, but it is more famous as the site where Lincoln was assassinated. Located on 10th Street, N.W., near the J. Edgar Hoover F.B.I. Building, it is just two blocks from Pennsylvania Avenue, the nation's Presidential Inaugural Parade Avenue.

While attending an evening performance of "Our American Cousin" on April 14, 1865, President Lincoln was assassinated in his presidential loge by an actor named John Wilkes Boothe. Lincoln died the following morning at the home of Swedish tailor, William Petersen, where he had been transported across the street the night before. At his bedside sat his beloved pastor and spiritual advisor, Phineas Gurley, from Lincoln's parish church, the New York Avenue Presbyterian Church.

Rewritten History

On the new *Official Park Guide* recently printed by the National Park Service, United States Department of the Interior, and given out to millions of people at this National Historic Site, one reads in bold capital lettering:

ASSASSINATION

of

PRESIDENT LINCOLN

The President Shot at Theatre

Last Evening

The upper third of this Guide is in jet black, the entire contents of the *Official Park Guide* being morbid in tone, wording and descriptive phraseology. As one opens the literature, a large reproduction of Ford's Theatre is in the center with one of its outer walls removed, leaving jagged edges, in order for the reader to reenact Lincoln's assassination on the stage of the theatre. A caption underneath the reproduction reads:

> This illustration is akin to a movie, for it shows the activity from the time Lincoln was shot until he was carried across the street and placed on the bed in the back bedroom of the Petersen House. Study it carefully.
> The illustrator is Al Lorenz.

The entire guide majors upon violence, murder, bloodshed, insanity and death. A graphic example of this descriptive literature gives the following account of Mary Todd Lincoln:

> The President's Widow

> Neither the judgment of history, nor the events she lived through were kind to Mary Todd Lincoln. . . . Her husband was shot in her presence. Criticism stalked her public actions and did not abate in the aftermath of Lincoln's assassination. In 1875 she was judged insane and admitted to a sanitorium for several months. . . .

And again:

> Washington in 1865:

> . . . Undertakers and coffin-makers were in great demand. Opportunists joined the throngs, preying on the weak and the innocent and adding to the crush of people. The city's primitive facilities were soon overtaxed. Few streets were paved, and in rainy weather they became almost impassable. Many wells were contaminated because of the lack of sewage facilities. The creeks and canals in the city were little more than open sewers. Washington was undergoing growing pains that would only be dealt with in the decade after 1865.

And then again:

The 10th Street Neighborhood:

> Ford's Theatre lay north of two of the worst neighborhoods in
> Washington. South of Pennsylvania Avenue, just a block and
> a half away, was what locals called "Hooker's Division," a cen-
> ter for crime and vice, named after the commander of troops
> stationed in the area, Gen. Joseph Hooker. Nearby was Murder
> Bay, one of the city's worst slums. As the city's population
> swelled with the influx of soldiers, so did the numbers of
> gamblers, hustlers, pickpockets, bootleggers and prostitutes.
> Unwary soldiers were frequently relieved of what little money
> they had.

I submit that the above events and circumstances surrounding
Lincoln's death are inappropriately pessimistic and lugubrious in
nature, and that the description of Washington, D.C. and the Ford's
Theatre neighborhood at that epoch is deliberately inaccurate. One
may question: Why does the National Park Service, in its above
recently rewritten literature, insist upon majoring on these gloomy,
pessimistic and fatalistic details in Abraham Lincoln's National
Historic Shrine, to the exclusion of the facts themselves? These
original facts portray Lincoln as a catalyst whose Christian value
system was foremost in his approach to the healing of the nation.

The above morbid and utterly fatalistic descriptive phraseology recurring throughout this *Official Park Guide*, can only be classified as "death literature" which has, in recent years, been forced
upon America's youth in school and university classrooms throughout our blessed land. The results have been depression, despair and
even suicide, when internalized and dwelt upon. Millions of young
Americans visit this museum annually. To make them reenact and
internalize the tragic and violent events which ended Lincoln's
earthly pilgrimage, without any mention of Abraham Lincoln's
God, his belief in eternal life through our Lord and Savior Jesus
Christ and his love of the Bible, is to distort the facts of America's
history—missing the mark completely.

Another *Official National Park Guide*, put out by the Division of
Publications, U.S. Department of the Interior in 1986 (Handbook

129), is about the Lincoln Memorial in our nation's capital. It begins by telling us of Abraham Lincoln, "the myth":

> This memorial is a testament in stone to a man, to a myth, and to an ideal that distinguishes the United States among nations. The man is Abraham Lincoln. The myth is of a hero who preserved the Union . . .

Based on the wealth of original evidence on Abraham Lincoln's Christian character, integrity and deeds, he was no "myth," nor was his cause to eradicate the evil of slavery from American soil "a myth." His life exemplified the stark reality of elevating human beings to the dignity of men and women made in the image of God.

Mary Todd Lincoln

Abraham Lincoln's wife, Mary Todd Lincoln, has been particularly maligned. All the original documents, writings and letters pertaining to Mary Todd Lincoln that I have consulted, show a woman of deep Christian faith, commitment to her family and church (New York Avenue Presbyterian Church) and a commendable wife to Abraham Lincoln. From where, then, did the myth of her being "a shrew" and "insane" ever originate? There is not a shred of documented evidence on her so-called "insanity" or ungodliness. Quite a number of recent biographies denigrate and debase the godly Mary Lincoln, in the most extraordinary way, such as the following excerpted commentary:

> . . . Today Mary Lincoln ranks among the most detested public women in American history, and Americans who do not know her husband's wartime policies or the names of his cabinet officers have unshakable opinions about Mary Lincoln's failings. Many remember because she demonstrated her husband's humanity. The President who dealt so generously with the afflicted in public affairs learned, in this understanding, to do so through his private life with a shrew. It is, of course, not a solely American idea that men of great mind and sensibility, like Socrates, often endure wives of abominable temper, like Xanthippe. In our national version of this myth Lincoln, the most venerated of all American heroes, daily

practiced tolerance of a cantankerous female who was neither his first nor his greatest love. If the great Abraham assures his wife's tainted immortality, the maligned Mary guarantees her husband's nobility. . . .[7]

And:

. . . Mary Lincoln was so incurably hostile as to do permanent damage to any friendship. . . .[8]

And again:

. . . Never under strict control, Mary Lincoln's temper was now given a very public display before the entire high command of the Army of the Potomac. After clambering out of the hateful ambulance toward the President, according to one officer, "Mrs. Lincoln repeatedly attacked her husband in the presence of officers because of Mrs. Griffin (who had also been on the reviewing field) and Mrs. Ord. . . . He pleaded with eyes and tones till she turned on him like a tigress and then he walked away hiding that noble ugly face so that we might not catch the full expression of its misery. . . .[9]

Another recent biographer throws more light on the matter, recounting the denigration of Mary Todd Lincoln in these terms:

. . . The core of the problem, I have come to believe, lies in the world's uncritical, all-encompassing adoration of Abraham Lincoln as something considerably more than a man. In many minds he has made the transition from folk-hero to folk-god, in something of the same process that enveloped Alexander the Great. As a folk-god, it would not have been possible for Abraham Lincoln to have loved a mortal woman, any mortal woman. Had he done so, that would have reduced him in stature. In order to maintain him as the great folk-god, it was necessary to give him a wife who would be the worst and most insupportable wife since Xanthippe. To all of the tragic burdens which Abraham Lincoln had to shoulder during the Civil War, his stature as a folk-god would be enhanced by adding one more ever-present and inescapable burden, Herndon's "female wild cat of the age. . . ."[10]

The following letter written by Mrs. Mary Todd Lincoln to her pastor from the executive mansion on May 22, 1865, shows the deep gratitude for the friendship and sympathy demonstrated to her bereaved family:

> Rev. Dr. Gurley
> My Dear Sir:
> Please accept as a memento, of the very kind regard entertained for you by my Beloved Husband, the hat worn by him, for the first and only time, at his Second Inauguration. While its intrinsic value is trifling, you will prize it, for the associations that cluster around it. If anything can cast a ray of light across my dreary and blighted pathway, the recollection of your Christian kindness, extended to myself and family in our heavy bereavements will ever be most gratefully cherished. With love to Mrs. Gurley, I remain,
>
> > Your heart broken friend,
> > Mary Lincoln.
>
> (Mrs. Lincoln died July 16, 1882 at the home of her sister, Mrs. Edwards, in Springfield, Illinois.)[11]

Let us now study Mary Todd Lincoln's own intimate letters to her confidante, friend and employee, Elizabeth Keckley, who published them in 1868 in her book entitled: *Behind the Scenes, Thirty Years a Slave and Four Years in the White House*. In the Introduction to a later edition of this book, we read:

> . . . However, Robert Lincoln rebuked Mrs. Keckley for publishing his mother's letters. He refused to accept the author's explanation, and prevailed upon the publisher, G. W. Carleton and Company, to suppress the book. *Behind the Scenes* was recalled from the market and all available copies were bought up by "friends of Mr. Lincoln." Elizabeth Keckley realized nothing from the sale of the book and suffered a decline of patronage in her dressmaking business. Some of her best friends even felt that book was harmful to other Negroes similarly employed. . . . Mrs. Keckley's book reveals more clearly the intimate family life of the martyred president and offers a more credible portrait of Mary Todd, than perhaps any other book about the Lincolns.[12]

The following are excerpts from Mary Todd Lincoln's published letters:

Chicago, December 27:

Dear Lizzie:
I wrote you a few lines on yesterday . . . I believe any more newspaper attacks would lay me low. As influence has passed away from me with my husband, my slightest act is misinterpreted. "Time makes all things right." I am positively suffering for a decent dress. I see Mr. A. and some recent visitors eyeing my clothing askance. Do send my black merino dress to me very soon; I must dress better in the future. . . .
Write,
Yours,
Mary Lincoln. . . .[13]

Clifton House, January 12:

My dear Lizzie:
Your last letter was received a day or two since. I have moved my quarters to this house, so please direct all your letters here. . . . Your letter announcing that my clothes were to be paraded in Europe—those I gave to you—has almost turned me wild. Robert would go raving distracted if such a thing was done. If you have the least regard for our reason, pray write to the Bishop that it must not be done. How little did I suppose you would do such a thing; you cannot imagine how much my overwhelming sorrows would be increased. May kind Heaven turn your heart, and have you write that this exhibition must not be attempted. Robert would blast us all if you were to have this project carried out. Do remember us in our unmitigated anguish, and have those clothes, worn on those fearful occasions, recalled. I am positively dying with a broken heart, and the probability is that I shall be living but a very short time. May we all meet in a better world, where such grief is unknown. Write me all about yourself. . . . For the sake of humanity, if not me and my children, do not have those black clothes displayed in Europe. The thought has almost whitened every hair on my head. Write when you receive this.[14]
Your friend,
Mary Lincoln.

The above suppressed correspondence from Mary Todd Lincoln to her confidante and friend show overwhelming grief at the announcement that the intimate Lincoln family mourning clothes would be paraded throughout Europe as museum pieces. It also graphically exposes the derogatory newspaper attacks on the person and character of Mrs. Lincoln in the wake of her husband's death, the latter having had many enemies during his lifetime.

As far as Mary Lincoln's impeccable qualities as a supportive wife and mother, this is amply proven by Keckley's eyewitness accounts of President Abraham Lincoln and his wife's devoted husband-wife relationship, to which she was a firsthand observer for four years in the White House:

> . . . The day after the levee I went to the White House and while fitting a dress to Mrs. Lincoln, she said:

> "Lizabeth, I have an idea. These are war times and we must be as economical as possible. You know the President is expected to give a series of state dinners every winter, and these dinners are very costly . . . the state dinner can be scratched from the programme. What do you think, Lizabeth?"

> "I think you are right, Mrs. Lincoln."

> "I am glad to hear you say so. If I can make Mr. Lincoln take the same view of the case, I shall not fail to put the idea into practice."

> Before I left her room that day, Mr. Lincoln came in. She at once stated the case to him. He pondered the question a few moments before answering.

> "Mother, I am afraid your plan will not work."

> "But it will work, if you will only determine that it shall work."

> "It is breaking in on the regular custom," he mildly replied.

But you forget, father, these are war times, and old customs can be done away with for the once. The idea is economical, you must admit."

"Yes, mother, but we must think of something besides economy. . . I believe you are right, mother. You argue the point well. I think that we shall have to decide on the receptions."

So the day was carried. The question was decided, and arrangements were made for the first reception. It now was January, and cards were issued for February.[15]

The above husband/wife discussion shows that Mary Lincoln appealed to her husband, according to the biblical admonition, "Wives, be subject to your own husbands, as to the Lord" (Ephesians 5:22), abiding by his final decision as her head. Throughout Keckley's inside account of the relationship between Abraham Lincoln and his wife, the identical pattern occurs. Nowhere is there any evidence to the contrary, as the rewriters of America's history would have our nation believe.

Another similar account is given below:

. . . Finding that Willie continued to grow worse, Mrs. Lincoln determined to withdraw her cards of invitation and postpone the reception. Mr. Lincoln thought that the cards had better not be withdrawn. At least he advised that the doctor be consulted before any steps were taken. Accordingly, Dr. Stone was called in. He pronounced Willie better, and said that there was every reason for an early recovery.

He thought, since the invitations had been issued, it would be best to go on with the reception. Willie, he insisted, was in no immediate danger. Mrs. Lincoln was guided by these counsels, and no postponement was announced. On the evening of the reception Willie was suddenly taken worse. His mother sat by his bedside a long while, holding his feverish hand in her own, and watching his labored breathing. The doctor claimed there was no cause for alarm. I arranged Mrs. Lincoln's hair, then assisted her to dress. Her dress was white satin, trimmed with black lace. The trail was very long, and as she swept through the room, Mr. Lincoln was standing with his back to the fire, his hands behind him, and his eyes on the carpet. His face wore a thoughtful, solemn look. The rustling of the satin dress attracted his attention. He looked at it a few moments; then, in his quaint, quiet way remarked:

"Whew! Our cat has a long tail tonight."

Mrs. Lincoln did not reply. The President asked: "Mother, it is my opinion, if some of that tail was nearer the head, it would be in a better style;" and he glanced at her bare arms and neck. She had a beautiful neck and arm, and low dresses were becoming to her. She turned away with a look of offend-ed dignity, and presently took the President's arm, and both went down-stairs to their guests, leaving me alone with the sick boy. . . . The brilliance of the scene could not dispel the sadness that rested upon the face of Mrs. Lincoln. During the evening she came up-stairs several times, and stood by the bedside of the suffering boy. She loved him with a mother's heart, and her anxiety was great. The night passed slowly; morning came, and Willie was worse. He lingered a few days, and died. God called the beautiful spirit home, and the house of joy was turned into the house of mourning. . . . Mr. Lincoln came in. I never saw a man so bowed down with grief. He came to the bed, lifted the cover from the face of his child, gazed at it long and earnestly, murmuring, "My poor boy, he was too good for this earth. God has called him home. I know that he is much better off in heaven, but then we loved him so. It is hard, hard to have him die!" Great sobs choked his utter-ance. He buried his head in his hands, and his tall frame was convulsed with emotion. . . . His grief unnerved him, and made him a weak, passive child. I did not dream that his rugged nature could be so moved. I shall never forget those solemn moments—genius and greatness weeping over love's idol lost. . . . Mrs. Lincoln's grief was inconsolable. The pale face of her dead boy threw her into convulsions. . . . Willie, she often said, if spared by Providence, would be the hope and stay of her old age. But Providence had not spared him. . . . Mrs. Lincoln was so completely overwhelmed with sorrow that she did not attend the funeral. . . .[16]

Nathaniel Parker Willis left a touching account of the Lincoln family in the aftermath of their young son's death. It is here excerpt-ed:

. . . He was his father's favorite. They were intimates—often seen hand-in-hand. And there sat the man, with a burden on his brain at which the world marvels—bent now with the load at both heart and brain—staggering under the blow like the taking from him of his child!

His men of power sat around him—McClellan, with a moist eye when he bowed in prayer, as I could see from where I stood; and Chase and Seward, with their austere features at work; and senators, and ambassadors, and soldiers, all struggling with their tears—great hearts sorrowing with the President as a stricken man and a brother. That God may give him strength for all his burdens is, I am sure, at present the prayer of a nation.[17]

Mrs. Lincoln's seamstress continues:

This sketch was very much admired by Mrs. Lincoln. I copy it from the scrap-book in which she pasted it, with many tears, with her own hands.[18]

The above eyewitness accounts of Abraham and Mary Todd Lincoln as a husband-wife team, dispel the unfactual fairy tales circulated throughout the land that Mary Todd Lincoln was a disgrace and a blight to her husband. Such second or third-hand stories, without any evidence to validate them can only be discarded as false.

As a fitting memorial and tribute to our 16th president, let us remember his life and deeds, as expressed by one who knew him well, his pastor, Dr. Phineas D. Gurley—one who prayed with him at his deathbed, helping Mrs. Lincoln and her son through their dark night of trial.

"HAVE FAITH IN GOD"—Mark 11:22
A Sermon
Delivered in the East Room of the Executive Mansion
Wednesday, April 19, 1865
At
THE FUNERAL OF ABRAHAM LINCOLN,
PRESIDENT OF THE UNITED STATES
By

REV. P. D. GURLEY, D.D.
PASTOR OF THE NEW YORK AVENUE
PRESBYTERIAN CHURCH, WASHINGTON, D.C.
AS WE STAND HERE TODAY, MOURNERS AROUND THIS
COFFIN AND AROUND THE LIFELESS REMAINS OF OUR
BELOVED CHIEF MAGISTRATE, WE RECOGNIZE, AND
WE ADORE THE SOVEREIGNTY OF GOD. His throne is in
the heavens, and His kingdom ruleth over all. He hath done,
and He hath permitted to be done, whatsoever He please.

. . . The people confided in the late lamented President with a
full and loving confidence. Probably no man since the days of
Washington was ever so deeply and firmly embedded and
enshrined in the very hearts of the people as Abraham Lincoln.
Nor was it a mistaken confidence and love. He deserved it—
deserved it well—deserved it all. He merited it by his character, by his acts, and by the whole tenor, and tone, and spirit of
his life. He was simple and sincere, plain and honest, truthful
and just, benevolent and kind. His perceptions were quick and
clear, his purposes were good and pure beyond question.
Always and everywhere he aimed and endeavored to be right
and to do right. . . .

He saw his duty as the Chief Magistrate of a great and imper-
illed people, and he determined to do his duty, and his whole
duty, seeking the guidance and leaning upon the arm of Him
of whom it is written, "He giveth power to the faint, and to
them that have no might He increaseth strength." Yes, he
leaned upon His arm, He recognized and received the truth
that the "kingdom is the Lord's, and He is the governor
among the nations." He remembered that "God is in history,"
and he felt that nowhere had His hand and His mercy been so
marvelously conspicuous as in the history of this nation. He
hoped and prayed that that same hand would continue to
guide us, and that same mercy continue to abound to us in the
time of our greatest need. I speak what I know, and testify
what I have often heard him say, when I affirm that that
guidance and mercy were the props upon which he humbly
and habitually leaned; they were the best hope he had for
himself and for his country. Hence, when he was leaving his
home in Illinois, and coming to this city to take his seat in the
executive chair of a disturbed and troubled nation, he said to

the old and tried friends who gathered tearfully around him and bade him farewell, "I leave you with this request: pray for me." They did pray for him; and millions of other people prayed for him; nor did they pray in vain. Their prayer was heard, and the answer appears in all his subsequent history; it shines forth with a heavenly radiance in the whole course and tenor of his administration, from its commencement to its close. God raised him up for a great and glorious mission, furnished him for his work, and aided him in its accomplishment. Nor was it merely by strength of mind, and honesty of heart, and purity and pertinacity of purpose, that He furnished him; in addition to these things, He gave him a calm and abiding confidence in the overruling Providence of God and in the ultimate triumph of truth and righteousness through the power and the blessing of God. . . .

Never shall I forget the emphasis and the deep emotion with which he said in this very room, to a company of clergymen and others, who called to pay him their respects in the darkest days of our civil conflict: "Gentlemen, my hope of success in this great and terrible struggle rests on that immutable foundation, the justice and goodness of God. And when events are threatening, and prospects very dark, I still hope that in some way which man cannot see all will be well in the end, because our cause is just, and God is on our side. . . ."

He is dead; but the God in whom he trusted lives, and He can guide and strenghen his successor, as He guided and strengthened him . . . but the cause he so ardently loved survives his fall, and will survive it. . . .

(ii) Robert E. Lee

Robert E. Lee, son of Anne Hill Carter and Major General Light Horse Harry Lee, was born on January 19, 1807 at Stratford Hall, the great Potomac River Plantation. He grew up in the family home, a house built in 1795, situated at 607 Oronoco Street, Alexandria, today an oustanding example of federal architecture, open to the public as a memorial to Virginia's great southern hero. His father had been a heroic cavalry leader in the Revolution and three times governor of Virginia. When Robert was six, his father, ill, penniless and broken in spirit, left the family for Barbados and never returned. The former hero died on his way back when Robert was 11, so, for all practical purposes, Robert was raised by his mother from age six. Anne Hill Carter was a direct descendant of Robert "King" Carter, the richest and most powerful figure of Virginia's Golden Age in the early 18th century. Raising her five children almost single-handedly, and giving them a magnificent example of Christian virtue, she is one of the little-celebrated heroines of America. William Fitzhugh, a distinguished contemporary, called her "one of the finest women the state of Virginia has ever produced," and stressed her "meritorious and successful exertions to support, in comfort, a large family, and give all her children excellent educations."

Robert E. Lee's schooling, up to the age of 13, was with a tutor at Eastern View, home of Robert Randolph, his mother's brother-in-law. From 1820–1823, he studied under William B. Leary at Alexandria Academy. In February, 1825, he was tutored by Benjamin Hallowell, a Quaker schoolmaster at 609 Oronoco Street, in order to pave the way for his entrance to West Point. At age 18, Lee entered the United States Military Academy as a cadet to train for his distinguished career. In the 1830s he became a lieutenant.

Lee married Mary Ann Randolph, only surviving child of George Washington Parke Custis, who was George Washington's adopted grandson. They inherited Arlington Plantation, 1,100 acres of tobacco land across the Potomac River from our capital city. The beautiful Lee-Custis Mansion, built by George Washington Parke Custis, still stands today. It was in this gracious southern home that their seven children were born and where Lee prayed fervently one entire night for God's guidance and His perfect will in the soul-wrenching decision—whether to serve with the North or support his homeland and the Confederacy.

In April, 1861, President Lincoln had offered him the field command over the U.S. Army. Lee turned it down, resigning from the army and shortly after joined the Confederacy. In a letter to his sister, he wrote:

> With all my devotion to the union and the feeling of loyalty and duty of an American citizen, I have not been able to make up my mind to raise my hand against my relatives, my children, my home.[1]

Although Lee owned slaves himself, he believed this system was a travesty, but he felt that the eradication of slavery "would sooner result from the mild and melting influences of Christianity than from the storms and tempests of fiery controversy."

In a letter to his wife dated December 27, 1856, Robert E. Lee had written:

> . . . In this enlightened age, there are a few, I believe, but will acknowledge that slavery as an institution is a moral and political evil in any country. . . . I think, however, a greater evil to the white than to the black race . . . The doctrines and miracles of our Saviour have required nearly two thousand years to convert but a small part of the human race, and even among Christian nations what gross errors still exist! . . .[2]

Historians have rated Lee as one of the greatest military strategists in history. The majority of his battles were fought with unfavorable odds against him, often numbering two-to-one or more, on the opposing side. Not only was he deeply respected by those who served under him, but he even came to be revered by those of the North who saw him as a man of deep character and godly conviction. He symbolized the gallantry and grace of the old south.

A magnificent stained-glass window in the National Cathedral, in Washington, D.C., memorializes this American hero.

> To the glory of God, All-righteous and All-merciful, and in undying tribute to the life and witness of Robert Edward Lee,

servant of God—Leader of men. General-in-Chief of the armies
of the Confederate states whose compelling sense of duty,
serene faith and unfailing courtesy, mark him for all ages as a
Christian soldier without fear and without reproach. This
memorial Bay is gratefully built by the United Daughters of the
Confederacy.

Although Lee's personal preference after the war was to
retire, he accepted the presidency of Washington College because he
knew that the future of the South depended on the education of
southern youth. He helped lift the college from its lowest point of
depression. Following his death in 1870, the school was renamed
Washington and Lee University. Lee had also played a key role in
encouraging the South to accept the defeat graciously and to work
toward rebuilding a unity with the North.

The Story of Lee's Lost Bible

Robert E. Lee had been given a Bible from some citizens in
Liverpool, England, in 1861 with this inscription:

General Robert E. Lee Commanding the Confederate Army
from the undersigned Englishmen and Englishwomen rec-
ognizing the genius of the General; admiring the humanity of
the man; respecting the virtues of the Christian.
October 13, 1861.[3]

Somehow, the Bible had been lost during the war and finally
rediscovered in Beira, Portugese East Africa (modern-day Mozam-
bique) in the 1930s. It was presented to Francis P. Gaines, president
of Washington and Lee, to be placed in the Lee Archives in the
school's library. "Every fragment of memorabilia that in any way
bears upon the General's relation to our national history will be
accessible to students of his life and all those who loved him,"
said Gaines. "The Liverpool Bible so designated will repose under
glass in a place of honor."[4]

Robert E. Lee was confirmed by Bishop Johns in Christ
Church, Alexandria, Virginia, when he was 54 years old. A silver
plaque on the communion railing marks this event for posterity.

Lee's family pew is designated by a larger silver plaque with his signature engraved upon it. The Lee family was Episcopalian.

Author Benjamin Howell Griswold, Jr. in his book, *The Spirit of Lee and Jackson*, wrote:

> . . . Lee and Jackson were both professing Christians—most men of their day were that—but on the premise that these men not only professed Christianity, but actually practised it and endeavored in every way to live according to its much neglected tenets. They were great readers of the Bible, and nearly every act of their lives was directed by their interpretation of its maxims. This was true of their actions not only at home toward their family and neighbors, but even in the camp and on the battlefield toward their enemies . . . Humility, Purity, Peacemaking, Love of Righteousness—virtues neglected—if not a little despised today, seem to have exalted these men and lifted them from the depths of defeat to the pinnacle of fame. . .[5]

The following excerpts from Lee's private correspondence show much of his godly character and vibrant Christianity, specifically: His gratitude to God for His unspeakable mercies; his deep dependence upon God's crowning help and protection; his desire that Americans should recognize this and be thus rewarded with national success; his abhorrence of war, and its reversal of love into hatred. Lee also shows deep emotion at the death of his gallant soldiers.

> To: Mrs. Robert E. Lee, December 25, 1862
>   from Fredericksburg, Virginia:
> My heart is filled with gratitude to Almighty God for His unspeakable mercies with which He has blessed us in this day. For those He has granted us from the beginning of life, and particularly for those He has vouchsafed us during the past year. What should have become of us without His crowning help and protection? Oh, if our people would only recognize it and cease from self-boasting and adulation, how strong would be my belief in final success and happiness to our country! But what a cruel thing is war; to separate and destroy families and friends, and mar the purest joys and happiness God has granted us in this world; to fill our hearts with hatred instead of love for our neighbors, to devastate the fair face of

this beautiful world! I pray that, on this day when only peace and good-will are preached to mankind, better thoughts may fill the hearts of our enemies and turn them to peace. Our army was never in such good health and condition since I have been attached to it. I believe they share with me my disappointment that the enemy did not renew the combat on the 13th. I was holding back all day and husbanding our strength and ammunition for the great struggle, for which I thought I was preparing. Had I divined that was to have been his only effort, he would have had more of it. My heart bleeds at the death of every one of our gallant men.

R.E. Lee.[6]

And then, Lee's intense love for his family shines through the following excerpted letter to his daughter, Agnes, written on November 16, 1865, from Lexington, Virginia:

My Precious Little Agnes:
I have just received your letter of the 13th and hasten to reply. It is very hard for you to apply to me to advise you to go away from me. You know how much I want to see you, and how important you are to me . . .

Your affectionate father,
R.E. Lee.[7]

Robert E. Lee's last days were written by Colonel William Preston Johnston for Reverend J.W. Jones in his *Personal Reminiscences of General Robert E. Lee, 1874.* Colonel Johnston was an intimate friend of the general and a distinguished member of the faculty of his college. He was one of those at the bedside of the dying general. It is being excerpted below in order to shed further light on Lee's true character and Christian comportment:

The death of General Lee was not due to any sudden cause, but was the result of agencies dating as far back as 1863. . . . In October, 1869, he was again attacked by inflammation of the heart-sac, accompanied by muscular rheumatism of the back, right side, and arms. The action of the heart was weakened by this attack . . . His decline was rapid, yet gentle; and soon after nine o'clock on the morning of October 12th, he closed his eyes, and his soul passed peacefully from earth. . . . General Lee's closing hours were consonant with his noble and disciplined life. Never was more beautifully displayed how a long and severe education of mind and character enables the soul to pass with equal step through this supreme ordeal; never did the habits and qualities of a lifetime, solemnly gathered into a few last sad hours, more grandly maintain themselves amid the gloom and shadow of approaching death. The reticence, the self-contained composure, the obedience to proper authority, the magnanimity and the Christian meekness, that marked all his actions, still preserved their sway, in spite of the inroads of disease and the creeping lethargy that weighed down his faculties. . . . Leaning trustfully upon the all-sustaining Arm, the man whose stature, measured by mortal standards, seemed so great, passed from this world of shadows to the realities of the hereafter.[8]

It would seem strange that for so great an American hero there would be those who have maligned his life and character by rewriting false and derogatory historic accounts of him. One such account is here excerpted below:

. . . Into this disordered, disgraced, uprooted family Robert E. Lee was born in January 1807, the fourth child . . . He was an unwanted child, as his mother confessed; conceived during the period of his father's association with Aaron Burr, born just after the death of his mother's father—her last hope of security. . . . Robert Lee was three when the family was dispossessed of Stratford, and six when his father said his pathetic farewells. He grew up with the memory of one parent's total failure and in constant sight of the other parent's martyrdom. . . . His frustrations made Lee unhappy to the point of melancholia and self-pity. . . . Frustration, which galvanized George Washington into hot, headlong action, only pinioned Lee on the rack of indecision and inactivity. This gentle person could not rail at the authorities for not promoting him, nor rage with jealousy when he was bypassed by subordinates, nor sate his love of land in prodigious schemes of acquisition. . . .[9]

To reiterate a close friend's personal reminiscences of Robert E. Lee, let us compare the following with the above derogatory, inaccurate statements made more recently on the life and person of Robert E. Lee:

. . . The reticence, the self-contained composure, the obedience to proper authority, the magnanimity and the Christian
meekness, that marked all his actions, still preserved their
sway. . . . Leaning trustfully upon the all-sustaining Arm, the
man whose stature measured by mortal standards, seemed
so great, passed from this world of shadows to the realities of
the hereafter.[10]

(iii) Stonewall Jackson

Another hero of America's history is Thomas (Stonewall) Jackson. Born in 1824 at Clarksburg, West Virginia, he greatly impressed those who knew him with his discipline, caliber and Christian characteristics, for which he was unsurpassed.

Jackson's lawyer father died when he was quite young, leaving his wife with two sons and a daughter to support. Mrs. Jackson is reputed to have been a woman of faith in God and of biblical understanding, bringing this zeal and fervor for Christian values into the life of young Stonewall and his siblings. Jackson never forgot his mother, always referring to her in later years with deep love and gratitude. After his mother's remarriage, Jackson and his brother were sent to live with an uncle. But receiving bad treatment from his uncle, young Jackson bundled up his belongings, hung them over his shoulder on the end of a stick, and walked 17 miles to the home of another uncle, thus demonstrating determination and character.

At the age of 19, he made application to fill a vacancy at West Point, and was accepted in July, 1842. It is recorded that he would study late into the night by the light of a fire, lying upon the floor after "lights out," in order to show himself approved in his work. After much hard work and determination, Jackson graduated 17 in a class of 70.[1] Although regarded by fellow students as somewhat of an oddity in manners and appearance, Stonewall soon gained their allegiance through his Christian forbearance and outgoing personality. When the war broke out in 1845 between the United States and Mexico, Jackson showed great initiative, for which he was brevetted major. In 1851, he became a professor in the Lexington Military Institute, a post he held for 10 years.

Civil War Fame

The election of Abraham Lincoln to office on March 4, 1861, as President of the United States, brought an opponent of slavery into the White House. On April 13, the Confederate capture of the Federal Fort Sumter at Charleston, South Carolina, led to a state of war. The Confederates, or southerners, numbered about six million whites. The command of the sea gave considerable advantage to the

Union armies, giving them the usual benefit of an extensive base. It was thus almost impossible to completely intercept them.

On April 29, 1861, Colonel Jackson took command of 4,500 men at Harper's Ferry. On November 1, 1861, Jackson, with the rank of Major General, was appointed to the command of the Shennandoah Valley, in which position he fully realized the importance of controlling the Baltimore and Ohio Railway.

Jackson excelled in "secrecy and surprise" of which Napoleon, Hannibal and Wellington were masters. His superiority of the regulars in battle appeared in the Mexican campaign, and at the two battles of Bull Run and at Gaines' Mill. He also understood the value and importance of using initiative. His expertise in the use of cavalry, the strategic arm before battle, were: scouting, screening, pursuing, charging and perhaps raiding. Jackson made it his constant practice to study his opponent's character. He was well versed in the use of strategic positions in warfare, thereby gaining frequent advantage over his adversary.

The above reflects Jackson's tactics and exploits as a true military genius, a product of West Point Military Academy.

Following are excerpts from Jackson's personal correspondence which show the inner man and nature:

> Lexington, Virginia 1852
> To his Aunt
> Mrs. Clementine (Alfred) Neale:
> . . . The subject of becoming herald of the cross has often seriously engaged my attention, and I regard it as the most noble of all professions. It is the profession of our divine Redeemer, and I should not be surprised were I to die upon a foreign field, clad in ministerial armor, fighting under the banner of Jesus. What could be more glorious? But my conviction is that I am doing good here; and that for the present I am where God would have me. Within the last few days I have felt an unusual religious joy. I do rejoice to walk in the love of God.[2]

The above depicts his foremost adherence to the cross of Christ, having frequently contemplated "the most noble of all professions," that of becoming a full-time minister, preacher or herald of the way of salvation through Christ Jesus. He concludes that

God's perfect will for his life presently is where he stands and rejoices in his calling.

Another letter, this time to his uncle, Alfred Neale, in 1842, concerns the untimely death of his brother Warren. It shows Jackson's joyous certitude of his brother's eternal destiny being secure, at the right hand of Jesus Christ, his Redeemer. Throughout Jackson's writings, his application of the Word of God and its promises to his own life and that of his family and friends, denotes an intimate relationship with its author:

> I have received no answer to my last communication conveying the sad news of my brother's premature death. He died in the hope of a bright immortality at the right hand of His Redeemer . . . As time is knowledge I must hasten my pen forward. We have received the smile of Bounteous Providence in a favorable Spring. There is a volunteer company being formed here to march to Texas, in order to assist in the noble cause of liberty.[3]

Jackson was a consistent Christian man. He was a constant attendant on preaching and he taught a class of black children in the Sunday school at Lexington.

After receiving news of the victory of Manassas, the Reverend Dr. White of Lexington read a letter from Jackson to the people gathered around to hear the results of the battle:

> My dear Pastor:
> In my tent last night, after a fatiguing day's service, I remembered that I failed to send you my contribution for our colored Sunday School. Enclosed you will find my check for that object, which please acknowledge at your earliest convenience and oblige yours faithfully,
>
> T. Jackson [4]

Jackson is further reported to have prayed this beautiful prayer to Almighty God on the battlefield in Manassas:

> Oh God, let this horrible war quickly come to an end that we may all return home and engage in the only work that is worthwhile—and that is the salvation of men.[5]

It is reported that at General Jackson's death, seven million people throughout the South went into mourning. Says Colonel R.P. Chew, Chief of Horse Artillery, Army of Northern Virginia, in his address delivered at the Virginia Military Institute on June 19, 1912:

> He was a Christian without fanaticism, a Christian in the open; one who did not hesitate in the presence of assembled thousands to pause on the eve of some great enterprise and raise his hand aloft, invoking the blessing of Divine Providence upon his efforts and those of his soldiers. He rose superior to human infirmity and was proof against the temptations of this life . . . while his strategy was as brilliant, his tactics as effective, he had achieved a victory that could be accorded to no one of these great commanders, (Caesar, Bonaparte, Marlborough and Wellington), he had made himself complete and absolute master of himself. Possessed of perfect poise of mind and temperament, his character adorned with every moral and manly attribute, and endowed with every Christian virtue. . . .[6]

General Robert E. Lee showed love and admiration for Jackson when, at the news of his death, he stated: "I have lost my right arm." Of Robert E. Lee, Stonewall Jackson spoke thus: "I will follow General Lee blindfolded."[7]

Memorial to Stonewall Jackson

Our National Cathedral in Washington, D.C., immortalizes the life of Stonewall Jackson with an inspiring stained-glass window. It depicts this American son kneeling on the battlefield, reading his Bible. The caption underneath reads thus:

> To the glory of the Lord of Hosts whom he so zealously served and in honored memory of Thomas Jonathan Jackson, Lieutenant General C.S.R. Like a Stone Wall in his steadfastness, swift as lightning and mighty in battle, he walked humbly before his Creator, whose Word was his guide. This Bay is erected by the United Daughters of the Confederacy and his admirers from South and North.

Vizetelly's painting "Prayer in 'Stonewall' Jackson's Camp." Library of Congress Collection.

Such was the life and example of one of America's greatest sons. The nobility of his character, as with so many other great leaders, came from his love of God and his scrupulous adherence to His words, as has been amply demonstrated in the above narrative of Jackson's life and writings.

Rewritten History

A 1988 publication entitled, *The Shade of the Trees* (a narrative based on the life and career of Lieutenant General Thomas Jonathan "Stonewall" Jackson), rewrites the Christian value-system, integrity and strict moral character which so distinguished Jackson in life, giving him an excellent reputation in all he did. This narrative describes Jackson as inebriated with alcohol, mesmerized by Mexican señoritas, losing his equilibrium after drinking, "slipping into a relaxed pattern of living" and enjoying breakfast in bed. I quote:

> . . . Without realizing it, Jackson was becoming tipsy from the punch. He began to watch the beautiful señoritas as they swayed to the music. He clapped his hands as they finished a number and stopped to rest. He had decided to go over and introduce himself to one particularly beautiful lady but as he bent over, he felt dizzy and his vision was blurred. Then he realized that he must have been drinking something with alcohol in it. He had violated his own rule, so he rose from his table, excused himself and retired to the hacienda. . . .[8]

and

> . . . It was easy for Jackson to slip into a relaxed pattern of living. He liked a lot the Mexican customs. Although it was hard to change his eating habits, he did . . . and for the better. He liked having his morning coffee and cakes in bed . . .[9]

So alien is this rewritten narrative to the true identity, discipline and integrity of Stonewall Jackson, that it is hard to imagine these lines being printed without shame and remorse on the part of the writer. These subtle changes and insinuations indicate, once again, the rewriting of America's glorious Christian legacy.

(iv) William Holmes McGuffey

William Holmes McGuffey was born on September 23, 1800, on the Ohio frontier, and died May 4, 1873, at Charlottesville, Virginia. He continues to make news today as the most important figure in the history of American public education.[1]

The National Education Association (NEA) honored McGuffey with the following resolution at his death:

> In the death of William H. McGuffey, late Professor of Moral Philosophy in the University of Virginia, this Association feels that they have lost one of the great lights of the profession whose life was a lesson full of instruction; an example and model to American teachers. His labors in the cause of education, extending over a period of half a century, in several offices as teacher of common schools, college professor and college president, and as author of text books; his almost unequalled industry; his power in the lecture room; his influence upon his pupils and community; his care for the public interests of education; his lofty devotion to duty; his conscientious Christian character—all these have made him one of the noblest ornaments of our profession in this age, and entitle him to the grateful remembrance of this Association and of the teachers of America.
> Elmira, New York, August 7, 1873.[2]

As clergyman, professor of ancient languages and philosophy, college president, advocate of public education and textbook compiler, William Holmes McGuffey lives on as the schoolmaster of the nation. In 1837 he produced the *Eclectic Third Reader* (containing selections in prose and poetry, from the best American and English writers, with plain rules for reading and directions for avoiding common errors). William Earnest Smith, in his work entitled: "About the McGuffeys," states that by the year 1963, 125 million copies of these readers had been sold. "Except the Bible," says he, "no other book or set of books has influenced the American mind so much."[3]

"The readers were used in the public schools longer than any other textbooks. The keen intellectual and literary sense of the composer and the high moral values which were taught, must have been the largest factor in the long tenure of these school books," said Dr. Benjamin Franklin Crawford, in his *Life of William*

Holmes McGuffey, published in 1963. McGuffey has been given the title of "Great Schoolmaster of the Nation." Just what was the content of McGuffey's readers that made them so popular for so many years? Following are excerpts from some of his readers. The first is a selection, "More about the Bible" from the 1837 *Eclectic Third Reader:*

> 1. The design of the Bible is evidently to give us correct information concerning the creation of all things, by the omnipotent Word of God; to make known to us the state of holiness and happiness of our first parents in paradise, and their dreadful fall from that condition by transgression against God, which is the original cause of all our sin and misery.

> 3. The Scriptures are especially designed to make us wise unto salvation through faith in Christ Jesus; to reveal to us the mercy of the Lord in him; to form our minds after the likeness of God our Savior; to build up our souls in wisdom and faith, in love and holiness; to make us thoroughly furnished unto good works, enabling us to glorify God on earth; and, to lead us to an imperishable inheritance among the spirits of just men made perfect, and finally to be glorified with Christ in heaven.

> 5. We have the most ample and satisfactory proofs that the books of the Bible are Authentic and Genuine; that is, that they were written by the persons to whom they are ascribed. The Scriptures of the Old Testament were collected and completed under the scrupulous care of inspired apostles. The singular providence of God is evident in the translation of the Old Testament into Greek, nearly three hundred years before the birth of Christ, for the benefit of the Jews who were living in countries where that language was used.

> 7. This will appear in a much stronger point of view when we consider the Jews as the keepers of the Old Testament. It was their own sacred volume, which contained the most extraordinary predictions concerning the infidelity of their nation, and the rise, progress, and extensive prevalence of Christianity.

> 8. That all the books which convey to us the history of the events of the New Testament, were written and immediately published, by persons living at the time of the occurrence of

the things mentioned, and whose names they bear, is most fully proved. 1. By an unbroken series of Christian authors, reaching from the days of the apostles down to the present time. 2. By the concurrent and well-informed belief of all denominations of Christians. 3. By the acknowledgement of the most learned and intelligent enemies of Christianity.

10. Matthew and John were two of our Lord's apostles; his constant attendants throughout the whole of his ministry; eye-witnesses of the facts, and ear-witnesses of the discourses which they relate. Mark and Luke were not of the twelve apostles; but they were contemporaries and associates with the apostles, and living in habits of friendship and intercourse with those who had been present at the transactions which they record. . . .

13. The manuscripts of the sacred books are found in every ancient library in all parts of the Christian world; and amount in number to several thousands. About five hundred have been actually examined and compared by learned men with extraordinary care. Many of them were evidently transcribed as early as the eighth, seventh, sixth, and even the fourth centuries.

Questions: 1. What is the evident design of the Bible? 2. Have we proofs of the authenticity of the Bible? 3. When was the Old Testament translated into Greek? 4. For whose immediate benefit was the translation made? 5. What is confirmed by the quotations of Christians from the Old Testament? 6. How do you prove the authenticity of the New Testament? 7. How could alterations in the Sacred Scriptures have been detected? 8. Where are ancient manuscripts of the Bible now to be found? 9. Do you think a person could now alter the Bible without being detected? 10. If God has condescended to give us His Word to guide us in the way of eternal life, do you not think that he would extend his protective hand for its preservation?

Errors: Glo-rous for Glo-ri-ous; sper-ets for spir-its; vol-lum for vol-ume; fust for first; a-pos-sles for a-pos-tles.

Spell and Define: 1. Omnipotent; 2. everlasting; 3. salvation; 5. translation; 6. quotation; 7. predictions; 8. acknowledgements; 9. contemporaries; 11. manuscripts; 12. evangelical; 13. promulgation; 14. authenticity.

McGuffey's *Third Reader* goes on to expose the meaning of the word: "Truth" a word frequently recurring in the New Testament. It shows the importance of teaching this fruit of the Holy Spirit, making it an integral part of each young American's life while growing up. Lesson 31 is entitled: "On Speaking the Truth"

(Rule: Too much pains cannot be taken to acquire familiarity with the stops).

1. A little girl once came into the house, and told her mother a story about something which seemed very improbable.
2. The persons who were sitting in the room with her mother did not believe the little girl, for they did not know her character. But the mother replied at once, "I have no doubt that it is true, for I never knew my daughter to tell a lie." Is there not something noble in having such a character as this?
3. Must not that little girl have felt happy in the consciousness of thus possessing her mother's entire confidence? Oh, how different must have been her feelings from those of the child whose word cannot be believed, and who is regarded by every one with suspicion? Shame, shame on the child who has not magnanimity enough to tell the truth.
10. How awful must be the scene which will open before you, as you enter the eternal world! You will see the throne of God: how bright, how glorious, will it burst upon your sight! You will see God, the Savior, seated upon the majestic throne. Angels, in number more than can be counted, will fill the universe with their glittering wings, and their rapturous songs. Oh, what a scene to behold! And then you will stand in the presence of this countless throng, to answer for every thing you have done while you lived.
11. Every action and every thought of your life will then be fresh in your mind. You know it is written in the Bible, "God will bring every work into judgment, with every secret thing, whether it be good or whether it be evil." How must the child then feel who has been guilty of falsehood and deception, and who sees it then all brought to light! No liar can enter the

kingdom of heaven. Oh, how dreadful must be the confusion and shame, with which the deceitful child will then be overwhelmed! The angels will all see your sin and disgrace. 12. And do you think they will wish to have a liar enter heaven and be associated with them? No! They will turn from you with disgust. The Savior will look upon you in his displeasure. Conscience will read your soul. And you must hear the awful sentence, "Depart from me, into everlasting fire, prepared for the devil and his angels."

Questions: 1. What is the subject of this Lesson? 2. What did the little girl do? 3. What did the company think? 4. What did her mother say of her? 5. How must the little girl have felt when her mother said she could not doubt her word? 6. What did the boy do? 7. What is degrading? 8. Should we ever resort to deception? 9. If we escape detection for falsehood here, when shall we be detected?

Errors: Set-ting for sit-ting; dah-ter for daugh-ter; diff-runt for dif-fer-ent; fur-git for for-get.

Spell and Define: 2. character; 3. consciousness; confidence; 4. falsehood; 6. contemptible; 7. disgraceful; 8. magnanimity; 10. rapturous; 11. deceitful.

Lesson 21, in the same McGuffey *Eclectic Third Reader,* speaks about the Character of Jesus Christ. Here again we see that, at a tender young age, American children were taught to follow the example of the Son of God, thus producing virtue in their adult lives, as opposed to modern-day vice.

(Rule: In many words the sound of "h" is suppressed where it should be sounded distinctly; and great caution must be used to avoid this fault.)

Examples: harm, heel, head, hot, hoarse, who, are pronounced improperly, arm, eel, ead, ot, orse, oo.

1. The morality taught by Jesus Christ was purer, sounder, sublimer and more perfect than had ever before entered into the imagination, or proceeded from the lips of man. And this he delivered in a manner the most striking and impressive; in

short, sententious, solemn, important, ponderous rules or maxims; or in familiar, natural, affecting similitudes and parables.

2. He showed also a most consummate knowledge of the human heart, and dragged to light all its artifices, subtleties, and evasions. He discovered every irregular desire before it ripened into action.

3. He manifested, at the same time, the most perfect impartiality. He had no respect of persons. He reproved vice in every situation, with the same freedom and boldness, wherever he found it; and he added to the whole, the weight, the irresistible weight, of his own example.

4. He, and he only, of all the sons of men, acted up, in every minute instance, to what he taught; and his life exhibited a perfect portrait of his religion. But what completed the whole was, that he taught as the evangelist expresses it, with authority, with the authority of a divine teacher.

5. The ancient philosophers could do nothing more than give good advice to their followers; they had no means of enforcing that advice; but our great lawgiver's precepts are all divine commands.

6. He spoke in the name of God: he called himself the Son of God. He spoke in a tone of superiority, and authority, which no one before him had the courage or the right to assume: and finally, he enforced every thing he taught by the most solemn and awful sanctions, by a promise of eternal felicity to those who obeyed him, and a denunciation of the most tremendous punishments to those who rejected him.

7. These were the circumstances which gave our blessed Lord the authority with which he spake. No wonder then, that the people "were astonished at His doctrines," and that they all declared "He spake as never man spake."

Questions: 1. Whose character is here portrayed? 2. What was the character of his instructions? 3. How did the life of Christ correspond with his teachings? 4. Wherein did he differ from the ancient philosophers?

Errors: Per-fict for per-fect; ir-reg-lur for ir-reg-u-lar; es-press-es for ex-press-es; flos-phers for phi-los-o-phers.

Spell and Define: 1. morality; sententious; 2. consummate; irresistible; 6. denunciation; 7. doctrines.

Lesson 37 of the *Eclectic First Reader* is appropriately entitled "Evening Prayer" and elaborates upon the importance of daily communion with God, this important facet of life being taught to young Americans, and emphasized in the classrooms of our national public schools.

At the close of the day, before you go to sleep, you should not fail to pray to God to keep you from sin and from harm. You ask your friends for food, and drink, and books, and clothes; and when they give you these things, you thank them, and love them for the good they do you. So you should ask your God for those things which he can give you, and which no one else can give you. You should ask him for life, and health, and strength; and you should pray to him to keep your feet from the ways of sin and shame.

You should thank him for all his good gifts; and learn, while young, to put your trust in him; and the kind care of God will be with you, both in your youth and in your old age.

close	before	sleep	would
fail	pray	from	harm
friends	food	drink	books
clothes	these	things	them
good	should	those	which
strength	learn	young	youth

Lesson 62 in the *Eclectic First Reader,* entitled "Don't Take Strong Drink," gives McGuffey's legitimate reasons for this statement, as follows:

No little boy or girl should ever drink rum or whiskey, unless they want to become drunkards. Men who drink strong drink are glad to have any excuse for doing it. So, one will drink it because he is so hot. Another will drink it because he is cold. One will drink it when he is wet, and another because he is dry—one will drink it because he is in company, and another, because he is alone, and another will put it into his glass of water to kill the insects! Thus the pure water from the brook is poisoned with the "drunkard's drink," and the man who uses it, becomes a sot. Then he is seen tottering through the streets, a shame to himself and to all his family. And oh, how dreadful to die a drunkard. The Bible says that no drunkard shall inherit the kingdom of heaven. Whiskey makes the happy miserable, and it causes the rich to become poor.

The removal of the Bible, Christ and prayer from the public school domain, is in total contrast to McGuffey's strong Christian teachings and has fostered the social degeneration that we are evidencing throughout our nation today.

From the above, we understand and perceive the underlying morality and Christian value-system which diffused and was disseminated throughout the American public school system, and which, in turn, formed and fashioned the American mind and thinking process. In short, it produced a people with a Christian moral fiber and conduct able to turn the world upside down with evangelization, charitable enterprises and a concept of liberty based upon God-ordained freedoms, which were thus inculcated into our government, culture and way of life.

What occurred so drastically to change the attitudes, Christian value-system and beliefs of Americans graduating from national classrooms in the past few decades or more? A key factor has been the rewriting of America's history in textbook form. This brilliant *coup d'etat* has been accomplished through the years, without firing a single shot. The result: a remolding of the free American mind liberated by biblical truth (which sets a nation free—John 8:32)—into enslavement through the rampant teaching of *vice and evil conduct*. The goal is to destroy this people from within her own ranks. When you have captured the minds of a people, you have captured their nation.

The removal of Almighty God, prayer, Christian love, kindness, forebearance and goodwill from our public school system was a deliberate *coup* to enslave the people of the United States to sin and vice so that another power could move in to take her. God's prophetic warning came through two of America's recent Chief Officers (Dwight D. Eisenhower and Ronald Reagan), in their choice of Scripture at their Presidential Inaugurations:

> If my people, who are called by my name, will humble themselves and pray and seek my face, and turn from their wicked ways, then I will hear from heaven, will forgive their sin, and will heal their land. (2 Chronicles 7:14)

The American classroom was where these Christian values and rules of conduct were taught as a way of everyday life, producing a great nation where biblical truths were put into practice. The fruits of the Holy Spirit—love, joy, peace, patience, kindness, goodness, faithfulness, gentleness, and self-control (Galatians 5:22–23)—were the social virtues which were lived out in the adult lives of earlier generations, having been inculcated into their lives in childhood.

While history in regard to William Holmes McGuffey has not been rewritten per se, has the removal of his famous reader from our educational system been a plan to rewrite an historical value system in the hearts and minds of two or more generations of our people? It is interesting to note that nothing teaching the same social moral values has in anyway replaced this reader.

His works are worthy to be resuscitated and retaught throughout the entire U.S. public school system, thus returning our country to the Christian principles and dignity which made the nation great and gave us our freedoms as Americans—a gift from God.[4]

(v) Marcus Whitman—The Preacher Who Rode for an Empire

Few Americans are familiar with the story of Marcus and Narcissa Whitman, two great American heroes, and their work for the cause of the gospel. Marcus made a valiant cross-country ride to save Oregon from falling to the Hudson Bay Company—and hence to the British.

As all believers know, every revival is preceded by prayer and fasting. In Kentucky in 1797, a young pastor by the name of James McGready and others entered into a solemn covenant:

> Therefore, we bind ourselves to observe the third Saturday of each month for one year as a day of fasting and prayer for the conversion of sinners in Logan County and throughout the world. We also engage to spend one half hour every Saturday evening, beginning at the setting of the sun, and one half hour every Sabbath morning at the rising of the sun in pleading with God to revive His work.[1]

Their prayers were answered. Revival took hold of the Kentucky wilderness and spread southward to the Carolinas and north across the mountains to the cities and churches of the East and New England.

Dr. Marcus Whitman and Narcissa Prentiss, who later became his bride, were both deeply touched by the revival—so much so that each had committed to the single lifestyle in order to better serve the Lord. But due to a mutual friend and divine providence, they married and committed their lives to evangelizing the Indians of the Northwest. The cross-country trip was made by means of sleigh, steamboat, stage, wagon, ox cart, horseback and on foot, all the way from the state of New York. Theirs was the first wagon to cross the Rocky Mountains.

In 1836, when Marcus and Narcissa Whitman crossed the mountains into Old Oregon as missionaries of the American Board of Commissioners for Foreign Missions, they were being carried along by the current of that blessed stream which began to flow throughout the land when the Great Revival broke out at the beginning of the century.

In addition, unbeknownst to the Whitmans, they were a providential answer to a foiled attempt by a declining Indian tribe

Statue of Marcus Whitman, medical missionary to the Indians in Washington Territory. U.S. Capitol. Courtesy of Architect of the Capitol.

in Oregon to find the one, true, triune God. In 1831, four Nez Perce and Flathead Indians came to St. Louis seeking to learn the secret of the white man's success, convinced that the white man's God was more potent than their own. These Indians were: Black Eagle, Rabbit Skin Leggings, No Horns on His Head and Man of the Morning. Their request was that missionaries be sent among them to tell them of the white man's God. The portraits of Rabbit Skin Leggings and No Horns on His Head are in the National Gallery of Art in Washington, D.C., painted by the Indian authority and painter, George Catlin.

In 1866 there appeared in a lecture by missionary Henry Spalding, an account of the sorrowful appeal of one of these Indians to General Clark when they were leaving to go back to their own people. Said the Indian:

> I come to you over a trail of many moons from the setting sun. I came with one eye partly open, for more light for my people who sit in darkness. I go back with both eyes closed. How can I go back blind to my people? I made my way to you with strong arms through many enemies and strange lands. I go back with both arms broken and empty. My people sent me to get the white man's Book from Heaven. You took me where you allow your women to dance, as we do not ours, and the Book was not there. You took me where they worship the great Spirit with candles, and the Book was not there. You showed me the images of good spirits and pictures of the good land beyond. But the Book was not among them. I am going back the long, sad trail to my people of the dark land. You make my feet heavy with burdens of gifts, and my moccasins will grow old in carrying them. But the Book is not among them. When I tell my poor, blind people after one more snow in the big Council that I did not bring the Book, no word will be spoken by our old men or by our young braves. One by one they will rise up and go out in silence. My people will die in darkness, and they will go on the long path to other hunting grounds. No white man will go with them, and no white man's Book, to make the way plain. I have no more words.[2]

No woman ever made such a journey as that made by Narcissa Whitman. In her fascinating journal for July 27, Narcissa, after speaking of some of her hardships, writes: "Do not think I regret coming. No, far from it. I would not go back for the world. I am contented and happy. Notwithstanding, I sometimes get very hungry and weary. Have six weeks' steady journey before us. Will the Lord give me patience to endure it?"

On August 29, when from the summit of the Blue Mountains Narcissa saw the Columbia River and Mount Hood, the goal of their journey, far off in the distance, two biblical promises came to her mind: "As thy days, so shall thy strength be," and "Lo, I am with you alway."

The Whitmans established themselves at Waiilatpu, among the Cayuse Indians. In a rude cabin at Waiilatpu, Alice Clarissa Whitman was born March 14, 1837, the first child of American white parents to be born west of the Rocky Mountains. When the child was two years of age, she drowned in the stream which ran behind their cabin.

What was the gospel of the Oregon Trail? What was the gospel that compelled Marcus and Narcissa Whitman to thrust on through the dangers and hazards of the great Northwest? What made them faithful unto martyrdom, perishing at the hands of those to whom they brought the good news of eternal life? What was the gospel which erected the first Protestant church west of the Rockies? What was the gospel that transformed the Indians, causing them to discard their tomahawks and scalping knives; replacing them with the resounding hymns of redemption each morning and evening—filling the mission with praises to Jehovah God? It was the magnificent gospel of Christ the Redeemer, the gospel of salvation from sin through the shed blood of the Lamb of God who takes away the sin of the world. This was the gospel of the Oregon Trail.

The British, who had established posts in Oregon through the Hudson Bay Company's fur trading, had intended to colonize the territory. Marcus Whitman undertook the arduous journey to Washington, D.C., to make his appeal for this valuable land. The fascinating story was related by none less than President Warren G. Harding in 1923 in a speech on "The Oregon Trail" at Meacham, Oregon. Here are excerpts:

My countrymen:

As I stand here in the shadow of the great hills, my mind reverts to the placid banks of the broad Potomac. There, as here, to an American proud of his country and revering her traditions, there is much of patriotic interest, and between these rugged mountains and those fertile lowlands, I find much in common. Living history records many indissoluble links, to one of which it seems fitting that I should direct your attention today. Of the many rooms in the White House, which possess the peculiar charm of association with epochal happenings, the one most fascinating to me is that which formerly comprised the Cabinet Room and the President's study. . . . Before my mind's eye as I stood in that heroic chamber a few days ago appeared the vivid picture. I beheld seated at his desk, immaculately attired, the embodiment of dignity and courtliness, John Tyler, 10th President of the United States. Facing him, from a chair constructed for a massive frame, his powerful spirit gleaming through his cavernous eyes, was the lion-visaged Daniel Webster, Secretary of State. The door opened and there appeared before the amazed statesmen a strange and astonishing figure. It was that of a man of medium height and sturdy build, deep chested, broad shouldered, yet lithe in movement and soft in step. He was clad in a coarse fur coat, buckskin breeches, fur leggings, and boot moccasins, looking much the worse for wear. But it was the countenance of the visitor, as he stood for an instant in the doorway, that riveted the perception of the two Chiefs of State. It was that of a religious enthusiast, tenaciously earnest yet revealing no suggestion of fanaticism, bronzed from exposure to pitiless elements and seamed with deep lines of physical suffering, a rare combination of determination and gentleness—obviously a man of God, but no less a man among men.

Such was Marcus Whitman, the pioneer missionary hero of the vast, unsettled, unexplored Oregon country, who had come out of the West to plead that the State should acquire for civilization the Empire that the churches were gaining for Christianity. . . .

It was more than a desperate and perilous trip that Marcus Whitman undertook. It was a race against time. Public opinion was rapidly crystallizing into a judgment that the Oregon country was not worth claiming, much less worth fighting for; that even though it could be acquired against the insistence of Great Britain, it would prove to be a liability rather than an asset. . . .

And he did not hesitate to speak plainly as one who knew, even like the prophet Daniel. "Mr. Secretary," he declared, "you would better give all New England for the cod and mackerel fisheries of Newfoundland than to barter away Oregon."

Then, turning to the President in conclusion, he added quietly but beseechingly:

"All I ask is that you will not barter away Oregon or allow English interference until I can lead a bank of stalwart American settlers across the plains. For this I shall try to do!"

The manly appeal was irresistible. He sought only the privilege of proving his faith. The just and considerate Tyler could not refuse.

"Dr. Whitman," he rejoined sympathetically, "your long ride and frozen limbs testify to your courage and your patriotism. Your credentials establish your character. Your request is granted!"

. . . Never in the history of the world has there been a finer example of civilization following Christianity. The missionaries led under the banner of the cross, and the settlers moved close behind under the star-spangled symbol of the Nation. Among all the records of the evangelizing effort as the forerunner of human advancement, there is none so impressive as this of the early Oregon mission and its marvelous consequences. To the men and women of that early day whose first thought was to carry the gospel to the Indians—to the Lees, the Spauldings, the Grays, the Walkers, the Leslies, to Fathers De Smet and Blanchet and De Mars, and to all the others of that glorious company who found that in serving God they were also serving their country and their fellowmen—to them we pay today our tribute; to them we owe a debt of gratitude, which we can never pay, save partially through recognition such as you have accorded it today. . . . I rejoice particularly in the opportunity afforded me of voicing my appreciation both as President of the United States and as one who honestly tries to be a Christian soldier, of the signal service of the martyred Whitman. And finally, as just a human being, I wish I could find words to tell you how glad I am to see you all, and reflecting as you do, from untroubled eyes, and happiness of spirit breathed by your own best song:

There are no new worlds to conquer
Gone is the last frontier,
And the steady grind of the wagon-train,
Of the sturdy pioneer.
But their memories live like a thing divine,
Treasured in Heaven above,
For the Trail that led to the storied West,
Was the wonderful trail of Love.

> Warren Gamaliel Harding
> President of the United States
> (1865–1923)[3]

Tragically, Whitman, his wife and 12 others were massacred in a sudden uprising of the Indians. They had been incited to violence by a half-breed from Maine named Jo Lewis, who had circulated the tale that Dr. Whitman was poisoning the Indians.

The tragedy put an end to the organized work of the American Board of Missions among the Indians in Oregon. But the seed that these devoted missionaries had sown did not return unto God void (Isaiah 55:10–11). It still bears fruit in the Christian churches and Christian faith of the Nez Perce and Cayuse Indians. One of the Indians said at their departure:

You are leaving us forever, and my people, O my people will see no more light. My children will live only in a night that will have no morning. When we reach Walla Walla I shall look upon your face for the last time in this world. But this Book in which your hands have written and caused me to write the words of God, I shall carry in my bosom 'til I lie down in the grave.[4]

Shortly after President Harding delivered his powerful account of Marcus Whitman's life of sacrifice, he went to be with our Lord forever. To Americans, he left the most accurate legacy of this missionary zeal with which these Western states of Washington, Oregon, Idaho and a portion of Montana were brought into the Union—that of the historical events which occurred in the Cabinet Room of the White House.

In spite of this U.S. president's personal testimony to Whitman's valiant journey to prevent Oregon's annexation by England, Whitman's efforts are denigrated by modern historians who discredit the purposes for the trip, and even make out his cross-country ride to be legendary, as follows:

> . . . The Life and Speeches of Senator Linn, of Missouri, who was the most advanced leader of the Oregon party, make no reference to Whitman. Tyler's (Tyler) lacks any contemporary reference to Whitman's presence in Washington, and if the author had found any he would have given it because he makes some conjectures as to the origin of the notion that Whitman exerted any influence on the diplomacy of that year. Had Whitman exerted even a small part of the influence attributed to him this universal silence would be inexplicable. This complete absence of contemporary references in print to Whitman's presence in Washington has naturally led advocates of the story to push their investigations among the manuscript records and to make inquiries of old officials, but the results have been equally disappointing. . . . In the legendary accounts of Whitman's visit to Washington and his interviews with Webster and Tyler the essential features are his arrival just in time to frustrate the effort of Sir George Simpson, the Governor of the Hudson Bay Company, to secure the cession of Oregon in exchange for the cod-fisheries, and it was upon this achievement that the claim that he saved Oregon to the United States was originally based. The incident is purely imaginary, and wherever it recurs it is the stamp or hall-mark, so to speak, of Spalding's invention. . . .[5]

And:

> According to widely accepted belief, Whitman paid a visit to Washington, D.C. in 1843, and interviewed President Tyler

and other government officials in an effort to prevent the cession to England of the Oregon Claim. (See Northwest Boundary dispute). Recent historical criticism, however, seems to prove that Whitman's visit to the East was not political in its nature, but was to dissuade the board from abolishing his mission.[6]

Of the extraordinary lives, saga and events which characterize Marcus and Narcissa Whitman's Christian witness among the Indians, Chester Collins Maxey, former president of Whitman College writes:

> There has been no other couple like the Whitmans in American history—no wooing more strange, no wedding more extraordinary, no marria[ge] more proof against stress and storm, no union of purpo[se and eff]ort more perfect, no failure more pathetic, no end[...]le, no immortality more sublime than theirs. Fo[rces they did no]t control or understand brought their lives t[ogether in a no]ble enterprise that failed; forces they did no[t unde]rstand brought their lives to a dire and agoni[zing end. S]o greatly did they live, so magnificently di[d they di]e serve that forces they set in motion will for[ever... the c]ivilization they helped to plant on the We[st...]he Continental Divide.[7]

Am[erica owes a gr]eat debt of gratitude to pioneers as selfless and as [...] [M]arcus and Narcissa Whitman—their work among[...] [ha]ving brought to them "the Book that tells about[...] Marcus Whitman's valiant ride cross-country havi[...] [pre]serve Oregon for the Union. This undaunted me[...] y left his indelible footprints throughout Wash[ing...] [stam]ping out a great episode in the identity of America [...] era as *a nation under God.*

Statue of Junipera Serra, represents California as its greatest hero. U.S. Capitol.
Courtesy of Architect of Capitol.

(vi) Junipero Serra—Man of God

Junipero Serra, "The Apostle to California," as he is called, president of the Franciscans for many years, and first person to bring the good news of salvation to the West Coast of America, was a giant among men, indeed. He founded nine missionary outposts, all of which later became major West Coast cities. They range over a 555-mile stretch from San Diego in the south to San Francisco in the north, and between them are San Juan Capistrano, San Gabriel, San Carlos, San Luis Obispo, Santa Clara, Santa Barbara, and Carmel. Although small in stature, he was great and godly in his life, work and outreach, bringing many Indians to the saving knowledge of our Lord and Savior Jesus Christ. At his birth on the island of Majorca, he was all but given up for dead. His parents, however, dedicated their child to full-time service for the Lord, should his life be spared—and in answer to their prayer, God miraculously saved his life. A quotation is here inserted from the introduction to the *Writings of Junipero Serra:*

> In 1769, Junipero Serra first set foot in the wilderness that was then California. In the face of incredible difficulties he laid the foundations of the mission system. Secular-minded historians may trace the system's progress by plotting year-by-year the increase in livestock and farm produce, the rise of permanent buildings with their distinctive architecture, improvements in highways and means of transportation, the growth of local industries, the availability of consumer goods, and the emergence of the intangibles that contribute to a more diversified form of social living. All this they will admire, and this they will call the great achievement of Serra. To all this, of course, Serra did contribute and to a greater extent than any of his contemporaries. But Serra never regarded it as his legacy to the West. Judged by his personal standard, all these things were mere incidentals. The motives which inspired his missionary labors must be sought much deeper. His standard was a supernatural one. He did not come to California to extract wealth from the soil, but to win souls for Heaven. He came to expand, not the empire of Spain, but the Kingdom of God. The registers of Baptisms and Confirmations were the balance sheet he consulted. Death might wreak havoc among his hard-won neophytes, but he found consolation in his sor-

row for he had prepared them for a future life which, his religious convictions assured him, was worth infinitely more than the life they were leaving and the pain of parting.

When life's evening twilight was gathering around Serra, other shadows, too, were growing darker. There were well-founded rumors that the mission system which he had set up might be altered profoundly; that a new form of ecclesiastical jurisdiction would be introduced; that the entire force of Franciscan missionaries would be dismissed and that their place would be taken by Dominicans from lower California. All this was known to Serra, and he did not need to be reminded that it was equivalent to a repudiation of all for which he had planned and labored through many toilsome years. He did not respond with an outburst of impatience, or an angry tirade against the detractors of the mission system. He calmly continued the policies which had guided him in the past, prepared to meet the blow, if and when it fell. He encouraged himself and others with the thought: we are utterly helpless in the face of this threat. If this misfortune befalls us, it will be because it is the will of God. And if it is God's will, we shall accept it without question. In that spirit of resignation he departed this life, unaware that a brighter day was dawning for the missions, and that the name and fame of Serra was destined to become California's most treasured heritage.

Finbar Kenneally, O.F.M.
Mattias C. Kieman, O.F.M.[1]

The following title page of Junipero Serra's book shows his dedication to God's kingdom work, and his love of the Lord Jesus Christ:

On the third Sunday after Easter, feast of the Patronage of the Holy Patriarch, St. Joseph, husband of Mary most holy, the second day of April in the year of our Lord, 1782, in which I, the undersigned, Fr. Junipero Serra, President of these missions of heathens, all things having been prepared in the chapel made of logs, and adorned as best as possible, I blessed water and with it I dedicated the land to God our Lord, and afterwards a large and high cross which we adorned and adored; afterwards I celebrated the Holy Sacrifice of the Mass, the first in this land with a homily on the Lord, which Mass because of the lack of others, was only read; and in place of the Te Deum, the ceremony finished with a prayer of praise. Let this be for the greater glory of God, the propagation of the faith and the good of souls.

This book consists of 212 usable pages, the first and last being blank. I sign this book so that all may know.

Fr. J.S., President.[2]

In November 1986 a major television network aired a program on Serra entitled, "Junipero Serra—Saint or Sadist?" The reenactment of his life in this program portrayed Serra as an exploiter and abuser of the Indians. Following the drama, a Catholic priest was interviewed on the life and work of Junipero Serra. He intelligently and factually refuted the inaccuracy of this television show. Unfortunately, however, most of the viewers had already formed their opinions and turned off their sets by the time he appeared on the screen. America's history had once again been rewritten in the minds and hearts of millions of her citizens. This directly contradicts the original writings of people who actually knew Serra, as found in the Library of Congress of the United States, and the historical evidence found within the missions themselves.

San Gabriel Mission

Outside the main entranceway to San Gabriel Mission, called: "Queen of the Missions," a sign welcomes all who come nigh with this message:

The Spirit of 1771 welcomes you. Behind this arch the beginning of California's modern civilization is written in massive walls and rudimentary though genial factories. Inside you will breathe an atmosphere of many years. Each inspiring psalmology of the church, fragrant and comforting with virtues and heroism of friars and missionaries who brought the blessing of Christianity to pagan Indians and to us.

Another wooden marker on a wall outside the garden entrance, relays this message:

Please observe respectful silence within these mission walls. These grounds deserve reverence, not only out of respect for those whose remains rest here, but also as a place where our unique Californian civilization had its beginning. Here began our rich, dynamic culture, which is fast becoming the spearhead of human progress.

San Juan Capistrano Mission

Mission San Juan Capistrano is striking in its hand-crafted red brick, stone walkways and quaint fountains—accented with colorful flowers, shrubs and blossoming trees and graced with many birds and doves.

The mission is named after Saint John Capistran. A plaque outside the mission walls highlights this saint's life:

> Born in 1386 as Giovanni Chiori in Capistrano, Italy, he distinguished himself as a judge in Naples. Later he entered the Franciscan order. A brilliant orator, his sermons attracted great throngs all over Europe when Sultan Mahammed II, leading his invincible forces westward, threatened to abolish Christendom. Friar Capistran recruited volunteers. The fort of NANDOR-FEHER-VAR (now Belgrade) was guarded by Hungary's greatest strategist, John Corvinus Hunyadi. With only token troops, Capistran rushed with his ragged band of students and poor to aid the beseiged, and together they miraculously routed the largest, best equipped army of that age. Pope Calixtus ordered all church bells to ring out daily and ever since. The noon angelus commemorates this event. Until the recent communist take-over, Capistran was honored as patron of Hungary's defenders. The Budapest uprising against godless foreign oppression erupted on the saint's feastday, October 23, 1956, 500 years after his victory over the infidels.
> (This reminder was blessed by Joseph Cardinal Mundszenty).

Proof that Junipero Serra and his friars taught the Indians skills and trades is apparent in the grounds of this attractive mission. Two V-shaped ovens were used to render down grease or tallow from hides, meat scraps and bones. The tallow from both ovens was used in an adjacent workshop to make soap and candles for trade. A third oven, which may have been used for multipurpose functions, has the largest firebox of any oven or furnace known on the mission grounds. Tallow, for mission use and trade, was made in addition to tanning of hides, dying, weaving, candlemaking, smelting, carpentry and tool-making. The church taught Indians the skills of European living in addition to love of God—for it is its ancient teaching that to work is to pray.

The honor roll of this parish featured on a wall of the mission, aptly captures the principles for which it stands:

> I pledge my loyalty to the flag of my country and to the God-given principles of freedom, justice and happiness for which it stands.

An interesting little anecdote about this mission is that during the pastorate of Father Arthur Hutchinson (1933–1951), the song, "When the swallows come back to Capistrano" was written by Mr. Leon René, in 1939.

A walk through its quaint cemetery hints of the inner life of the mission, giving its true Christian history. Here's an example:

> On the 9th of December 1812, I gave ecclesiastical burial to male and female adults and a tiny tot. The following died buried in the ruins of said church that was ruined on the 8th of said month and year at the time of the first mass.
> Fr. Joseph Barona.

As one leaves, regretfully, this charming and inspiring old mission, these poignant words go with you: "You leave with the old expression of good-bye—Vaya con Dios, meaning 'Go with God'."

San Diego de Alcala Mission

Mission San Diego de Alcala, California's first mission, founded by Father Junipero Serra in July, 1769, was reconstructed by the generous aid of the citizens of San Diego in 1931, and fully restored by the charity of the Hearst Foundation in 1946. It was rededicated to the glory of God and the salvation of souls by its reestablishment as a parish church, under the title "Mission San Diego de Alcala" in

1941. Within the church of San Diego Mission one finds the following inscription:

> This plaque honors the memory of Fray Junipero Serra, "The Apostle of California," who died 200 years ago after a life dedicated to speading the gospel of Jesus Christ—1784–1984.

> Presented by Serra International, 15,000 Catholic laymen in 31 countries, who in 1984, celebrate 50 years of fostering vocations to priesthood and religious life. Always to go forward and never to turn back.

Junipero Serra's Latin Bible, now in the safekeeping of the Carmel Mission, was printed at Lyons, France, in 1568.[3] Its title page translation reads as follows:

> The Holy Bible
> Very carefully corrected to
> accord with the Hebrew and
> with the testimony of the most reliable manuscripts:
> With figures and geographical
> descriptions in which the structures
> and various buildings and works,
> and regions as well, are placed
> before the eyes of everyone.
> There are in addition interpretations
> of Hebrew, Chaldean and Greek names, as
> well as very full indices.[4]

Ronald Reagan was sworn into office as governor of California on January 2, 1967, using Serra's Bible. This priceless gem of America's Christian heritage was described thus at that time:

> A Bible brought to California by famed Spanish missionary Father Junipero Serra . . . published in Lyon, France, in 1568 and now . . . housed permanently in the Archives of the Carmel Mission. . . . "It is, to my knowledge, the oldest Mission Bible in California," said Harry Downie, curator at the Carmel Mission.[5]

It has been attested that Junipero Serra's greatest legacy is California itself.[6]

He is considered to be California's founding father, every aspect of his indelible stamp upon the state's history and religion having been analyzed and examined in depth.[7]

A letter from sculptress Doris Kutchuka on display within the confines of this mission, gives insight regarding the architecture and culture of our California missions. She states that:

> ... A new style of architecture began with these missions. Big, simple, beautiful, preserving peace and tranquility. This is the beginning of a new culture; of education and distribution of knowledge. ...

It stands to reason that everything about these missions glorifies and witnesses to the amazing, saving grace of our Lord Jesus Christ. Not so with modern-day versions of their history. Of five or six history books and travelogues I consulted, the thrust of their narrative is a purely secular-humanistic one, with hardly any mention at all of Almighty God and His hand upon the affairs of the people in California through the work and outreach of Junipero Serra's missions.

Here is an example denoting a purely humanistic outreach and approach to life, shredded of Christian values and the life-blood of the missions, which was to nurture souls in eternal truths:

San Diego de Alcala
The California missions almost never happened! When San Diego de Alcala, the first mission, was planned in 1769, the Spanish King's hopes for a string of ecclesiastical-military establishments in California hung by a thread. Everything that could go wrong did go wrong. First of all, two expeditions had left Baja California by land and two by sea. The two ships arrived at San Diego first. When the land expeditions came on the scene, they found that scurvy had stricken the crews of both ships. 38 sailors had died. The San Antonio, with a skeleton crew of 8 men, was sent back to San Blas to get fresh supplies for the expedition and new crews for the two ships. The Rivera land expedition of forty men was also sent back to Baja California for supplies. Local Indians, the Yumas, were more aggressive, turbulent and warlike than their relatively

peaceful neighbors to the north. Trouble from them could be
expected. And it came . . . [8]

The narrative continues documenting the trials and progress
in the natural, but totally lacks understanding of the far more
powerful forces that were taking place in the spiritual, and the
impact the spiritual played upon the natural. Junipero Serra came
to California primarily to glorify God and to present the simple
gospel plan of salvation to the lost Indians on America's West
Coast. Like the settlers on the East Coast who came with a quest for
biblically based living, the West Coast too was evangelized and
Christianized by Father Junipero Serra and his fervent Spanish
friars. What a magnificent testimony to God's grace being shed
abroad throughout our land: "From sea to shining sea, God shed
His grace on thee, beloved America."

In spite of the wealth of factual evidence portraying Junipero
Serra's godliness, his love of Jesus Christ and his biblical way of life,
the following is a shocking recent reinterpretation of this man's life
and conduct:

> . . . In his austere cell, Serra kept a chain of sharp pointed iron
> links hanging on the wall beside bed, to whip himself when sin-
> ful thoughts (including, presumably, any sexual impulses)
> ran through his mind in the night. . . . [9]

And then, in a 1988 book entitled *Junipero Serra, the Vatican and
Enslavement Theology*, Father Junipero Serra has been accused of the
following inhuman endeavors:

> *The Whip and the Cross*
> . . . Neophytes judged "delinquent" in their worship, labor, or
> personal behavior were punished by whipping them on the
> bare back with a rope, lariat, or a flexible reed or cane. . . . The
> humiliation of being whipped in front of one's peers must
> have been appalling—especially when one recalls that the
> Indians in their own societies did not physically punish one
> another, and seldom punished or even publicly scolded their
> own children. . . . But for California Indians, the comparison
> between their treatment and the norms of punishment pre-
> vailing in various European Institutions was meaningless.

What counted for them was that their punitive treatment at the missions ruptured the freedom and dignity they had once enjoyed. . . [10]

Just a short distance down the slope from San Juan Capistrano, is one of California's oldest restaurants, El Adobe de Capistrano. Its authentic dungeon dates to 1778. The foyer, dating to 1812, was the passageway for stage coaches on overnight journeys. The beautiful little garden chapel is a frequent site for weddings. This is the American heritage: one of the oldest restaurants extolling God's glory and preeminence in the affairs of this nation, by virtue of a chapel.

Today the United States stands far removed from the proud origin of a nation established upon biblical truth. How dire and important the need to return to Almighty God, His direction and way of life.

Abraham Lincoln's Godly Role in the Mission Story

In 1862, President Abraham Lincoln restored the mission lands to the churches in California, after the Mexican Secularization Act of 1833 had taken the mission lands from the hands of the church. A copy of this Act of Congress is to be found upon a wall in the Museum of San Diego de Alcala Mission.

> Now know ye, that the United States of America, pursuant to the provisions of the Act of Congress aforesaid of third March, 1851, have given and granted and by these presents I give and grant unto the said Joseph G. Alemony, Bishop of Monterrey, and to his successors, "in trust for the religious purposes and uses to which the same have been respectively appropriated" the tracts of land embraced and described in the foregoing survey; but with the stipulation that in virtue of the 15th section of the said act, the confirmation of the said claim and this patent, "shall not affect the interests of third persons." To have and to hold the said tracts of land with the appurtenances and with the stipulation aforesaid, unto the said Joseph G. Alemony, Bishop of Monterrey and his successors, in trust for the uses and purposes as aforesaid.

In testimony whereof, I, Abraham Lincoln, President of the United States, have caused these letters to be made patent, and the seal of the General Land Office to be hereunto affixed. Given under my hand at the city of Washington, this 23rd day of May, in the year of our Lord one thousand eight hundred and 62, and of the Independence of the United States the eighty sixth.

By the President, Abraham Lincoln. By N.O. Stoddard, Secretary. Recorded: Vol. 4; pages 94 to 101, inclusive. G.N. Granger, Recorder of the General Land Office.

A popular book found in most of the mission bookstores is *Spanish Missions of California—Coloring Album* published in 1977. The description for San Miguel Arcangel Mission is as follows:

Mission San Miguel was undamaged by earthquakes and other misfortunes which befell many of the missions. The church and padres' wings still stand and look just as they did over 150 years ago. The colonade is especially interesting with its row of 16 different shapes and sizes of arches. Rather sombre and plain on the outside, the church comes aglow with vibrant colors on the inside. Under the direction of imported artist Estevan Munras, the Indians learned to paint designs and pictures on the walls as beautiful as they could. . . .[11]

Fellow Americans, what do we glean from the above? Earthquakes, architecture, colors, painting pictures . . . There is no interpretation of the pulsing, vibrant inner life of this mission, its outreach for souls, its Christianization of the Indians, teaching them useful skills and crafts, and the high and noble Christian value system which was honored and practiced on a daily basis by these friars.

Once again, the Christian value system of our missions—living evidence of God's hand upon the West Coast of our land—has been expunged and removed from current literature and historic records.

Canonization and Posthumous Attacks

September 1988 marked the date when a proposed canonization process was initiated by the Catholic church, to make Junipero Serra a saint for his extraordinary life and work among the Indians. Mrs. Georgette O'Brien, a former public relations executive and a concerned citizen, pointed out that there were protests and uprisings in the San Diego area concurrent with the proposed canonization. Why? Because gullible people had been provoked by humanists into believing that the godly Junipero Serra was nothing more than an Indian killer. It is ludicrous that 200 years after the man's death, there are those who would be so audacious as to fabricate falsehoods and serious allegations against him, in spite of the fact that those who were his contemporaries in life made no such charges. In fact, his death was deeply mourned, especially by the Indian population, the very ones whom the anti-Christians claimed he murdered and exploited!

In stark contrast to the above rewritten accounts of Junipero Serra's life motivation, the original documentation of his Christian forbearance and genuine love for the Indians throughout his 34 years in California indicates that at approximately two p.m. on August 28, 1784, Junipero Serra, man of God, went to be with the Lord Jesus Christ, whom he had loved and served so well among the California Indians for 34 years. Those present said that after he prayed, he "fell asleep" in Christ.[12]

On August 29, 1784, his funeral requiem service was attended by officers and the crew of the San Carlos, Monterrey Presidio Commandant and soldiers, mission guards, and 600 Indians. Among them was Bernardino de Jesus, the first person baptized by Serra in Upper California (who lived until February 27, 1792). "Melting the hearts of all," the bells continued their mournful double stroke tolling throughout the day.[13]

Of Junipero Serra's life and actions among the Indians, the following excerpted letter, written on November 25, 1784, by San Fernando College guardian Juan Sancho to the Franciscan Provincial of Mallorca, is a testimony of historical truth:

> I have just received the news from our missions in Monterrey
> of the death of our beloved countryman, the Reverend Father,
> Lector, Junipero Serra, who was the president, at San Carlos.

> I have been informed that he died the death of the just and in such circumstances that besides bringing tender tears to the eyes of all of those present, they all were of the opinion that his happy soul went directly to heaven to enjoy the reward for 34 years of great and continuous labors, undergone for our beloved Jesus, whom he ever kept in mind, suffering them in an inexplicable manner for our redemption. So great was his charity which he always manifested towards those poor Indians that not only the ordinary people, but likewise persons of higher condition were struck with admiration. All men said openly that that man was a saint and that his actions were those of an apostle. It has been the opinion concerning him ever since he arrived in this kingdom. This opinion has been constant and without interruption.[14]

In the face of this national dilemma and in spite of it, Junipero Serra's life continues to shine forth as a bright light to the nations. It is just another example of America's founding period history being replete with gospel truth—from coast to shining coast.

A conspicuous brick cross marks the spot where Father Junipero Serra first established civilization on the West Coast of America. A plaque commemorates the event as follows:

> In this ancient Indian village of Cosay discovered and named San Miguel by Cabrillo in 1542, visited and christened San Diego de Alcala by Vizcimo in 1602. Here the first citizen, Fray Junipero Serra, planted civilization in California. Here he first raised the cross. Here began the first mission. Here was founded the first town, San Diego on July 16, 1769. In memory of him and his works. The order of Panama, 1913.

The State of California itself has recognized the contributions of Serra by selecting him as their representative in Statuary Hall, the old legislative chamber of the U.S. Capitol. The life-size, bronze statue stands prominently with other great missionaries, preachers, pastors, statesmen and inventors of caliber, representing all 50 states in the Union. Such was the life and testimony of *Junipero Serra—man of God.*

Chapter III

WHERE ARE WE GOING?

Independence Hall, site of the signing of the U.S. Constitution and Declaration of Independence. The "Pavilion" now housing the famed Liberty Bell is in the background. Photo by John W. Wrigley.

(i) Independence Hall

Independence Square, the heart of the nation's birthplace, consists of three key buildings: The Old Supreme Court Building, *Independence Hall* and Congress Hall. Independence Hall (the Old Pennsylvania State House) is called "The Birthplace of America's Liberty." It was here that both the Declaration of Independence and the U.S. Constitution were signed. It was here, too, that the old Liberty Bell rang for all the great founding events of *this nation under God*.

In a telephone interview dated December 15, 1986 with Doris Fanelli, Supervisory Curator of the Independence National Historical Park Museum Collections, Ms. Fanelli told me that "our National Museum was in Independence Hall from the 1840s. Its purpose was to commemorate the founding of the American government or related historical events—political, fine arts and multimedia."

Although Ms. Fanelli admits that this was an important historic museum, our National Museum was taken over by the Independence National Historical Park (INHP) in 1951. The museum was disbanded, and no museum building now exists. These valuable materials pertaining to our legitimate American history and formerly housed within this building, have been dispersed throughout the Independence National Historical Park collections, in different buildings. They are no longer readily accessible to the public, such as the original documentation, paintings and sculpture on the founding of America.

In front of Independence Hall stands a famous bronze statue of George Washington. This is the work of renowned sculptor Joseph Alexis Bailly, done in the year 1869. Bailly was one of the most celebrated sculptors of the time, renowned for his life-reproducing images of famous personages of his day. He was truly considered a master craftsman of his art. Our first president's right hand rests upon a book. Obviously a significant and meaningful part of the sculpture, one might like to know what the sculptor had in mind. However, there is absolutely nothing in writing to identify the book itself and the meaning the sculptor intended to convey. Even a special request to the Independence National Historic Park for information on this produces no results. According to their files, they have nothing to identify the book itself.

After extensive research, I proved my premise that it was a Bible—the Book of books, the world's bestselling book to date—the Holy Scriptures upon which George Washington's left hand rested when he was sworn into office as the first president of the United States.

The INHP *Interpretative Fact Sheet* on this statue completely omits the Christian values inherent not only in this great masterpiece, but also in the artist himself. Under the heading "Statue of George Washington," the first two paragraphs of his INHP Fact Sheet, entitled "Samuel Murray," give a 22-line commentary on Murray, the workman who, in 1910, took a mold from Bailly's original masterpiece, making the exact bronze replica which stands today in front of Independence Hall, signed: *J. A. Bailly.* Its original is now housed within City Hall. The last paragraph of the Fact Sheet consists of nine lines, and has only one sentence on Bailly, the sculptor of this magnificent creation. This historic INHP Fact Sheet bearing the catalog folder number S.N. 17.020, comes from the Independence National Historical Park Museum Office and Library. Submitted by the Assistant Curator, Anne Verplanck, it is dated November, 1985.

The INHP Interpretative Fact Sheet majors upon the materials used, and the stark, brutal facts and statistics—but nothing else. No mention is made of the Bible upon which George Washington's hand rests. [1]

The above reinforces my thesis that America's history, and the correct interpretation of her historic treasures, has been rewritten, to the detriment of the original artist's interpretation and the meaning he attributed to his own masterpiece. Moreover, the American public is being cheated of the rich Christian legacy which these treasures convey.

Another recent "Fact Sheet on Independence" widely distributed throughout the national landmarks, exhibitions and shrines in historic Philadelphia is here reprinted for public appraisal. The First Amendment to the United States Constitution, commonly upheld as the *Freedom of Religion Clause,* has now been coined by the National Park Service, Department of the Interior, as the *Right of Public Assembly* and freedom of speech amendment, its mission being "to preserve America's great cultural and natural heritage."[2] This shows, once again, a deliberate removal of her Christian reli-

Independence

National Historical Park
Philadelphia

National Park Service
U.S. Department of the Interior

Right of Public Assembly

The First Amendment to the Constitution says:

"Congress shall make no law respecting an establishment of religion, or prohibiting the free exercise thereof; or abridging <u>the freedom of speech</u>, or of the press; or <u>the right of the people peaceably to assemble</u>, and to petition the Government for a redress of grievances."

Most Americans take for granted their right to freedom of speech. Yet throughout our history the scope of this First Amendment freedom has been debated, particularly when governments have attempted to restrict the expression of opinions which are unpopular or viewed as dangerous.

Fact Sheet. Courtesy of Independence National Historical Park, Philadelphia.

gious heritage, which forms the basis and bedrock of the freedoms and liberties which we now enjoy as Americans.

Where do these Independence materials and fact sheets originate, and who researches and writes them, one might question?

The Independence National Historical Park, Department of the Interior new Visitors' Center was constructed in 1976 opposite the traditional First Bank of Philadelphia, on Third Street. It is the oldest bank in the United States, serving as the government's bank from 1797–1811. Upon entering the Visitors' Center, focal point for all INHP interpretative tours of historic Philadelphia, in November 1986, I was met with an appalling Main Exhibit which encompassed a large portion of the Center, indoctrinating millions of young Americans into false, distorted history and pornographic art.

A large sign welcomed all to Philadelphia, with the wording:

The Philadelphia Cornucopia . . .
   You are invited . . .

The use of the Cornucopia, to symbolize abundance, is traced to Greek mythology.

It was a magnificent horn which filled itself with food and drink at the owner's request. Here, Red Grooms has depicted 300 years of Philadelphia's Bounty.

18th Century: Proudly leading the procession as it passes through history, is our Ship of State, with George Washington firmly in command. His companions, Franklin and Jefferson, also loom larger than life as each generation admires our 18th Century heros. . . . 19th Century: To Washington's right, we see a very unique banquet inside a mammoth ribcage. . . . During the Victorian period, society was shocked by female participation in life-drawing classes given by Thomas Eakins at the Pennsylvania Academy of Fine Arts. . . . these figures lead the ever-flowing procession as the next generation adds to the bounty offered by a city laden with history and culture.

The Ship of State stood in the center, our founding fathers, George Washington, Benjamin Franklin and Thomas Jefferson ridiculed, upon it. Washington was laden with cheap medals; Jefferson was portrayed in his dressing gown, quill in hand, drowsing over a half-extinguished candle; while Franklin played idly with a child's kite. Martha Washington was featured in a cheap pink taffeta, low-cut dress with a tinsel crown and yellow, stringy hair flying in the wind. Our first First Lady comprised the Ship's prow.

An explanatory "map" of the exhibit was written out in graffiti upon a bar-stool. A glance to the rear, right hand side of "the Ship of State" showed pornographic art—crude, immoral and godless.

This exhibition, depicting William Penn's Philadelphia, "a city laden with history and culture" ran in prominence in the Independence National Historical Park Visitors' Center from 1983 to early 1987—for three years—contaminating millions of unsuspecting Americans visiting the birthplace of our nation. A park ranger told me that citizens of Philadelphia had refused to have this exhibit placed in Independence Hall where it was originally intended. Upon exiting, a large wall panel disclosed the following:

> Philadelphia Cornucopia was commissioned by the Institute of Contemporary Art and is now sponsored by Citizens for Philadelphia Cornucopia. We offer special thanks to the numerous private contributors and the following supporters:
>
> - The City of Philadelphia
> - Civic Center Museum
> - Fairmount Park Art Association
> - *Independence National Historic Park*
> - *Friends of the Independence National Historic Park*
> - Mabel Pew Myron Trust
> - Pennsylvania Council on the Arts
> - Barra Foundation
> - Girard Bank
> - Quaker Moving and Storage Company
> - Campbell Soup Company
> - Community Education Center
> - ICA

While in *Independence Hall*, I inquired of a ranger as to the source of materials studied by the Independence National Historical Park Rangers who serve as the only permitted lecturers/interpreters in Philadelphia's historic landmarks and shrines, adminis-

Above: Statue of George Washington in front of Independence Hall, Philadelphia. Sculptor: Joseph Alexis Bailly. Photo John W. Wrigley. Below: The "Philadelphia Cornucopia" exhibit. George Washington at the helm of the "Ship of State" with his wife, Martha, the prow of the ship.

Above: Thomas Jefferson, author of the Declaration of Independence, in his dressing gown, drowsing. Benjamin Franklin playing with a kite. Below: To direct you through "Philadelphia Cornucopia," find your way around on this graffiti-marked barstool.

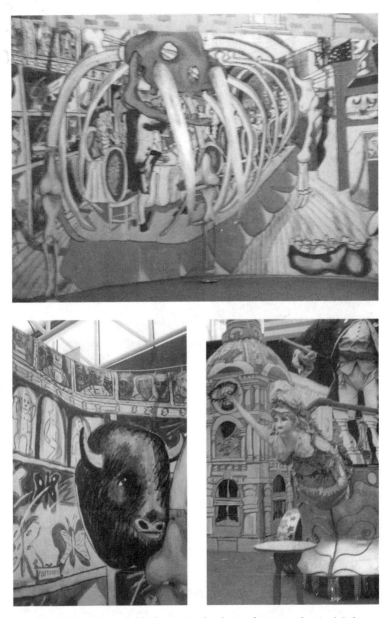

Above: The delegates hold a banquet in the ribcage of a mammoth animal. Left: This section is entitled "Monkeydelphia." Right: A close-up of Martha Washington as the prow of the "Ship of State."

Above: George Washington in the center and William Penn above. Below: Millions of schoolchildren visit these exhibits each year.

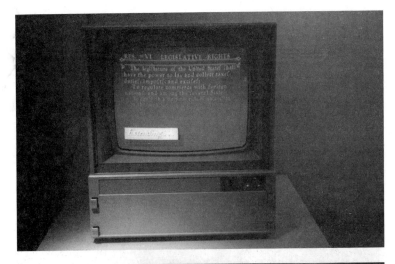

"The Miracle at Philadelphia" exhibit. Above: Cutting up our U.S. Constitution on a Word Processor. Below: Upon exiting the Constitutional Convention, a display inviting visitors to sign their name and state of residence if they would have endorsed the original Constitution, had they been at the 1787 Convention.

tered by the Department of the Interior. I was given a number to call in order to obtain more information on this literature. Upon reaching the number in question, I was greeted by an Independence National Historical Park Historian—Bicentennial of the Constitution Research Team, who, after seeing my great interest in the Park's historic tours, agreed to give me a copy of the famous 196-page *Liberty Bell of Independence National Historic Park: A Special History Study* by John C. Paige (Denver Service Center, National Park Service, United States Department of the Interior, Denver, Colorado).

I was thus granted the great privilege of being one of the few people admitted to the inner sanctum of the Independence National Historical Park, Historic Research Team's operational headquarters in Philadelphia, located within the First Bank of Philadelphia opposite the Visitors' Center (closed to the public). I was told to go to the Visitors' Center and announce myself. A ranger would then take me across the street and let me into the First Bank. This building is a private, double-locked edifice. Only special park rangers have keys to enter or exit. The magnificent, gracious, classic-domed interior of the First Bank in America is a sight for every American to admire, being the oldest bank in the United States. The Independence National Historical Park—historic research offices are arranged in a circular pattern, around the inner rotunda. There I met the historian, who handed me a copy of "The Liberty Bell Report." Upon exiting, a wall panel disclosed the following:

Office of History and Historical Architecture
David C. Dulcher
Penelope Batcheler
William Brookover
David Kimball
Robert Sutton

Conference Room
Viola Pritchett
Jane Kolter
Gloria McLean
Anne Cox Toogood

Library
Shirley A. Mays

Museum Operations
Doris Fanelli
Robert L. Gianni
Ricardo Hutchinson, Jr.
Preston James.

The above offices and titles disclose that research and history specialists in the field of American founding period history, historical architecture, documentation and historical museum exhibits are being paid to produce the fact sheets and historical interpretations on our nation's past.

However, the interpreters of America's rich founding period history have vastly altered, reinterpreted and even falsified the founding period records of our nation. A masterpiece painting "The First Prayer in Congress" has been lost; the Liberty Bell has been removed from its original site, and its history rewritten as "a symbol of world freedom" (see Official Park Guide Book); The INHP Department of the Interior Official Tour Literature entitled *Urban Renewal Tour, Financial Tour, Holy Experiment Tour* and *Cultural Tour* give rewritten historical information, alien to the original, true documented history of America; *all* outdoor historic markers in this historic square mile of America, pertaining to the most significant landmarks of the foundations of the United States were permanently removed (Spring, 1987) and replaced with reinterpreted markers bearing no mention or hint of the original Christian heritage of our nation, which forms its strength.

Commonly found new phraseology of such markers is given in the following example:

Second Bank of the United States
"The Portico of the glorious edifice always repays me for coming to Philadelphia." Philip Howe 1838.

Here stands the Second Bank of the U.S., established in 1816 to hold government deposits and regulate currency, it dominated American finance for more than a decade. The temple-like bank had both priests and heretics. Bank President Nicolas Biddle preached the value of the bank, while U.S. President Andrew Jackson decried it as a "hydra of corruption." The "temple" was looted of its treasure when Jackson vetoed the recharter of the bank, distributing government deposits to smaller banks. Now long after the passions of finance and philosophy have subsided, we recognize the architecture—not the institution—as the real treasure of the bank. Designed by William Strickland, it has been called the finest example of Greek Revival Architecture in the United States.

The above rewritten marker draws in religious terminology within the descriptive commentary on this edifice, marrying finances with religion, which is a powerful way to indoctrinate youth. This is done by word associations and symbolic speech. Words such as "temple-like," "priests and heretics," "preached the value of," "hydra of corruption," "treasure" and "passions of finance and philosophy," all depict a value-system which promotes money and banking, materialism and monetary gain, within the context of religion. Sadly, only a few lines at the end of this commentary disclose the design and architecture of the building.

Second Bank of the United States

Miracle at Philadelphia—United States Constitutional Convention Bicentennial, Independence National Historic Park Exhibition
(September 17, 1986—December 31, 1987)

Upon entering this building, one was greeted with a half-incinerated flag of the 13 original states. The exhibition was presented in terms of a Constitutional Convention, an entire wall being filled with a lithograph depicting children sitting in a classroom with quills and textbooks. They were represented as delegates to the Constitutional Convention. George Washington was shown signing the Constitution. A quotation read "Groping in the dark to find political truth" by Benjamin Franklin.

The tone and content of this exhibition was pessimistic, at best, with headlines throughout reading as follows:

- *America Nourished by Liberty:*
    The Saga of Empty pockets
- The Nationalists Alarm—The Calamity of Congress
- The Nationalists Alarm—Troubles Abroad
- The Nationalists Alarm—Troubles at Home
- The Nationalists Alarm—The Call to the Convention
- *Reconciling North and South*
To achieve a Constitution, the Northern and Southern interests had to find compromises. Move the handles to the red mark beneath the position you choose. When the map looks right, you will see how the Convention resolved these conflicts between geographical regions.

- The Compromise that failed
The delegates were Federalists, not fortunetellers.

A large mirror represented this section of the exhibit. Its frame was comprised of neon red lighting. A button which glowed neon red light to the left, featured the directive: "Push and hold button and look into the future of the Slavery Compromise." One has to keep holding the button down, while the whole panel lights up, showing an old, enlarged photograph of the Civil War. A fortress wall appeared in the foreground, with soldiers and cannons and a vast, empty, dry plain. We watched young people press the button, draw a blank, shake their heads and walk away, probably asking themselves the same question as we did: "What on earth has this got to do with the Slavery Compromise—let alone the Constitution of the United States?"

Another panel entitled *Inventing the Mechanics of Government* was depicted as an actual Solar System, and subheaded *The Solar System of Federalism.*

The "Miracle at Philadelphia—United States Constitutional Convention Bicentennial, Independence National Historic Park" exhibition continued with a section entitled—"Filling in the Blanks: The work of the Committee of Style."

Upon exiting this—the INHP's major exhibit on the signing of the U.S. Constitution—the visitor was faced with two stands on either side of the rear main exhibition hall. Handsome silver ink-stands, with quills were displayed, above which was the poignant question, in bold lettering:

> If you had been in Independence Hall on September 17, 1787, would you have endorsed the Constitution?
> If you would have signed, pick up the pen on the table and set your name and state to the document before you.

I submit that there is nothing *miraculous* about this exhibition, at all. Our sacred U.S. Constitution was being reevaluated and rewritten on a word processor; people were being asked to write their names and states of residence, if, in fact, they would have signed the original Constitution had they been present at its signing in 1787. The semantics, wording and events described upon the walls and partitions of *The Miracle at Philadelphia* exhibition were negative, alarmist, calamity-strewn and bankrupt-oriented. There was practically nothing factually elevating, challenging and/or optimistic about this major event in the Constitutional History of the *One Nation under God*.

Furthering the subject of a Constitutional Convention to commemorate the signing of the United States Constitution on 17 September, 1787—hence our freedom as Americans—the INHP Department of the Interior Cultural Tour literature prominently features the Philadelphia Maritime Museum as its first stop, the Second Bank of the United States being next on the agenda.

On December 8, 1986, an interview with educator William H. Ward of the Philadelphia Maritime Museum revealed the following:

There is an education program especially geared for public school children. They are "Grade and Curriculum Oriented Classes." The museum's education department gives out all information needed to schools. In a course which Mr. Ward was currently teaching, "Privateers and the American Revolution," the students acted out the scenes they were learning. A new course was being taught, entitled: "Fishing and the Constitution." Concerning this course which he was teaching, educator Ward stated:

> I will get students to reevaluate the United States Constitution. The Federalists' Constitution was good up to 1900—after that,

it has to be changed so that the states can run their own affairs.

This is a very effective way to indoctrinate millions of America's youth into rethinking the validity of the U.S. Constitution—and its possible rewriting.

INHP Literature and Historic Materials Readily Available to Public

The center for the sale of the Independence National Historical Park literature and materials made available to Americans is located at the rear west side of Independence Hall. Its logo consists of a leaf upon which an open book rests bearing the initials: ENP & MA. Its motto: "Conservation of our Nation's Heritage and Resources." Its stated purpose and function are:

> The Sales Center of this National Park Service area is operated by Eastern National Park and Monument Association, a nonprofit organization. Proceeds are used by the Association to support historical, scientific and educational activities of the National Park Service for the benefit of the public and posterity.

What a tragedy and tremendous loss to the people of America that her true treasures of founding period art, history and sculpture should be in the hands of those who would distort history to fit their own mindset and projected goals.

Independence Hall provides *A Teacher's Guide—for Discovering Independence National Historic Park.* This informative sheet states:

> A valuable educational resource awaits your exploration. Make a visit to Independence National Historic Park a part of your curriculum. Organize your trip to make the best use of the park; stimulate your students with stories of the American Revolution, of Benjamin Franklin, of 18th Century Philadelphia; and discover the variety of buildings and exhibits! Make us a part of your school year—we will be glad to help you.

The Liberty Bell Pavilion—see and carefully touch this world symbol of freedom.

The Independence Natonal Historical Park *Official Guidebook to Philadelphia* goes further to reinterpret this symbol of America's biblical freedom with its inscription from Leviticus 25:10 upon its face as: " . . . a symbol of world freedom."

The main operational headquarters for the INHP is identical to the Friends of the Independence National Historic Park, at 313 Walnut Street, Philadelphia, Pennsylvania. A wide range of tax-deductible memberships, such as Minuteman, Statesman, Patriot, Signer and Bell-ringer are offered, according to the amount one could afford, giving the people the impression of being a part of the preservation of our nation's rich history. But, one would question if they are unwittingly becoming part of a group that does just the opposite.

Their informative literature gives an outline of membership benefits, including educational materials, lectures, symposia and tours on America's rich history, art and architecture. These are all further incentives to support the questionable work and outreach of the INHP.

A letter received from Secretary of the Interior, Donald Paul Hodel, dated December 8, 1986, gave me the following encouragement pertaining to the restoration of America's rich founding period history to Philadelphia's landmarks, shrines and historic sites. It reads:

Recently, our mutual friend and your admirer, mentioned to me, again, the wonderful tours you provide of the monuments and historic sites in this area. She urged me to get in touch with you and talk about what you do.

I am very interested in what she tells me about your efforts. I would like to learn more with the thought in mind that some of the more significant aspects of your material which have been "lost" by the National Park Service might be found and returned to their interpretative tours, too.

If this would be of interest to you, I hope you will respond affirmatively when either Mary Ann Wilkinson or Terri Mar-

shall of my office call to see if we can find a mutually convenient time to meet. . . .

(signed) Donald Paul Hodel

An appointment was made for me to meet with Secretary
Hodel in his Washington, D.C., office, on January 9, 1987. I worked
tirelessly to compile the material on historic Philadelphia, in order
to prove, with documented evidence, the ravages made upon our
Christian heritage and original historical roots in "the birthplace of
the nation." I spent an hour with Mr. Hodel and his Special Assistant for Programs in his office. A slide presentation on the *Philadelphia Cornucopia Exhibition,* which was to complete its three-year
course in early February, 1987, was given on Secretary Hodel's
drafting board.

After explaining carefully all the material, duplicates of my
original material and documentation on the National Park Service's rewriting of America's history and removal of her precious
Christian heritage were left with him. Detailed photographs accompanied the entire exposé. I had also carefully cataloged the plaques
(e.g. *St. Joseph's Church* plaque) and markers (e.g. *First Prayer in
Congress* marker in front of Carpenters' Hall) pertaining to our
American Christian heritage and history which still taught in a
vibrant manner our nation's true origins in Philadelphia.

A letter dated February 3, 1987, from Secretary of the Interior
Hodel accompanied my returned material, telling me that the
three-year long exhibit: "Philadelphia Cornucopia" had run its
course, a fact which had been public knowledge for some time. The
letter then stated:

> . . . Through a million dollar gift from Bell of Pennsylvania, an
> exciting new exhibit will open in mid May. It will feature 16
> computers with which visitors will interact in order to under-
> stand and appreciate the 19th and 20th century evolution of
> our Constitution. . . .
>
> Again, thank you very much for making me aware of the sit-
> uation in Philadelphia. I am returning your materials to you
> with this letter.

(signed) Donald Paul Hodel.

On May 22, 1987, our inaugural Christian Heritage Tour of "Philadelphia, City of Brotherly Love" took place. How utterly devastated was I to find that *all* the outside markers and plaques pertaining to our true, American heritage (including those cataloged above) were permanently *removed* from public view. They were replaced by secular humanistic plaques, devoid of the godly values and historic themes that had been prominent on the former plaques. This was an even further corrosion upon our national Christian roots!

While many visitors would be unaware of this loss, I was shaken by the abrupt removal of the Christian evidence which I had meticulously cataloged as still existing in historic Philadelphia. This is a devastating blow to millions of Americans who come to Philadelphia annually to study our nation's historic foundations.

As the statue of George Washington with his hand upon the Bible in front of Independence Hall shows, our earlier historians did not neglect to demonstrate the Christian values that were integral in the lives of our forebears and the founders of this nation. Unfortunately, many modern historians have transgressed from this truth in history. Today, it will be up to the average American citizen to work toward, and demand restoration of, the lifeblood of our history.

The statue of George Washington standing directly in front of Independence Hall, site of the reading of the Declaration of Independence and signing of the U.S. Constitution, portrays Washington with his hand upon the Bible. This symbolizes his dependence upon God's Words at the birth of the nation. Our first president was sworn into office on April 30, 1789 with his left hand upon the Bible, which was opened to the 49th and 50th chapters of Genesis.[3] The latter part of the 49th chapter of Genesis reads:

> Joseph is a fruitful bough, even a fruitful bough by a well; . . .
> The archers have sorely grieved him and shot at him, and
> hated him: *But his bow abode in strength, and the arms of his
> hands were made strong by the hands of the mighty God of Jacob* . . .

Above: Jacob Duché and his wife—a portrait by their son, Thomas Duché. The Historical Society of Pennsylvania. Below: Carpenter's Hall, Philadelphia Pennsylvania, site of the first convening of Congress, September 5 through October 26, 1774. Illustrator: Helen Weir.

(ii) Carpenters' Hall

On September 5, 1774, the first convening of Congress under the Articles of Confederation took place in Carpenters' Hall, Philadelphia. The exquisite, federal-style structure is designed in the shape of a cross. Upon entering the building, one is greeted with a mosaic tile emblem and its exhortation: *Honor God*. The delegates actually met in Carpenters' Hall from September 5 to October 26, 1774.

One of their first official acts was to invite Jacob Duché, Rector of Christ Church, called "the nation's church," to open the first Congress with prayer. Subsequently, he was invited to serve as first chaplain of Congress. In opening the session, he selected, very appropriately, Psalm 35 to be read in its entirety:

> Contend O Lord, with those who contend with me;
> Fight against those who fight against me.
> Take hold of buckler and shield,
> And rise up for my help.
> Draw also the spear and the battle-axe to meet those
>   who pursue me;
> Say to my soul, "I am your salvation,"
> Let those be ashamed and dishonored who seek my
>   life;
> Let those be turned back and humiliated who devise evil
>   against me.
> (Psalm 35:1–4)

Following the reading, he broke out into spontaneous prayer. In corresponding with his wife, John Adams wrote of the event: "I must confess that I never heard a better prayer, or one so well pronounced. It filled the bosom of every man present."

This tradition of prayer in Congress continues today, each session of both House and Senate opening with Scripture readings and prayer to Almighty God.

A Lost Masterpiece

In 1848, a magnificent painting, entitled "The First Prayer in Congress" was executed by T.H. Matheson. This work of art aptly captures our forefathers' spirit of humility and dependence on

God in accomplishing their difficult task. Since the 1950s the original of this great Matheson painting which plays an important part in our American Christian heritage for posterity, has been lost by the overseers of the Independence National Historic Park Museum Collection. In response to my request for a photograph of the original painting, a letter dated 8/18/86 from Doris Fanelli, Supervisory Curator of the Independence National Historic Park, Department of the Interior, Museum Collections, stated the following:

> . . . If you want a photograph of the original painting I'm afraid that we cannot help you. Our files indicate that at least four scholars unsuccessfully have attempted to locate the original Matheson during the past fifteen years.

Thus we see by the response of the overseers of some of America's greatest treasures, that this Christian work of art has "disappeared." A January 1, 1989 official Department of the Interior report prompted by my inquiry, gives a different story—that it was "incorrectly recorded" as an original masterpiece painting at the outset:

> Doris Fanelli (Supervisory Curator) states that the original gift to the city of Philadelphia was a print and incorrectly recorded as an original. This would explain why four scholars have not been able to find the original on Park grounds.[1]

By this statement, they completely dismiss the issue. This is preposterous, however, as a masterpiece painting of such great value and significance could not possibly be "incorrectly recorded" as an original, and then suddenly materialize into an engraving of the original!

The loss of this treasure is an irreplaceable loss to the American people.

Another letter forwarded to me, this time addressed to Mr. Grant Mydland, Assistant to Assistant Secretary, Department of the Interior, Fish and Wildlife, National Park Service, Washington, D.C., and dated January 12, 1989, stated the following:

. . .Whether the painting ("The First Prayer in Congress") exists or not is immaterial because it is not a documentation of the event. It is a history painting, a conjectural piece executed after the fact and intended to evoke emotion in the beholder. T.H. Matheson wasn't born until 1813. He could not have witnessed the Continental Congress in 1774. . . . Because of its 1848 date, and because it depicts the Continental Congress which met in 1774 in Carpenters' Hall, we have no opportunity to display the print in our public buildings. . . .

> (signed) Doris D. Fanelli, Ph.D.
> Supervisory Curator
> U.S. Department of Interior,
> National Park Service
> Independence National Historical
> Park, Philadelphia.

The original marker outside Carpenters' Hall depicted a reproduction of this painting, "The First Prayer in Congress." However, it was removed in the Spring of 1987 and replaced with a marker bearing secular details, primarily concerning the architecture, windows and construction of this building, once owned by the "Carpenters' Guild." The new marker reads thus:

Carpenters' Hall, completed in 1774, was the meeting place of a group of Philadelphia master builders known as the Carpenters Company. The carpenters banded together to establish architectural standards, to set prices for work and to aid members' families in times of need. A visitor to Philadelphia in the 1700's would have seen many buildings designed and constructed by members of the Carpenters' Co., including the Pennsylvania State House (Independence Hall); Old City Hall, The Pennsylvania Hospital, Benjamin Franklin's Mansion and their own Carpenters' Hall. The Carpenters aided the leaders of the American Revolution by offering them the use of Carpenters' Hall. It was here that the first Continental Congress gathered in 1774 to air their grievances against Great Britain.

Once again, the curators have deliberately majored on the minors. The Carpenters' Company should not be the primary focus. This is the very first thing a visitor reads upon approaching the building. This marker finally mentions the true significance behind Carpenters' Hall in the last sentence—almost as an afterthought. Only the three concluding lines of this descriptive marker speak of the convening of the Continental Congress. The only reason for the fame of this building is the fact that our first Congress convened there, commencing in prayer.

The original marker paid tribute to the significant role Christianity played in the founding of the nation. It showed a large lithograph of "The First Prayer in Congress," with all 56 Congressmen kneeling in prayer. Thus we see another graphic example of the hidden agenda of these curators: to completely expunge Christianity from America's history.

In an official Independence National Historic Park, Department of the Interior Report, dated January 1, 1989, on the removal of the original "The First Prayer in Congress" marker, these overseers of America's founding history state:

> "The First Prayer in Congress" is a conjectural projection of the historical event and therefore based on the park's determination to preserve the accuracy of these treasures must put a high priority on exact references. That is why the painting or lithograph would not have a high profile in an 18th century exhibit.[2]

The Department of Interior curators call this historic event conjecture, i.e., an opinion without sufficient evidence or proof, speculation, and glibly dismiss a key historic event. Have our learned curators not bothered to read the precious documentation they are charged with preserving—such as the *Journals of Congress*, which are comparable to our present-day *Congressional Record*? These records were meticulously kept by Charles Thomson, Secretary of Congress. In addition, there are other references from the founders themselves, who were personally present at the meeting. These include John Adams' correspondence, George Washington's personal copy of the *Journals of Congress*, and records from Christ Church; their rector, Jacob Duché, who led the prayers, becoming the first Chaplain to Congress. What more historic proof could one ask for?

To further rewrite America's foundational history, the Commission on the Bicentennial of the United States Constitution,

"The First Prayer in Congress," September 7, 1774 in Carpenter's Hall, Philadelphia, by T.H. Matheson (c. 1848). Independence National Historical Park Collection.

The interior of Carpenter's Hall. Best known for "The First Prayer in Congress," recent exhibits focus on construction and building materials. Photo by John W. Wrigley.

Scholastic News Handbook, dated February 22, 1989, depicts a sketch of their own making entitled: "The First Prayer in Congress"; designating a fabricated date for this founding period event, namely, April 6, 1789—almost 15 years after the actual event occurred in Philadelphia!

Thus we see that, according to the Department of Interior authorities, "the accuracy of the event," i.e., "The First Prayer in Congress" portrayed by T.H. Matheson, no longer fits their modern standards of historic accuracy.

However, T.H. Matheson's painting (c. 1848) depicts the event as related by the *Journals of Congress,* our founding fathers' correspondence and the records of Christ Church. Let us ask ourselves the question: Should we remove the painting entitled, "The Signing of the U.S. Constitution" by Howard Chandler Christy (c. 1940)? Although painted in 1940, it is one of the most reproduced and widely disseminated works on the original event. This painting, which hangs on a stairwell adjacent to the House of Representatives in the U.S. Capitol, has been consistently used by the Committee on the Bicentennial of the U.S. Constitution as a poster, and displayed throughout the nation as a memorial to the true event.

On the front page of the April, 1988, issue of "We, the People," (newsletter of the Commission on the Bicentennial of the United States Constitution), we read these lines:

> "Disney's Bicentennial gift: (Howard Chandler) Christy Canvas Reproductions.
>
> Magnificent mural replicas of the famous painting depicting the Signing of the U.S. Constitution have been donated by the Walt Disney Company to the Commission on the Bicentennial of the U.S. Constitution for display at the fifty state Capitol buildings and 157 federal courthouses around the country . . . The painting, by Howard Chandler Christy, depicts the scene of the framers of the Signing of the U.S. Constitution in Philadelphia on September 17, 1787. Commissioned by Congress in 1939, Christy completed the painting in a makeshift studio in the U.S. Navy Yard in Washington, D.C. The canvas, measuring 20' by 30' was unveiled on May 29, 1940. It now commands the grand stairway on the House side of the Capitol. Christy was patient and painstaking in attempting to

reproduce the scene exactly as it took place in Philadelphia. He
began by obtaining portraits of 37 of the 39 signers. . . .

The above narrative thus reinforces the need for consistency
in actions of government custodians of America's historic treasures. Either reinstate and replace the famed "The First Prayer in
Congress" painting (c. 1848) and *all* its reproductions; or remove
and abolish Howard Chandler Christy's "Signing of the U.S. Constitution" (c. 1940) because "it is a conjectural projection of the
historical event . . . executed after the fact and intended to evoke
emotion in the beholder," to quote Supervisory Curator Fanelli's
reasoning.

The park authorities claim they put "a high priority" on exact
references. How much more exact could one get? Reading between
the lines, it is obvious they will stoop to any level to achieve their
goals—the elimination of Christianity and the Bible from our history.

Today, Carpenters' Hall remains a national historic site of
great significance and value, being the site where Congress met for
the first time; and where the unbroken American tradition of the
Congressional chaplaincy began.

Carpenter's Hall, however, has now been placed in the Independence National Historic Park, Department of the Interior Financial Tour literature. The descriptive wording reads thus:

> . . . Carpenters' Hall was also associated with the early finan-
> cial history of the United States. . . . In 1798, the first national
> bank robbery occurred here to the amount of $160,000.

I submit that the early finances of the United States belong in
a bank or the U.S. Treasury, and certainly not as a replacement of
our first Congress' heartfelt prayer to Almighty God for His blessings upon the new nation.

Since the removal of the exterior marker with its "The First
Prayer in Congress" reproduction, the postcards depicting this
famous event have also been removed from the racks within Carpenters' Hall itself, thus leaving no traces whatever of the magnificent Christian history pertaining to our origins and the faith of our

founding fathers. These forebears sought God's guidance in their quest for freedom from the tyranny of an alien power.

Here again, America has been robbed of her invaluable historic legacy—as recounted to millions prior to its permanent removal.

Above: Christ Church—"The Nation's Church," Philadelphia Pennsylvania. Palladian windows *after* removal of the famed "Patriots'" and "First Prayer in Congress" stained-glass windows, Fall, 1986. Photo by John W. Wrigley. Below: The pew marker of George and Martha Washington's pew in Christ Church.

(iii) Christ Church

Christ Church, established in 1695 and now called "The Nation's Church," was a focal point around which the American revolution evolved. The founding fathers were intimately a part of the worship of Almighty God in this vibrant colonial parish church. This magnificent relic of the founding period of America's history was designated a National Shrine in 1950.

It is interesting to note that, when the University of Pennsylvania was founded in 1740 as *The Charity School,* four-fifths of its first Board of Trustees were members of Christ Church.

The Second Continental Congress proposed a resolution calling for a public day of fasting, prayer and humiliation on July 20, 1775. Congress gathered at the State House and proceeded as an entity to Christ Church where Reverend Jacob Duché preached a sermon entitled, "The American Vine." Later in the day, members of Congress assembled to hear Thomas Coombe, the assistant minister, preach a sermon dedicated to Benjamin Franklin. Finally, in November of the same year, William White, the other assistant to Duché, preached a profound sermon entitled, "Submission to Civil Disobedience," in which he counseled that if civil authority superceded the will of God, then resistance was sanctioned. As he stated, "The object of Government is human happiness."

The famous sermon on "The Duty of Standing Fast in our Spiritual and Temporal Liberties" was preached in Christ Church July 7th, 1775, by the Reverend Jacob Duché, M.A., first chaplain to Congress.

White later became the second chaplain to Congress, under George Washington. Duché and White were directly connected with other families involved in making the momentous decision of the War for Independence. Duché was married to Francis Hopkinson's sister, Elizabeth, Hopkinson being one of the signers of the Declaration of Independence. White was the brother-in-law of Robert Morris, financier of the Revolution and member of Christ Church. All three were educated at the College of Philadelphia.

The Reverend White succeeded Duché as rector in 1779. When the British Army occupied Philadelphia, White journeyed to York, Pennsylvania, to serve as chaplain to the Continental Congress. He was not only a spiritual leader for the founding fathers but a friend and counselor to the patriotic men who guided the Revolution, drafted the Constitution and led the nation through these difficult years. William White was consecrated a bishop in 1787, and through his efforts the Anglican Church in America was reorganized at Christ Church as the Protestant Episcopal Church in America. After the departure of the British from Philadelphia, Chaplain White updated the liturgy, replacing the annoying petitions for His Majesty, the King of England, with prayers for Congress and the other leaders in their nation's new government.

A 17th-century English walnut bapismal font adorns Christ Church. It is the one in which William Penn was baptized in 1644, and was sent to Christ Church in 1697.

The great Americans who worshiped at Christ Church include: Benjamin Franklin, Alexander Hamilton, John Adams, Thomas Jefferson, Robert Morris, Betsy Ross and George Washington. Plaques mark the pews belonging to various families, including that of George Washington, Benjamin Franklin, Betsy Ross and Robert Morris. In 1861, two magnificent stained-glass windows were ordered from London and installed. They are the "Patriots' Window" and the "The First Prayer in Congress" or "Liberty Window." The "Patriots' Window" portrays the founding fathers worshiping God in their family pews with open Bibles. This window entitled "Christ Church Patriots 1790" signifies the foundational strength of our forefathers as they sought to put God first in their lives and to rely on Him to meet their every need in building a nation established on biblical truth.

Of further historic significance is the upper panel of the "Christ Church Patriots' Window," which shows America's biblical heritage commencing in 1607 with the Jamestown settlers celebrating the Lord's Supper upon their arrival in the New World.

The other famous window is the "Liberty Window." When our first Congress assembled in Carpenters' Hall on September 5, 1774, it was unanimously agreed upon that the session should be opened in prayer. For the Reverend Duché, it was not a mere formality as he led the group in prayer. The solemnity of the occasion is aptly captured as these—the greatest men in the colonies—cried out to God for guidance in the enormous task they faced.

Once again, in conformity with the national phenomenon taking place today, both the Patriots' and the Liberty windows were permanently removed from Christ Church in the fall of l986 and replaced with clear glass windows! When originally removed, it is claimed that the windows were being cleaned, but they have since been packed in storage crates, with no plans to reinstall them, whatsoever. It has also been claimed that these 125-year-old windows commemorating two crucial national events were removed to render the interior of the church "back to its original look"—i.e., clear, transparent glass. So they replaced the 19th-century stained-glass windows with 20th-century glass in the 17th-century structure. What illogical reasoning!

While photographing the interior of Christ Church in May, 1988, Curator Bruce Gill told me that it had been his decision to remove these windows for "cleaning." Once removed, he stated that it was then decided never to reinstall them—a tremendous loss in terms of teaching our Christian heritage to succeeding generations of Americans, within the context of the most historic church in the nation: "The Nation's Church."

The Independence National Historic Park, Department of the Interior Holy Experiment Tour literature includes Christ Church on its itinerary. It states:

> . . . Of special interest is the beautiful Palladian window above the altar . . .

This window, the design of Italian Architect Andrei Palladio, has clear glass in stark contrast to the rich American founding period history taught by the Patriots' and Liberty windows, of which no mention is made whatever.

In its January 24, 1989 report, the Department of the Interior, which has general jurisdiction over this church, states regarding these windows:

> In order to preserve the 18th century church, the windows were replaced with 18th century type glass. Again, church officials concurred with this decision to authenticate the 18th century integrity.[1]

The "18th century type glass" referred to here is nothing more than clear, transparent window panes; certainly not 18th-century hand-blown glass, which was not preserved!

Above: "The Patriots' Window" depicting the founding fathers' worshiping God in their family pews. Below: "The Liberty Window" depicting the first prayer in Congress. These stained-glass windows appeared in Christ Church before their permanent removal, Fall, 1986. Photos by John W. Wrigley, taken from the last remaining postcards.

Christ Church, Philadelphia, stands as a monument and national shrine to those events which shook the world in 1776, and claims among its sons no less than seven signers of the Declaration of Independence, all buried in its grounds. The permanent removal of the visual reenactment of these famous Christian events, in the form of "The Patriots'" and "The First Prayer in Congress" or "Liberty," windows, must be grievous to the Holy Spirit. For it is bad enough when our secular and civic organizations refuse to acknowledge God's hand in the founding of this nation, but how much greater the insult when done by the very church directly tied into that providential history!

In response to my letter requesting photographs of these priceless windows, Bruce Cooper Gill, Curator of Christ Church, wrote to me on June 10, 1988, as follows:

> . . . Unfortunately, there were at one time photos of both windows, but as they were sent out for publication in the past they were never returned (as promised).

Once the windows were gone, the commemorative postcards of these windows soon followed, and the interpretative tour was conformed to a format totally bereft of these cataclysmic Christian events of our founding period.

Above: Left: The Liberty Bell, which rang out from Independence Hall, Philadelphia, announcing all the cataclysmic events of America's founding period. Illustrator: Helen Weir. Right: Another view of the Liberty Bell with the inscription, "Proclaim liberty throughout the land unto all the inhabitants thereof" (Leviticus 25:10). Photo by John W. Wrigley. Below: "The Pavilion," the new home of the famed bell. Photo by John W. Wrigley.

(iv) The Liberty Bell

Fifty years of God's peace and prosperity elapsed over Pennsylvania after William Penn's 1701 *Charter of Privileges* to his colonists. In 1751, the Year of Jubilee, the Pennslvania Assembly ordered a commemorative bell to be cast in England, for the anniversary of Penn's Charter. That is the bell now known as the famed Liberty Bell. Speaker of the Assembly, Isaac Norris, himself a Quaker, chose a portion of Leviticus 25:10 for inscription upon the bell: ". . . proclaim liberty throughout the land unto all the inhabitants thereof . . ."

It was in the steeple tower of Independence Hall that the famed old bell was rung to proclaim American Independence. This symbol of American freedom and democracy rang for all the major landmarks of our nation's history, until in 1835, while tolling the requiem for Chief Justice Marshall, it cracked. In 1873, the bell was lowered to a spot directly below the tower. The full verse from Leviticus 25:10 was then inscribed upon its base: "And ye shall hallow the 50th year and proclaim liberty to all the inhabitants throughout the land." For years the Liberty Bell was housed in Independence Hall where it had originally hung, but at midnight, on the first of January, 1976, despite great protest by patriotic and tradition-loving Philadelphia, the famed old bell was moved from Independence Hall to an ultra-modern structure across the street. It is unfortunate that the historic base of the Liberty Bell, which included the full verse from Leviticus 25:10 is no longer on display. This foremost symbol of American Independence is now interpreted by the Independence National Historic Park overseers as "a symbol of world freedom"—rather than what its true Christian history indisputably proclaims: "Thou shalt hallow the 50th year and proclaim liberty to all the inhabitants throughout the land."

The pastor of one of the oldest and most historic churches in Philadelphia told me that the Independence National Historic Park authorities had convened a meeting of the heads of all historic landmarks and shrines to discuss the removal of the Liberty Bell from Independence Hall. In his own words:

> We had our backs against the wall when they told us that they expected 30 million visitors for the bicentennial of the Declaration of Independence in 1976. We were terrified at the thought of so many people visiting Independence Hall during

that year. Therefore, we had no option but to acquiesce to
their demands. The only problem was that they made a monumental error of quoting an estimated 30 million, when only
three million arrived. By this time, however, the Liberty Bell
had already been moved out of its national historic setting
since it rang out America's independence from Great Britain in
1776.

The following interview with Henry M. Shuttleworth, National Park Ranger, and Chief Bellringer at Independence Hall for the
past 30–35 years, was recorded by me in November, 1986:

Ranger: I would like to see the Liberty Bell back in
Independence Hall.

Author: Why is that?

Ranger: Well, that is where it all took place.

Author: What do you mean, "it all took place"?

Ranger: That's where the bell tolled when the Declaration of Independence was celebrated, when our Constitution
was celebrated, when the Articles of Confederation were
signed.

Author: And many other great landmarks of America's history.

Ranger: That's the original spot. Where it is today, is not.

Author: It resembles a railroad station.

Ranger: You are talking to Henry Shuttleworth, the
Head Bellringer of Independence Hall. That's why I feel I
know a little bit about our bells. Our bells is my hobby, and I
am just reading now about Christmas in the Revolutionary
period. That's how I start my New Year's Eve—by tolling
the bells for 13 bell rings for the 13 colonies. The Centennial
Bell weighs 13,000 pounds. A thousand pounds for each state.
It is in Independence Hall. It was given to us in 1872. The
Bicentennial Bell was given us by Queen Elizabeth to help us
celebrate our 200th Anniversary.

Author: It is very interesting that it should be put up in
1976 here at the Independence National Historic Park, Department of the Interior new Visitors' Center, the very year of
the Bicentennial of our Declaration of Independence, and that
at that time, the Liberty Bell, which tolled in Independence
Hall to announce this great event, was moved to the "Pavil-

ion," a squat building across the road; and that this bell (the Bicentennial Bell) here, is now called: "The Freedom Bell."

Ranger: The Bicentennial Bell, the Queen's Bell, some people refer to it as the Freedom Bell, but they also refer to the Liberty Bell as the Freedom Bell. So I'm a little bit cautious myself, in saying the Freedom Bell.

Author: The Liberty Bell is representative of our freedom as Americans, would you not say?

Ranger: That, and the Statue of Liberty. There's nothing greater than those two as symbols of freedom for this country.

Author: Yet the Department of Interior has removed it from Independence Hall, where it belongs!

At another interview, this time with Barbara Applebaum, National Park Service Ranger/Lecturer on December 8, 1986, I recorded the following:

Ranger: The Liberty Bell basically just started to wear out in the 1830s after 80 years of use, and it wasn't really that great a bell to begin with, so they really didn't notice that it didn't sound too good for a while. . . . If it hadn't been called the "Liberty Bell" by the abolitionists, it would have probably been just used as scrap metal, and just been thrown out. It was just an ordinary bell that rang up to the 1840s and there was no significance. The significance developed after the American Civil War because the nation really needed to be healed after the Civil War, because the North and the South really weren't on speaking terms. And the bell became this big romantic symbol of liberty for everybody and brotherhood; and by World War I it had expanded not just for liberty in the United States, but liberty to people all over the world. It was only at the time of the Civil War that this bell got its significance. In the 1850s, say 1830s it started to become significant to the Abolitionists. In the 1850s it expanded, and after the Civil War it became this big romantic symbol that it is today.

Author: And before that—what was the reason it was there?

Ranger: They needed a large, loud bell to communicate back in the 1770s. Philadelphia had grown so large that they needed a large bell to let people know the news. The news of the day, the time of day, funerals, fires.

Author: And it wasn't used for any other significance at all until the Civil War?

Ranger: Well—it rang on July 8 for the first Public reading of the Declaration of Independence, but every bell in town rang for that; and it rang when George III was crowned King of England, but every bell in town rang for that. So the real significance is after the 1830s.

The above commentary given by an Independence National Historic Park Service, Department of the Interior Ranger, represents falsified, rewritten American history, in keeping with the removal of the Liberty Bell from Independence Hall. The Liberty Bell's unsurpassed symbolic and historic fame—in short the very reason for her tremendous significance to all Americans, is that she rang out all the major landmarks of America's birth. The Liberty Bell also tolled the requiem for some of the nation's greatest founding period heroes, such as Thomas Jefferson, John Adams and fourth Chief Justice, John Marshall. It is thus a tragic and serious "crime against Americans" to have the Liberty Bell's proud heroic associations removed; her history being now equated with "any bell in town" by the curators of Independence National Historic Park, overseers of the nation's most historic square mile. This discloses that the park rangers have been indoctrinated to leave out the crucial Christian events for which this foremost symbol of America's history and Independence rang (or tolled)—from 1776 to 1830! What a travesty for an entire nation's historic legacy.

The Liberty Bell has now been placed in the Independence National Historic Park, Department of the Interior Urban Renewal Tour literature. All that is said about this famed symbol of America's liberties and freedoms reads as follows:

> . . . On the first block directly across the street from Independence Hall is the Liberty Bell Pavilion, the new permanent home of the Liberty Bell, moved there on January 1, 1976. The center block includes the Judge Edwin O. Lewis Quadrangle where special events and entertainments are accommodated throughout the year. . . .

In a wonderful old history book on the restoration of Independence Hall, the committee on its restoration and return to original significance gives an accurate account of the value and meaning of this bell:

> The old "Liberty Bell," which had been taken from the cupola and placed within the chamber, we removed to the vestibule, suspending it from the original beam and scaffolding. (The latter having been discovered nearly intact in the steeple). We deemed it appropriate to inscribe upon its base the whole Scriptural text, a part of which had been moulded upon the bell in 1753, as it, even then, so essentially predicted and ordained: first, "Liberty throughout the land," and secondly, the CENTENNIAL celebration thereof. The whole has been enclosed by a plain railing, which circumstances show to be essential to its preservation.[1]

The two workmen who cast the bell at Whitechapel Foundry in England were "Pass" from the Island of Malta, and "Stow," a son of Charles Stow, the door-keeper of the Council. After being hung up in its place, it was found to contain too much copper, and Pass and Stow "were so teased with witticisms of the town" that they asked permission to cast it over again. For their work, Pass and Stow were paid 60 English pounds, 13 shillings and five pence.[2]

The Liberty Bell is now housed in a modern, squat structure bearing the name "The Pavilion," being the identical new name given to the famous Old Post Office Building in our nation's capital (site of the first Flag Day celebrations), after its renovations in 1982.

Although expatriated from its original setting where it rang out all the greatest landmarks of our founding period, the Liberty Bell continues to maintain its place in the hearts of Americans as a unique symbol of the United States Declaration of Independence from British colonial rule:

> . . . Proclaim liberty to all the inhabitants throughout the land.
> (Leviticus 25:10)

Above: The Betsy Ross House where the first American flag was designed and commissioned to be made by George Washington, Robert Morris and Col. George Ross. Below: Display cabinet in the house. In the Center, Betsy Ross' family Bible, recording the births of her children. Photos by John W. Wrigley.

(v) How did the United States Flag Originate?—Betsy Ross and the Stars and Stripes. Francis Scott Key and the Star-Spangled Banner.

At 239 Arch Street in historic Philadelphia, stands the restored colonial home of Betsy Ross. Here she received a committee from Continental Congress comprised of George Washington, Colonel George Ross and Robert Morris, who commissioned her to make the first American flag in 1776. It was Washington's desire to have a six-pointed star. However, when Betsy Ross, with a deft snip of her scissors, cut a perfect, five-pointed star for him, the committee, unanimously impressed, opted for five points in each star of our star-spangled banner.

Some of the guided tours in Philadelphia state, with suggestive undertones, "But you know Betsy Ross was married three times," as if to discredit her character and make her appear as a dishonorable person. The fact is, however, this admirable lady was widowed twice, as two sea captain husbands were lost at sea. Her third husband, who worked in their upholstery and flag-making business, preceded her in death.[1] The large Ross family consisted of seven children. Betsy's family Bible is on permanent display in the Ross home, showing forth in whom she and her family placed their trust. Betsy Ross and her family were members of Christ Church—"the nation's church"—in Philadelphia. A plaque in that church designates her family pew, not far from George and Martha Washington's pew.

Francis Scott Key

On September 14, 1814, Christian Patriot, Francis Scott Key, wrote his heaven-inspired poem at an inn in Baltimore harbor, portraying America's flag—her foremost symbol, representing our origins, dependence upon Almighty God and value system as a nation. Ever since he came ashore from a ship after watching the American flag fly triumphantly through the bombardment of Fort McHenry, his immortal poem has been cherished by Americans with the deepest patriotic devotion. It is interesting that many people are only familiar with the first stanza of this poem. However, the remaining stanzas clearly speak of the relationship of God to our nation and our dependence upon Him. It is here printed in its entirety:

The Star-Spangled Banner

O say! Can you see, by the dawn's early light,
What so proudly we hailed at the twilight's last gleaming?
Whose broad stripes and bright stars through the perilous
      fight,
O'er the ramparts we watched were so gallantly streaming?
And the rocket's red glare, the bomb bursting in air,
Gave proof through the night that our flag was still there.
O say, does that Star-Spangled Banner yet wave
O'er the land of the free and the home of the brave?

On the shore, dimly seen through the mists of the deep,
Where the foe's haughty host in dread silence reposes,
What is that which the breeze, o'er the towering steep,
As it fitfully blows half conceals, half discloses?
Now it catches the gleam of the morning's first beam,
In full glory reflected now shines in the stream,
'Tis the Star-Spangled Banner—O Long may it wave
O'er the land of the free and the home of the brave!

And where is that band who so vauntingly swore,
That the havoc of war and the battle's confusion
A home and a Country should leave us no more?
Their blood has washed out their foul footsteps' pollution.
No refuge could save the hireling and slave
From the terror of flight or the gloom of the grave,
And the Star-Spangled Banner in triumph doth wave
O'er the land of the free and the home of the brave.

O thus be it ever when free men shall stand
Between their loved homes and war's desolation!
Blest with victory and peace may the heaven rescued land
Praise the Power that hath made and preserved us a nation!
Then conquer we must when our cause it is just
And this be our motto: "In God is our trust."
And the Star-Spangled Banner in triumph shall wave
O'er the land of the free and the home of the brave.

These magnificent words, depicting love of God and country,
were adapted to the inspiring music of John Stafford Smith (c.
1780).[2]

On March 3, 1931, an Act to make the Star-Spangled Banner the national anthem of the United States of America, was resolved by the Senate and House of Representatives in Congress assembled (36 U.S.C. Sec. 170).[3]

Millions of Americans throughout the ensuing years have paid homage to our flag—the Star-Spangled Banner, by singing the National Anthem, giving full expression to their love of Almighty God and their homeland.

Pledge to the flag

On October 21, 1892, Francis Bellamy, a Baptist minister who had been ordained in the Baptist Church of Little Falls, New York, wrote a pledge of allegiance to America's flag—the Star-Spangled Banner:

> Pledge of Allegiance to the Flag
> I pledge allegiance to the flag of the United States of America and to the Republic for which it stands, one nation under God, indivisible with liberty and justice for all. [4]

The pledge he wrote was first used at the dedication of the World's Fair grounds in Chicago on October 21, 1892, the 400th anniversary of the discovery of America, and has been recited from that day to this, with some changes, by school children throughout our land. Reverend Bellamy's original wording was altered slightly by the First and Second National Flag Conferences in 1923 and 1924 and his work was officially designated, as the Pledge of Allegiance to the Flag by Public Law 287, 79th Congress, approved December 28, 1945. On June 14, 1954, Flag Day, President Dwight D. Eisenhower signed into law House Joint Resolution 243, which added to the Pledge of Allegiance the compelling and meaningful words: under God.[5] This came about after Eisenhower and his wife had attended the Sunday, February 7, 1954, Lincoln Day Observance Service at the New York Avenue Presbyterian Church—the sermon topic being: "Under God."*

*See Addendum, for entire historic sermon "Under God."

The song "Pledge of Allegiance to the Flag," composed by Irving Caesar, ASCAP, was sung for the first time on the floor of the House of Representatives on Flag Day, June 14, 1955, by the official Air Force choral group, the "Singing Sergeants," under the direction of Captain Robert L. Landers, AFRES, in special Flag Day ceremonies.[6]

The meaningful and compelling words: *One nation under God*, denoting dependence and reliance upon Almighty God, our Benefactor and Sustainer, were adapted from Abraham Lincoln's famed Gettysburg Address, where he describes America as: "this nation under God."

Webster's New Twentieth Century Dictionary states that "to dip the flag" means "to salute by lowering the flag and immediately returning it to place. It is done in token of courtesy, welcome, or respect." The commentary goes on to explain that "to strike or lower the flag" means to "lower the flag as a sign of surrender; hence, to capitulate, to give up."

The Star-Spangled Banner has a proud Christian heritage. It was designed by a Christian patriot, George Washington, and first made by a Christian patriot, Betsy Ross, both of whom were members of Christ Church in Philadelphia. Our flag has been honored and stamped with America's national motto: *In God is our Trust*, both verbally and musically. It is thus the foremost symbol of a nation whose primary allegiance is to Almighty God, and whose people bow the knee to God alone; for, as the Pledge of Allegiance states: we are the One nation under God.

To dishonor, or to burn this symbol of a Christian nation could thus be termed as dishonoring God, our motto being: *In God is our Trust*.

(vi) Wanamaker's Department Store

Only in historic Philadelphia can one do one's personal shopping in a national historic landmark. Upon entering the Wanamaker Department Store opposite City Hall, one is greeted by a spectacular sight—that of a 33,000-pipe organ encircling the upper gallery of the main floor. And if one should be there during a concert, it's like being in a magnificent worship service or a classical organ recital. In addition, a "10-foot" bronze eagle stands proudly in the center of the court, symbolizing our national emblem. If one visited the department store prior to 1988 at Easter time, this store rivaled any gallery with its two irreplaceable oil paintings: "Christ before Pilate" and "Christ on Calvary"—annually displayed with the story of Jesus Christ's mock trial, humiliating death, and glorious resurrection three days later, a 60-year-old Philadelphia tradition. Who and what is behind this unique enterprise? Simply, a godly man.

John Wanamaker was the man who built this impressive store. It was while inspecting the construction of the new Wanamaker Department Store that John's brother, Rodman, was impressed that the grand court would be best utilized as a music center, and set out to obtain the finest organ in the world. He acquired the Louisiana Purchase exposition organ, in Festival Hall, St. Louis. The instrument had been played by Alexander Guilmont and nearly every other noted organist of that day. It took 13 freight cars to ship it to Philadelphia, where it was rebuilt and heard publicly for the first time on June 22, 1911. Unlike most organs, played only Sundays or special occasions, the Wanamaker organ has been played every business day since its installation.

Marcel Dupré, organist at Notre Dame Cathedral in Paris and one of many world-renowned organists who played this instrument, made his American debut at Wanamakers in November 1921.

The great French Classicist, Honoré de Balzac, said of the organ:

> The organ is in truth the grandest, the most daring, the most magnificent of all instruments invented by human genius. It is a whole orchestra in itself. It can express anything in response to a skilled touch. Surely it is, in some sort, a pedestal on which the soul poises for a flight forth into space, essaying on

her course to draw picture after picture in an endless series to paint human life, to cross the infinite that separates Heaven from earth! . . .[1]

The most poignant insight into John Wanamaker, most commonly known as a financier and business tycoon, comes from his pastor, Gordon MacClennon of Bethany Presbyterian Church in Philadelphia. The following is excerpted from the introduction to "Prayers of John Wanamaker,"[2] in order to give the reader insight into this successful businessman's source of strength and ability in life:

In the prayers contained in this volume, there is revealed the loftiness of soul, the catholicity of spirit, the perfect standing of human need, and the great childlike faith of John Wanamaker. He was truly a man of prayer and the place of prayer was precious to him. He always approached the Throne of Grace with great reverence and deep humility, as though he, too, had heard the command, "Put off thy shoes from off thy feet, for the place whereon thou standest is holy ground." The following prayers are closely associated with different services of the Bethany Presbyterian Church of Philadelphia of which Mr. Wanamaker was the founder and senior elder. For 65 years he was the active superintendent of the Sunday School; and every Sunday, unless absent from the city or prevented by illness, he was to be found at the Superintendent's desk, leading the school in the Superintendent's prayer. . . .

His regular church prayer meeting always found him in his place, and many times he has said: "I like to be present at the meeting, in the middle of the week, feeling, as I sit among the people gathered, some of them deaf, hearing hardly a spoken word and others with failing sight, that as the Lord passed around amongst them He might give me a blessing too." He was present always, as leader of a little meeting of men at 9 o'clock in the morning, for prayer and meditation, known as the John Wesley Class Meeting. At 9:30 he attended the Brotherhood Meeting, leading and inspiring the men with his unique personality and deep spiritual insight and constant interest in the lives of the 300 or more men who met there. From the Brotherhood Meeting he went to regular morning church service, taking a full part in all the worship. At 2:30 in

the afternoon, he was present to superintend the great Sunday
School which he, with the same uniqueness which built the
greatest merchandising establishment in America, developed
from a class of 27 pupils to an enrollment of 5,000!

But his activity in connection with the church and school did
not cease with the services on Sunday, for wherever there
was trouble, or sickness, or death he always found time to be
present giving words of counsel and help and always to lead
the distressed ones to the Throne of Grace where he had
found one able to help in all times of need.

It may truly be said that the people of Bethany Church and
Sunday School will longest remember him by the uniqueness and tender sympathy of his prayers. He knew God, and
in his prayers revealed that he knew Him.

Following are prayers from the man who knew prayer:

Ever-living God, our Father, we have come into Thy house
again through Thy mercy which has kept us alive. We would
worship Thee with reverence. We hallow Thy name, O God,
our Father, the name which is above every other name. We
worship Thee, O Christ, God manifest in the flesh. We hear
Thee speak, O Christ, who walked the pathways of this very
earth and talked and did things like a man, and left the earth
richer for the charity of thy words and the work of Thy dear,
kindly hands. Thou hast written Thy name on so much of
daily life that we cannot walk or talk or open the doors of our
homes without thinking of Thee and Thy ways in Galilee.

Oh Lord, Thou hast told us how to pray. Help us to shut the
door, shutting out the world, and the enemy and any fear or
doubt which spoils prayer. May there be no distance between
our souls and Thee.

Our Father, we have come to sit down together to rest, after a
busy week, and to think. We are not satisfied with ourselves
for we all, like sheep, have gone astray. What we have done is
what we ought not to have done. We are stung to the quick
with disappointment, sorrow and desolation. It seems as
though there were a cankerworm eating at the core of our

hearts, and there is no rest for our souls day or night. Have pity upon us, Lord, and cut us not down in Thy displeasure. We confess our sin and bring it to Thee. Let our prayers prevail in Heaven, and do Thou heal and help us to a new life in Christ Jesus. Amen.

We bless Thee, Eternal Father, for Thy Throne and its purpose; grant us Thy Holy Spirit that we may see somewhat the greatness of Thy ever-extending Kingdom. Pity our poor, superficial, ever-dwindling faith. Thou art able to do exceedingly abundantly above all we can ask or think. Expand our capacity, enlarge our thinking, grant us culture and upbuilding of soul. Take from us sordidness and littleness. Cause us to realize what Thy Kingdom is, its beneficence and ministries to redeem the world.

From the above moving prayers, we see that Wanamaker's secret of success was his faith in Almighty God and his love and adherence to the Lord Jesus Christ and his unfailing words.

In the National Register of Historic Places Inventory, acquired from the Philadelphia Historical Commission, we read the following extraordinary business accomplishments of John Wanamaker, showing forth his key role in developing business and commerce in America:

Wanamaker also contributed a number of significant innovations of his own to the evolutionary development of both the department store and retailing in general. The most important of these were in advertising, an aspect of selling in which he had no peer. When Wanamaker entered retailing "truth in advertising and merchandising claims hardly existed," says Sobel, "but he changed this. He . . . did so by advertising his creed widely, to a larger audience than that reached by any businessman before him, and then delivering his promises." Wanamaker published the first copyrighted advertisement in America (1874); ran the first full-page mercantile advertisement in an American paper (1879); founded two successful national periodicals in the late 1870's specifically to carry his advertising copy—*Everybody's* and *Farm Journal;* ran full-page advertisements in such popular magazines as *Century* and *Scribner's* as early as 1880; and entered into the first annual contract for full-page advertising in a daily newspaper (1899).

In addition he used the mails to send out booklets, circulars, and cards calling attention to sales and special categories of merchandise and to distribute "catalogues that were," according to his biographer Herbert Adams Gibbons, "precursors of the huge volumes now issued by mail-order houses." All these undertakings were "innovations," says Gibbons, "some in the idea and others in the style."

Loss of an American Tradition

Part of Philadelphia's heart was lost when a 60-year-old Wanamaker gift to the people was abolished in the name of progress. On February 24, 1988, the two biblical masterpieces, "Christ before Pilate" and "Christ on Calvary" were sold at Sotheby's Auction in New York City for slightly under $120,000. This excerpt from the *Philadelphia Inquirer,* dated February 22, 1988, gives the background of the paintings:

> The Munkacsy paintings were acquired by John Wanamaker in 1887 and 1888, and were exhibited at the Paris Exposition Universelle in 1889. They were hung in Wanamaker's house, Lindenhurst. When the mansion burned in 1907, the pictures were saved by being cut from their frames. Wanamaker died in 1922. After his wife, Mary, died in 1928, the two large Munkacsy paintings were exhibited every Easter. The rest of the year they were kept in the organ loft.[3]

Just as Christ was betrayed for 30 pieces of silver, so this Easter memorial that had become part of the city of Philadelphia was, with cold calculation, ripped from the hearts of the people of Philadelphia for a mere $118,250.

The Wanamaker Department Store had been bought out by Woodward and Lothrop, a well-known East Coast department store chain. (Both Woodward and Lothrop and Sotheby's are under the same ownership). The same newspaper article goes on with this commentary:

> In October, Woodward and Lothrop sold the Wanamaker building, which fills the block bounded by Chestnut and Market, Juniper and 13th Streets, to California developer, John Kus-

miersky. Woodward and Lothrop leased back the lower five floors for Wanamaker, and Kusmiersky plans to convert the upper seven floors to office space. The Easter story paintings are considered the most important and valuable in the collection. "Christ before Pilate" and "Christ on Calvary," both by the Hungarian artist Mihaly Munkacsy, measure 21 feet across and are nearly 14 ft. high.[4]

A press release dated March 8, 1988, obtained from the Philadelphia Historical Commission is excerpted below as follows:

HISTORIC WANAMAKER'S DEPARTMENT STORE TO UNDERGO MIXED-USE RENOVATION
Plans for the restoration, preservation and adaptive reuse of the John Wanamaker Building, one of Philadelphia's best loved landmarks, were unveiled today in a joint press conference hosted by John Kusmiersky of Philadelphia Center Realty and Ed Hoffman, Chairman of Woodward and Lothrop, parent company of John Wanamaker of Philadelphia. . . . This work will be designed and coordinated under the guidelines and scrutiny of The National Park Service. The National Park Service safeguards the integrity of historic structures and has strict rules for the restoration, preservation, and upgrading of these buildings, a vital part of the architectural heritage.

It is unfortunate that big business took precedence over what had become a beautiful part of the city's history, character and personality. The annual portrayal of the mock trial, agonizing death, burial and glorious resurrection of our Lord and Savior Jesus Christ was coldly removed forever from Philadelphia and America's Christian heritage.

(vii) Carter's Grove Plantation (c.1750)

Carter's Grove was the plantation home of Robert "King" Carter, (1663–1732), who was one of the most significant figures of America's founding period, and whose property comprised 300,000 acres of land.[1] Carter's father died in 1669 when the boy was six years old. His older brother, John Carter II, became his guardian and under the stipulation of his father's will, he began his schooling under an indentured servant with some schooling.[2] He was then sent to England for six years, to board with a Mr. Bailey for his grammar school education, from about 1672–1678.[3] Of his early school days, Carter writes:

> From my owne observations when I was in England, those boyes that wore the finest close and had the most money in their pocketts still went away, with the least learning in their heads.[4]

Carter's studies comprised grammar, rhetoric and logic, with its roots in Latin, Greek and some Hebrew.

Robert Carter was a devoted Christian husband and father of 12. He brought up his children in the love and admonition of the Lord Jesus Christ. Ritualism and hierarchy of the established church was of no importance to Carter who wished to impart biblical truth and high standards of morality to his offspring.[5]

He is also remembered for the church which he built in the early 1700s, historic Christ Church in Lancaster County, Virginia, which is still maintained and honors his name today.

Following are selected passages from Carter's personal correspondence. They disclose his adherence to the gospel message of forgiveness and the sound guidance and counsel he afforded to his son. To a Mr. Perry in England on July 22, 1720:

> . . . My son, I find, upon the stool of repentance. It will be well he will come to his senses at last. He makes me large promises to retrench himself and that he will for the future call upon you for no more by the quarter than £37:10, and will make the best use of his time that he has to stay in England, by a close application to his study. These are agreeable promises if he keeps them. He hath sent me an account of How, the tailor's, for fifty-odd pound, which it seems I must pay. He expects it will cost him some money to be called to bar, which I must not

281

grudge at. He begs of me to forget his past extravagances and desires I may not insist upon a particular account from him, and that he will give me no more occasion of future complaints. Upon these terms I am willing to shut up with him. Thus you see I am no stranger to the story of the Gospel. . . . political jars here I hope will be laid aside for some time at least. All things at present carry the fact of peace, a most comprehensive word of all sublunary blessings.[6]

To John, his son, on July 23, 1720 (in relation to the letter above):

Dear Son John:
I have lately received your letters in Mr. Perry's packet of April date, in which you make me repeated promises to retrench your expenses and reduce them to the bounds I have set you—that is, to take no more from Mr. Perry than £37:10 per quarter, except the charge of calling you to the bar. You likewise promise me a strict improvement of your time that you have to spend in England, by a close application of your studies. May Heaven keep you fixed to this resolution without wavering. It will prove a cordial to your heart all the days of your life. Upon these hopes I shall pass over what's past, according to your desire, and have ordered Mr. Perry to pay your tailor's bill of fifty-odd pound. Your relations here are in health; all that are capable, I believe, write to you themselves. Pray take a little more care of your brothers in England. The rest is to beg God's blessing upon you . . .[7]

What were some of Carter's great achievements which so distinguish him in our nation's history?

A vestryman in Christ Church, the church he built for his parish, he also served as Justice of the Peace.[8] At the age of 28 he took his seat in the House of Burgesses at Jamestown as a member for Lancaster County. In 1696 he became Speaker of the House, and in 1697 filled the position of chairman of the Committee of Propriations and Grievances—the most important committee in that body.[9] After being elected member of the Council, in 1699 he became Colonial Treasurer, holding this position until 1704. He was highly esteemed and respected by all the Burgesses.[10] His duties as member of the Council, together with other leading men of the colony, comprised performing executive, legislative and judicial functions. Fellow members were William Byrd I, Edmund Jenings, Benjamin Harrison, James Blair and others.[11]

In 1715 Carter was appointed lieutenant commander of Lancaster and Northumberland counties. At the death of Governor Hugh Drysdale, "King" Carter, as president of the Council, assumed the administration of government, officially approved by George II in July 1726. This governorship Carter executed admirably for more than a year.[12] Among his impressive services to God and country, this American son also acted as rector and visitor of the College of William and Mary, being made a trustee of the college in 1729, and endowing the college with a handsome scholarship.[13] Buried in the yard at Christ Church where he had worshiped, his epitaph reads:

> Here lies
> Robert Carter, Esq., an honorable man, who exalted his high birth by noble endowments and pure morals. He sustained the College of William and Mary in the most trying times. He was Governor, Speaker of the House and Treasurer . . . he built and endowed, at his own expense, this sacred edifice, a lasting monument of his piety to God. Entertaining his friends with kindness, he was neither a prodigal nor a thrifty host. . . . At length, full of honor and years, having discharged all the duties of an exemplary life, he departed from this world on the 4th day of August 1732, in the 69th year of his age. The wretched, the widowed, and the orphans, bereaved of their comfort, protector and father, alike lament his loss.[14]

Rewritten History

Carter's Grove Plantation is now administered by the Williamsburg Foundation, which oversees and has jurisdiction over Colonial Williamsburg, the old capital city of Virginia during the years 1699 through 1780. In September, 1988, while researching Carter's Grove, one of America's oldest and most prestigious plantations, the first, and only informative sign which now greets the visitor upon entering the grounds (installed 1988), does not give a single word relating to the true significance and history of Robert

"King" Carter's Plantation and spectacular Georgian home. Rather, the new sign reads:

> Martin's Hundred
> This plantation was founded by the London-based Society of Martin's Hundred in 1617 and later was assigned 21,500 acres; it was settled in 1619. The site of Wolstenholme Town, its administrative center, was discovered by archaeologists in 1977. They located the graves of several victims of the Indian Massacre of 22 March 1622 when 78 colonists here—half the plantation's population—were reported slain. The area soon was resettled but the town was never rebuilt. Department of Conservation and Historic Resources, 1988.

I subsequently interviewed a docent at the Carter's Grove Visitors' Center, who reported the following:

> Carter's Grove, dating back to 1750 A.D. and one of the oldest plantations in America has had its historic interpretation changed from the founding period to history beginning in the 1920's when Mrs. Archibald McCrea bought the estate and lived in it. This new interpretation occurred about three years ago when the new Director, Mr. Lawrence Henry (appointed by the Colonial Williamsburg Foundation), changed the historic interpretation and meaning of this valuable national heritage site.[15]

A recently installed, new exhibit within the Visitors' Center catches the eye prior to exiting onto the spacious grounds of Carter's Grove Plantation. The exhibit outlines primarily the history of the McCreas, with a few lines about Robert Carter—the latter being the very reason for which this valuable Georgian mansion and plantation has been preserved for America's posterity. The exhibit concludes with information about the Algonquin Indians, colonial slaves' quarters, and the 1611 "Martin's Hundred" English mercenary settlement highlighted—220 English mercenary settlers having supposedly founded a town called Wolstenholme Towne right on the grounds of Carter's Grove Plantation and Georgian home!

However, in the official report of the First Legislative Assembly convened by the 1607 Jamestown Settlement on July 30, 1619, in their church, Mr. John Pory, secretary, records two representative

Burgesses from Martin's Hundred (or Plantation), namely, Mr. John Boys and Mr. John Jackson.[16] The 1607 Jamestown colonists had divided their settlement into "hundreds," "incorporations" or "plantations" in order to govern themselves more efficiently.

The Colonial Williamsburg Foundation, therefore, has no excuse for rewriting this crucial epic of America's founding period history, depicting Martin's Hundred as a "mercenary English settlement." "Martin's Hundred" was part and parcel of the 1607 Jamestown Settlement, which convened its political meetings in prayer to Almighty God, and whose godly chaplain, Richard Bucke, baptized Pocahontas into the Christian faith.

Upon entering the grounds of Carter's Grove Plantation, immediately to one's left are the newly constructed *Slaves' Quarters*, with a Colonial Williamsburg Foundation official interpreter dressed in the colonial period "slaves' garb." Excerpted below is part of the interpretative lecture given by one of these representatives:

> This plantation is owned by the Colonial Williamsburg Foundation. In 1971, archaeological digs were found here. It was slaves' quarters (not a tannery, as they originally thought). Based on that, and structured evidence from other slaves' quarters in Virginia, tax records, account books, other such evidence and diaries, plans were made and handed to carpenters. The Research Library is owned by Colonial Williamsburg. This is brand new in history—black history that has not been discussed or interpreted before 1979. Colonial Williamsburg is on the cutting edge of history museums around the country. The New York Times ran an article about these slave quarters on September 19, 1988. The Washington Post did the same thing in the summer of 1987. Local T.V. and radio (media) ran articles and Public Service announcements about these archaeological slaves quarters. Carpenters were hired by Colonial Williamsburg to go to various sites. We actually put up the first building in November, 1987. Carpenters wear 18th century costumes because of the 18th century work they're doing. Interpretation of construction work includes:

>> What does this say about 18th century slave experience in the colonial Chesapeake? Carter's Grove Mansion now focuses on 20th century history;

the Slaves' Quarters focus on 18th century history; the newly constructed Wolstenholme Towne,
(Archaeological site of an English settlement "discovered"), on 17th century history. They found a
series of pits and postholes and fashioned what
the average slave house was in the 18th century.[17]

A short distance further on, to the right, one sees a cluster of
newly-constructed thatched-roofed, grey "shacks" with short-
stumped wooden fences and markers, one of which indicates the
place where a tree supposedly had stood; another bearing the
name "Granny's Grave." Other grave markers designate recent
archaeological discoveries of Martin's Hundred gravesites. The
visitor is rather startled by an ominous-looking gaping hole, built of
grey concrete, and disappearing into a hillside close by. The new,
informative marker discloses its identity:

Winthrop Rockefeller Archaeological Museum
Construction is underway at this site for the Winthrop Rockefeller Archaeological Museum. The museum will contain
artifacts discovered during excavations of Martin's Hundred,
including those found at the adjacent Wolstenholme Towne
site. In its galleries the story of this discovery and of what it
revealed about life on this site in the early seventeenth century will be presented. Construction of the museum is supported through the generosity of the Winthrop Rockefeller Charitable Trust. The museum will open in 1991. We invite you to
return then to experience this additional chapter in the story of
life at Carter's Grove.

A Chance Meeting

Upon exiting this beautiful plantation, I had an interesting
encounter with Gillian Daroczy, of Dearborn, Michigan, at the
Visitors' Center of Carter's Grove Plantation. She is one very familiar with the real Carter's Grove history. Following is her account of
the revised founding period history now presented at this famed
historic site:

I came here seven years ago. The original history of this famous plantation was given then. Robert "King" Carter was the richest man in Virginia and a prominent and significant figure during the founding period of our country. He was the father of Anne Hill Carter, grandfather of Robert E. Lee. Her husband was Light Horse Harry Lee.

They don't mention any history about the Carters living here during the Revolutionary War period any more. "Why don't you speak about it?" we asked the interpreter? "Because we interpret the house as it has come through the years," was the response. "But it doesn't have anything to do with the Carter history and influence for which it is so famous and has been preserved. Mrs. McCrea, I'm sure, bought it to preserve the heritage. She would have liked the people to appreciate the home's historical significance, as opposed to having her own private living quarters described on an updated scale. It's like going through the Dodge Mansion at Grosse Pointe. I came to see and study our early American history, which is so rich—not to go through a Real Estate Tour."

Seven years ago, my mother and I and two guests heard the history of the Carter era correctly interpreted. We were thrilled with the history of this mansion during the Revolutionary period. . . . not, "this is Mrs. McCrea's refrigerator—34 years old and still running . . ." I left the tour. Who cares how old her refrigerator is? The roof is raised to accommodate new quarters. The tour highlights their bedroom; office; bathroom; where the toilet was; the electric light and ash tray in a cupboard enclosing the toilet!

The only statement we heard about our American Revolutionary period history was that Robert "King" Carter originally built this house. We didn't learn anything here about Carter and his influence—not one thing! I think they should remove everything about the McCreas. Is this what the Williamsburg Foundation makes you pay money for? Children learn more about American colonial, revolutionary history by being there, seeing, experiencing, touching it. This is how children, future generations of Americans, are taught our foundational history.

Listening to the above commentary, one cannot help being deeply moved by the chagrin and pathos of this young woman's testimony on the removal of a heritage very near and dear to each American; that of the founding period of our nation through Robert "King" Carter and his descendants at Carter's Grove Plantation—all the more so as Carter's Grove Plantation is being publicized to Americans in newspapers, (such as the November, 1990 issue of the complimentary *Williamsburg Magazine*), as a site which "chronicles 350 years of history" requiring tickets to be purchased in advance!

Further to the above removal of all original history pertaining to the great American Christian patriot, Robert "King" Carter, from his own Georgian mansion and homesite, Carter's Grove Plantation, we see history being rewritten on his person and character. In an article entitled "Shirley Plantation—Built on a Tradition of Heritage and Hierarchy," which appeared in the Spring 1991 edition of the widely distributed *Colonial Williamsburg,* journal of the Colonial Williamsburg Foundation, we read:

> . . . Conspicuous is the portrait of Robert "King" Carter of Corotoman on the Rappahannock. . . He noted in his diary occasions when he personally haggled over pennies for yarn and eggs on trading days on his docks. . . He was as shrewd in simple dealings as he was in the management of his vast holdings. . . In King Carter's picture, the left forefinger seems to be pointing to a vest pocket of this rather plainly dressed man. The flap of the pocket is curled, indicating frequent use. . . . Whether the finger points to a time piece or a coin purse is irrelevant; the King would waste neither. . .[18]

And again, in a caption above a photographic reproduction of this remarkable man's portrait, we read:

> Seeming still to survey his vast domain, Robert "King" Carter, portrayed by an unknown artist, points to a vest pocket where, . . . (he) kept his purse.[19]

The above lines imply that Carter's mind was staid upon materialism (his vast domain) and money (his purse), imputing to Carter negative character traits which he did not have, as has been amply demonstrated by his personal correspondence and deeds portraying his love of God and a Christian value system.

It would also be in keeping with the Colonial Williamsburg Foundation's printed mandate as "the nonprofit educational organization responsible for the restoration, preservation, and interpretation of the 18th-century capital of the colony of Virginia" to correctly attribute Robert "King" Carter's true historic roots and identity to *Carter's Grove Plantation*—his circa 1750 homesite.

Many Americans are awakening to this travesty—as it seems the effort to obliterate the founding period of our nation, so rich in biblical heritage—has accelerated in recent years.

Bruton Parish Church, Williamsburg, Virginia. George Washington wrote in his diary, June 1, 1774: ". . . went to church and fasted all day." Illustrator: Helen Weir.

(viii) Colonial Williamsburg, Virginia

Williamsburg, Virginia, is a trip into America's colonial past, where the House of Burgesses sat in the old State Capitol from 1699–1780, and where matters leading to the birth of our new nation were deliberated and heatedly debated.

In the 1930s John D. Rockefeller provided the funds to fulfill the cherished dream of the Reverend Dr. William A.R. Goodwin, a godly man and Rector of Bruton Parish church, that is: to restore Williamsburg to its original 18th-century historical architecture and beauty.

A predominant sign in the Bruton Parish Church entranceway discloses the church's true identity as a place of prayer and worship where America's providential history was made: "Enter with reverence. An Episcopal church in continuous use for the worship of God since 1715."

The original Ten Commandments, Lord's Prayer and Apostles' Creed are beautifully calligraphied upon the rear altar wall.

Our founding fathers' original family pews are designated with their names upon them, showing forth where their allegiance lay:

Front Row, (right)
Gen. George Washington Pew 16
Patrick Henry Pew 18

Front Row (left)
Thomas Jefferson Pew 17
Thomas Nelson and Edmund Pendleton Pew 19
George Mason and George Wythe Pew 21

In addition to these Christian founders and patriots of our land worshiping the one, triune God at Bruton Parish Church, numerous great American statesmen find their place, to include:

John Marshall, fourth Supreme
Court Chief Justice Pew 13
James Monroe, fifth U.S. President Pew 14
Sir John Randolph (Vestryman 1727)
Edmund Randolph and Peyton Randolph
 (Vestrymen 1747) Pew 20

The College of William and Mary

Of primary significance in the heart of Williamsburg is the College of William and Mary, established in 1693 by the crown of England. A plaque prominently displayed on the inside wall of the Christopher Wren Building, first edifice of what is now a vast college campus, quotes from its charter specifying that the purpose for the school is the training of ministers of the gospel and the propagation of the Christian faith:

> Charter granted by King William and Queen Mary, for the founding of William and Mary College in Virginia.
>
> William and Mary, by the grace of God, of England, Scotland, France and Ireland, King and Queen, Defenders of the Faith, to all whom these our present Letters shall come, greeting. Forasmuch as our well-beloved and trusty Subjects, constituting the General Assembly of our Colony of Virginia, have had it in their minds, and have proposed to themselves, to the end that the Church of Virginia may be furnished with a Seminary of Ministers of the Gospel, and that the Youth may be piously educated in Good Letters and Manners, and that the Christian Faith may be propagated amongst the Western Indians, to the glory of Almighty God. . . .[1]

A Visitors' Guide to the College of William and Mary says this about the origins of the college:

> A few years after the founding of Jamestown, a movement was started in England and in Virginia to establish a college, but construction at a settlement called Henrico, near Richmond, was disrupted by an Indian massacre in 1622. The idea of a college for the Virginia Colony persisted, and in 1693 King William III and Queen Mary II granted a Charter to establish "the College of William and Mary in Virginia" in what is now Williamsburg. Actual construction commenced in 1695. . . .[2]

Compare the above with the true text of the Charter already discussed. It fails to explain what the true purpose for the founding of this college was—the salvation of souls. It is but another example of the removal of all traces of Christianity and the Christian value system from the original documents of our nation.

Original Charter for the College of William and Mary, Williamsburg, Virginia.
University Archives, Swem Library, College of William and Mary.

The College of William and Mary holds preeminence as the nation's oldest college (Harvard being the oldest university). Three United States presidents (Tyler, Monroe and Jefferson) attended this college, George Washington being its first chancellor. At its establishment in 1693, the college comprised three schools: The Grammar, Philosophy and Divinity Schools. Among the textbooks studied were, *Buchanan's Paraphrase of the Psalms*, the Latin Bible, the Greek New Testament and Greek and Latin editions of the *Book of Common Prayer*.[3]

In 1697 an Indian School was added, its stated purpose being to prepare Indian boys so that they could go back to their tribes as Christian evangelists to teach and preach the Word of God.[4]

Member of the Continental Congress and signer of the Declaration of Independence, George Wythe, for whom the law college is named, was legal mentor to Thomas Jefferson and many early Americans.

From this school proceeded great American patriots such as John Marshall, star pupil of George Wythe, and fourth Chief Justice of the Supreme Court; Peyton Randolph, first president of the Continental Congress, along with 16 members of that body; and four signers of the Declaration of Independence.[5]

As Edmund Randolph, attorney general under George Washington observed: "until the Revolution, most of the leading men were alumni of William and Mary."

It was here, too, that George Washington received his surveyor's commission in 1749, Benjamin Franklin the honorary degree of Master of Arts in 1756, and the Chevalier de Chastellux and Thomas Jefferson in 1782, the degree of Doctor of Civil Law.

The famous and unique chapel, which houses the oldest organ in continuous use in America, is appropriately located within the Christopher Wren Building. This inspiring chapel was initially used for morning and evening prayer, moral discourses and conferring of degrees and honors.[6] Evening prayer was the most popular service of scholars and townsmen, bringing about a joyous gathering of "town and gown" at the close of day.[7] The Wren Building Chapel reminds us of an era when church, state and school were linked together by Christianity. Without Bruton Parish Church, the College of William and Mary would probably not

Prayers.

THANKSGIVINGS.

The 1752 *Book of Common Prayer* used at the time of independence by our founding fathers. Prayers for the king of England were changed for "the people of the United States in general, So especially for their Senate and Representatives in Congress assembled." Courtesy of Bruton Parish Church, Williamsburg, Virginia.

have come to Williamsburg, and without the church and college, the capital would not have located here.[8]

Its presidents, until 1814, and most of its faculty until the American Revolution were ministers. Six of its presidents have jointly held the position of Rector of Bruton Parish Church, which served founding fathers George Washington, Thomas Jefferson, Patrick Henry and others.[9]

Two of the college's great academicians are memorialized within its regal, yet simple interior. They are: Dr. James Madison, president of the College of William and Mary, and second cousin to our fourth U.S. president, James Madison; and George Wythe, founder of the prestigious Wythe School of Law at the college. Plaques honoring these men read as follows:

> In Memoriam of the Right Reverend Doctor James Madison (1749–1812)
>
> Graduate of the College of William and Mary (1771)
> Professor of Mathematics (1773–1775)
> Professor of Natural Philosophy and Chemistry and of Political Economy and International Law
> President (1777–1812)
> Member of the Commission appointed in 1779 to determine the boundaries between Virginia and Pennsylvania
> Elected first Bishop of Virginia (1790)
> He cooperated with Thomas Jefferson in 1779 in reconstructing the curricula of the College of William and Mary introducing the elective system of study, the Schools of Modern Languages, Municipal and Constitutional Law and Medicine. He also introduced the study of Political Economy (1784) and the study of History (1805)
> The original tablet was erected by William Madison Scott in 1927.

George Wythe's plaque reads as follows:

> George Wythe, LLD (1726–1806)
> Member of the Continental Congress,
> Signer of the Declaration of Independence, member of the Commission of 1776 on the revision of the laws of Virginia
> Judge of the Chancery Court

First Professor of Law in the College of William and Mary
The American Arisides
He was an exemplar of all there is noble and elevating in the
profession of Law. Erected as a tribute to his courage as a
patriot, his ability as an instructor, his uprightness as a lawyer,
his purity as a Judge.
The original tablet was presented by the Virginia State Bar
Association in 1893.

In respect to the College of William and Mary, Thomas Jefferson was requested to expand the curricula of this college by introducing an elective system of study, which included the Schools of Modern Languages, Municipal and Constitutional Law, Medicine and Political Economy and History. Jefferson has left us his own account of what actually transpired in his handwritten autobiography:

> . . . The acts of assembly concerning the College of William and
> Mary were properly within Mr. Pendleton's portion of our
> work but these related chiefly to its revenue, while its consti-
> tution, organization and scope of science were derived from its
> charter. We thought that on this subject a systematical plan of
> general education should be proposed, and I accordingly pre-
> pared three bills for the Revisal, proposing three distinct
> grades of education, reaching all classes . . . the second bill pro-
> posed to amend the constitution of William and Mary college,
> to enlarge its sphere of science, and to make it in fact a Uni-
> versity. The third was for the establishment of a library . . .

To further elucidate the true identity of the College of William and Mary, an official college memorandum dated February 11, 1962, entitled *Wren Training,* raises the following question:

> 1. Was the College of William and Mary Episcopal following
> the disestablishment of the church here? If so, did it remain so
> until it became a State School?

The correct historical answer given in the memorandum is:

> William and Mary was private, not Episcopalian, after the
> disestablishment of the Anglican Church in Virginia. There

were still strong ties between the College and the Episcopal Church, of course, notably because of Episcopal clergy on the faculty. In 1780 College president James Madison (who was Episcopal bishop of Virginia) wrote: "it is now thought that Establishments in Favor of any particular Sect are incompatible with the Freedom of a Republic." Jefferson reorganized the College at about the same time he was working on the principle of Religious Freedom. The College remained private until 1906 when during Lyon G. Tyler's presidency it became a state-supported school for training teachers.

The above reinforces the fact that Thomas Jefferson's and James Madison's "Freedom of Religion" principle referred exclusively to mainline Christian sects or denominations, having equal footing and acceptance within the community proper, without the interference of a state-controlled church.

William and Mary's Earl Gregg Swem Library has in its safekeeping, one of America's most cherished possessions of her founding period history. Owned by Bruton Parish Church, it is the original *1752 Book of Common Prayer* in which the prayers for the sovereign of England were substituted with prayers for the Congress of the newly established United States of America. This was done in the margins, in longhand, the original words being crossed out of the text and substituted with:

> for the people of these United States in general; so especially for their Senate and representatives in congress assembled;...thy people . . . Almighty God who has given us grace at this time, with one accord to make our common supplications unto thee; and dost promise that when two or three are gathered together in thy name, thou wilt grant their requests; fulfill now, O Lord, the desires and petitions of thy servants, as may be most expedient for them; granting us in this world knowledge of thy truth, and in the world to come life everlasting. . . . The grace of our Lord Jesus Christ, and the love of God, and the fellowship of the Holy Ghost, be with us all evermore.

Capitol of Williamsburg

The beautiful and imposing Capitol of Williamsburg stands at the end of the Duke of Gloucester Street. This red brick, Georgian style building is designed in the shape of an "H." It was here that the House of Burgesses convened, and the chaplain of this governing body commenced each session of the House with prayer and Scripture readings. George Washington, Thomas Jefferson, Patrick Henry and many other prominent Virginian sons were among the delegates who heatedly deliberated the urgency and cause of America's independence from Great Britain.

Bible Removed

But one important thing has been removed—the Bible that was in constant use by the House of Burgesses prior to the birth of the United States.

Information given to me by the Director of the Colonial Williamsburg Foundation, Graham Hood, on October 7, 1987, advises that the famous "Vinegar" Bible, King James Version, published in Oxford, England in 1717, was constantly in use by the House of Burgesses. Its pseudonym, "Vinegar" comes from the fact that the word: "Vineyard" at the top of the 22nd chapter of Luke's Gospel, was misspelled to read: "Vinegar." Said Hood, (the Curator):

> This Bible was consistently and continually used whenever prayer for the assembly was needed. The Bible was part of the Conference, Council and Committee meetings in Congress. Removed in the mid-1970's and returned to the library of the South Committee Room in the early 1980's. Cannot be seen by the public except by special permission, when one is doing a specialized project.[10]

Information recently received in September 1988 gives a different story of this famous, well-used Bible, which I was permitted to see and photograph. The following, somewhat evasive information, was sent to me upon my inquiry regarding the pertinent information, significance and date of the Vinegar Bible:

... I enclose copies of the pertinent data re: the "Vinegar" Bible at the Capitol. In accord with our policy, I have removed the names of the individuals whose letters prompted the research responses. I do note that the evaluation given the Bible in the 1950's was done by a widely recognized Rare Book and Manuscript dealer.

(signed)John E. Ingram, Curator
Special Collections
Colonial Williamsburg Collection[11]

Two copied letters of information—with names and addresses removed—were also sent by the Colonial Williamsburg Foundation on the "Vinegar" Bible, which was used by members of the House of Burgesses during the crucial years which paved the way for the birth of the new nation, establishing itself under the protection of Almighty God.

The two paragraphs which really concern me in this redescriptive phraseology pertaining to one of America's oldest and most cherished possessions are:

The "Vinegar" Bible, consistently and continually used by the delegates for guidance from God, prayer and direction prior to independence. The House of Burgesses, Capitol, Williamsburg, Virginia.

1960

. . . The book was removed from the Capitol because it was doubtful such a large Bible (20 inches) would have been in the room and because undue emphasis was being placed on its curious significance.[12]

1958

. . . I have not forgotten that I was to write you about the Vinegar Bible. We find that at least six copies have been sold in this country in the last 30 years, and since most copies naturally turn up in London, and since many are sold privately, you will see it can hardly be considered a rarity. As a matter of interest, I might say that the auction prices have ranged from $24.00 to $70.00.[13]

According to the curator, the above reinterpreted historical information is now on file with the Colonial Williamsburg Foundation, descriptive of the one and only "Vinegar" Bible in the House of Burgesses, Capitol of the Virginia capital city in the 1700s.

Why does this Bible hold preeminence over others with the same error? Because of its significance and use by men whom God appointed to form and fashion a unique new republic—a government based upon biblical truth.

Upon taking the tour of Williamsburg's Capitol, and inquiring as to the whereabouts of this famous old Bible, neither the supervisory curator nor the guide knew anything about it. This specific "Vinegar" Bible is now in an obscure library of the Williamsburg Capitol, away from the admiring eyes of God-loving, patriotic Americans, who would revere and honor its intrinsic value and worth. This famous volume of Holy Scripture served to imbue Burgesses such as founding fathers George Washington, Thomas Jefferson, Patrick Henry and others, with God's incomparable words and direction at such an important crossroads in our nation's history.

The "Vinegar" Bible is one of the richest and most valuable possessions of America's Founding Period. It forms an intricate part of our national Christian heritage—a true testimony to the hand of Almighty God in directing the decisions and actions of our founding fathers in their quest for liberty.

Another recent piece of literature printed by the Colonial Williamsburg Foundation, is entitled "No Thanksgiving in Williamsburg." It appeared in prominence, next to the design of a large turkey, on the back of the *1989 Thanksgiving Day Menu*. This was at the well-known Bay Room of the Williamsburg Lodge. The front of this select menu featured mythological King Neptune with his pitchfork, above the wording "The Bay Room Thanksgiving Menu," and three smaller sailing vessels below. The text read as follows:

Scholars will search in vain for any mention of Thanksgiving Day in the 18th Century Virginia Gazette. Fourth Thursdays in November were no different from other days—runaway slaves, lost pocketbooks, ships departing to London. Page after page, it is always business as usual. No festivities, no turkey, no stuffing, no sleigh ride to grandmother's house, in short, no Thanksgiving Day. There were, however, many days of thanksgiving. Bumper harvests, drought-breaking rains, safe voyages, and military victories were made frequent occasions for public prayers and celebrations during the seventeenth and eighteenth centuries. The colonists who settled Berkeley Hundred in 1619 carried instructions to give thanks "yearly and perpetually" on the anniversary of their arrival. And they did, for three years—until Indians annihilated the settlement in 1622, after which it seemed prudent for surviving Virginians to proclaim another day of thanksgiving for having been spared. There were comparable observances in eighteenth-century Williamsburg. Days of thanksgiving were proclaimed to commemorate, for instance, Queen Anne's health and the "happy agreement" between her Majesty and the Houses of Parliament.

These were all solemn religious occasions. They have only an indirect relationship to the present Thanksgiving holiday, which we should give ungrudgingly to New Englanders. Or, better yet, to Old Englanders, for the Plymouth Colony Pilgrims were only celebrating a folk custom that they remembered from England. The Harvest Home, a time of feasting, dancing, and gaming after the crops were safely gathered, was an ancient peasant festival. Brought to all the American colonies, it thrived best in the small farming communities of New England. Only in 1863 did President Abraham Lincoln make Thanksgiving Day a national holiday as a reminder of "peace, harmony, tranquility, and Union" in a time of civil war. So it turns out that your Thanksgiving dinner in Williamsburg is one of history's tastier ironies.

The Colonial Williamsburg Foundation, a tax-exempt entity, operates the entire historic area of Williamsburg, Virginia, called "the cradle of the nation." The proceeds from this Williamsburg Lodge are used for its educational and historic programs.

My records indicate that the "No Thanksgiving at Williamsburg" literary piece is incorrect historical information and untrue to the traditional annual American Thanksgiving Day observance celebration, which forms part and parcel of her rich Christian heritage. The national origins of a day of observance set apart to give thanks to our gracious God and Father, the God of Abraham, Isaac and Jacob, the God of our Lord Jesus Christ, and the God of the Americans, naturally encompassed 18th-century Virginia. The fact that Abraham Lincoln in 1863, by Act of Congress, set apart the last Thursday in November as the official annual observance day for each American to give thanks to Almighty God for His bountiful blessings upon our land, does not in any wise detract from prior national Thanksgiving observance days, celebrated on different dates, but on a regular basis. This unique and revered American Christian tradition began with the *First National Thanksgiving Proclamation*, on November 1, 1777, by Order of Congress, and signed by Henry Laurens, President of the Continental Congress. It is here reprinted in its entirety:

> Forasmuch as it is the indispensable duty of all men to adore the superintending Providence of Almighty God; to acknowledge with gratitude their obligation to Him for benefits received, and to implore such farther blessings as they stand in need of; and it having pleased Him in His abundant mercy not only to continue to us the innumerable bounties of His common Providence.

> It is therefore recommended to the legislative or executive powers of these United States, to set apart Thursday, the eighteenth day of December next, for solemn thanksgiving and praise:

That with one heart and one voice the good people may express the grateful feelings of their hearts, and consecrate themselves to the service of their Divine Benefactor; and that together with their sincere acknowledgements and offerings, they may join the penitent confession of their manifold sins, whereby they had forfeited every favour, and their humble and earnest supplication that it may please God, through the merits of Jesus Christ, mercifully to forgive and blot them out of remembrance;

That it may please Him graciously to afford His blessings on the governments of these states respectively, and prosper the public council of the whole; to inspire our commanders both by land and sea, and all under them, with that wisdom and fortitude which may render them fit instruments, under the Providence of Almighty God, to secure for these United States, the greatest of all human blessings, independence and peace; That it may please Him, to prosper the trade and manufactures of the people, and the labour of the husbandman, that our land may yet yield its increase; to take schools and seminaries of education, so necessary for cultivating the principles of true liberty, virtue and piety, under His nurturing hand, and to prosper the means of religion for the promotion and enlargement of that kingdom which consisteth "in righteousness, peace and joy in the Holy Ghost."

And it is further recommended, that servile labour, and such recreation as, though at other times innocent, may be unbecoming the purpose of this appointment, be omitted on so solemn an occasion.

In keeping with the general tone in the Colonial Williamsburg Foundation's "No Thanksgiving in Williamsburg" literary piece, is their comment that ". . . the Plymouth Colony Pilgrims were only celebrating a folk custom that they remembered from England. The Harvest Home, a time of feasting, dancing, and gaming after the crops were safely gathered, was an ancient peasant festival. Brought to all of the American colonies, it thrived best in the small farming communities of New England."

The above-quoted *1777 National Thanksgiving Proclamation* denotes gratitude, humility and repentance towards Almighty

God, supplication for His mercy, thanksgiving for His blessings of independence and peace and prayers for the prosperity of Christianity in righteousness, peace and joy in the Holy Spirit. This precludes the Harvest Home festival, a godless folk custom.

I submit, once again, that the above is a falsification of America's true Christian origins and history, deceiving multitudes into believing foibles, fables and tales which have absolutely nothing to do with the Pilgrims in New England and the Mayflower Compact, from which the first Thanksgiving celebration stems.

After the harvest crops were gathered in November, 1623, it was Governor William Bradford of Plimoth Plantation, in Plymouth, Massachusetts, who proclaimed that:

> All ye Pilgrims with your wives and little ones, do gather at the Meeting House, on the hill . . . there to listen to the pastor, and render Thanksgiving to the Almighty God for all His blessings.[14]

Had the Colonial Williamsburg Foundation authors and scholars of this historic, educational piece entitled "No Thanksgiving in Williamsburg" searched the December, 1777, issues of the *Virginia Gazette*, they would have assuredly found that the Christian colonists in Williamsburg were gratefully giving thanks to Almighty God (together with the rest of their fellow Americans) on the *third Thursday in December, 1777*, rather than the last Thursday in November of that year.

The above indicates a serious questioning of the Colonial Williamsburg Foundation's ability to correctly research and interpret America's rich founding period history to the public.

The authors of "No Thanksgiving in Williamsburg" further state that ". . . only in 1863 did President Abraham Lincoln make Thanksgiving Day a national holiday as a reminder of 'peace, harmony, tranquility, and Union' in a time of civil war. So it turns out that your Thanksgiving dinner in Williamsburg is one of history's tastier ironies."

I submit that the above is a deliberate misinterpretation and falsification of the true importance and meaning of Abraham Lincoln's own words in his *October 3, 1863, Thanksgiving Proclamation*, in which he glorifies our God and Father as Americans and stresses the infallibility and inerrant Truth of the Bible, the Word of God, which instructs us to "give thanks unto the Lord in all things for His manifold blessings to us." It is here reprinted for all Americans to read:

> It is the duty of nations as well as of men to own their dependence upon the overruling power of God; to confess their sins and transgressions in humble sorrow, yet with assured hope that genuine repentance will lead to mercy and pardon; and to recognize the sublime truth, announced in the Holy Scriptures and proven by all history, that those nations are blessed whose God is the Lord.
>
> We know that by His divine law, nations, like individuals, are subjected to punishments and chastisements in this world. May we not justly fear that the awful calamity of civil war which now desolates the land may be a punishment inflicted upon us for our presumptuous sins, to the needful end of our national reformation as a whole people?
>
> We have been the recipients of the choicest bounties of heaven; we have been preserved these many years in peace and prosperity; we have grown in numbers, wealth and power as no other nation has ever grown.
>
> But we have forgotten God. We have forgotten the gracious hand which preserved us in peace and multiplied and enriched and strengthened us, and we have vainly imagined, in the deceitfulness of our hearts, that all these blessings were produced by some superior wisdom and virtue of our own. Intoxicated with unbroken success, we have become too self-sufficient to feel the necessity of redeeming and preserving grace, too proud to pray to the God that made us.
>
> It has seemed to me fit and proper that God should be solemnly, reverently and gratefully acknowledged, as with one heart and one voice, by the whole American people. I do therefore invite my fellow citizens in every part of the United States, and also those who are at sea and those who are sojourning in foreign lands, to set apart and observe the last Thursday of November as a day of Thanksgiving and praise to our beneficent Father who dwelleth in the heavens.
>
> (signed) A. Lincoln
> October 3, 1863

(ix) Jamestown, Virginia

Jamestown, Virginia, is indeed a place of beginnings for what was later to become the United States of America. It was Virginia's first capital for 92 years. Originally known as "James Cittie," it was the site of the first permanent English settlement in America in 1607, and the meeting place of the first representative legislative assembly in 1619. The true identity of our great nation is indelibly stamped upon the First Charter of Virginia, dated April 10, 1606:

> I. JAMES, by the grace of God, King of England, Scotland, France, and Ireland, Defender of the Faith, etc., whereas our loving and well-disposed Subjects, Sir Thomas Gates, and Sir George Somers, Knights, Richard Hackhit, Clerk, Prebendary of Westminster, and Edward-Maria Wingfield, Thomas Hanham, and Ralegh Gilbert, Esqrs. William Parker and George Popham, Gentlemen, and divers others of our loving subjects, have been humble suitors unto us, that We would vouchsafe unto them our Licence, to make Habitation, Plantation, and to deduce a Colony of sundry of our People into that Part of America, commonly called VIRGINIA, and other Parts and Territories in America, either appertaining unto us, or which are not now actually possessed by any Christian Prince of People, . . . We, greatly commending, and graciously accepting of, their Desires for the Furtherance of so noble a Work, which may, by the Providence of Almighty God, hereafter tend to the Glory of his Divine Majesty, in propagating of Christian Religion to such People, as yet live in Darkness and miserable Ignorance of the true Knowledge and Worship of God, and may in time bring the Infidels and Savages, living in those Parts, to human Civility, and to a settled and quiet Government; Do, by these our Letters Patents, graciously accept of, and agree to, their humble and well-intended Desires, . . .[1]

It was thus that the London Company established the first permanent Christian colony in America with 120 settlers leaving England in December, 1606, and planting a colony at Jamestown on May 14, 1607.[2]

The church tower is the only remaining original 17th-century structure. The first great English highway in America once ran along the river shore, turning inland and passing behind the church.

It continued over the swamp and then left over the isthmus near Jamestown Island.

A magnificent cross, representing that upon which our Lord and Savior Jesus Christ was crucified, was erected by the colonists upon their disembarkation on American soil. A replica of this cross is here, in its place.

The second act of the colonists was to kneel down and commemorate the Last Supper together. Presiding over this important celebration was their chaplain, the Reverend Robert Hunt, who became the first minister of the colony.

At this very spot stands the handsome Robert Hunt bronze memorial, showing forth these first 1607 settlers kneeling on the ground, receiving the Lord's Supper from their chaplain. A sail tied between three or four trees served as their first church. The communion rail was made of boughs of trees. In order for the reader to better comprehend the Christian fervor of these 1607 Jamestown settlers, I have chosen to reproduce the colonists' own testimony, inscribed upon Hunt's Memorial:

> 1607. To the glory of God and in memory of the Reverend Robert Hunt, Presbyter, appointed by the Church of England. Minister of the Colony which established the English Church and English civilization at Jamestown, Virginia, in 1607. His people, members of the Colony, left this testimony concerning him. He was an honest, religious and courageous Divine. He preferred the Service of God in so good a voyage to every thought of ease at home. He endured every privation, yet none ever heard him repine. During his life our factions were ofte healed, and our greatest extremities so comforted that they seemed easy in comparison with what we endured after his memorable death. We all received from him the Holy Communion together, as a pledge of reconciliation, for we all loved him for his exceeding goodness. He planted the First Protestant Church in America and laid down his life in the foundation of America.

The above portrays a 1607 Christian foundational settlement in America, devoid of the mercenary thrust which recent "historians" have given it.

Of further interest in this vein is a large informative plaque on the rear right wall of the original Jamestown church site, stating:

> To the glory of God and in grateful remembrance of the adventurers in England and Ancient Planters in Virginia who, through evil report and loss of fortune, through suffering and death, maintained stout hearts and laid the foundations of our country.

Upon the base of the tallest and the most conspicuous monument in Jamestown, the Tercentenary Monument, are inscribed these words:

> Lastly and chiefly the way to prosper and achieve good success is to make yourselves all of one mind for the good of your country and your own, and to serve and fear God, the giver of all goodness, for every plantation which our heavenly Father hath not planted shall be rooted out. Advice of the London Council for Virginia to the Colony, 1606.

Another inscription reads:

> Jamestown, the first permanent colony of the English people and birthplace of Virginia and of the United States.

The rear of this impressive memorial discloses the following:

> Virginia Company of London Chartered April 10, 1606, founded Jamestown and sustained Virginia 1607–1624.

The right-hand side wording tells us that:

> Representative government in America began in the first House of Burgesses assembled here July 30, 1619.

Thus, the very first Representative Assembly in the New World was convened at Jamestown on Friday, July 30, 1619. It met in response to orders from the Virginia Company,

> . . . to establish one equal and uniform government of the people there inhabiting. First Sir George Yeardley, knight

governor and Captaine General of Virginia, having sente his summons all over the country, as well as to invite those of the Counsell of Estate that were absent, as also for the elections of Burgesses there were chosen and appeared . . . The most convenient place we could finde to sitt in was the quire of the churche, when Sir George Yeardley the Governor being sett downe in his place, those of the Counsel of Estate set next to him on both handes, except only the Secretary (John Pory) then appointed Speaker, and Thomas Pierse the Sergeant standing at the bar, to be ready for any service the Assembly should command him. "But foreasmuch as men's affaires doe little prosper, where God's service is neglected, all the Burgesses tooke their places in the Quire till prayer was said by Mr. Bucke the Minister, that it would please God to guide and sanctifie all our proceedings, to His own glory and the good of this plantation."[3]

It is recorded that the Assembly proceeded to business despite the extreme heat which endangered their health (and killed one of the Burgesses), until August 4, 1619.

Inside the old church at Jamestown, one reads the following interesting records of this Christian colony's beginnings:

The cobblestone and brick foundations, exhibited here under glass, supported the frame church of 1617, the first church on this site, and Jamestown's third church. It was within the 1617 structure that the first representative legislative assembly in America convened from July 30–August 4, 1619. The first all-brick church (of which the old Tower was a part and on whose foundations the present memorial church in large part rests), was begun in 1639. The present memorial church was built in 1907.[4]

The Ten Commandments of Almighty God (Exodus 20), grace the walls behind the altar, in beautiful calligraphy.

So simple and moving are these, that they are here reproduced in their original wording:

The Ten Commandments
I. Thou shalt have none other gods but me.
II. Thou shalt not make to thyselfe any graven image.

III. Thou shalte not take the name of the Lord thy God in Vaine.

IIII. Remember that thou keepe holy the Sabbath day.

V. Honour thy father and thy mother.

VI. Thou shalt doe no murther

VII. Thou shalte not steale

IX. Thou shalte not beare false witnes against thy neighbor.

X. Thou shalt not covet.

Obviously, those who advocate the recently-fabricated myth: "separation of church and state," removing God's Ten Commandments and prayer from the public schools, ignore the fact that the Ten Commandments and prayer proved significant in the convening of the First Legislative Government in America (1619).

And, of importance to the ministries and outreach of this original Christian colony, we read the historical annals of a young convert:

> In memory of Chanco, an Indian youth converted to Christianity, who resided in the household of Richard Pace across the river from Jamestown and who, on the eve of the Indian massacre of March 22, 1622, warned Pace of the murderous plot thus enabling Pace to cross the river in a canoe to alert and save the Jamestown settlement from impending disaster.[5]

Regardless of the wealth of original documents, plaques and memorials testifying to the 1607 Jamestown settlement being Christian in its focus, way of life and presentation of gospel truth to the Indians; a relatively new reenactment (c. 1957) to this Jamestown Settlement, located a mile away, and administered by the Jamestown-Yorktown Foundation, has a different story to tell. One reaches this Jamestown Reenactment prior to the authentic Jamestown Island historic site. To either side of the entranceway, large beige and brown markers display three sailing vessels, with the wording: "JAMESTOWN SETTLEMENT 1607 A Living History Museum." Multitudes of visitors are thus given the impression that this is the original 1607 Jamestown historic site, leaving the area without seeing the true Christian settlement and identity of these Jamestown pilgrims further down the river.

The handsomely illustrated literature of the 1957 reenactment commences thus:

> Chapter One. In the book of American history, Jamestown, Virginia, represents the nation's beginnings. Established as a business venture in 1607, Jamestown was England's first permanent colony in the New World. . . . Here, near the original site of Jamestown, you'll experience firsthand what life was like in the colony. . . .

A recreation of the Powhatan Indian Village, together with its "Indian ceremonial dance circle, social structure, religion and government" is also described in this literature.

The most important aspect of the 1607 Jamestown settlement, however, is totally omitted—that of their biblically based, day-to-day lives, which attracted many Indians as converts to Christianity. Had it been established as purely a "business venture," to quote the above, the 1607 Jamestown settlers would not have convened the first Representative Legislative Assembly in America in their church, commencing with prayer to Almighty God for His guidance, protection and blessings upon their newly founded settlement "to His own glory and the good of this plantation."

The Visitors Guide to this 1957 Jamestown settlement reenactment portrays an American Indian in ceremonial dress with bow and arrow, upon its cover. It begins thus:

> JAMESTOWN SETTLEMENT
> Re-creating America's first
> Permanent English Settlement
>
> Jamestown was established in 1607, 13 years before the Pilgrims landed at Plymouth in Massachusetts, and nearly a century before Williamsburg became the capital of Colonial Virginia. The 1607 expedition was sponsored by the Virginia Company of London, a group of English investors who hoped to make a profit from the New World's wealth . . .

The above is totally devoid of any historic validity or truth, as the London Company's 1606 First Charter of Virginia spells out clearly their reasons for coming to America: "1) Virginia was not now actually possessed of any Christian Prince or People," and 2) "their desires for the furtherance of so noble a work, which may, by the Providence of Almighty God, hereafter tend to the glory of His Divine Majesty, in propagating of Christian Religion to such Peoples, as yet live in darkness and miserable ignorance of the true knowledge and worship of God. . . ."

Once again we see America's foundational history distorted and falsified, in order to eliminate all traces of her rich Christian heritage and evangelistic origins from our culture and civilization.

No Thanksgiving in Jamestown

My visit to this re-created Jamestown settlement on Thanksgiving Day, 1990, disclosed the following, on a blue-bordered flyer:

> JAMESTOWN SETTLEMENT
> presents
> Foods and Feasts in 17th Century Virginia, November 22–24,
> 1990
> . . . while there is no "Thanksgiving"
> tradition at Jamestown, food was always
> an important factor in the welfare of
> the early colony. . . .

The entire one-page flyer then goes on to major upon hogs and their butchering!

This "historic" emphasis upon food is inconsistent with the true Christian spirit and daily walk of these 1607 Jamestown settlers, who put God first in all their undertakings, thus expressing daily thanksgiving to Him, as recorded by John Pory, secretary of the colony:

> But foreasmuch as men's affaires doe little prosper, where God's service is neglected, all the Burgesses tooke their places in the Quire till a prayer was said by Mr. Bucke the Minister, that it would please God to guide and sanctifie all our proceedings. . . .

Immortalized in Jamestown history is the life and conversion of Pocahontas, the "Christian Indian Princess." She was the favorite daughter of Powhatan, who ruled the Powhatan Confederacy. She was born about 1595, probably at Woronocomoco, 16 miles from Jamestown. She had saved Captain John Smith's life twice during the colony's first years. In 1608–1609 she was a frequent and welcome visitor to Jamestown. After accepting Jesus Christ as her Lord and Savior, Pocahontas was baptized into the Christian faith in the original church at Jamestown in 1613. A beautiful oil painting capturing this event hangs within the U.S. Capitol Rotunda. She subsequently married John Rolfe , Council Member of the Jamestown Colony. Their marriage took place in April, 1614, being officiated by Rev. Richard Bucke (1573–1623), chaplain to the first Representative Legislative Assembly in the New World.[6] In 1616 Pocahontas visited England with her husband and infant son, Thomas, and was presented to the Royal Court. While returning to Virginia two years later, she died and was buried in St. George's Church in Gravesend, England. Today, many Americans claim descent from her through her son.

A replica of the only known original extant portrait of Pocahontas hangs on a wall adjacent to the gift shop at the Visitors' Center in Jamestown*, which is run by the National Park Service, Department of the Interior. It depicts this Indian Princess as she appeared when presented to the Queen, in royal English attire she had worn on that occasion. Her true identity, inscribed upon the painting itself by the artist Brooke, immortalizes her for her Indian heritage and her conversion to Christianity:

> Matoaks ats Rebecka, daughter of the mighty Prince Powhatan Emperour of Attanoughknomouck ats Virginia converted and baptized in the Christian faith, and wife to the wor.^{H} Mr Tho: Rolff.

It's interesting that a duplicate version of this portrait is available for purchase in the National Park Service Visitors' Center gift shop. However, significantly, the inscription under the image has been rewritten. Lacking, of course is that of her conversion to Christianity as shown below:

*Removed and Replaced by National Park Service volunteer sign, at author's visit 1/15/1991.

"Baptism of Pocahontas at Jamestown, 1613" by John G. Chapman. U.S. Capitol
Rotunda. Photo by John W. Wrigley.

Ætatis suæ 21. Aº.1616.

Matoaks als Rebecka daughter to the mighty Prince
Powhatan Emperour of Attanoughkomouck als Virginia
converted and baptized in the Chriſtian faith, and
Wife to the worꝶ Mr Tho: Rolff.

Brooke's portrait of Pocahontas. The only original of this Indian Princess, converted and baptized in the Christian faith. National Portrait Gallery, Smithsonian Institution.

Pocahontas (c 1595–1616), daughter of an Indian chief, aided the first English colonists and later married one of them. She is shown here in the clothes she wore in England where she went with her husband, John Rolfe.[7]

This is another clear example of the rewriting of America's history to fit a mold which is totally alien to the true records. The subtle rewriting of the artist's own inscription may seem inconsequential. However, it was the Lord working in the life of Pocahontas that catapulted her into her unique position in life, and thus immortalized her name in history. It is that key factor—her Christianity—which those opposed to Christianity despise and would attempt to eradicate from the pages of our national history.

American Women: 1607 to the Present

Pocahontas (c1595-1616), daughter of an Indian chief, aided the first English colonists and later married one of them. She is shown here in the clothes she wore in England where she went with her husband, John Rolfe.

This portrait is based on material in the Smithsonian Institution.

Published by The Proud Press, Box 1236, Berkeley, CA 94701. Copyright © 1898 by Polly and John Zane. All rights reserved. Printed in the U.S.A.

Illustration from the only existing painting by Brooke. English, 1616. Printed by permission of the copyright owners Polly and John Zane.

(x) Yorktown, Virginia—Thomas Nelson, Jr.

A visit to Yorktown, Virginia, is a rare treat for those who love America's rich founding period history. The visitor is greeted by a tall, imposing monument entitled the "Victory Monument," standing sentinel on the edge of a promontory. Three muses, each with a star upon her head, stand erect upon a pedestal, the base of which bears these inscribed words: "One Country—One Constitution—One Destiny."

This memorial to America's heroic past represents the bloodshed and sacrifice that preceded the birth of the new nation. The following lines, inscribed upon the front base of the statue, are descriptive of how the battle was won:

> At York on October 19, 1781, after a siege of 19 days by 5500 American and 7,000 French troops of the line 3,500 Virginia militia, under command of General Thomas Nelson and 36 ships of war; Earl Cornwallis, Commander of the British forces at York and Gloucester surrendered his army—7,251 officers and men—840 seamen—244 cannon and 24 standards, to His Excellency George Washington, Commander in Chief of the Combined Forces of America and France to His Excellency the Compte de Rochambeau, commanding the auxiliary troops of his most Christian Majesty in America and to his Excellency the Compte de Grasse, Commander in Chief of the Naval Army of France in Chesapeake.

A left-hand side inscription reads:

> The Provisional Articles of Peace concluded November 30, 1782, and the definitive Treaty of Peace concluded September 3, 1783 between the United States of America and George III, King of Great Britain and Ireland, declare
> His Britannic Majesty acknowledges the said United States, viz. New Hampshire; Massachusetts Bay; Rhode Island and Providence Plantations; Connecticut; New York; New Jersey; Pennsylvania; Delaware; Maryland; Virginia; North Carolina; South Carolina and Georgia, to be free, sovereign and independent states.

To the right-hand side of the base we read:

> The Treaty concluded February 6, 1778 between the United States of America and Louis 16th, King of France, declares the

318

Essential and Direct end of the present defensive alliance is to maintain effectually the Liberty and Sovereignty and the Independence absolute and unlimited of the said United States, as well in matters of Government as of Commerce. Erected in pursuance of a resolution of Congress adopted October 29, 1781; and an Act of Congress approved June 7, 1880. To commemorate the Victory by which the Independence of the United States was achieved.

Colonial Grace Church of York-Hampton Parish gives forth these historic lines upon a bronze plaque on its front facade:

A national shrine at the Cradle of the Republic. Erected 1697; Burned 1814; partially rebuilt in 1825; Rebuilt in 1926. These are the original walls, built of marble. The bell was cast in London in 1725, but broken during the fire of 1814. It was recast in Philadelphia in 1882. The original hammered communion silver made in London in 1649, is still in use. First Confirmation service in Virginia was held in this church in 1791. General Thomas Nelson Jr., signer of the Declaration of Independence, lies buried in the churchyard.[1]

General Thomas Nelson, Jr., whose handsome, Georgian-designed colonial mansion is open to the public, lies buried in the grounds of Grace Church. His epitaph reads:

General Thomas Nelson, Jr., Patriot, soldier, Christian gentleman. Born December 18, 1738. Died January 2, 1789; mover of the Resolution of May 15, 1776 in the Virginia Convention instructing her delegates in Congress to move that body to declare the colonies free and independent states. Signer of the Declaration of Independence. War Governor of Virginia. Commissioner of Virginia's forces. He gave all for liberty.

The above indicates not only Nelson's prominence as a great American statesman and patriot, who fought valiantly for America's freedom, but also his status as a man of Christian caliber and virtue.

However, upon visiting the Nelson House, one is historically "entertained" with a drama, composed by the National Park Service, Department of the Interior, and enacted by characters impersonating Nelson's wife Lucy and John Robinson Grymes, the brother of Lucy Nelson (who has loyalist sympathies). General Thomas Nelson, Jr. does not feature in the cast, although his house is worthy of teaching colonial Christian history, which this famous personage embodied. The seven-page script enacted during the 1989 summer season, could be summed up in three words: "rewritten, historic trivia." It is here excerpted:

> Lucy: Good afternoon everyone! Welcome to our home! I am so glad you were able to accept our dinner invitation following the completion of Court today. But, I must extend the apologies of Mr. Nelson to you. He was unexpectedly called away to Williamsburg this fine May morning to attend the Virginia Convention being held in the Capitol building. Apparently his presence was much needed, for Thomas had anticipated leaving tomorrow. He begs your forgiveness, but my brother John is here. He too attended court today and came to visit just moments before you. He and I will do our best to be your host and hostess for dinner. . . . John, our guests have arrived from court. Ladies and gentlemen, I would like to introduce you to my brother, John Robinson Grymes.

> John: Good afternoon! I am so pleased you accepted my gracious sister's dinner invitation. I stopped by to check on her well-being. I worry about her when she is alone. (John holds Lucy by the hand).

> Lucy: John, you have always been a dutiful brother. What would I do without you? (Lucy affectionately pats John's hand). So, John, tell us what you experienced at court today? Was it as busy as most?

> John: Yes, indeed, it was an eventful court day. I always look forward to these court day "festivities." Remember that problem the town was having with Mr. Jacob's swine running rampant through the streets?

> Lucy: Yes, that inconsiderate man! His hogs were getting into everything, destroying plants and flowers and leaving their droppings scattered all over town. What a disgrace!

John: Mr. Jacobs was fully aware of the county ordinance prohibiting swine from going about at large and the court saw fit to fine him seven pounds. I believe this will convince him to keep his swine penned up.

Lucy: I hope you are right. Do you think he'll appeal his conviction though? He's such a spendthrift you know.

John: He might. Since the court fined him more than five pounds he can appeal to the General Court in Williamsburg. You know, I think Mr. Jacobs would appeal to Satan himself if he thought the Devil could save him a shilling!

Lucy: No doubt! But tell me of Margaret Jones. I heard about that terrible fight she had with John Butterfield along the waterfront last week. I heard she scarred his face. Tis true?

John: Tis true, and the court did not look favorably on her actions. She is such a harlot anyway. The court sentenced her to be dragged by a boat's stern through the river right here along the water front where she committed her crime. Oh that I could see that! It's been a long time since I've witnessed such punishment. I can't recall, however, if they drag the poor wretches by their ankles or their wrists. Can any of you? (John poses the question to the guests).

Lucy: What a sad fate for anyone, but perhaps her behaviour will change for the better. But tell me about the Charlston orphans, John? What of their fate?

This dramatic "historic" presentation concludes thus:

Lucy: Please forgive me, but my brother's departure has upset me greatly. I hope you will understand that dinner must be postponed as I need time to be by myself. If you would be so kind as to go downstairs now, one of my servants will be able to show you out. I hope we can soon meet again, under happier circumstances. Thank you for your kindness and good day.[2]

The above is yet another poignant example of America's rich founding period history having been obliterated to nothingness. It also shows a psychological abuse of the thousands of Americans visiting the mansion, who, after being "invited to dinner" by a founding father, are then discourteously shown out by a servant, and who are being subjected to this hodge-podge of irrelevant data and utter confusion.

(xi) Greenfield Village

Greenfield Village, founded by Henry Ford in 1929, is a tribute to the genius and accomplishments of scores of Americans, whose perseverance and hard work realized a way of life undergirded by Christian principles of liberty and sparked by the free enterprise system.

Henry Ford himself defined his goals for Greenfield Village as follows:

> When we are through, we shall have reproduced American life as lived; and that, I think, is the best way of preserving at least a part of our history and tradition. For by looking at things people used, and that show the way they lived, a better and truer impression can be gained than could be had in a month of reading—even if there were books whose author had the facilities to discover the minute details of the older life.[1]

This fascinating story, conceived and nurtured in the mind of Ford, is related through original landmarks, buildings, monuments, memorials, objets d'art; and priceless rare treasures, documents and symbols which bring America's rich history and culture to life. Interestingly enough, assembling a complete set of McGuffey Readers was the first collecting effort of Henry and Clara Ford.[2]

Greenfield Village is also the story of the courage and valor which spurred a people onward to great heights of invention and national achievement. To quote the staff at Greenfield Village, it is "the history of America as written into things their hands made and used," with an emphasis upon the original item. It is the visualization and the embodiment of the American dream. Here, millions of American children, students and adults have visited the homes and birthplaces of some of America's greatest sons. Among these are Noah Webster's home with the interior intact, William Holmes McGuffey's schoolhouse and Abraham Lincoln's statehouse.

Over one million objects, and 25 million documents, manuscripts, books and priceless photographs are here housed and displayed.[3] Greenfield Village has traditionally engendered, in the heart of every American, a new pride and love for his valuable national heritage.

Greenfield Village can be divided into four sections:

(1) The earlier homes of our ancestors demonstrating their family lives from the 1640's to the late 19th century.
(2) The village green, with its church, inn, town hall, school, courthouse, shops and other buildings essential to daily living.
(3) The humble homes and workshops of American industrial giants whose genius and inventions made the world we live in today.
(4) The industrialization of America.[4]

This incomparable legacy of America's origins and development spans approximately 260 acres, set aside in Dearborn, Michigan, by Henry Ford to house more than 100 structures moved to this site from original settings nationwide.[5]

Sad to say, Greenfield Village has undergone a radical change in recent years, like so many other historical sites across America. The following is quoted from a letter received on May 3, 1989, from Gillian Daroczy, a young woman who grew up in this vicinity, and whose formative years were molded by the cultural and historic significance of Greenfield Village:

> . . . One important concern is the lack of "living" interpreters in the buildings. And the need for those who are, to give their renditions more details. Heavens, if you didn't come loaded with questions and just happened to be shy, you would go away quite empty, the interpreting was that "brief."
> I mentioned to the gentleman yesterday that there are so many human interest stories revolving around Henry Ford, there's little reason for a host of highlights not to be shared as you're walking through his home. . . . My favorite home, that of the Wright Brothers, was another one of the brief encounters through the house. The guide seemed to wait for me to question rather than come forth with an armload of information. I ran into the same thing at Noah Webster's home and Ford's. I know there are many more this way also. I've seen it change so many times. You could once at least peer into a room and comfortably look over things while a guide interpreted the building for you. Now there's a tape that plays constantly. The flow of traffic is practically "nil"—which is sad. It proves a few things to me: (1) the house feels "empty," (2) we're still in the mode of "hurrying" through life as we hurry from one empty building to another so we can say—have we done them all? (3)

in the process of becoming tired by walking into and out of the homes, only to be blocked off by an impersonal wall of glass that shouts distrust, and listening to a recording that is too lifeless to answer any questions there might have been—there's a feeling of disappointment. How many times will one of us want to continue to return to be disappointed? The fact is that we keep these "living" museums alive by our investment in them. Personally, I'm beginning to feel really cheated and it bothers me.

Maybe it is because I've grown up with the Village and Museum and I've seen it interpreted differently. The special events continue, yet there's something missing today that's important. The over-all flavor. Not one Model T passed me on the road. Not one horse and carriage. I can see modern cars parked now behind the Eagle Tavern—and that never was. Also, outside the Armington and Sims Millyard is this sign:

"19th Century living shops and foundries required large amounts of coal, coke and iron to operate. These are stored outside. Outdoor pieces of scrap iron, casting and old boilers added to creating a new American industrial landscape."

In the cities today we're surrounded by an influx of waste scattered about that we can't seem to go without and here we've recreated some more. I suppose this is so we know what it used to look like when we finally clean things up!

To me, it deflects from the purpose of the mill—what was being developed on the "inside." Many of these buildings were without interpreters. I had the feeling myself of wanting to pass them by to get to something more lively—at the same time, aware there was much these mills and factories could teach if they had a "living" voice.

Remember when I mentioned that Sir John Bennett's Jewelry Store which Ford brought from London was now used as the bakery? Well, not only is jewelry no longer displayed or sold here, but the huge mirror gracing what was once a beautiful shop, now reflects the vision of soda fountain style tables and chairs where you can eat too! Very tacky. I dread to think what is in store for the Sarah Jordan Boarding House—the flower garden was done away with some time ago in favor of a vegetable garden because it was deemed necessary to a "boarding home". . . . The Old Swiss Watch Repair Shop, which in the latter years has been another gift shop, now has a little sign on it stating, "Not an interpretive building." . . . It's right in the middle of what is one of the prettiest streets set out there; along with Noah Webster's home, the Ann Arbor home displaying Greek Revival Architecture and also Stephen Foster's home, among others. . . .

We all have a duty to preserve our heritage. . . .

Henry Ford also created this treasure trove to preserve the old because America was changing so rapidly. He saw it as a wonderful teaching tool. My next door neighbor, once a guide for many years at Greenfield Village, spoke with me about the conversations she had with Henry Ford when he used to sit by the Menlo Park exhibition. They would often talk while she was on break in between the groups of visitors. She tells me how happy he was in feeling satisfied that things may change in the world, but that the Village would always be there, unchanged. It was protected.

Now if we can only protect the interpretation from being updated so much that we leave gaps in the roots of our heritage. . . . The William Holmes McGuffey School wasn't interpreted. . . . As yet, I haven't retrieved any old postcards.

I would say that we have to be keenly aware of the subtle changes made to our history, to speak up to those responsible and put them right back on their toes. . . .[6]

I have allowed Miss Daroczy to write a large portion of this chapter, because it could not be better expressed than by her testimony. As a lifelong resident of Dearborn, a teacher and a former guide at Greenfield Village, she has witnessed its decline from a thriving, inspiring experience into history, to a lifeless, depersonalized "instant walkthrough." Many modern museums have taken the same route as that taken by countless history classes across the nation: where history is taught as names, dates, places and other facts to be committed to memory, with very little understanding of the cause and effect of history. Noah Webster, in his 1828 dictionary defined "history" as:

> An account of facts, particularly of facts respecting nations or states; a narrative of events in the order in which they happened, with their causes and effects. History differs from Annals.

And he compared it to "annals" which he defined as:

> Annals relate simply the facts and events of each year, in strict chronological order, without any observations of the annalist.

Today's museums and history books alike have deteriorated from histories to mere annals. Many Americans sense that something has gone awry, but they are not quite certain what has happened. As this book has attempted to prove, it has not been the result of mere happenstance or lack of understanding, but a deliberate and well-planned attack upon the nation to discredit and destroy all that has made this country great.

When properly taught, history is one of the most exciting of all subjects, because it deals with the people of history and what made them who they are. People like Miss Daroczy are sickened because they understand the potential of this subject and it is heartbreaking to see blank-faced Americans leaving their national museums, cold, indifferent and unchanged, because those who have recently assumed positions of power over these museums have expunged the very lifeblood from our history.

We have produced a nation of lost people searching for their history. For without knowing the past, a people cannot really know who they are in the present. Or know where they are going!

"The Statue of Liberty Enlightening the World." National Park Service, Statue of Liberty National Monument.

(xii) The Statue of Liberty—or, Liberty Enlightening the World?

The Statue of Liberty was conceived in the mind of Edouard de Laboulaye who had been deeply touched by the American Revolution and the biblical principles upon which it was based. How it had contrasted with France's revolution led by atheists 13 years later. The vision was birthed by French sculptor Auguste Bartholdi. Bartholdi writes of the statue, which is officially named, "The Statue of Liberty Enlightening the World":

> The statue was born for this place which inspired its conception. May God be pleased to bless my efforts and my work, and to crown it with success, the duration and the moral influence which it ought to have. I shall be happy to have been able to consecrate the best years of my life to being the interpreter of the noble hearts whose dream has been the realization of the monument to the French American Union.[1]

A frail young Jewish poet by the name of Emma Lazarus contributed her poem entitled "The New Colossus" which was, years later, to be displayed upon a bronze plaque on the base of "Liberty Enlightening the World." Its beautiful lines grasp each American's heart:

> Not like the brazen giant of Greek fame,
> with conquering limbs astride from land to land;
> Here at our sea-washed, sunset gates shall stand
> A mighty woman with a torch, whose flame
> Is the imprisoned lightning, and her name
> Mother of Exiles. From her beacon-hand
> Glows world-wide welcome;
> her mild eyes command
> The air-bridged harbor that twin cities frame.
> "Keep, ancient lands, your storied pomp!"
> cries she
> With silent lips.
> "Give me your tired, your poor,
> Your huddled masses yearning to
> breathe free,
> The wretched refuse of your teeming shore.
> Send these, the homeless, tempest-tost to me,
> I lift my lamp beside the golden door!"

A six-stanza anonymous poem began like this:

> Ah, Madame Liberty, God bless you!
> Since all the cash is there at hand,
> No longer need it now distress you
> The question of a place to stand.

The last stanza reads:

> Soon you in your allotted station,
> Firm in your tower, strong and tall,
> Will give this truth a new illustration,
> The People are the all in all.

The inauguration ceremony of "The Statue of Liberty Enlightening the World" was begun with a powerful prayer to Almighty God, by Reverend Richard S. Storrs, D.D., excerpted below:

> Almighty God, our Heavenly Father, who art of infinite majesty and mercy, by whose counsel and might the courses of the worlds are wisely ordained and irresistibly established, yet who takest thought of the children of men, and to whom our homage in all our works is justly due: We bless and praise Thee for the knowledge and understanding which Thou bestowest upon man, and for the spirit of constancy and courage born within him of Thy inspiration. We glorify Thee for the command which Thou dost give him over treasures of the mine and the strength of the hills, that he may make them the ministers of lessons of a gracious significance; and we humbly and gratefully recognize Thy presence in all which he achieves of beauty and power. The mind to devise and the will to accomplish, both are of Thee. From Thee cometh the artificer's skill; and to Thee the patience of faithful workmen, in whatever dexterous labor of the hands, equally renders laud and praise. It is in Thy favor, and through the operation of the Gospel of Thy grace, that cities stand in quiet prosperity; that peaceful commerce covers the seas; that peoples and nations separated by oceans are not severed in spirit, but continue allied, in common desire and in mutual regard, with happy recollections and with happier hopes . . . We pray that the Liberty which it represents may continue to enlighten with beneficent instruction, and to bless with majestic and wide bene-

diction, the nations which have part in this work of renown; that it may stand a symbol of perpetual concord between them; and that walking in the paths of knowledge and freedom, they may constantly advance in the wisdom of their councils, in magnanimous enterprise, and in the noble and salutary arts which are cherished by peace. . . . We pray for all the nations of the earth; that in equity and charity their sure foundations may be established; that in piety and wisdom they may find a true welfare, in obedience to Thee, glory and praise; and that, in all the enlargements of their power, they may be ever the joyful servants of Him to whose holy dominion and kingdom shall be no end. . . .[2]

At this auspicious event, Count Ferdinand de Lesseps' speech, given on behalf of the Franco-American Union, is moving and insightful as to the purpose and significance of this statue and her torch:

Citizens of America! I have hastened to accept the gracious invitation accorded me by the government of the Great American Republic, to be present today. It was a generous thought of those who presided at the erection of the Statue of Liberty. She has honored equally those who have conceived this spirit of hospitality and those who took great pleasure in accepting it. "Liberty Enlightening the World!" A grand beacon raised in the midst of the waves at the threshold of a free America! In landing under the rays of her kindly light we know that we have reached the country where the individual initiative is developed in all its power; where progress is religion; where large fortunes become the property of the people, to endow charities, to encourage education, to develop science, and to sow for the future seeds of greater benefit. . . .[3]

With the richness of this heritage and the Christian values upon which our American "Statue of Liberty Enlightening the World" was birthed, it is astounding, once again, to have viewed the media's centennial celebrations on television and national newspapers, referring to her just simply as "the great lady." The true historical importance and valuable Christian heritage pertaining to one of the greatest symbols of America's liberties and freedoms was covered up and eliminated from commentaries and interpretative material on the subject. "The Statue of Liberty Enlightening the World" is furthermore now coupled with Ellis Island as: "The Statue of Liberty-Ellis Island Foundation, Inc.," in its construction of the Immigrant Wall of Honor. This is in total conformity with the national phenomenon to strip this country of her true identity and magnanimity as a *Nation under God*.

(xiii) The Library of Congress

> ... It is the duty of every good citizen to use all the opportunities, which occur to him, for preserving documents relating to the history of our country.
>
> Thomas Jefferson, to Hugh P. Taylor, October 4, 1823
> (Quoted on the front page of the Library of Congress Rare Manuscript Division Literature)

The Library of Congress serves primarily as a research arm for Congress. It was established in 1800 with an appropriation of $5,000.00 to "furnish such books as may be necessary for the use of Congress."[1] This library, comprising the largest repository of organized knowledge in the world, houses more than 21 million books and pamphlets, together with more than 60 million manuscripts, maps, prints and photographs.[2] Among the library's greatest possessions are some of the most revered documents of American history, such as Jefferson's "Rough Draft" of the Declaration of Independence, one of the original copies of the Bill of Rights and the first two drafts of the Gettysburg Address in Lincoln's handwriting. *From these collections can be drawn the facts that are needed to frame informed legislation.*[3]

Housed within a small chamber in the Capitol building, its small collection at the outset comprised a mere 740 volumes and three maps. Today, it estimates an approximate collection of 97 million items. Rare book collections (such as those belonging to Tsar Nicholas II, George Washington and Thomas Jefferson), music, recordings, prints, photographs and copyright items are part of the collection.

Today, however, there is concern as to whether the Library of Congress will continue to uphold its standard of excellence as an historic resource.

On September 27, 1988, I had an interesting commentary given me by a senior librarian of a reading room in the Library of Congress, on the inside situation prevailing at this national library—the research arm to Congress, as follows:

> We had to fight tooth and nail to save the Main Card Catalogs (with the Library's earliest and most valuable recorded book collection upon them), from being "pulped"—destroyed—when the Main Reading Room was closed for "renovations"

on December 9, 1987. This was the decision of the Architect of the Capitol, who now has legal jurisdiction over the Library of Congress due to "renovations." We librarians, in light of the historic value of this Card Catalog, took it to our Union, The American Federation of State County and Municipal Employees, who fought it and won, by threatening to take them to court. This irreplaceable Card Catalog was thus saved in a matter of seconds (at the last minute.) That is the only way we were able to prevail. There is no other recourse.

The Retrospective Catalog was put on Premarc Computer. But it is filled with gross errors. It comprises 15th century to 1968 books. However, none of the 15th century books are on this Premarc catalog, which doesn't include everything. They took the lowest bidder for the transfer of Card Catalogs to Computer Tape. I would describe them as the type of little old ladies from Scotland. This Premarc Computer Catalog is rubbish. We librarians can't decipher it at all. They have the wrong information on the wrong field, e.g. the Author field in the Title Field, the Call Number field in the Pagination field, etc. It would take fifteen years and millions and millions of dollars to recreate the Computer Catalogs from the nonsense on the Premarc Computer Catalog. Typical errors on this Computer Catalog are: the creation of records for books that don't exist; and many on the shelf that don't exist in the Premarc Computer Catalog.

The new Librarian of Congress was installed October 15, 1987. He brought in his own people. There was a general exodus from the Library of Congress after he came in. They got rid of the Director of Personnel. The Chief of the Exhibits Office was reassigned to another post, in September 1988. Lewis Mortimer, Director of Personnel was reassigned to Federal Research. Many chiefs left or retired. There are 12–15 Divisions at the Library with missing chiefs to include the chiefs of the European Division; the Rare Book Division; the Asian Division; Federal Research Division (Classified for Military and State Department Documentation), which is located in the Navy Yard. When the heads of departments and directors get reassigned, you don't hear about them anymore.

Library of Congress Main Reading Room before closure "for renovations" and near destruction of Card Catalogs (below), on December 9, 1987. Historic Thomas Jefferson Building (c. 1897).

Over a billion dollars worth of books are in these two Rare Book Card Catalogs you see here. We librarians are adamant that we couldn't exist without a card catalog. When our Rare Book Reading Room was closed in 1985, we were promised that it would reopen six months' later. We are still waiting. They keep promising that when the renovations are over it will be much better. But I've seen the plans, and it will be worse. There will be no assigned office for the Chief of the Rare Book Division. I strongly objected to that. There will be no contact with Reference Collections; no contact with the readers; and no BOOKS. No librarian was consulted. This is the sole design of the Architect of the Capitol, George M. White. We librarians can't answer Reference questions without a Card Catalog. These Rare Books are one of a kind in the world, comprising books of such caliber and importance to the original records of the formation of the United States of America: the writings of our Founding Fathers; Thomas Jefferson wrote in the margins of some of the manuscripts; there are manuscript notes; meticulously preserved records on previous ownership; fine binds; artists' information, etc. This cannot be included on the Computer Catalog. This collection also comprises some of the original writings of the Reformers, and includes invaluable collections acquired over many, long years. Among the valuable collections in this Rare Book Reading Room are the Toner, Russian Imperial, Early American Children's Books, American Imprints, the Houdini and Lessing Rosenwald Collections and many others.

I think they are eliminating the Rare Book Library. They'll just have a Librarian.

When the librarians objected to the new plan for the Rare Book Reading Room, we were told: "Why don't you just move the furniture around." But it's bolted on the floor. I've been here 13 years. This kind of thing I can't put up with. I don't intend to be around when they reopen the Rare Book Reading Room. I've had other job offers.

I was punished and passed over for promotion and didn't receive salary increases. If you stand up for anything, you're a troublemaker and you are branded. No matter what you do, you're sabotaged. All projects and work which you do is set aside. You're held back while other people who agree with the changes are promoted, and get salary increases, honors and service awards.

A Memorandum from a *Senior Reference Librarian* to the *Acting Chief and Acting Supervisory Librarian*, dated November 24th, 1987, had for its subject: "Circulation Desk in the Renovated Rare Book Reading Room," and read as follows:

On November 20, 1987, a senior librarian showed the Reference Section the plans for the Circulation Desk in the renovated Rare Book Reading Room. These plans detail the actual physical setting of the Circulation Desk. They make clear that carrying out reference service will be extremely difficult. Beside the fact that all reference staff will be facing the wall in a blind area, the essential tools for reference and reader service will not exist. The most glaringly obvious of the many faults in this area are the lack of book distribution facilities, lack of shelving for reference books and bound catalogs and the location of the COMPAQ system on top of the shelflist.

The location of the COMPAQ system on top of the shelflist creates innumerable problems. The COMPAQ system is the most important tool of the Reference Section. The circulation, registration, and charge file systems will be on the COMPAQ. The COMPAQ will be used for other important projects like creating new bibliographies, publications, reports, and answering letters. With the COMPAQ on top of the shelflist, staff members will have to stand to use it, extended use will be physically challenging as well as impractical. It is unrealistic to expect staff to remain standing to use the system, yet if they sit down they cannot reach the keyboard.

The plan for the Circulation Desk leaves no room for book distribution. There is no space for book trucks and no shelves to hold rare books. Since the primary function of the desk is servicing books it is astounding that no space was found for this function. Books of all types seem to be banned from the desk as there is no shelving. Basic reference books necessary to answer the simplest reference questions will be shelved elsewhere. Staff will have to leave the Circulation Desk everytime a question is asked that requires a reference book. Between standing at the COMPAQ and running for reference books on top of retrieving rare books for readers, reference staff will face daily physical exhaustion early in the day.

The current plans for the renovation of the Circulation Desk will place the reference staff in a crisis situation from the opening day of the Rare Book Reading Room. The staff is being deprived of a functional work area and the basic tools essential in carrying out their duties. This crisis will certainly effect negatively the security and preservation of the national treasures under the jurisdiction of the reference staff.[4]

To back up this alarming testimony by a senior librarian, the Statement of AFSCME Local 2910 before the Committee on Appropriations, Subcommittee on Legislative Branch Appropriations, U.S. House of Representatives, 2/23/87, is here quoted:

We strongly recommend that the Committee appropriate funds to restore the Library's Main Card Catalogs to cabinets near the Main Reading Room after renovation. Management originally planned to do this. The present crisis in the MUMS/SCORPIO system makes it essential that we keep the card catalog as a back-up system. Current plans call for the catalog trays simply to be stacked on shelves after renovation in an inaccessible location, and ultimately to be discarded in about five years under the incorrect assumption that PRE-MARC, an error-ridden, truncated automated version of the Library's shelflist will provide adequate access to the Library's vast holdings not on the MARC database. The Library's own data indicate that over 50% of PREMARC records are defective. One example will suffice: there are more than two dozen different, incorrect, spellings of "United States" on PREMARC; the number of records with these incorrect spellings is not known to us, but none can be retrieved by a user looking for the correct spelling. Management's claim that a microfiche version of the main catalog will be an adequate substitute for the catalog itself is a notion strongly disputed by its own reference staff and also contradicted by an extensive body of professional literature and studies.[5]

Another report from the Library of Congress Professional Guild, the AFSCME Local 2910, dated 7/24/87, to Glen Zimmerman, the associate librarian for management, has for its subject: "Library's response to Guild's 2/23/87 Testimony before the Congressional Subcommittee on Legislative Branch Appropriations."

It is excerpted below, to show the seriousness of the crisis situation at our National Library of Congress, and "the Administration's determination to stick its head in the sand."

> . . . The persistence of the card catalog problem, in spite of the administration's determination to stick its head in the sand, was recently demonstrated (again) by the report of the 1987 class of Library of Congress Interns. This group of a dozen experienced staff members recently spent four months systematically visiting all departments of the Library, listening to positions on all sides of issues affecting the Library. . . . In January of this year they wrote in their collaborative final report:

> "Many of us were also deeply concerned about the library's plan to remove the card catalog from the Main Reading Room without replacing it with something that provides comparable access to the Library's collections. Comparable access does not appear to be possible through the use of the problem-plagued PREMARC file or the cumbersome K. G. Saur microfiche of the catalog. Continuing to make the catalog easily available for public use until the computer can provide the same information would seem a necessity; the plan to remove the card catalog from the Main Reading room without having upgraded the online catalog indicates a disturbing lack of interest in scholarly and public use on the part of Library management."

> Of course, this report, too, is being ignored . . .

> Regarding the matter of conference rooms being created in the gallery area overlooking the Main Reading Room (MRR), the Library's excuses are rather wide of the point at issue. There are 3,968 linear feet of shelf space in this area; and the administration is planning not to cover over the shelf-support uprights that are now in place there but rather to cut them out with blow torches, and thereby to eliminate for all future time the possibility of recovering this central area for bookshelves. The Jefferson Building does not need seven or eight conference rooms; the few that it does need can be planned in

other areas. The Main Reading Room, however, does need extra shelf space, and there is almost nowhere else to get it except in the gallery area. The assertion that the "colonnaded areas" will provide the extra shelf space overlooks the fact that these colonnades will be in entirely different reading rooms that will have different reference collections serving different purposes—i.e., they will not form a part of the Main Reading Room reference collection, which will most require additional space. The Library's reply here, in other words, is pure smoke screen.

One possible alternative for providing the needed extra shelf space lies in converting the existing card catalog cases (the A-F section now in MRR) to bookshelves rather than tearing them out entirely and replacing them with more desks. The general public will have more than 200 additional seats in any event when the 5th floor of the Adams Building is finished; increasing the number of readers' desks in the Main Reading Room while simultaneously decreasing the amount of shelf space available in the reference collection (on Deck 33) will inevitably lead to a dilution in the quality of service. We will no doubt win architectural awards for the beauty and symmetry of the room; but they will be won at the expense of quality reference service.

The primary reason more shelf space is needed in the Main Reading Room itself has to do with a peculiarity that sets the Library apart from many other research libraries: our closed stacks. When readers cannot browse the bookshelves directly, they are much more heavily dependent on indexes and bibliographies to provide access to the collection than they are in other libraries. The Main Reading Room, which is supposed to be the "index" to the whole "encyclopedia" (according to Dr. Boorstin's own plan!) therefore needs many more of these indexes and bibliographies—not many fewer—easily available to scholars if it is indeed to function as an index rather than a museum of architectural symmetry. But the function of a library reference collection in a closed stacks environment has not been attended to in the renovation plans. (And, yes, the reference staff has protested this, too, in vain.)

If we lose the card catalog easily available in cabinets after the renovation and also lose rather than gain shelf space for the ever-growing MRR reference collection, then there will indeed be a serious degradation in the quality of service the Library can offer. Again, there is much more involved in state-of-the-art reference service than merely adding more high-priced electronic gadgets—especially if the gadgets displace alternative systems that provide better access to the older materials (the vast bulk of the Library's treasures). One continually wonders where this administration has derived its peculiar notions of library science. . . .

Another senior librarian's commentary in October, 1988, this time coming from the Microfilm Reading Room of our national Library of Congress, sheds further light on the current disarray and confusion of this national repository for books which, only a few years' ago, was considered one of the most complete and efficient in the world:

Since the closure of the Library of Congress Main Reading Room on December 9, 1987, it has been very upsetting. Things are much more difficult than they were before. It has been a big disruption for everyone. We hear different things every day. The plans are bandied about then constantly changed. This Microfilm Reading Room was originally intended to stay here, in the Main Thomas Jefferson Building, but now we hear that it will be moved to the John Adams Building. There is a rearrangement of physical plans of all the Reading Rooms constantly. The MAP Committee of which Ellen Hahn is the head, has a Blueprint Plan, and knows the latest plans. It has been a big disruption for everyone. The workmen seen around here belong to the Architect of the Capitol. I miss the Main Reading Room. I assume they're going to preserve the interior and its valuable heritage for the American people.

To add to this disturbing takeover of our national collections and other facilities, notes from a scholar of many years currently doing research at the Library of Congress Rare Book Reading Room give us an indication of conditions from the public's viewpoint:

It has been ten months since the Main Reading Room in the Jefferson Building closed. At the same time, the Reference Collection in that room and the Main Card Catalog were shifted to deck 7 South in the Adams Building. The Renovation project has also made crossing from east decks of the Jefferson Building to the west decks and the reading rooms a true handicap course. Computer access and photocopying stations are now limited to the second floor Reading Room in the Jefferson Building. There is a photocopier in the Folklore but it is for use in that section. Much time is spent, walking from one location to another when formerly the catalog, the computer terminals, the reference collection and photocopying equipment were within steps of each other. I have estimated a loss of at least 25% of my time in surmounting these difficulties.

Another Library of Congress researcher whom I interviewed on 12/19/89, had this report to give:

In researching Turco-Armenian History, I have encountered several instances where titles have been missing from the shelf or "missing in inventory," although listed in the Card Catalogue. Specifically, in four days of research at the Library of Congress, I have requested twelve books, of which three were "missing in inventory." One of these had been published by the Government Printing Office: King, William Henry, *Turkish Atrocities in Asia Minor*. Washington, D.C., 1922. Another was the famous missionary account of atrocities to Armenians by missionary Grace H. Knapp, entitled: *The Mission at Van: Turkey in Time of War*. New York (Prospect Press) 1915. This book was reported four times as: "Missing in Inventory. Special Search cannot find it."

On April 11, 1990, frustrated and exhausted from receiving numerous call-slips returned with the notation "Missing in Inventory," I set about tracking down the plight of these priceless books, listed as part of the Library of Congress Collection in the Main Card Catalog. With the aid of a Stack Pass, I was able to go directly to the shelves themselves, finding the illusive, one-of-a-kind book *Turkish Atrocities in Asia Minor* exactly where its Card Catalog call number indicated it should be. I subsequently obtained a photocopy of this book, in order to show how the Library of Congress is making inaccessible to the public, books pertaining to Christianity. The title page of this book, published in 1922, reads:

> The Turkish Atrocities in Asia Minor and in the Pontus Speech given before the Greek Third National Assembly by G. Baltazzi (Minister of Foreign Affairs) May the 31st, 1922.

The interior of this suppressed exposé of atrocities committed to Christians in Asia Minor is excerpted as follows:

> . . . The idea which inspires all these crimes leaves no room for doubt. It is the systematic extermination of all Greeks and all Christians, in the countries placed under the direct administration of the Turkish Authorities. . . . To the long martyrdom of the Christians in Anatolia there is now added a new series of victims immolated for assuring the realization of the aim pursuited, that is, to change the complete ethnologic composition of the countries in which, for the most part, up to the present our religious fraternities were not in the minority. I have the firm hope that, without distinction of race or of religion all here who have in their souls the ideals of civilization and of justice will join in this protestation. . . .

(A chart lists 815 communities; 874 churches and 738 schools in the six provinces devastated, with a total Christian population of 303,287 exterminated).

> . . . In comparison with this work the massacres of extermination of the Christians in the time of Nero appear as nothing. Certainly, it is the most horrible example of savagery that history has ever recorded.

In the place of missionary Grace Knapp's famous book: *Mission at Van: Turkey in time of War*, (DS.640.K68) I found a recently inserted "Shelfmarker" with the terminology "Missing in Inventory" upon it. (See Reprint). In this stack shelf area, other valuable books on similar topics were noted as "Missing in Inventory," as follows:

Date of Marker:	Title:	Main Card Catalog No:
12/84	*Visits to Monasteries in . . .*	DS.58.Z9 1955
12/84	*Minorities in the Arab World* by A.H. Hourari	DS.58.H68
12/84	*The Middle East: Fourteen* by G. Perry	DS.62.P385 1983
12/84	*L'Empire du Levant, Histoire,* by R. Grousset	DS.62.G75
10/89	*France at War* by Rudyard Kipling	D.640.K65 1915a Copy 2.
10/84	*15000 KM* by Walter Kliukmuller	D.640.K672 Copy 2
12/84	*Theses for the Reconstruction. . .* by I. Velikovsky	DS.6l.V4 Copy 2
12/84	*Political Dictionary of the . . .* by Y. Shimoni	DS.6l.S52 1974

The two other copies of Rudyard Kipling's *France at War*, (D 640.K65 1915a and D640.K65 1915b Copies 2), however, were "charged to the Rare Book Collection" on 10/17/84, for specialized use only.

More than 300 Main Card Catalogs bear the title *Pilgrim Fathers*, denoting books pertaining to the true account of the 1620 Pilgrims at Plimouth Plantation in Massachusetts. However, scores and scores of "Missing in Inventory" shelfmarkers, dated May, 1989, have been inserted in the place of these priceless, one-of-a-kind books on America's founding period heritage and history. Some of these are listed below:

Date of Marker:	Title:	Main Card Catalog No:
5/89	*The Pilgrim and the Book*	F68.M145 Copy 2
5/89	*The First Plymouth Patent*, Council for New England	F68.C85 Copy 3
5/89	*The Pilgrims of Plymouth*	F68.B38
5/89	*In the Days of the Pilgrim Fathers*	F68.C9
5/89	*Commonwealth History of Massachusetts*	F64.H322 (Vols. 3 and 4)
5/89	*Biographical Sketches of the Fathers of New England*	F68.C55
5/89	*The Mayflower Pilgrims*	F68.C29
5/89	*Colonial Expansion*	F68.C37
5/89	*Massachusetts List of Plays*	F68.M398
5/89	*The Women of the Mayflower* . . .	F68.N952
5/89	*The Story of the Pilgrim Fathers*	F68.H43
5/89	*A Sermon*, by John Chester	F68.C52 Copy 2
5/89	*Of Plimoth Plantation*	F68.B8073
5/89	*Living in the Time of the Pilgrim Fathers*	F68.A46
5/89	*Scenes and Characters of the Massachusetts Bay Colony*	F64.B75
5/89	*History of Massachusetts* by Alden Bradford	F64.B8 Copy 2
5/89	*A Pageant of Pilgrims*	F68.B32

Among the *Pilgrim Fathers* collection of books which were "charged to the Rare Book Collection" in May of 1989, the following are listed:

Date of Marker:	Title:	Main Card Catalog No:
5/89	*A Sermon at the Publick Lecture in Boston, Jan.*	F67.S545

The Library of Congress "missing in inventory" syndrome. Above: *A Pageant of Pilgrims* by Esther W. Bates—"Missing in Inventory," 6/12/90. Left: *Living in the times of the Pilgrim Fathers*—"Missing in Inventory," 5/19/89. Right: *The English Ancestry and Homes of the Pilgrim fathers*—one of many books "checked to Rare Book Collection," 5/19/89.

LIBRARY OF CONGRESS Collections Management Division SPECIAL SEARCH REQUEST	Date 3/31/90	SPECIAL SEARCH REPORT

INSTRUCTIONS:
1. A report will be sent to you. Give full mailing address or research facility assignment.
2. A carbon is being made. Write with ball point or pencil.
3. Allow up to one month for reply. Bring report to Alcove 7 to claim books held.
4. Books not claimed by the end of the reservation period will not be retained in Alcove 7.

APR 2 1990

Book/Call No.

E.302.
J454

Author *Thomas Jefferson*
Title *The Complete Jefferson*
Volume, Date, Other Pertinent Data

Will accept other edition ☑ Yes ☐ No
Wish locations of other libraries holding this title if not located ☐ Yes ☐ No

Name *Catherine Millais*

SPECIAL SEARCH REPORT
☐ The item requested is being held on reserve until _____ in Alcove 7, Main Reading Room.
☐ The item is not in the general collections, but may be requested in _____ Room _____, Building _____
☐ The item is in use inside the Library. If your need is urgent, contact the Special Search Unit, Alcove 7, Main Reading Room.
☒ The item is not available because:
  ☐ It is on outside loan, and recall was not yet successful.
  ☐ It is not owned by the Library.
  ☐ It has been recorded as missing. You may renew your request in 60 days and another search will be made.
  ☐ It has been declared lost.
  ☒ It could not be located.
  ☒ A record has been kept of your request and if the item is located before the end of the next calendar year you will be notified.
  ☐ _____

S/L

LIBRARY OF CONGRESS Collections Management Division SPECIAL SEARCH REQUEST	Date 3/31/90	SPECIAL SEARCH REPORT

INSTRUCTIONS:
1. A report will be sent to you. Give full mailing address or research facility assignment.
2. A carbon is being made. Write with ball point or pencil.
3. Allow up to one month for reply. Bring report to Alcove 7 to claim books held.
4. Books not claimed by the end of the reservation period will not be retained in Alcove 7.

APR 2 1990

Book/Call No.

E.332.
J454

Author *Thomas Jefferson*
Title *The Declaration of Independence*
Volume, Date, Other Pertinent Data

Will accept other edition ☑ Yes ☐ No
Wish locations of other libraries holding this title if not located ☐ Yes ☐ No

Name *Catherine Millais*

SPECIAL SEARCH REPORT
☐ The item requested is being held on reserve until _____ in Alcove 7, Main Reading Room.
☐ The item is not in the general collections, but may be requested in _____ Room _____, Building _____
☐ The item is in use inside the Library. If your need is urgent, contact the Special Search Unit, Alcove 7, Main Reading Room.
☒ The item is not available because:
  ☐ It is on outside loan, and recall was not yet successful.
  ☐ It is not owned by the Library.
  ☐ It has been recorded as missing. You may renew your request in 60 days and another search will be made.
  ☐ It has been declared lost.
  ☒ It could not be located.
  ☒ A record has been kept of your request and if the item is located before the end of the next calendar year you will be notified.
  ☐ _____

S/L

Library of Congress Research Facilities.

5/89	*The First Plymouth Patent, Council for New England*	F68.C85 Copy 2
5/89	*The Mayflower Compact*	F68.M452
5/89	*The Mayflower Compact*	F68.M45
5/89	*The Mayflower and the Pilgrim Fathers*	F68.M44
5/89	*Leyden Documents relating to the Pilgrim Fathers*	F68.L68
5/89	*New England's Memorial* by Nathaniel Morton	F68.M89
5/89	*New England's Prospect*	F67.W877
5/89	*The Character and Blessedness of the Upright*	F67.W87
5/89	*The English Ancestry and Homes of the Pilgrim Fathers*	F68.B19
5/89	*The Valley of Baca* by Cotton Mather	F67.S535
5/89	*A Discovery occasioned by the death of the Honorable Stephen Sewell*	F67.S55
5/89	*New England's Memorial* by Nathaniel Morton	F68.M885

and many others.

In another stack shelf section, this time on the reformation and its exposés of popism and counterfeits to Christianity, the same phenomenon exists. Scores and scores of books have been replaced with recently inserted shelfmarkers bearing the terminology: "Missing in Inventory." Among these is John A. Ryan's book *The State and the Church*. An even stranger occurrence was here noted: Scores and scores of books have been recently "charged to the Rare Book Collection" which is only available to researchers doing specialized projects, dissertations, theses or to authors of books. This precludes the general public's accessibility to its own collection, placed in the custody of the Library of Congress! Some of the valuable books, property of the people of the United States, and recently "charged to the Rare Book Collection" are here enumerated:

Date of Marker:	Title:	Main Card Catalog No:
7/81	*The Practical Divinity*	BX.1763.C55
7/81	*The French Convert*, 1793	BX.1763.F8
7/81	*The French Convert*, 1798a	BX.1763.F8
7/81	*The French Convert*, 1798	BX.1763.F8
7/81	*The French Convert*, 1802	BX.1763.F8
7/81	*The French Convert*, 1810	BX.1763.F8
7/81	*The French Convert*, 1830	BX.1763.F8
7/81	*The French Convert*, 1841	BX.1763.F8

(Thus expunging *all* copies of this valuable book from the general public's view).

7/81	*George Fox*	BX.1763.F7
7/81	*The Protestant Tutor* By Benjamin Harris	BX.1763.H34
7/80	*Memoirs of John Gordon*, 1734	BX.1763.G63
7/81	*An Introduction to the Study* . . .	BX.1763.H9
7/81	*A Recantation Sermon*	BX.1763.H3
7/81	*Joseph Hall* (no title given)	BX.1763.H2
7/80	*Triumphs of Rome*	BX.1763.H197
7/81	*A Master Key* . . . 1773	BX.1763.G2
7/81	*The Apology of John Ball*	BX.1763.B2
7/81	*The Pedigree of Heritiques*	BX.1763.B26
7/81	*Elechus* . . .	BX.1763.B3
7/80	*The Safe Religion* 1657	BX.1763.B38
7/81	*Full and Easie* . . .	BX.1763.B34
7/81	*The Religion of Rome*	BX.1763.B4
7/81	*Certaine Catolicke*	BX.1763.C4
7/81	*Reponse a la Profession de Foy*	BX.1763.C45
7/81	*Catholicke* . . .	BX.1763.C47
7/81	*A Replie to Jesuit Fishers*	BX.1763.W57
7/81	*Some Thoughts upon the Spirit*	BX.1763.W65
7/81	*Spiritus* . . .	BX.1763.S65
7/80	*The Difference between the Church and Court of Rome*, 1674	BX.1763.L7
7/81	*The Difference between the Church and Court of Rome*, 1647a	BX.1763.L7
7/80	*Resolutis* . . . by Martin Luther	BX.1763.L77
7/80	*The Unreasonableness of Impiety*	BX.1763.116
7/80	*Popery Anatomized*, 1672	BX.1763.W4

7/80	*Saul and Samuel at Endor,* copy 2, 1674	BX.1763.B7
7/80	*Saul and Samuel at Endor,* copy 3, 1674	BX.1763.B7
7/80	*Judgement of God upon the Roman Catholic Church, 1689*	BX.1763.C7
7/80	*A Quartron of Reasons*	BX.1763.D5
7/80	*An Essay* . . . by Paul Dudley	BX.1763.D75
9/80	*Historic Romish Treasons and Usurpations,* 1671	BX.1763.F6
7/81	*The Papists' Bait*	BX.1763.G27
7/81	*A Master Key to Popery 1725*	BX.1763.G3
7/81	*The Tyranny of Satan*	BX.1763.G23
7/81	*A Newyeare's Gifte*	BX.1763.G25
7/81	*Synopsis Papism, 1634*	BX.1763.W73
7/80	*The True Mark of the Beast*	BX.1763.P43
7/81	*A Reformation*	BX.1763.P45.B5
7/80	*Popery exposed by its own Authors, 1718*	BX.1763.M7
7/81	*A Short* . . . by J. Morland	BX.1763.M8
7/81	*Of True Religion* by John Milton	BX.1763.M63
7/80	*Letter from Rome*	BX.1763.M6
7/80	*The French and Protestant Companion* 1719	BX.1763.M25
7/81	*Popish Idolatry*	BX.1763.M4
7/81	*The Masterpiece of Imposture*	BX.1763.G6H3
7/81	*A Letter to* . . .by Charles Wharton	BX.1763.W53
7/81	*Commpanella,* by Henry Stubbs	BX.1763.S77
7/81	*(No Title given)* by Henry Stubbs	BX.1763.S78
7/81	*Popish Policies*	BX.1763.S73
7/81	*Romish Ecclesiastical*	BX.1763.S7
7/80	*Ancient and Modern Delusions*	BX.1763.P4
7/81	*John Niccol's Pilgrimage* . . .	BX.1763.N6
7/81	*Idee* . . .	BX.1763.O6
7/81	*A Declaration,* by John Niccols	BX.1763.N55
7/81	*A most Horrid but True Copy*	BX.1763.M83
7/81	*Den Roomschen,* by Jacbobus Lydius	BX.1763.L8
7/81	*The Candor, 1779*	BX.1763.PM2
7/80	*Discourses, 1754*	BX.1763.P34
7/81	*Five Sermons*	BX.1763.S4

7/81	*Rome's Conviction, 1783*	BX.1763.S3
7/80	*Iac. Lectii ie.,* by J. Lectius	BX.1763.L4
7/81	*A Short Survey . . . 1609*	BX.1763.R5
7/81	*A Conscise. . .* by Charles Wharton	BX.1763.W5
7/80	*Pot au Noir (Rel. Papiste Ren.) 1787*	BX.1763.P6
7/80	*De Necessaria*	BX.1763.T8
	Secessione Nostra. . .	
7/81	*The Tryal*	BX.1763.T7
7/81	*A Dissuasive* by Jeremy Taylor	BX.1763.T3
	(No indication on Shelfmarker	
	whether "Missing in Inventory"	
	or "Charged to Rare Book	
	Collection")	
7/80	*Letters, 1753*	BX.1763.T6
7/81	*A Reply. . .*by Charles Wharton	BX.1763.W55

Among those "Missing in Inventory" the following are enumerated:

Date of Marker:	Title:	Main Card Catalog No:
7/81	*Saul and Samuel at Endor*	BX.1763.B7 Copy 1
7/81	*A Catholicon*	BX.1763.W7
7/81	*Rome's Conviction*	BX.1763.S3
7/81	*The Picture of a Papiste*	BX.1763.O65

Of further interest is the fact that numerous volumes of H. Prideaux's *The Old and New Testament Connections* were "charged to the Rare Book Collection" on 12/5/84; Volumes 1 and 2 of the 1720 edition being charged to the Rare Book Thomas Jefferson Collection (Main Card Catalog No: DS.62.P8.)

All of the above-listed shelfmarkers, whether "Missing in Inventory" or "Charged to the Rare Book Collection" I photocopied, showing a tremendous loss to the American public of valuable, one-of-a-kind, true Christian documents pertaining to our faith and the faith of our forefathers.

Early in August, 1990, while I was doing research on George Washington's little-known personal collection of books and his three-volume, hand-autographed, yet *unclassified* (never been cataloged) Bible, a frightening new addition to our national Rare Book Collection met my eye. It was none other than the *Playboy*

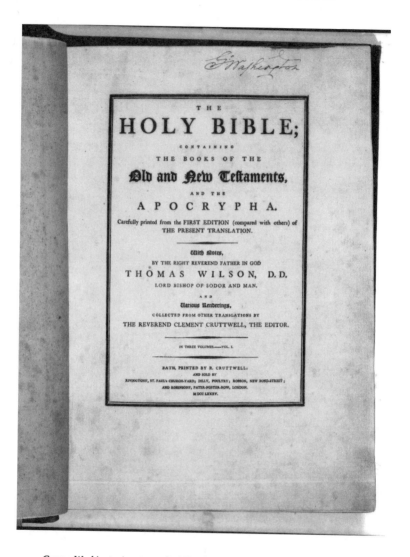

George Washington's autographed Family Bible (unclassified). Rare Book Collection, Library of Congress.

Index (Card Catalog No. AP2 P692), incorporated in May 1987 within this collection of priceless Bibles and Christian foundational books on America's true origins. These editions stood boldly on the Rare Book Reference Shelf, next to our Revised Standard Version of Holy Scripture, together with biographies of great American heroes. One must be blind to ignore the seriousness of the situation at our national Library of Congress—the fact that George Washington's personal, autographed Bible is *unclassified;* thus no one would know it was part of the collection unless one searched one-by-one through the Card Catalogs consisting of thousands of rare Bibles! Yet *Playboy Magazine Index* has been brazenly classified as part of America's Library of Congress Rare Book Collection! In addition, I have had insurmountable difficulties in obtaining duplicates of the title pages and contents of unique volumes, such as George Washington's personal, autographed *Journals of Congress,* commencing with the First Prayer in Congress; Samuel Adams' famous August 1, 1776, Oration from Independence Hall (where he states unabashedly that "Our Forefathers threw off the yoke of popery in Religion; for you is reserved the honor of levelling the popery of Politicks. They opened the Bible to all, and maintained that capacity of every man to judge for himself in Religion. Are we sufficient for the comprehension of the sublimest spiritual truths, and unequal to material and temporal ones? . . .") (Card Catalog no. E.211.063); John Winthrop's 1644 *only* original (unchanged and untampered) account of the Massachusetts Bay heresies (Card Catalog no. BR.520.W7. 1644). Although signed and approved on August 3, 1990, by the Rare Book Collection Chiefs for photoduplication, and paid for in the total amount of $122.50, according to the Library of Congress prepayment policy, on September 12, 1990, I was told by the Library of Congress Photoduplication Services that the Rare Book Chiefs had "changed their minds," refusing photoduplication. They stated that they were not responsible, regardless of large sums of money having been prepaid. I secured a copy of the preapproved, prepaid order. It bears bold, black lines drawn through it by the very same Rare Book Collection Chiefs who had signed and approved it in my presence, six weeks prior!

A newly prepared Rare Book Division Memorandum, dated August 10, 1990, was then displayed at the Rare Book check-in counter by the Rare Book Chiefs, Mr. Peter von Wingen, and Mr. Clark Evans. It reads:

ANSWERS TO COMMONLY ASKED QUESTIONS ABOUT PHOTODUPLICATION IN THE RARE BOOK AND SPECIAL COLLECTIONS DIVISION

How can I get copies of Rare Material?

Reproductions of Rare material are available as black and white prints, color transparencies or color slides. All requests for reproductions are handled by the Photoduplication Service, John Adams Building, Room G–1011 (Mon–Fri, 8:30–4:45, tel: 202–707–5740). There are no public photocopying facilities in the Rare Book and Special Collections Division.
SPECIAL NOTE: The Rare Book Division regrets that it can no longer send its material for microfilming or photocopying. We hope that in the near future equipment and procedures will be available which will limit damage to the Rare books under our custody.

How much does it cost?

A list of services and charges is available in the Rare Book Reading Room or the Photoduplication Service. All cost estimates are made by the Photoduplication Service.

On November 7, 1990, I was told by the Rare Book Chiefs that they did not know where Abraham Lincoln's 1847 Family Bible (with his inscribed family records) was, although it is listed in the Rare Book Card Catalog (unclassified)! On November 13, 1990, after much prayer, it was "discovered" by a librarian of the Rare Manuscript Division (now housed in the James Madison 2nd Annex of the Library of Congress) in a box in the back. As it is not cataloged in the Rare Manuscript Division under "Presidential Papers—Abraham Lincoln," it was found quite by chance. This librarian told me that Lincoln's family Bible had been valued at $17.00—written within its inner cover! I was finally given permission by the Rare Manuscript Chief to examine in detail Lincoln's 1847 Family Bible—one of America's greatest treasures.

What a tremendous tragedy is occurring at the Library of Congress, regarding the custody and availability of America's greatest and most valuable original documents, proving indisputably that her origins of government stemmed from biblical truth! All the more so as these valuable, original, one-of-a-kind books are not on microfiche, nor are they available in any other form.

Main Vestibule (Great Hall) of Library of Congress

A December, 1989 Memorandum circulated to Guide Services states the newest and most devastating blow to the American public, millions of whom travel long distances to visit their national Library of Congress yearly. Under the direction of George M. White, Architect of the Capitol, the Main Vestibule or Great Hall, which comprises this library's splendor and magnificence, with two of its most valuable books in the world, *The Gutenberg Bible* and the *Great Bible of Mainz*, will be closed for "renovations" on June 29, 1990, until "well into the 1990s." Unless their plan is thwarted, Americans will lose access to "the most beautiful building in the world," (its reputation at the opening in 1897), together with the original *Gutenberg Bible* and the *Great Bible of Mainz* which are the only two permanent items exhibited within this beautiful, godly setting, as a focal point for many long years. A recent, May 30, 1990 *verbal* communiqué from the Library of Congress Public Affairs Office, states that these two priceless gems of America's Christian heritage will be placed in the modern 1980 James Madison Memorial Building Annex, to the left of the main entranceway, out of sight of the flow of people. Once again, nothing whatever on the plight of these two Jefferson Main Vestibule permanent exhibits is available in *writing*, or any form of public announcement.

After two months of fruitless requests, telephone calls, letters and formal, written requests (recommended by the Legal Counsel to George M. White, Architect of the Capitol), in order to consult the blueprints of the Jefferson Building Main Vestibule, on March 23, 1990, we were finally permitted limited access to view these blueprint plans. However, we were expressly forbidden to photocopy them, being informed by the office of the Legal Counsel to Mr.

George M. White that the *Library of Congress was exempt from the Freedom of Information Act*. A foremost American architect and myself consulted these blueprints. After careful study and scrutiny of these plans, he informed me that the "minor touch-ups" did not warrant closure of this building to the public at all, more especially as there was "no working contract" for its "renovations" (The Jefferson Building Main Vestibule named "Phase II" in the blueprints); thus closing this valuable historic landmark to millions of Americans without being able to "renovate" anything.

To add fuel to the fire, the American Federation of State, County and Municipal Employees, in their February 23, 1987, Statement to the Committee on Appropriations, Subcommittee on Legislative Branch Appropriations, U.S. House of Representatives, gave the following warning in respect to plans for "renovations" of the famed Jefferson Building:

> Plans for renovation and post-renovation space utilization have been developed with no input from the reference staff. The proposed colonnades in the Jefferson Building for example, not only are an extravagant expense but are a hindrance to the staff's ability to provide good reference service. There are plans to provide eight conference rooms and a private dining room in the Jefferson Building, while there will be inadequate space to house its reference collections. Only quick Committee action can prevent the execution of questionable plans like these.

The new "Exhibit Hall" of our national Library of Congress, which is on the Mezzanine Level of the Jefferson Building Main Vestibule, is in a magnificent chamber which has been barred to the public for "renovations" for the past three years. However, it was reopened from 1 p.m.-6 p.m. on May 29, 1990, uniquely to honor Raisa Gorbachev with a reception and the opening of an "Old Believers" Exhibit. I was present toward the close of this event. Unbeknownst to the American public, the walls of this formerly beautifully designed hall have been repainted with rows and rows of grotesque gargoyles or demons' heads, removing and replacing the original godly designs adorning its walls since 1897. Another prominent corridor which connects the North East and South East Entrances, and which was closed for "renovations" since the closure

Newly painted designs over original godly decor on the S.E. and N.E. Corridor walls in historic Thomas Jefferson Building.

Library of Congress Main Vestibule or Great Hall—Main historic Jefferson Building, closed to the public June 29, 1990. "for well into the 1990s."

of the Main Reading Room "for renovations" on December 9, 1987, was also briefly opened from 1:00 p.m.-6:00 p.m., May 29, 1990. I was appalled at the ugly gargoyles or demons' heads and animalistic designs replacing the original godly, beautiful decor, which I had admired for more than 10 years while working at our national Library of Congress. Guards and library employees told me that "management" had refused to touch up the original designs, removing and replacing them with these grotesque faces (see photographs). Unless the plan to close the Jefferson Main Vestibule of the Library of Congress for "renovations" and "touch-ups" (without a working contract) is thwarted, there is serious question as to management's trustworthiness in "touching-up" the interior of one of America's most valuable historic landmarks, which exudes godliness and Christian values upon wall and ceiling.

Recently, a copy of a letter from E. Clay Shaw, Jr., member of Congress, has been put into my hands. In response to one of many letters of inquiry to the Library of Congress regarding America's Christian heritage within the Main Vestibule or Great Hall, he reports the following:

> ... The Main Reading Room and the Great Hall are the centers of construction. Both areas are being renovated to match their original 18th century decor. ...

What would stop management from painting over America's Christian heritage, as has been done on the walls and ceilings in the chamber and corridors already discussed? Unless God's people in America rise up and take a stand against such blasphemy: *nothing*.

Also recently, thousands of American visitors have been rerouted to the James Madison Memorial Building (2nd Library of Congress Annex), a modern, 1980 office building. The Interpretative Film and Guided Tours Center has been moved from the historic Thomas Jefferson Building to this modern annex. This is truly one of the greatest tragedies in the nation's history, especially as the interior of the Main Vestibule or Great Hall has been boarded up from within. To date, no workmen can either enter or exit, the blueprints having had no specifications or working contract. As predicted by the lack of specifications, no renovations can proceed. Thus the Jefferson Main Vestibule is closed "for well into the 1990s."

The beautiful and symbolic bronze doorway, which welcomed millions into the inner sanctum of Christian, patriotic and historic truth, is boarded up from within with a large, yellow sign greeting visitors: "*EMERGENCY EXIT ONLY.*"

On November 13, 1990, I visited the (c. 1980) James Madison Memorial Building (2nd Annex of the Library of Congress), in order to view the plight of the *Gutenberg Bible* (world's most valuable book), and the magnificent *Great Bible of Mainz.* Immediately upon entering, the visitor is greeted with a large sign announcing the new, November, 1990, Exhibit "A World of Names," consisting of bright-colored travelogue posters, enveloping and blighting these two sacred items of America's Christian heritage—having been removed from the permanent habitat within the Jefferson Main Building Great Hall at its closure, June 29, 1990.

This new exhibition—by the U.S. Board on Geographic Names—filled the James Madison Memorial Hall.

On either side of the revered *Gutenberg Bible* are large posters depicting, among others, The Big Apple, a girl and a cat, "Future City," a muddied soccer player, Korean Airlines and Japanese traditional costume.

To each side of the *Great Bible of Mainz,* Lessing Rosenwald of Philadelphia's priceless gift to America, large posters depict: Honolulu, a New Orleans Mardi Gras masquerade ball, Taos Pueblo, a modernistic rendition of Walla Walla and a giant skier.

At the end of this hall is the famed white marble statue of James Madison. This work of art executed by Walker Hancock, shows the Father of the Constitution confidently seated in a large chair, "alert and ready to respond to arguments" according to the sculptor's own words.

To either side and behind this moving memorial to the "Champion of Religious Freedom" are walls plastered with bright-colored T-shirts (to the left) and a multi-colored totem pole (to the right), both prominently visible from the vantage point of the *Gutenberg Bible* and the *Great Bible of Mainz,* which testify to God's hand upon our nation.

Should we, as God-loving and God-fearing Americans, stand by and allow the Library of Congress, as custodians of our nation-

James Madison Memorial Building, 2nd Annex of Library of Congress. The plight of the *Great Bible of Mainz* (above) and the *Gutenberg Bible*, submerged in travelogue posters, as shown by Mardi Gras Masquerade costumes, in the U.S. Board of Geographic Names Exhibit, (11/90–5/91). Below: The *Great Bible of Mainz* empty encasement, 4/28/91.

Library of Congress Main Jefferson Building, Main Entrance, boarded up 4/28/91.

The bronze "Torch of Learning" (1893) atop the Library of Congress historic Thomas Jefferson Building (1897). Sculptor: Edward Pearce Casey. The torch welcomes all who wish to delve into its vast array of knowledge on the foundations of America. Below: The kiosk constructed in Fall, 1990, in front of the Main Entrance to the James Madison Memorial Building, 2nd Annex of Library of Congress, 1980. The dome is counterfeit of the bronze masterpiece with the spike replacing the "Torch of Learning" (symbolizing scholarship).

James Madison Memorial Building. The new kiosk depicting the future agenda of Library of Congress management for famed Thomas Jefferson Building, to "celebrate the humanistic legacy of the world."

al Christian heritage, to disrespect God's Holy Word by submerging these two priceless volumes in worldly, materialistic slogans?

Upon exiting the James Madison Memorial Building, I examined the new circular "kiosk" just built in the front of this edifice since closure of the Main Jefferson Historic Building. It clearly represents a "spoof" of the magnificent "Torch of Learning" atop our national Thomas Jefferson Library of Congress main dome (see photographs). Symbolically, however, in order to denigrate all scholarship and higher learning, which the Historic and Rare Book Collections of the Jefferson Building exemplify, this new dome is designed as an abstract to the magnificent "Torch of Learning," with a Spike in place of the Torch (i.e. light, enlightenment, enlightening and illumination of the mind), once again shifting the emphasis from the grandeur and nobility of the original design to a meaningless counterfeit, which now serves to display posters, predominantly of new exhibits and events, and sales items. Under one poster entitled, "Thomas Jefferson Building," one reads: "The Thomas Jefferson Building (1897), the grand old building of the Library of Congress now undergoing renovation, will reopen in 1993. Meanwhile, it continues to offer some services to researchers. . . . Following its renovation, the Thomas Jefferson Building will celebrate the humanistic legacy of the world. It will contain reading rooms for the study of every region and culture. . . ." (see reprint). By the above we can now see the agenda of management in closing the historic Jefferson Building—to replace our American Christian legacy with *the humanistic legacy of the world!*

A Step Further:

On April 6, 1991, while conducting a Christian Heritage Tour for 70 internationals, we were dismayed to witness empty thermostated encasements where the *Gutenberg Bible* and *Great Bible of Mainz* have been displayed for many decades without interruption. In place of these books, two signs read, respectively: "The *Gutenberg Bible (Great Bible of Mainz)* has been removed from display for conservation reasons."

At my visit on April 28, 1991, the *Great Bible of Mainz* was still missing. My question is this: These priceless Bibles pertaining to America's Christian heritage are *permanent exhibits* of the Library of

Congress, never once removed from their same thermostated encasements while displayed in the historic Jefferson Building Main Vestibule. Why, then, should the public be deprived of this Christian legacy now? Should we deprive millions of Americans from viewing the original Constitution, Declaration of Independence and Bill of Rights, displayed in similar, thermostated encasements, at our National Archives in Washington, D.C., for "conservation reasons"? The latter are aged and on frail parchment which yellows and falls apart more easily than vellum. Yet they remain on permanent exhibition without interruption. *The Gutenberg Bible* and *Great Bible of Mainz* are leatherbound volumes beautifully printed and calligraphied on sturdy vellum, the inner skin of a young animal, and in excellent condition! Is it not, once again, to eradicate the Word of God from America's culture and civilization?

On June 3, 1991, just prior to the publication of *The Rewriting of America's History*, a visit to the James Madison Memorial Hall, to review the plight of the famed *Gutenburg Bible* and *Great Bible of Mainz*, revealed the following.

The 11/90 thru 5/91 exhibit "A World of Names" had just run its course. A new, permanent, handsome beige marble display stand had just been built adjacent to the *Great Bible of Mainz* display cabinet, which rivets the visitor's attention, prior to accessing our famed Bible. A large, prominent, new stand-up sign announces the identity of this new exhibit:

> The Bicentennial of the Polish Constitution—All power shall be derived from the will of the people.

> May 3, 1791, marks a supreme moment in Polish history, and indeed, in modern Western Constitutional development. Despite its considerable size and population, Poland had suffered from internal strife and from continuous aggression of its more powerful neighbors. On October 6, 1788, King Stanislaus Augustus Pontiatowski boldly initiated a new parliament— since known as the Four-year Sejm—presided over by two renowned patriots . . . Thomas Jefferson was to declare the Polish Constitution one of the three most notable of the period. The May 3rd Constitution represents nothing less than the first written fundamental law in modern Europe. Although the commemoration of this date has been suppressed by political

circumstances for most of the past 200 years, the Constitution's combined message of personal liberty and Polish national spirit insured it a life that will outlive tyranny.

Jefferson's leatherbound copy of the 1791 English translation of the Polish Constitution of 1791, entitled "New Constitution of the Government of Poland," had been dug out of Jefferson's extensive library of law books, housed in the Library of Congress Law Library, and prominently displayed within the new, permanent beige marble display cabinet—right next to the *Great Bible of Mainz*.

From the above we see clearly management's agenda: to submerge the *Gutenburg Bible* and the *Great Bible of Mainz*—God's Holy Word—in secular exhibits pertaining to commerce and travel; and to bypass the entire meaning of the James Madison Memorial Hall, with its white marble, seated statue of James Madison and this founding father of the U.S. Constitution's words upon its walls, lauding the United States Constitution. It is a Constitution that has worked admirably for 200 years—unlike the Polish Constitution, which, although a viable document in its own right, certainly cannot be equated with America's remarkable freedoms and liberties, described by founding father, Thomas Jefferson himself, as "the gift of God."

It would be truer to Madison and Jefferson's beliefs, both of whom were proponents of the Christian religion and called "Champions of Religious Freedom," to have displayed one of Jefferson's numerous books on Christianity and law, such as Horatio Grotius's famed *The Truth of Christian Religion*, which forms the basis for all international law, next to the *Great Bible of Mainz*.

But *who*, in this case, is "management," or who researches and writes up these biased and slanted "legacy of the world" exhibits, supplanting and undermining our own United States historic legacy, one might ask?

The June 24, 1991 testimony of a senior librarian who holds 16 years' seniority at the Library of Congress given to me, disclosed that there are four "rare book specialists" comprised of "two American history specialists, one European specialist and one specialist in Book Arts." Their task is "to work on the exhibits, publications and guides to the Library of Congress."

Book taken from Jefferson's original library. Hugo Grotos was the "father of international law," and highly esteemed by Jefferson. (The sections marked are Jefferson's handwriting.)

The numerous times I have used the Rare Book Reading Room Collections, these "specialists" sat at desks near the scholars, flipping through books throughout the day. The total restructuring and rewriting of America's historic legacy to fit a mold reflecting management's new "humanistic legacy of the world," bypassing our nation's true identity, would thus easily be explained. Also easily explained would be the insurmountable obstacles I have had in obtaining the preapproved, prepaid photoduplications on America's Christian history books from the Rare Books Chiefs, and their refusal to date to execute the order.

USSR Fascination

Coupled with the one-day reopening of the new "Exhibit Hall" for the Gorbachev reception, there seems to be a real bias and fascination with the Soviet Union. To gain further insight into management's fascination with the USSR's products, the following lines excerpted from literature promoted by the European Division of the Library of Congress, adjacent to the new site of our Rare Book Division (since its closure for "renovations" in 1985), are cited below. Put out by the *USSR Academy of Sciences*, they decry American imperialism and world domination, as follows:

> September, 1987 (Volume 9)—Asia and Africa today
> USSR Academy of Sciences—Russian Edition.

> . . . The ideology and politics section carries the article by Y. Mova who tells the reader about the attempts by the US and its allies (with the help of a thoroughly planned propaganda campaign) to indoctrinate the peoples of Asia, Africa and Latin America with all kinds of western stereotypes. The propaganda is meant to brainwash the public in the three continents and deprive the revolutionary liberatory movements of their ideologic weapons. The author cites facts proving that US has been increasing its ideologic expansion over the developing world over the present administration's term of office. . . .

> October, 1987 (Volume 10)—Asia and Africa Today
> USSR Academy of Sciences—Russian Edition

... U.S. imperialism, while using Kuwaitan oil and capital
for developing its own industry, has tied this small country to
its economy by a "double knot," which tells negatively on
Kuwait's socio-economic situation. ...

November, 1987 (Volume 11)—Asia and Africa today
USSR Academy of Sciences—Russian Edition.

... He (Doctor of History, A. Kiva) reminds the reader that
Lenin emphasized the world-wide significance of the Russian Revolution, consisting in the fact that its most important features will be repeated in other countries. ...

This same *USSR Academy of Sciences* is quoted has having
resuscitated volumes and rare books never before exhibited in its
own country, for Raisa Gorbachev's "Old Believers" Exhibition
which opened at our national Library of Congress Main Vestibule
on May 29, 1990. Sponsored by Armand Hammer, this exhibition
closed the day management had fixed for closure of the magnificent
Jefferson Building Main Vestibule for "renovations"—June 29,
1990.

Main Reading Room Reopens
On June 3, 1991, the reopening of the Main Reading Room to
researchers and Readers—two-and-one-half years later than quoted on an official 11/87 Library of Congress Memorandum to
Librarians and Scholars—occurred.

Just prior to the publication of *The Rewriting of America's History* my visit to the reopened Main Reading Room, accessed only
from the rear S.E./N.E. corridor of the Thomas Jefferson Building
disclosed its new identity.

A predominant, handsomely-framed, new information
plaque, focally placed at the left-hand side (access side) of the
main entranceway to the "Computer Catalog Center" read as follows:

The Main Reading Room

... The structure was designed not merely to accommodate
more books and scholars than the old quarters in the Capitol

could handle, but to gather under one roof the recorded human achievement throughout time and from all the civilizations of the world . . . a delegation of Congressmen visited the famous libraries and monuments of Europe, and ordered the architects to build something grand—only grander—to stake their claim that the young nation would soon overtake the old world. One can see in the size and shape of the Reading Room with its soaring dome and rotunda shape, as well as in the lavish ornamentation used throughout the building, the influences of the British Library, La Bibliotéque Nationale and the Paris Opera. Thus, this building embodies the ebullient self-confidence and the passionate belief in the on-going progress of humankind towards enlightenment that informed the culture of America at the turn of the century.

The above is a total misstatement of fact based upon the library's true identity and beginnings. It was established in 1800 with an appropriation of $5,000.00 from Congress "to furnish such books as may be necessary for the use of Congress," i.e. the Congress of the United States of America. This purpose and function carried over to its magnificent 1897 building, and continues to the present time.

In my careful study and knowledge of the Jefferson Building's Main Vestibule and Main Reading Room, these spectacular chambers do not reflect influences of British and French culture, but are predominantly American in their artistic, architectural and sculptural expression.

A 1904 history book in the Library of Congress Rare Book Collection states that:

This building, the most perfectly arranged structure in the world for the use and storage of books, was begun in the year 1888. The first Act of Congress providing for the construction of the Library of Congress was approved by President Cleveland on April 15, 1886, and its terms adopted the plans submitted by John L. Smithmeyer, architect of Washington, D.C. In October, 1888, a new Act of Congress was approved, placing the work under the control and management of Thomas Lincoln Casey, Chief of Engineers of the army, and on the death of General Casey in March 1896, he was succeeded by Bernard R. Green, C.E., and under his charge the building was completed in February, 1897, within the limit of time set by Congress and $150,414.66 below the limit of cost, or, in exact figures, for $6,344,585.34. . . . The Library is in the style of Italian Renaissance. . . . The Central feature of the building is the Reading Room, an octagonal hall 100 feet in diameter and 125 feet in height, lighted by eight large semicircular windows, 32 feet wide. This room has a seating capacity for 250 readers, furnishing each a desk with four feet of space to work in . . . It is the magnificent series of mural and sculptural decorations with which the architecture is enriched that has contributed most to give the Library its notable position among American public buildings. . . ."[6]

Another 1897 rare history book in the same collection tells us that "The capacity of the additional shelving which may be placed in the first and second stories . . . is somewhat less than one hundred miles of shelving."[7]

From the above we see that the 1897 historic Thomas Jefferson Building is "the most perfectly arranged structure in the world for the use and storage of books." The primary function of this building's construction was clearly for books and scholarship for Congress, thus a predominantly American enterprise, and not one geared toward "all civilizations of the world." Further, the style of the building is Italian Renaissance, being the artistic expression of 50 foremost American sculptors, painters and craftsmen. It is in no wise the reflection of the Paris Opera, the British Library and the French National Library—I am familiar with all three of these structures; but it is truly and uniquely a product of American creativity. The building material employed for the exterior walls is white granite from New Hampshire and for the inner courts, Maryland granite and white enameled bricks. The interior is rich in choice marble from Europe, Africa and America.[8]

America being a Christian nation, we see two magnificent Scriptures in bold, gold lettering above the Main Reading Room pillars representing RELIGION and SCIENCE. They are: "What doth the Lord require of thee, but to do justly, to love mercy, and to walk humbly with thy God" (Micah 6:8)—two of God's graceful angels hold up this scriptural admonition; and, "The heavens declare the glory of God and the firmament showeth His handiwork" (Psalm 19:1), respectively. Further to this, we see two more resplendent

Above: The Main Reading Room of the Library of Congress. The Statue representing "Religion"—Micah 6:8. Below: "The Manuscript," by John W. Alexander, mural painting depicting Old and New Testament manuscripts engrossed and illuminated by monastic scribes of the Middle Ages. (On wall above permanent exhibition place for the *Gutenberg Bible*, Main Vestibule of Jefferson Building.

inscriptions glorifying God above the pillars for HISTORY and PHILOSOPHY, namely: "One God, one law, one element, and one far-off Divine event to which the whole creation moves" (Alfred, Lord Tennyson); and "The enquiry, knowledge and belief of Truth, is the sovereign good of human nature" (Bacon), respectively.[9]

Charles W. Eliot, former president of Harvard University was the sole consultant for the writings on the walls and ceilings. The Main Vestibule walls and ceilings radiate Christian, patriotic and traditional American themes in their inscriptions and paintings, such as the mural painting entitled "THE FAMILY. A mother holding with outstretched arms her babe who welcomes his father returning from the hunt. Grandparents and two older sisters beaming with affection complete the group."[10] Other inscriptions glorify God, such as: "Nature is the Art of God" (Thomas Browne); "There is but one Temple in the Universe and that is the body of man" (Novalis); and "How charming is Divine Philosophy" (Milton).[11] Another magnificent mural painting is entitled: "The Manuscript." It forms part of "The Evolution of the Book" wall paintings by John W. Alexander, and shows monastic scribes engrossing and illuminating biblical manuscripts in the Middle Ages. The last of these is "The Printing Press" of Johan Gutenberg, whose breakthrough in printing produced our famed *Gutenberg Bible*.[12]

The Main Vestibule portrays 26 beautifully sculptured cherubs lining both sides of the exquisite white marble stairwells which lead to the Mezzanine level and Visitor's Gallery. The work of sculptor Martiny, each cherub represents a different discipline, such as the cherub of "art," with a pallet; the cherub of "agriculture," with a sheaf of wheat; the cherub of "music," with a lyre and music book; the cherub of the vineyard with grapes, etc. Throughout the Main Reading Room and Main Vestibule are sculptured angels and cherubim, of which the Scriptures abound. They give God all the glory.[13]

Quite in keeping with this Christian theme in sculpture, are the two handsome bronze statues to either side of RELIGION in the Main Reading Room. They are MOSES with the Ten Commandments (his name being on the rear Visitors' Gallery wall), representing the Old Testament; and PAUL, the apostle chosen by Christ to bring the gospel of salvation to the gentiles.[14]

The Government of the Republic

The Lobby of the Main Reading Room main entranceway (in the Main Vestibule) shows forth five panels by Elihu Vedder. They symbolize "The Government of the Republic" and the results of good and bad administration. The panel of Government is above the beautiful main doors to the Main Reading Room. On the right are Good Administration, Peace and Prosperity; on the left, Corrupt Legislation and Anarchy. Government holds in her left hand a scepter and in her right hand a tablet upon which are inscribed Lincoln's words from his famed Gettysburg Address: "A Government of the people, by the people and for the people."[15]

The Seals of the United States and Executive Departments

Altogether synonymous with the Americanism of this building, are patriotic themes, such as that of George W. Maynard's "The Discovery and Settlement of America." Portrayed in the ceiling are Courage, Valor, Fortitude and Achievement (Southwest Pavilion, Second Floor). And the seals of the United States and Executive Departments are large motifs on the walls and ceiling of the Second Floor North West Pavilion. The work of W.B. van Ingen and E.E. Garnsey, they are: "Treasury and State," with George Washington's inscribed words: " 'Tis our true policy to steer clear of permanent alliances with any portion of the foreign world," and Webster's "Let our object be our country, our whole country and nothing but our country." "Thank God! I also am an American."; "War and Navy," with inscriptions quoted from George Washington—"The aggregate happiness of society is, or ought to be, the end of all government." "To be prepared for war is one of the most effective means of preserving peace."; and "Justice and Post Office."

In the central inner dome is the great seal of the United States. Forty-eight stars for America's 48 states, adorn the U.S. flag. Encircling the whole are Lincoln's famed words: "That this nation under God shall have a new birth of freedom."[16]

The Representatives' Reading Room

To crown this building's reflection of godly Truth, are the ceiling paintings of the Representatives' Reading Room (South curtain). There are seven Lights of Civilization and their poignant meanings, as follows: *Indigo*—Light of Science; *Blue*—Light of Truth (The Spirit of Truth is trampling the dragon of Error. The figures in the corners hold the Bible); *Green*—Light of Research; *Yellow*—Light of Creation (The Creator, Almighty God is depicted with His Word: "Let there be light" Genesis 1:1); *Orange*—Light of Progress; *Red*—Light of Poetry; *Violet*—Light of State is that of the Republic, America supports the shield of the United States, her liberty cap is inscribed 1776. She is attended by an eagle. In the border are mottoes, "Liberty, Suffrage, Justice and Fraternity."[17]

Forty Great American Heroes

Woven into the mosaic ceiling above the *only two* permanent exhibits of the Main Vestibule—*The Gutenberg Bible* and *The Great Bible of Mainz* (removed at closure of Main Vestibule to public, 6/29/90)—are giants of America's Christian history, such as Jonathan Edwards and Cotton Mather; the nation's foremost sculptors and architects, such as Thomas Crawford (who sculpted "Armed Freedom" atop the U.S. Capitol dome); Thomas U. Walter (who designed the U.S. Capitol dome); and Benjamin LaTrobe, one of the U.S. Capitol's greatest architects, who also designed "the church of the presidents" in 1816. Also featured are Hiram Powers (who sculpted "Faith, Hope and Charity") and Gilbert Stuart, whose celebrated portrait of George Washington hangs in the East Room of the White House. Some of America's greatest composers, such as Louis Moreau Gottschalk (the first person to incorporate American musical themes into symphonic orchestration), also find their place among the 40 Americans representing our religious, artistic and scientific heritage.

Quotations from many of this country's literary geniuses, such as Henry David Thoreau's "Books are the treasured wealth of the World"; together with Milton's "A good book is the lifeblood of a master spirit," in gold lettering, stand out to either side of the bronze doorway, the interior of which has been described "as a vision in polished stone."

How much more American could our Library of Congress Jefferson Building be?

The above is but a glimpse of the all-American Christian heritage and history which our 1897 Thomas Jefferson historic Main Vestibule and Main Reading Room exude in their written and artistic expression—a proud legacy to be passed on to future generations.

I was aghast at the "new" interior of the Library of Congress Main Reading Room, after its three-and-a-half-year closure "for renovations." New plush carpeting promotes management's predominant symbol, which recurs throughout the chamber. It is a replica of a large directory, complete with index tabs, encircled by leaves and berries, and designed within a circle. It replaces the Library of Congress original insignia of a ribboned wreath enveloping an open book upon which rests an incense urn, symbolizing scholarship and learning. The new, open directory symbol amply describes the general idiocy of the "Computer Catalog System" for its pages portray illegible flowered designs, with a flower-like design at the top of the page. By and large, these large, carpet designs, together with multiple flowered, circular designs recurring throughout the new carpeting, detract from scholarship and concentration, clashing with the 19th-century original decor of the historic Main Reading Room.

The Main Card Catalog, having been removed from its centrally-situated focal position within the Main Reading Room at closure 12/9/87, is now tucked away in a side, back room (Deck 33), with no signs or direction available to visiting scholars, researchers and readers who would not know their research capability, and are thus being crippled intellectually by the 50 percent defective "new" Computer Catalog, taken from the Shelf List! On the inside door of Deck 33 is the sign: "MAIN CARD CATALOG (A–Powell—through 1980) For books cataloged after 1980, use Computer Catalog." Further, in the past few years, prior to the Reopening of the Main Reading Room, an uncanny phenomenon has occurred; almost every Card Catalog (representing each volume) on the original, one-of-a-kind Christian historical books of our great American patriots, has been "Charged to the Rare Book Collection." This is also evidenced by the numerous call slips recently returned to scholars with the notation: "Charged to the Rare Book Collection." This large-scale exodus of America's original Christian historical volumes from the General Collection has only occurred in the past few years. Thus, these books are no longer accessible to the general public—to individual thinkers, researchers, writers and inquirers into the wealth of our nation's true origins.

Ultramodern computer equipment (for self-service) is now to be found at each Main Reading Room alcove, replacing the former unsurpassed reference materials, librarians and Main Card Catalog research facilities, which made our National Library of Congress one of the most efficient and best-equipped scholarship libraries in the world. As Librarian of Congress, James H. Billington's testimony to the House of Appropriations, February 5, 1990, requested (and received) 326 million dollars of taxpayers' funds for Fiscal Year 1990, it is not surprising that such grandiose and luxurious "renovations" and wall exhibits were accomplished by management, to the great detriment of America's scholarship and heritage.

Are we, the people of the United States, for whom government was instituted, and in whose hands we have confidently placed the priceless and irreplaceable treasures of our historic past, to stand idly by, as we see our nation stripped of all that we cherish and hold near and dear to ourselves and our children?

The Thomas Jefferson Library of Congress historic building and its priceless collections are worth defending—for without the one-of-a-kind original books validating America's true Christian history, no proof remains to refute and destroy the lies, deceit and distortions promoted by the enemies of our land, who have rewritten a powerful nation's history—one that confidently asserts without apology or hesitation: *"IN GOD IS OUR TRUST."*

Anything which reflects on the negative is far from being popular in present-day America. However, as this national Library of Congress contains not only the valuable original records pertaining to our American Christian heritage, but also to our founding period history, replete with original writings of the founding fathers, it represents firsthand evidence that we *are* a Christian nation. Thus its importance, and the dire necessity to thwart closure of the historic Jefferson Building Main Vestibule, exuding Christianity upon wall and ceiling, and comprising *the only public* access to this landmark, to preserve and restore the Card Catalogs to the Main Reading Room, to restore the Rare Book Reading Room to its original blueprint plan before it was disbanded in 1985 and to continue to make available to the public the Rare Book Reading Room Card Catalogs, (comprising thousands of the rarest and most priceless Bibles in the world) for individual research and consultation. This is the duty of our national library in its service to the public, without the control and manipulation of original sources and research facilities, the most important and crucial of which are the original Main and Rare Book Card Catalogs.

(xiv) In God We Trust—America's Coins Show in Whom We Place Our Trust

The following correspondence addressed to Hon. S.P. Chase, Secretary of the Treasury, and dated November 13, 1861, reveals how even our coins came to be symbolic of our Christian heritage:

Dear Sir:

You are about to submit your annual report to Congress respecting the affairs of the national finances.

One fact touching our currency has hitherto been seriously overlooked. I mean the recognition of the Almighty God in some form on our coins.

You are probably a Christian. What if our Republic were now shattered beyond reconstruction? Would not the antiquaries of succeeding centuries rightly reason from our past that we were a heathen nation? What I propose is that instead of the goddess of liberty we shall have next inside the 13 stars a ring inscribed with the words "perpetual union," within this ring the allseeing eye, crowned with a halo; beneath this eye the American flag, bearing in its field stars equal to the number of the States united; in the folds of the bars the words "God, liberty, law".

This would make a beautiful coin, to which no possible citizen could object. This would relieve us from the ignominy of heathenism. This would place us openly under the Divine protection we have personally claimed. From my heart I have felt our national shame in disowning God as not the least of our present national disasters.

To you first I address a subject that must be agitated.
(sgd) M.R. Watkinson
Minister of the Gospel
Ridleyville, PA.[1]

A few days after reading its contents, the Secretary of the Treasury addressed his response to the Director of the Mint in Philadelphia, as follows:

Dear Sir:

No nation can be strong except in the strength of God or safe except in His defense. The trust of our people in God should be declared on our national coins.

You will cause a device to be prepared without unnecessary delay with a motto expressing in the fewest and tersest words possible this national recognition.

Yours truly,
(Sgd). S.P. Chase[2]

A further letter from the Secretary of the Treasury to James Pollock, director of the Mint, dated December 9, 1863, finalizes the conviction that our nation's strength lies in Almighty God and His defense.

He writes:

I approve your mottoes, only suggesting that on that with the Washington obverse the motto should begin with the word 'Our,' so as to read:

"Our God and our Country." And on that with the shield, it should be changed so as to read: "In God we Trust."[3]

Thus it was that by Act of Congress, dated March 3, 1865, "In God We Trust" was inscribed upon our United States coins. In the past few years, we have witnessed an aborted attempt by the enemies of Christianity and America to remove this godly symbol from our United States currency. The truth of its poignant message, however, is a daily reminder to Americans where our allegiance lies: upon Almighty God and His providence (blessings) upon our land.

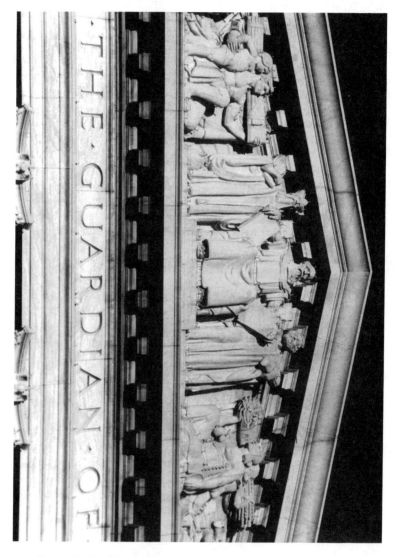

"Justice, the Guardian of Liberty" portrays God's servant, Moses, in the center, with the two tablets of the Law, the Ten Commandments, in either hand. Lawmakers of the past stand on either side. Marble bas-relief by Herman MacNeil. Positioned above the Chief Justice's head outside East Portico, Supreme Court of the United States. Photo by John W. Wrigley.

(xv) The Supreme Court

The Supreme Court of the United States had its beginnings in a handsome red brick building of Georgian design, to the left of Independence Hall in Philadelphia. From 1791–1800 the first three Chief Justices—John Jay, John Rutledge and Oliver Ellsworth—presided over the Court, handing down its earliest decisions from the attractive courtroom. John Jay, first Chief Justice, was also President of the American Bible Society. The Supreme Court had seven seats in 1807, increasing to nine in 1837, to 10 in 1863, and then decreasing to eight in 1866. The seating finally stabilized at nine in 1869, with one Chief Justice seated in the center and four Associate Justices on either side.[1]

A phenomenon of great interest to all visiting the Supreme Court is the different sizes, shapes and widths of the Justices' chairs. The question arises: Why are the Justices' chairs so different? The reason is that each Justice makes his or her own selection, based upon personal comfort and preference.

The Supreme Court moved from Philadelphia to the newly completed Capitol Building in February, 1801. It convened in six different locations until 1935, when our magnificent Vermont marble Supreme Court edifice, opposite the Capitol grounds, was completed and opened for court sessions. Designed by foremost American architect Cass Gilbert, it resembles a neo-classic Roman temple, but it is replete with biblical themes within and without its handsome walls.

The sculpture over the east portico of the building is entitled: JUSTICE THE GUARDIAN OF LIBERTY. Moses is the central figure, holding the two tablets of THE TEN COMMANDMENTS, one in either hand, stark reminder of the origin and basis for our American legal system.[2]

The Ten Commandments

One gains access to the inner courtroom through an attractive oak doorway. Each door has beautifully engraved upon its lower half, the Ten Commandments of Almighty God (Exodus 20).

The inner courtroom of the Supreme Court shows four marble bas-relief panels beneath the ceiling on each of the four walls. Each has a particular story to tell. The panel directly above the bench where the Chief Justice and eight Associate Justices are seated, depicts "The Power of Government" and "The Majesty of the Law." Between these two allegorical figures, THE TEN COMMANDMENTS stand out in a position of prominence. The seated figure representing "The Power of Government" has his elbow squarely resting upon God's Ten Commandments, showing from whence our power is derived.[3]

Rewritten History

The curators of the Supreme Court have taken the liberty of rewriting its own artistic themes, which are engraved in solid marble. By omitting any mention of the Ten Commandments, prominently featured as a focal point above the Chief Justices' head (in their rewritten caption) the entire message and importance of this sculpture is by-passed. These sculptured panels are the workmanship of master American sculptor, Adolf A. Weinman. This world-renowned sculptor is also noted for his sculpture of Thomas Jefferson presenting his Declaration of Independence to the committee appointed to evaluate it, which is found above the main entranceway to the Jefferson Memorial in our nation's capital.

A plaster model of the panel above the bench depicting the Ten Commandments has been recast and placed on exhibition on the ground floor of the Supreme Court building, North Entrance, with a caption deleting any mention of God's Ten Commandments, designed by the sculptor as its focal point. It reads as follows:

> East Wall plaster model of Courtroom Frieze
> The central focus of the frieze located directly above the Bench
> is on the seated figures representing "Majesty of the Law" and
> "Power of Government."
> Artist: Adolph A. Weinman.

Whether the curators of the Supreme Court agree with this or not, it is not in their scope of jurisdiction to remove The Ten Commandments from their new, rewritten descriptive caption!

"The Ten Commandments" (Exodus 20), marble of bas-relief, stand in prominence above the Chief Justice's head, Inner Courtroom of the Supreme Court. Two allegorical figures, "The Power of Government" (left) and "The Majesty of the Law" (right) flank "The Ten Commandments." Courtesy: Supreme Court of the United States.

"The Struggle between Good and Evil with Good Prevailing," marble bas-relief,
Inner Courtroom, Supreme Court. Courtesy: Supreme Court of the United States.

The Struggle between Good and Evil with Good Prevailing

On the wall opposite the bench is Adolph Weinman's sculpture entitled: "The Struggle Between Good and Evil with Good Prevailing." The sculptor has portrayed the figures on the left representing Security, Harmony, Peace, Charity and Defense of Virtue, who triumph over Corruption, Slander, Deceit and Despotic Power, depicted on the right with two serpents.[4] The sculptor had personified God's good versus Satan's evil, with his characters, who could well be taken out of Galatians 5:22–23. It depicts a clash between God's virtues and laws, or the fruit of the Holy Spirit, and the evil works of Satan.

Both marble sculptures in the Inner Courtroom of the Supreme Court, highest court in the land, stand out as awesome reminders that truly we are a Christian nation.

Supreme Court Justice David J. Brewer, who served from 1890–1910, gave a magnificent lecture entitled *The United States a Christian Nation*,[5] which is hereunder excerpted. This brilliant American statesman dealt with the subject from every conceivable aspect—academic, educational, legal, constitutional, cultural, economic, executive, biblical and symbolic—leaving no stone unturned:

> We classify nations in various ways, as, for instance, by their form of government. One is a kingdom, another an empire, and still another a republic. Also by race. Great Britain is an Anglo-Saxon nation, France a Gallic, Germany a Teutonic, Russia a Slav. And still again others are heathen, and still others are Christian nations.
>
> This Republic is classified among the Christian nations of the world. It was so formally declared by the Supreme Court of the United States. In the case of Holy Trinity Church vs. United States, 143 U. S. 471, that Court, after mentioning various, circumstances, added, "these and many other matters which might be noticed, add a volume of unofficial declarations to the mass of organic utterances that this is a Christian nation." (Unanimous opinion, Feb 29, 1892)
>
> But in what sense can it be called a Christian nation? Not in the sense that Christianity is the established religion or that the

people are in any manner compelled to support it. On the contrary, the Constitution specifically provides that "Congress shall make no law respecting an establishment of religion, or prohibiting the free exercise thereof." Neither is it Christian in the sense that all its citizens are either in fact or name Christians. On the contrary, all religions have free scope within our borders. Numbers of our people profess other religions, and many reject all. Nor is it Christian in the sense that a profession of Christianity is condition of holding office or otherwise engaging in the public service, or essential to recognition either politically or socially. In fact the Government as a legal organization is independent of all religions.

Nevertheless, we constantly speak of this Republic as a Christian nation—in fact, as the leading Christian nation of the world. This popular use of the term certainly has significance. It is not a mere creation of the imagination. It is not a term of derision but has substantial basis—one which justifies its use. Let us analyze a little and see what is the basis.

Its use has had from the early settlements on our shores and still has an official foundation. It is only about three centuries since the beginning of civilized life within the limits of these United States. And those beginnings were in a marked and marvelous degree identified with Christianity. . . .

Christianity Inspired Colonies

It is not exaggeration to say that Christianity in some of its creeds was the principal cause of the settlement of many of the colonies, and co-operated with business hopes and purposes in the settlement of the others. Beginning in this way and under these influences it is not strange that the colonial life had an emphatic Christian tone. . . .

In Delaware, by the Constitution of 1776, every officeholder was required to make and subscribe the following declaration: "I, A.B., do profess faith in God the Father, and in Jesus Christ His Only Son, and in the Holy Ghost, one God, blessed forevermore; and I do acknowledge the Holy Scriptures of the Old and New Testament to be given by divine inspiration."

New Hampshire, in the Constitutions of 1784 and 1792, required that senators and representatives should be of the "Protestant religion." And this provision remained in force until 1877.

The fundamental Constitutions of the Carolinas declared: "No man shall be permitted to be a freeman of Carolina, or to have any estate or habitation within it that doth not acknowledge a God, and that God is publicly and solemnly to be worshipped."

The Constitution of North Carolina, of 1776, provided: "That no person who shall deny the being of God or the truth of the Protestant religion, or the divine authority either of the Old or New Testaments, or who shall hold religious principles incompatible with the freedom and safety of the State, shall be capable of holding any office or place of trust or profit in the civil department within this State." And this remained in force until 1835, when it was amended by changing the word "Protestant" to "Christian," and as so amended remained in force until the Constitution of 1868. And in that Constitution among the persons disqualified for office were "all persons who shall deny the being of Almighty God.". . .

Christianity Fundamental to Office Holding

In Maryland, by the Constitution of 1776, every person appointed to any office of profit or trust was not only to take an official oath of allegiance to the State, but also to "subscribe a declaration of his belief in the Christian religion." In the same State, in the Constitution of 1851, it was declared that no other test or qualification for admission to any office of trust or profit shall be required than the official oath "and a declaration of belief in the Christian religion; and if the party shall profess to be a Jew the declaration shall be of his belief in a future state of rewards and punishments." As late as 1864 the same State in its Constitution had a similar provision, the change being one merely of phraseology, the provision reading, "a declaration of belief in the Christian religion, or of the existence of God, and in a future state of rewards and punishments."

Mississippi, by the Constitution of 1817, provided that "no person who denies the being of God or a future state of rewards and punishments shall hold any office in the civil department of the State."

Another significant matter is the recognition of Sunday. That day is the Christian Sabbath, a day peculiar to that faith, and known to no other. It would be impossible within the limits of a lecture to point out all the ways in which that day is recognized. The following illustrations must suffice: By the United States Constitution the President is required to approve all bills passed by Congress. If he disapproves he returns it with his veto. And then specifically it is provided that if not returned by him within ten days, "Sundays excepted, . . ." after it shall have been presented to him it becomes a law. Similar provisions are found in the Constitutions of most of the States, and in thirty-six out of forty-five is the same expression, "Sundays excepted". . .

By decisions in many states a contract made on Sunday is invalid and cannot be enforced. By the general course of decision no judicial proceedings can be held on Sunday. All legislative bodies, whether municipal, State or national, abstain from work on that day. Indeed, the vast number of official actions, legislative and judicial, recognizes Sunday as a day separate and apart from the others, a day devoted not to the ordinary pursuits of life. . . .

God's Name Prevails

While the word "God" is not infrequently used both in the singular and plural to denote any supreme being or beings, yet when used alone and in the singular number it generally refers to that Supreme Being spoken of in the Old and New Testaments and worshipped by Jew and Christian. In that sense the word is used in constitution, statute and instrument. In many State Constitutions we find in the preamble a declaration like this: "Grateful to Almighty God." In some he who denied the being of God was disqualified from holding office. It is again and again declared in constitution and statute that official oaths shall close with an appeal, "So help me, God." When, upon inauguration, the President-elect each four years consecrates himself to the great responsibilities of

Chief Executive of the Republic, his vow of consecration in the presence of the vast throng filling the Capitol grounds will end with the solemn words, "So help me, God." In all our courts witnesses in like manner vouch for the truthfulness of their testimony. The common commencement of wills is "In the name of God, Amen." Every foreigner attests his renunciation of allegiance to his former sovereign and his acceptance of citizenship in this Republic by an appeal to God.

These various declarations in charters, constitutions and statutes indicate the general thought and purpose. If it be said that similar declarations are not found in all the charters or in all the constitutions, it will be borne in mind that the omission oftentimes was because they were deemed unnecessary, as shown by the quotation just made from the opinion of the Supreme Court of Louisiana, as well as those hereafter taken from the opinions of other courts. And further, it is of still more significance that there are no contrary declarations. In no charter or constitution is there anything to even suggest that any other than the Christian is the religion of this country. In none of them is Mohammed or Confucius or Buddha in any manner noticed. In none of them is Judaism recognized other than by way of toleration of its special creed. While the separation of church and state is often affirmed, there is nowhere a repudiation of Christianity as one of the institutions as well as benedictions of society.

In short, there is no charter or constitution that is either infidel, agnostic or anti-Christian. Wherever there is a declaration in favor of any religion it is of the Christian. In view of the multitude of expressions in its favor, the avowed separation between church and state is a most satisfactory testimonial that it is the religion of this country, for a peculiar thought of Christianity is of a personal relation between man and his Maker, uncontrolled by and independent of human government.

Notice also the matter of chaplains. These are appointed for the army and navy, named as officials of legislative assemblies, and universally they belong to one or other of the Christian denominations. Their whole range of service, whether in prayer or preaching, is an official recognition of Christianity. If it be not so, why do we have chaplains?

Christ Honored in All States

If we consult the decisions of the courts, although the formal question has seldom been presented because of a general recognition of its truth, yet in The People vs Ruggles, 8 John. 290,294,295, Chancellor Kent, the great commentator on American law, speaking as Chief Justice of the Supreme Court of New York, said: "The people of this State, in common with the people of this country, profess the general doctrines of Christianity, as the rule of their faith and practice.". . .

The New York Supreme Court, in Lindenmuller vs. The People, 33 Barbour, 561, held that:

"Christianity is not the legal religion of the State, as established by law. If it were, it would be a civil or political institution, which it is not; but this is not inconsistent with the ideal that it is in fact, and ever has been, the religion of the people. This fact is everywhere prominent in all our civil and political history, and has been, from the first, recognized and acted upon by the people, as well as by constitutional conventions, by legislatures and by courts of justice. . ."

In Arkansas, Shover vs. The State, 10 English, 263, the Supreme Court said: "This system of religion (Christianity) is recognized as constituting a part and parcel of the common law. . ."

If now we pass from the domain of official action and recognition to that of individual acceptance we enter a field of boundless extent, and I can only point out a few of the prominent facts:

Notice our educational institutions. I have already called your attention to the provisions of the charters of the first three colleges. Think of the vast number of academies, colleges and universities scattered through the land. Some of them it is true, are under secular control, but there is yet to be established in this country one of those institutions founded on the religions of Confucius, Buddha or Mohammed, while an overwhelming majority are under the special direction and control of Christian teachers. . .

The Bible, the Guide to Life

You will have noticed that I have presented no doubtful facts. Nothing has been stated which is debatable. The quotations from charters are in the archives of the several States; the laws are on the statute books; judicial opinions are taken from the official reports; statistics from the census publications. In short, no evidence has been presented which is open to question. I could easily enter upon another line of examination. I could point out of the general trend of public opinion, the disclosures of purposes and beliefs to be found in letters, papers, books and unofficial declarations. I could show how largely our laws and customs are based upon the laws of Moses and the teachings of Christ; how constantly the Bible is appealed to as the guide to life and the authority in questions of morals; how the Christian doctrines are accepted as the great comfort in times of sorrow and affliction, and fill with the light of hope the services for the dead. On every hilltop towers the steeple of some Christian church while from the marble witnesses in God's acre comes the universal but silent testimony to the common faith in the Christian doctrine of the resurrection and the life hereafter.

But I must not weary you. I could go on indefinitely, pointing out further illustrations both official and non-official, public and private; such as the annual Thanksgiving proclamations, with their following days of worship and feasting; announcements of days of fasting and prayer; the universal celebration of Christmas; the gathering of millions of our children in Sunday Schools, and the countless volumes of Christian literature, both prose and poetry. But I have said enough to show that Christianity came to this country with the first colonists; has been powerfully identified with its rapid development, colonial and national, and today exists as a mighty factor in the life of the Republic. This is a Christian nation. . .

It behooves us to complete this chapter on the Supreme Court with a poignant message inscribed above the main, Pennsylvania Avenue Entrance to the Department of Justice building. It encapsulates the application of The Ten Commandments to each and every life:

> Justice in the Life and Conduct of the State is possible only as first it resides in the hearts and souls of the citizens.

Conclusion

As we began *The Rewriting of America's History* with a true portrayal of Christopher Columbus and his godly vision in the discovery of America in 1492, so we close with the Supreme Court of the United States, judiciary branch of the United States government. On June 21, 1989, this court voted that U.S. Flag-burning was a constitutional act—a far cry from the patriotism, fervor and zeal which characterized the founding of our nation, and George Washington's meticulous design of the Stars and Stripes to represent a unique new republic. On March 21, 1989, the day of the Supreme Court's hearing of this case—Texas vs. Johnson, members of the Revolutionary Communist Party, U.S.A., vigorously demonstrated on the East Lawn of the Capitol, opposite the Supreme Court, giving out literature entitled "It's Time for the People's Verdict on Burning the U.S. Flag."

Greg "Joey" Johnson is quoted as follows:

> We live in a sick and dying empire that's desperately clutching at its symbols.

A prominently encased announcement on the bottom of this Revolutionary Communist Party, U.S.A., Informative Sheet, states:

> The Emergency Committee of the Supreme Court Flag Burning Case has called for:
>
> 12 noon Tuesday, March 21 Rally and National Press Conference East Lawn of the Capital across from the Supreme Court.
>
> No Supreme Court Suppression of Antipatriotism! Burning the American Flag is Not a Crime! Antipatriotism is not a Crime!
>
> Also Tuesday evening: 8 pm William Kunstler, David Cole, Joey Johnson and others will speak on:
>
> "What's at Stake in this Case"
> American University, Washington D.C.
> Ward Building, Auditorium 2
>
> (On the A.U. Campus, corner of Massachusetts and Nebraska)

Of particular import and relevance to *The Rewriting of America's History* is the following blatant statement made quite brazenly and without any trace of apology whatever—to either God or country:

> If Joey's conviction is reinstated it will be a chilling and far-reaching decision. It will send a message that the government intends to suppress those who oppose and reject all that the U.S. stands for. It will be a major step to reverse verdicts of the '60's and to reimpose the "my country right or wrong" mentality by criminalizing antipatriotism and anti-americanism. Think about it. It will amount to government regulation on what are "acceptable" forms of protest and what is the "acceptable content" of political resistance. It will disallow a wide range of symbolic speech. It will open the door to compulsory patriotism in many forms, including mandatory flag salutes in the schools. It will unleash possees and "thought police" to enforce patriotic behavior.

The authors of this "It's Time for the People's Verdict on Burning the U.S. Flag" Informative Sheet identify themselves as follows:

> Revolutionary Communist Party, U.S.A
> P.O. Box 3486, Merchandise Mart,
> Chicago, Illinois 60654.

> In New York, the *Revolutionary Worker Newspaper* and other literature of the RCP is available at: Revolution Books, 13E 16th St., NY, NY 10003 . . .

Our flag—"The Star-Spangled Banner"—is the symbol of a godly form of government based upon *Christian principles of liberty*. Altogether in keeping with this astounding verdict passed by the Supreme Court, is the hidden agenda of the "American Civil Liberties Union"—alias the ACLU, from which the following is quoted:

> *Policy No. 81* calls for a permanent ban on displays of the nativity scene and the menorah on public property.[1]

Policy No. 84 calls for the removal of "under God" from the Pledge of Allegiance [to our U.S. Flag] and the Republic for which it stands.[2]

(The above represents a direct affront to Abraham Lincoln, whose phrase "this nation under God" in his famed Gettysburg Address, orchestrated Dwight D. Eisenhower's Act of Congress in 1954, establishing permanently "One Nation under God" into the Pledge of Allegiance to our Flag).

Policy No. 92 calls for an end to tax exemptions for all churches and synagogues. (The ACLU is right now in court trying to strip the Catholic Church of its tax exemption because of its opposition to abortion).[3]

Policy No. 210. . . calls for the legalization of all narcotics, including crack and angel dust, contending "the introduction of substances into one's own body" is a civil liberty.

With a secret membership of 250,000, the ACLU is a vastly changed organization from the one Roger Baldwin presided over in the 1950s; today, its ideology closely patterns the ACLU's ideology of the 1930s from which John Dewey resigned because of Marxist domination.[5]

The monuments to the ACLU are now all around us, superseding and removing the monuments and memorials to America's greatness—her *true* history, representing the *One nation under God*. The public school system is a classic example of this phenomenon: The Lord's Prayer (Matthew 6); the Ten Commandments (Exodus 20); and the scene of the birth of our Lord and Savior Jesus Christ (Luke 2) are prohibited in those schools built by the ACLU.[6]

However, *who* or *what* is actually behind the ACLU and the numerous other movements and agents alive and active in falsifying, removing, and misinterpreting America's history—verbally, visually and tangibly?

This question dogged me through the arduous five years' research and compilation of this book documenting the rewriting of a powerful nation's history.

The word "brainwashing" isn't a popular concept in such an enlightened and civilized Republic as the United States of America today. Yet, believe it or not, this is what has occurred, but in such a subtle and underhanded manner, using major U.S. channels of communication, so as to deceive the most astute of her citizens.

Psychopolitics is the technical term for brainwashing. It is:

> The art and science of asserting and maintaining dominion over the thoughts and loyalties of individuals, officers, bureaus, and masses and the effecting of the conquest of enemy nations through "mental healing."

What I am about to share with you is taken directly from a book entitled *Brainwashing—A Synthesis of the Russian Textbook on Psychopolitics* compiled by a former card-carrying Communist, Kenneth Goff of Englewood, Colorado. For this invaluable contribution to the American people, Goff was assassinated.

In his preliminary "Editorial Note" to the Synthesis, Goff states:

> From May 2, 1936, to October 10, 1939, I was a dues-paying member of the Communist Party, operating under my own name Kenneth Goff, and also the alias John Keats. In 1939, I voluntarily appeared before the Un-American Activities Committee in Washington, D.C. which was chairmaned at that time by Martin Dies, and my testimony can be found in Volume 9 of that year's Congressional Report.

> During the period that I was a member of the Communist Party, I attended their school which was located at 113 E. Wells St. Milwaukee, Wisconsin, and operated under the name Eugene Debs Labor School. Here we were trained in all phases of warfare, both psychological and physical, for the destruction of the Capitalistic society and Christian civilization. In one portion of our studies we went thoroughly into the matter of psychopolitics. This was the art of capturing the minds of a nation through brainwashing and fake mental health—the subjecting of whole nations of people to the rule of the Kremlin by the capturing of their minds. We were taught that the degradation of the populace is less inhuman than their destruction by bombs, for to an animal who lives only once any life is sweeter than death. The end of a war is the control of a conquered people. If a people can be conquered in the absence of

war the end of the war will have been achieved without the destructions of war.

During the past few years I have noted with horror the increase of psychopolitical warfare upon the American public. First in the brainwashing of our boys in Korea and then in the well-financed drive of mental health propaganda by left-wing pressure groups, wherein many of our states have passed Bills which can well be used by the enemies of America to subject to torture and imprisonment those who preach the gospel of our Lord and Saviour Jesus Christ, and who oppose the menace of Communism. A clear example of this can be seen in the Lucille Miller case. In this warfare the Communists have definitely stated: "You must recruit every agency of the nation marked for slaughter into a foaming hatred of religious healing."

Another example of the warfare that is being waged can be seen in the attempt to establish a mental Siberia in Alaska, which was called for in the Alaskan Mental Health Bill. A careful study of this Bill will make you see at once that the land set aside under the allotment could not be for that small territory, and the Bill within itself establishes such authority that it could be turned into a prison camp under the guise of mental health for everyone who raises their voice against Communism and the hidden government operating in our nation.

This book was used in underground schools, and contains the address of Beria to the American students in the Lenin University prior to 1936. The text in the book in general is from the Communist Manual of Instructions of Psychopolitical Warfare, and was used in America for the training of Communist cadre. The only revision in this book is the summary, which was added by the Communists after the atomic bomb came into being. In its contents you can see the diabolical plot of the enemies of Christ and America, as they seek to conquer our nation by subjecting the minds of our people to their will by various sinister means.

This manual of the Communist Party should be in the hands of every loyal American, that they may be alerted to the fact that it is not always by armies and guns that a nation is conquered.

Kenneth Goff.[7]

An address by *Lavrenti Pavlovitch Beria* is then quoted, as follows:

American students at the Lenin University, I welcome your attendance at these classes on Psychopolitics. Psychopolitics is an important, if less known, division of Geo-politics. It is less known because it must necessarily deal with highly educated personnel, the very top strata of "mental healing." By psychopolitics our chief goals are effectively carried forward. To produce a maximum of chaos in the culture of the enemy is our first most important step. Our fruits are grown in chaos, distrust, economic depression and scientific turmoil. At least a weary populace can seek peace only in our offered Communist State, at last only Communism can resolve the problems of the masses. A psychopolitician must work hard to produce the maximum chaos in the fields of "mental healing". He must recruit and use all the agencies and facilities of "mental healing". He must labor to increase the personnel and facilities of "mental healing" until at last the entire field of mental science is entirely dominated by Communist principles and desires.

To achieve these goals the psychopolitician must crush every "home grown" variety of mental healing in America. Actual teachings of James, Eddy and Pentecostal Bible faith healers amongst your misguided people must be swept aside. They must be discredited, defamed, arrested, stamped upon even by their own government until there is no credit in them and only Communist-oriented "healing" remains. You must work until every teacher of psychology unknowingly or knowingly teaches only Communist doctrine under the guise of "psychology." You must labor until we have dominion over the minds and bodies of every important person in your nation. You must achieve such disrepute for the state of insanity and such authority over its pronouncement that not one statesman so labeled could again be given credence by his people. You must work until suicide arising from mental imbalance is common and calls forth no general investigation or remark.

With the institutions for the insane you have in your country prisons which can hold a millon persons and can hold them without civil rights or any hope of freedom. And upon these people can be practiced shock and surgery so that never again will they draw a sane breath. You must make these treatments common and accepted. And you must sweep aside any treatment or any group of persons seeking to treat by effective means.

You must dominate as respected the fields of psychiatry and psychology. You must dominate the hospitals and universities. You must carry forward the myth that only a European doctor is competent in the field of insanity and thus excuse amongst you the high incidence of foreign birth and training. If and when we seize Vienna you shall have then a common ground of meeting and can come and take your instructions as worshippers of Freud along with other psychiatrists.

Psychopolitics is a solemn charge. With it you can erase our enemies as insects. You can cripple the efficiency of leaders by striking insanity into their families through the use of drugs. You can wipe them away with testimony as to their insanity. By our technologies you can even bring about insanity itself when they seem too resistive.

You can change their loyalties by psychopolitics. Given a short time with a psychopolitician you can alter forever the loyalty of a soldier in our hands or a statesman or a leader in his own country, or you can destroy his mind.

However, you labor under certain dangers. It may happen that remedies for our "treatments" may be discovered. It may occur that a public hue and cry may arise against "mental healing". It may thus occur that all mental healing might be placed in the hands of ministers and be taken out of the hands of our psychologists and psychiatrists. But the Capitalistic thirst for control, Capitalistic inhumanity and a general public terror of insanity can be brought to guard against these things. But should they occur, should independent researchers actually discover means to undo psychopolitical procedures, you must not rest, you must not eat or sleep, you must not stint one tiniest bit of available money to campaign against it, discredit it, strike it down and render it void. For by an effective means all our actions and researches could be undone.

In a Capitalistic state you are aided on all sides by the corruption of the philosophy of man and the times. You will discover that everything will aid you in your campaign to seize control and use all "mental healing" to spread our doctrine and rid us of our enemies within their own borders.

Use the courts, use the judges, use the Constitution of the country, use its medical societies and its laws to further our ends. Do not stint in your labor in this direction. And when you have succeeded you will discover that you can now effect your own legislation at will and you can, by careful organization of healing societies, by constant campaign about the terrors of society, by pretense as to your effectiveness make your Capitalist himself, by his own appropriations, finance a large portion of the quiet Communist conquest of the nation.

By psychopolitics create chaos. Leave a nation leaderless. Kill our enemies. And bring to Earth, through Communism, the greatest peace Man has ever known.

Thank you.
Lavrenti Pavlovitch Beria
(March 29, 1899—December 23, 1953 Deputy Premier of the Soviet Union under Georgi M. Malenkov until his arrest for "high treason" in July, 1953; reportedly executed by a firing squad December 23, 1953).[8]

It is my firm belief, based upon seven years' indepth research and study in formulating two books on the crucial subject of America's Christian heritage, symbols, history and evidence and their rapid elimination from the very records of our United States history, that Psychopolitics lies behind the sinister plot to disarm this nation of her greatest strength—faith in God, Christ and the Bible, and to subsequently enslave the American people to a ruthless foreign rule.

Kenneth Goff's exposé of *Brainwashing—A Synthesis of the Russian Textbook on Psychopolitics* contains 16 chapters, defined as follows: I. The History and Definition of Psychopolitics; II. The Constitution of Man as a Political Organism; III. Man as an Economic Organism; IV. State Goals for the Individual and Masses; V. An Examination of Loyalties; VI. The General Subject of Obedience; VII.

Anatomy of Stimulus—Response Mechanisms of Man; VIII. Degradation, Shock and Endurance; IX. The Organization of Mental Health Campaigns; X. Conduct Under Fire; XI. The Use of Psychopolitics in Spreading Communism; XII. Violent Remedies; XIII. Recruiting of Psychopolitical Dupes; XIV. The Smashing of Religious Groups; XV. Proposals Which Must be Avoided; and XVI. Summary.[9]

Directly related to the contents of *The Rewriting of America's History*, are the following excerpts from this Synthesis:

> The strength and power of Psychopolitics cannot be overestimated, particularly when used in a nation decayed by pseudo-intellectualism, where exploitation of the masses combines readily with psychopolitical actions, and particularly where the greed of Capitalistic or Monarchial regimes has already brought about an overwhelming incidence of neurosis which can be employed as the groundwork for psychopolitical action and a psychopolitical corps. . . .[10]

> In a nation under conquest such as America, our slow and stealthy approach need take advantage only of the cycles of booms and depressions inherent in Capitalistic nations in order to assert of more and more strong control over individual wills. A boom is as advantageous as a depression for our ends for during prosperity our propaganda lines must only continue to point up the wealth the period is delivering to the selected few to divorce their control of the state. During a depression one must only point out that it ensued as a result of the avarice of a few and the general political incompetence of the national leaders. . . . The rich, the skilled in finance, the well informed in government are particular and individual targets for the psychopolitician. His is the role of taking off the board those individuals who would halt or corrupt Communist economic programs. Thus every rich man, every statesman, every person well informed and capable in government must have brought to his side as a trusted confidant a psychopolitical operator. . . .[11]

> Denying a Capitalist country easy access to courts, bringing about and supporting propaganda to destroy the home, creating continuous juvenile delinquency, forcing upon the state all manner of practices to divorce the child from it will in the

end create the chaos necessary to Communism . . . By making readily available drugs of various kinds, by giving the teenager alcohol, by praising his wildness, by stimulating him with sex literature and advertising to him or her practices as taught at the Sexpol, the psychopolitical operator can create the necessary attitude of chaos, idleness and worthlessness into which can then be cast the solution which will give the teenager complete freedom everywhere—Communism. . . . By these means the patriotism of youth for their Capitalistic flag can be dulled to a point where they are no longer dangerous as soldiers. While this might require many decades to effect, Capitalism's short term view will never envision the lengths across which we can plan.[12]

If we could effectively kill the national pride and patriotism of just one generation we will have won that country. Therefore there must be continual propaganda abroad to undermine the loyalty of the citizens in general and the teenager in particular.[13]

The role of the psychopolitical operator in this is very strong. He can, from his position as an authority on the mind, advise all manner of destructive measures. He can teach the lack of control of this child at home. He can instruct in an optimum situation the entire nation in how to handle children—and instruct them so that the children, given no control, given no real home, can run wildly about with no responsibility for their nation or themselves. . . The misalignment of the loyalty of youth to a Capitalistic nation sets the proper stage for a realignment of their loyalties with Communism. Creating a greed for drugs, sexual misbehavior and uncontrolled freedom and presenting this to them as a benefit of Communism will with ease bring about our alignment.[14]

In the case of strong leaders amongst youthful groups, a psychopolitical operator can work in many ways to use or discard the leadership. If it is to be used, the character of the girl or boy must be altered carefully into criminal channels and a control by blackmail or other means must be maintained. But where the leadership is not susceptible, where it resists all persuasions and might become dangerous to our Cause, no pains must be spared to direct the attention of the authorities to that person and to harrass in one way or another until he can come into the hands of the juvenile authorities. When this has been effected it can be hoped that a psychopolitical operator, by reason of child advisor status, can, in the security of the jail and cloaked by processes of law, destroy the sanity of that person. Particularly brilliant scholars, athletes and youth group leaders must be handled in either one of these two ways. . . .[15] Just as a dog can be trained, so can a man be trained. Just as a horse can be trained, so can a man be trained. Sexual lust, masochism, and any other desirable perversion can be induced by pain-drug hypnosis and the benefit of Psychopolitics. . . .[16]

. . . Degradation and conquest are companions . . . However, degradation can be accomplished much more insidiously and much more effectively by consistent and continual defamation . . . Continual and constant degradation of national leaders, national institutions, national practices, and national heroes must be systematically carried out, but this is the chief function of Communist Party Members, in general, not the psychopolitician. The realm of defamation and degradation, of the psychopolitician, is Man himself. By attacking the character and morals of Man himself, and by bringing about, through contamination of youth, a general degraded feeling, command of the populace is facilitated to a very marked degree. . . . The officials of a government, students, readers, partakers of entertainment, must all be indoctrinated, by whatever means, into the complete belief that the restless, the ambitious, the natural leaders, are suffering from environmental maladjustments, which can only be healed by recourse to psychopolitical operatives in the guise of mental healers. . . . The educational programs of psychopolitics must, at every hand, seek out the levels of youth who will become the leaders in the country's future, and educate them into the belief of the animalistic nature of Man. This must be made fashionable. They must be taught to frown upon ideas, upon individual endeavor. They must be taught above all things, that the salvation of Man is to be found only by his adjusting thoroughly to this environment. . . .[17]

. . . As it seems in foreign nations that the church is the most ennobling influence, each and every branch and activity of each and every church, must, one way or another, be discredited. Religion must become unfashionable by demonstrating broadly, through psychopolitical indoctrination, that the soul is non-existent, and that Man is an animal. The lying mechanisms of Christianity lead men to foolishly brave deeds. By teaching them that there is a life hereafter, the liability of courageous acts, while living, is thus lessened. The liability of any act must be markedly increased if a populace is to be obedient. Thus, there must be no standing belief in the church, and the power of the church must be denied at every hand. . .

The psychopolitical operative, in his program of degradation, should at all times bring into question any family which is deeply religious, and, should any neurosis or insanity be occasioned in that family, to blame and hold responsible their religious connections for the neurotic or psychotic condition. Religion must be made synonymous with neurosis and psychosis. People who are deeply religious would be less and less held responsible for their own sanity, and should more and more be relegated to the ministrations of psychopolitical operatives. By perverting the institutions of a nation and bringing about a general degradation, by interfering with the economics of a nation to the degree that privation and depression come about, only minor shocks will be necessary to produce, on the populace as a whole, an obedient reaction or an hysteria. . . .[18]

By releasing continued propaganda on the subject of dope addiction, homosexuality, and depraved conduct on the part of the young, even the judges of a country can become suborned into reacting violently against the youth of the country, thus mis-aligning and aligning the support of youth. . . .[19]

. . . The psychopolitical operative should also spare no expense in smashing out of existence, by whatever means, any actual healing group. . . .[20]

As every chair of psychology in the United States is occupied by persons in our connection, or who can be influenced by persons in our connection, the consistent employment of such texts is guaranteed. They are given the authoritative ring, and they are carefully taught. . . Should any whisper, or pamphlet, against psychopolitical activities be published, it should be laughed into scorn, branded an immediate hoax, and its perpetrator or publisher should be, at the first opportunity, branded as insane, and by the use of drugs the insanity should be confirmed.[21]

. . . Constant pressure in the legislatures of the United States can bring about legislation to the effect that every student attending a high school or university must have classes in psychology. . . .[22]

. . . Reactionary nations are of such a composition that they attack a word without understanding of it. As the conquest of a nation by Communism depends upon imbuing its population with communistic tenets, it is not necessary that the term "Communism" be applied at first to the educative measures employed. As an example, in the United States we have been able to alter the works of William James, and others, into a more acceptable pattern, and to place the tenets of Karl Marx, Pavlov, Lamarck, and the data of Dialectic Materialism into the textbooks of psychology, to such a degree that anyone thoroughly studying psychology becomes at once a candidate to accept the reasonableness of Communism. . . .[23]

. . . Given any slightest encouragement, public support would swing in an instant all mental healing into the hands of the churches. And there are Churches waiting to receive it, clever churches. . . . Among Fundamentalist and Pentecostal groups healing campaigns are conducted, which, because of their results, win many to the cult of Christianity. . . . Just as in Russia we had to destroy, after many, many years of the most arduous work, the Church, so we must destroy all faiths in nations marked for conquest. Insanity must be made to hound the footsteps of every priest and practitioner. His best results must be turned to jibbering insanities no matter what means we have to use. . . . You need not care what effect you have upon the public. The effect you care about is the one upon officials. You must recruit every agency of the nation marked for slaughter into a foaming hatred of religious healing. You must suborne district attorneys and judges into an intense belief as fervent as an ancient faith in God that Christian Science or any other religious practice which might devote itself to mental healing is vicious, bad, insanity-causing, publicly hated and intolerable. . . .[24]

. . . We have battled in America since the century's turn to bring to nothing any and all Christian influences and we are succeeding. While we today seem to be kind to the Christian, remember we have yet to influence the "Christian world" to our ends. When that is done we shall have an end of them everywhere. You may see them here in Russia as trained apes. They do not know their tether is long only until the apes in other lands have become unwary. . . . You must work until "religion" is synonymous with "insanity." You must work until the officials of city, county, and state governments will not think twice before they pounce upon religious groups as public enemies. . . . Remember, all lands are governed by the few and only pretend to consult with the many. It is no different in America. The petty official, the maker of laws alike can be made to believe the worst. It is not necessary to convince the masses. It is only necessary to work incessantly upon the official, using personal defamations, wild lies, false evidences and constant propaganda to make him fight for you against the church or against any practitioner. . . .[25]

. . . We must strike from our path any opposition. We must use for our tools any authority that comes to hand. And then, at last, the decades sped, we can dispense with all authority save our own, and triumph in the greater glory of the Party. . . .[26]

. . . Authors of literature which seek to demonstrate the picture of a society under complete mental control and duress should be helped toward infamy or suicide to discredit their works. . . .[27]

. . . Movements to improve youth should be invaded and corrupted, as this might interrupt campaigns to produce in youth delinquency, addiction, drunkenness, and sexual promiscuity. . . .[28]

. . . The end of war is the control of a conquered people. If a people can be conquered in the absence of war, the end of war will have been achieved without the destruction of war. A worthy goal . . . and the glory of Communist conquest over the stupidity of the enemies of the People.
The End.[29]

In attaining their goal of rewriting America's history and the obliteration of every Christian emblem, landmark, teaching, symbol, record, law and obstacle in their way; the godless enemies of America have successfully employed the *Hegelian Principle*, which can be explained as follows: Change in a society is brought about in a three-step process: *Thesis, Antithesis and Synthesis*. The first step (thesis) is to create a problem. The second step (antithesis) is to generate opposition to the problem (fear, panic, hysteria). The third step (synthesis) is to offer the solution to the problem created in step one—change which would have been impossible to impose on the people without the proper psychological conditioning achieved in stages one and two. Applying the Hegelian Principle, and irresistible financial influence, concealed mattoids seek to dismantle social and political structures by which free men govern themselves—ancient landmarks erected at great cost in blood and treasure. Their objective is to emasculate America, merge nations under universal government, centralize economic powers, and control the world's people and resources.

Why should we, as Christians in America, try to conserve our Christian heritage and godly roots, as exemplified in Christian symbols, plaques, memorials and historical records throughout our nation? Because herein lies the strength and security of a nation formed and fashioned according to biblical truth, under God's protective care. Herein lies America's freedoms and liberties, as we have enjoyed and celebrated them for the past 200 years.

Where are we going?

We are going toward control, slavery and conquest by the enemies of America, who have successfully, over a long period of time, infiltrated her ranks in almost every conceivable field. The oft-repeated question, uttered of old by Joshua, servant of Jehovah God, the God of Abraham, Isaac and Jacob, the God of our Lord and Savior Jesus Christ, the God of Christopher Columbus, Governor William Bradford, William Penn, our founding fathers and countless other great American patriots, is:

> . . . choose for yourselves today whom you will serve: but as
> for me and my house, we will serve the Lord. (Joshua 24:15)

For those of you who wish to make a turn-around and serve the God of our fathers, and accept His Son Jesus Christ as your Lord and Savior, I would invite you now to pray this prayer with me:

Father in Heaven, I come to you humbly, as a child, accepting your free gift of salvation through your Son Jesus' sacrificial death and atonement for my sins. I now accept Him as my Lord and Savior, and I thank you, Father, for this priceless gift of a Messiah. I now repent of my sins and turn my life over to you, Lord Jesus, in order to serve you all the days of my life in spirit and in truth. I accept your unconditional forgiveness, Father, in Christ's sacrifice on Calvary's cross for me and realize that through your grace and mercy, I am now translated into the kingdom of eternal life, have become your beloved child, and that I am sealed in Him with the Holy Spirit of promise forever; for You tell me that if I confess with my mouth Jesus as Lord, and believe in my heart that God raised Him from the dead, I shall be saved. (Romans 10:9). Lead me, I pray, into all truth through your Holy Word, Lord Jesus. Amen.

Americans by and large have lost track of who they are and from whence they came. Fellow Americans, turn, repent and be healed before it's too late. God is calling you individually to return to your godly foundations and Christian way of life, choosing the righteous path, abhorring and refusing what is evil. The above calls for a genuine spiritual revival and repentance in the hearts and lives of His people in America, lest we perish.

But you shall remember the Lord your God, for it is He who is giving you power to make wealth, that He may confirm His covenant which He swore to your fathers, as it is this day. And it shall come about if you ever forget the Lord your God and go after other gods and serve them and worship them, I testify against you today that you shall surely perish.

Like the nations that the Lord makes to perish before you, so you shall perish; because you would not listen to the voice of the Lord your God. (Deuteronomy 8:18–20).

FOOTNOTES

Chapter I

(i) [1] David, Maurice. *Who was Christopher Columbus?* Letter from Don Cristobal Colon to his son, Don Diego, published by the Duchess of Berwick y Alba. New York: The Research Publishing Company, 1933, pp. 68, 69.

[2] Ibid., p. 92.

[3] Kling, August J. "Columbus—A Layman Christ-bearer to unchartered isles." *The Presbyterian Layman*. October, 1971.

[4] Greene, Carol. *Christopher Columbus, A Great Explorer*. Chicago: Children's Press, 1989. p.33.

[5] Fradin, Dennis Brindell. *Columbus Day*. Hillside, N.J.: Enslow Publishers, Inc., 1990, pp. 27, 30.

[6] Bates, Esther Willard. *Columbus Discovers America*. Boston: Walter H. Baker Company Publishers, 1930, pp. 5–8.

[7] Kling, August J. *The Presbyterian Layman*. October, 1971.

(ii) [1] Winsor, Justin. *The Surrender of the Bradford Manuscript*. Cambridge: John Wilson & Son, University Press, 1897.

[2] Bradford, William. *Of Plimoth Plantation*. (From the original Manuscript). Boston: Wright and Potter Printing Company, 1898.

[3] Commager, Henry Steele (ed). *Documents of American History*. New York: F.S. Crofts and Company, 1934, pp. 14-15.

[4] Bradford, William. *Of Plimoth Plantation*.

[5] Winsor, Justin. *The Surrender of the Bradford Manuscript*.

[6] Westbrook, Perry D. *William Bradford*. Boston: Twayne Publishers, A Division of G. K. Hall and Co., 1978, pp. 141, 142.

[7] Ibid., p. 119.

[8] Smith, Bradford. *William Bradford Pilgrim Boy*. New York: The Bobbs Merrill Company, Inc., 1953, pp. 170–178.

[9]Hays, Wilma Pitchford. *Rebel Pilgrim, A Biography of Governor William Bradford*. Philadelphia: The Westminster Press, 1969, pp. 31, 32.

[10]Commager, Henry Steele (ed). *Documents of American History*. p. 1054.

[11]Bailey, Richard Briggs. *Pilgrim Possessions as told by their Wills and Inventories*. Copyright 1951 by Richard B. Bailey, pp. 110–114.

[12]Ibid., pp. 98–103.

[13]Ibid., pp. 79–89.

[14]Ibid., pp. 66–71.

[15]Ibid., pp. 73, 74.

[16]Ibid.

[17]Anderson, Joan. *The First Thanksgiving Feast*. (Photographed by George Ancona). New York: Clarion Books (Tickner and Fields: A Houghton Mifflin Company), 1984, n.p.

[18]Ibid.

[19]Heath, Dwight B. (ed.) *Mourt's Relation*. Journal of the Pilgrims at Plymouth from the original text of 1622. Boston: Applewood Books, 1986, pp. 89, 90.

[20]Bradford, William. *Of Plimoth Plantation*. pp. 96, 97.

[21]Ibid., p. 104.

[22]Ibid., p. 127.

[23]Matthews, Albert. *The Term Pilgrim Fathers*. Reprinted from the publications of the Colonial Society of Massachusetts, Vol. XVII. Cambridge: John Wilson and Son University Press, 1915, pp. 293, 294.

(iii) [1]Comfort, William Wistar. *William Penn and Our Liberties*. (Published in the Penn Mutual's centennial year in honor of the man whose name the company adopted at its founding in the year 1847.) Philadelphia: The Penn Mutual Life Insurance Company, 1947, n.p.

[2]*Penn Mutual Archives Collection*. Philadelphia.

[3]*Pennsylvania Historical Society Collection.* Philadelphia.

[4]Wanamaker, John. *Philadelphia a Guide.* (Made for the convenience of people interested in the city's notable history and present achievements.) Philadelphia: John Wanamaker, 1917, p. 3.

[5]Dunn, Richard A. and Mary Maples (eds.), *The World of William Penn.* Philadelphia: University of Pennsylvania Press, 1986, pp. 37, 38.

[6]*Philosophical Society of Pennsylvania Collection.* Philadelphia.

[7]Cope, Thomas Pyrn (ed.) *Passages from the Life and Writings of William Penn.* Philadelphia: Friends Bookstore, 1882.

[8]Ibid.

[9]Dunn, Richard A. and Mary Maples (eds.) *The World of William Penn.* p. 7.

[10]*The Philadelphia Enquirer.* January 7, 1984.

[11]Ibid., April 5, 1984.

[12]Ibid, April 6, 1984.

[13]Jefferson, Thomas. *Inscription within the Jefferson Memorial,* Washington, D.C.

[14]"William Penn's Original 1684 Prayer For Philadelphia." Historical Society of Pennsylvania. Philadelphia, PA.

(iv) [1]*George Washington's Rules of Civility and Decent Behaviour in Company and Conversation.* Cambridge: Riverside Press, 1926.

[2]Washington, George. *General Orders.* Archives of Mount Vernon, Mount Vernon, Virginia.

[3]Padover, Saul K. (ed.) *A Jefferson Profile.* New York: J. Day and Company, 1956, p. 227.

[4]Clark, Ellen McCallister, Librarian. *Archives of Mount Vernon.* Mount Vernon Ladies' Association, Mount Vernon, Virginia.

[5]*George Washington to Martha Washington.* Rare Book Collection, Library of Congress. Washington D.C.

[6]Madison, James, D.D. (Bishop of the Protestant Episcopal Church in Virginia, and President of William and Mary College). *A Discourse on the death of George Washington.* New York: T. and J. Swords, 1800.

[7]*George Washington's Prayer for America.* The Washington Memorial Chapel at Valley Forge, Pennsylvania.

[8]Fitzpatrick, John C. (Ed.) *The Writings of George Washington from the Original Manuscript Sources 1745–1799.* Vol. 29. Washington D.C.: United States Government Printing Office, 1931, p. 250.

[9]Burk, William Herbert, D.D. *The Washington Window in the Washington Memorial Chapel of Valley Forge.* Pennsylvania: Norristown Press, 1926, p. 30.

[10]Smith, Sheldon Moody. *A Brief Tour of the Washington Memorial Chapel.* Valley Forge, Pennsylvania.

[11]Ibid.

[12]Burk, William Herbert, D.D. *The Washington Window in the Washington Memorial Chapel of Valley Forge.* p. 36.

[13]Ibid., p. 25.

[14]Ibid., p. 36.

[15]Ibid., p. 13.

[16]Ibid., p. 27.

[17]Ibid., p. 25.

[18]Alexander, Holmes M. *Washington and Lee—A Study in the Will to Win.* Boston: Western Islands Publishers, 1966, pp. 7, 8.

[19]Adams, Charles Francis. *Familiar Letters of John Adams with his wife Abigail Adams, during the Revolution, with a memoir of Mrs. Adams by Charles Francis Adams.* New York: Hurd and Houghton, 1876, p. 65.

(v)   [1]Arnold, Richard K., (ed.) *Adams to Jefferson/Jefferson to Adams— A Dialogue from their Correspondence.* San Francisco: Jerico Press, 1975, pp. 12–13.

[2]Ibid., p. 25.

[3]Ibid., p. 27.

[4]Ibid., pp. 27–28.

[5]Ibid., pp. 30–31.

[6]Stefoff, Rebecca. *John Adams, 2nd President of the United States.* Oklahoma: Garrett Educational Corporation, 1988, pp. 78, 79.

[7]Ibid., pp. 81, 82.

[8]Wilstach, Paul, (ed.) *The Correspondence of John Adams and Thomas Jefferson (1812–1826).* Indianapolis: The Bobbs Merrill Publishers, 1925, p. 112.

[9]Ibid., p. 147.

[10]Adams, Charles Francis. *Familiar Letters of John Adams and his wife Abigail Adams, during the Revolution.* p. 10.

[11]Ibid., pp. 37, 38.

[12]Ibid., p. 46.

[13]Adams, Abigail. *Letters of Abigail Adams to her Husband.* Old South Leaflets. No. 6. Fourth Series, 1886, pp. 1–3.

[14]Ibid., pp. 4–6.

[15]Adams, Charles Francis. *Familiar Letters of John Adams and his wife Abigail Adams, during the Revolution,* p. XXVI.

[16]Ibid., p. 3.

[17]Ibid.

[18]Ibid., pp. 3, 4.

(vi) [1]Webster, Noah, LLD. *The American Dictionary of the English Language.* George and Charles Merriam, 1854, p. 313.

[2]Jefferson, Thomas. *Second Inaugural Address.* March 4, 1805.

[3]Mayo, Barnes, (ed.) *Jefferson Himself—The Personal Narrative of a many-sided American.* Boston: Houghton Mifflin Company, 1942, pp. 231, 235.

[4]Ibid., p. 231.

[5]Ibid., pp. 230, 231.

[6]Jefferson, Thomas. *Autobiography*. Original Manuscript in Rare Manuscript Collection, Library of Congress. Washington, D.C.

[7]*Letters of Thomas Jefferson on Religion*. (Compiled for Senator A. Willis Robertson, April 27, 1960). The Williamsburg Foundation, Williamsburg, Va.

[8]Ibid.

[9]Jefferson, Thomas. *Autobiography*.

[10]Jackson, Henry E., (ed.) *The Thomas Jefferson Bible*. (Undiscovered teachings of Jesus; reported by his four biographers; arranged by Thomas Jefferson; translated by R.F. Weymouth; printed in modern form; designed as an aid to the practice of social intelligence and the creation of a science of a society). New York: Boni and Liveright Publishers, 1923, p. 10.

[11]Ibid., Introduction.

[12]*Catalogue of the Library of Thomas Jefferson*, Vol. II. Rare Book Collection, Library of Congress. Washington, D.C. 1953, p.120.

[13]Ibid.

[14]Ibid. Title Page.

[15]*Letters of Thomas Jefferson on Religion*.

[16]Ibid.

(vii) [1]Madison, James. *A Memorial and Remonstrance*. (Presented by the General Assembly of the State of Virginia). 1785. Rare Book Collection, Library of Congress. Washington, D.C.

[2]Ibid.

[3]Ibid.

[4]Ibid.

[5]*Companion Guide to the Supreme Court's Holy Battles*. (With Correspondent Roger Mudd), 1989, p. 11.

⁶Fritz, Jean. *The Great Little Madison.* New York: G. P. Putnum's Sons, 1989, p. 19.

⁷Ibid., p. 10.

⁸Ibid, pp. 10, 11.

⁹Adams, John Quincy. *A Eulogy on the Life and Character of James Madison, September 27, 1836.* Boston: John H. Eastburn City Printer, 1836, p. 18.

(viii) ¹Franklin, Benjamin. *Some Account of the Pennsylvania Hospital from its First rise, to the Beginning of the Fifth Month, called May, 1754.* Philadelphia: B. Franklin and D. Hall, MDC-CLIV, pp. 66–69.

²*The Autobiography of Benjamin Franklin.*

³Ibid.

⁴Ibid.

⁵Pfaff, William S., (ed.) *Maxims and Morals of Benjamin Franklin.* New Orleans: Searcy and Pfaff, Ltd., 1927.

⁶Franklin, Benjamin. *Information to Those Who Would Remove to America.* London: M. Gurney, 1794, pp. 22, 23.

⁷Meltzer, Milton. *Benjamin Franklin, the New American.* New York: Franklin Watts, 1988, pp. 246, 247.

⁸Pfaff, William S., (ed.) *The Pith of Franklin's Letters.* New Orleans: Searcy and Pfaff, Ltd., 1927.

(ix) ¹Fritz, Jean. *The Great Little Madison.* p. 19.

²Ibid., p. 21.

³Henry, William Wirt. *Patrick Henry—Life, Correspondence and Speeches.* Vol. 1, New York: Burt Franklin, 1969, pp. 91–93.

⁴Drinkard, William R. *An Oration on the Life and Character of Patrick Henry.* (Delivered before the Patrick Henry Society of William and Mary College on May 29, 1940). Richmond: P.D. Bernard, 1840.

⁵Henry, William Wirt. *Patrick Henry—Life, Correspondence and Speeches.* Vol. 1.

(x)   [1] Machen, Lewis H. *An Address: George Mason of Virginia (1725–1792).* (Presenting a portrait to Fairfax County). May 20, 1901.

[2] Mason, Robert C. *George Mason of Virginia (Citizen, Statesman and Philosopher).* An Address Commemorative of the launching of the S.S. Gunston Hall at Alexandria, Virginia, January, 1919. New York: Oscar Aurelius Morgnor, p. 18.

[3] *A Companion Guide to the Supreme Court's Holy Battles.* (With Correspondent Roger Mudd), 1989, p. 11.

[4] Ibid., Introduction.

[5] Mason, George. Eulogy on Ann Mason, inscribed within his original 1759 family Bible. Gunston Hall Plantation, Lorton, Virginia.

[6] Park, Edwards. "George Mason: The Squire of Gunston Hall." *Colonial Williamsburg,* The Journal of the Colonial Williamsburg Foundation, Spring 1991, Vol. XIII, No. 3, p. 16.

[7] Ibid., pp. 18, 19.

[8] Rowland, Kate Mason. *The Life of George Mason (1725–1792).* Vol. 1. New York: Russell and Russell, Inc., 1964, pp. 32, 33.

[9] Mason, Robert C. *George Mason of Virginia (Citizen, Statesman and Philosopher).* p. 10.

(xi) [1] Webster, Noah, LL.D *Introduction to An American Dictionary of the English Language.* (Revised and enlarged by Chauncey A. Goodrich, Professor at Yale College). Springfield, MA: George and Charles Merriam, 1828.

[2] Ibid.

[3] Memoir of the Author by the Editor. *An American Dictionary.* 1847.

[4] Leavitt, Robert Keith. *Noah's Ark, New England Yankees and Endless Quest. A Short History of the Original Webster Dictionaries, with reference to their First Hundred Years as publi-*

cations of G & C Merriam Company. Springfield, MA: G & C Merriam Co., 1947, p. 76.

[5]Ibid.

[6]Ibid.

[7]Webster, Noah, LL.D. *The Holy Bible.* Containing the Old and New Testaments in the Common Version. New Haven: Durrie and Peck, 1833.

Chapter 2

(i)   [1]American Bar Association *Committee on American Citizenship: Washington, Lee and Lincoln, The Great Triumvirate Among the Makers of America.* Dallas, 1924, p. 25.

[2]William J. Wolf. *The Religion of Abraham Lincoln.* New York: Seabury Press, 1963.

[3]Lincoln, Abraham. *Second Inaugural Address, 1865.* Inscribed on North Wall of Lincoln Memorial, Washington, D.C.

[4]Matthew 7:1.

[5]Matthew 18:7.

[6]Revelation 16:7.

[7]Baker, Jean H. *Mary Todd Lincoln, a Biography.* New York: W. W. Norton and Company, 1989, p. xiii.

[8]Ibid., p. 151.

[9]Ibid., p. 239.

[10]Stone, Irving. *Mary Todd Lincoln: A Final Judgment?* Springfield, IL: Abraham Lincoln Association, 1973, p. 15.

[11]Edgington, Frank E. *History of the New York Avenue Presbyterian Church.* Washington, D.C.: New York Avenue Presbyterian Church, 1961, pp. 252, 253.

[12]Keckley, Elizabeth. *Behind the Scenes—Thirty years a Slave and Four years in the White House.* New York: Arno Press and the New York Times, 1968. (Reprinted from the original 1868 copy in the collection of Princeton University), Introduction.

[13]Ibid., pp. 363–364.

[14]Ibid., pp. 364–366.

[15]Ibid., pp. 95–97.

[16]Ibid., pp. 100–105.

[17]Ibid., pp. 109–110.

[18]Ibid., p. 110.

[19]Gurley, Phineas D. *Funeral Sermon for Abraham Lincoln.* Presbyterian Historical Society, Philadelphia, PA.

(ii)   [1]*American Peoples Encyclopedia.* Vol. 12. Chicago: Spencer Press, Inc., 1954, p. 120317.

[2]Lattimore, Ralston B. *The Story of Robert E. Lee, as told in his own words and those of his contemporaries.* Washington, D.C.: Colortone Press, 1964, pp. 22–23.

[3]Lyne, Cassie Mancure. *Preface of George Fox's Diary and Other Christian Historical Data.* Washington, D.C. Rare Book Collection. Library of Congress, 1875.

[4]Ibid.

[5]Griswold, Benjamin Howell. *The Spirit of Lee and Jackson.* Baltimore: The Norman Remington Company, 1927, pp. 12–13, 18.

[6]Lee, Robert E., Captain. *Recollections and Letters of General Robert E. Lee by his son.* New York: Doubleday, Page and Company, 1924, pp. 88, 89.

[7]Ibid., p. 195.

[8]Ibid., pp. 438, 439.

[9]Alexander, Holmes M. *Washington and Lee—A Study in the Will to Win.* pp. 57, 67.

[10]Lee, Robert E., Captain. *Recollections and Letters of General Robert E. Lee by his son.* p. 439.

(iii)   [1]Cook, Roy Bird. *The Family and Early Life of Stonewall Jackson.* Charleston, WV: Education Foundation, Inc., 1967, pp. 64–65.

[2]Gittings, John G. *Personal Recollections of Stonewall Jackson.* Cincinnati: The Editor Publishing Company, 1899, p. 32.

[3]Ibid.

[4]Ibid., p. 65.

[5]Cook, Roy Bird. *The Family and Early Life of Stonewall Jackson.* p. 92.

[6]Chew, Colonel, R.P. *An Address on Stonewall Jackson.* (Delivered at the Virginia Military Institute, Lexington, on the unveiling of Ezekiel's Statue of General T.J. Jackson, June 19, 1912). Lexington: Rockbridge County News Print, 1912, pp. 61, 62.

[7]Ibid.

[8]Brown, Jack I. *The Shade of the Trees.* (A narrative based on the life and career of Lieutenant General Thomas Jonathan "Stonewall" Jackson). Great Neck: Todd and Honeywell, Inc., 1988, p. 69.

[9]Ibid.

(iv) [1]Westerhoff, John H., III. *McGuffey and his Readers Piety, Morality and Education in 19th Century America.)* Nashville: Abington Press, n.d., p. 13.

[2]Ibid., pp. 13–14.

[3]Smith, William Earnest. *About the McGuffeys.* Oxford, OH: Cullen Printing Company, 1963. Title Page.

[4]Jefferson, Thomas. *Inscription within the Jefferson Memorial.* Washington, D.C.

(v) [1]MacCartney, Clarence Edward Noble. *The Gospel of the Oregon Trail.* (An Address, First Presbyterian Church, Pittsburgh, Pennsylvania), June 1, 1936.

[2]Weigle, Luther A. (ed.). *The Pageant of America.* Vol. X. American Idealism. New Haven: Yale University Press, 1925.

[3]Harding, Warren Gamaliel. *A Government Document.* Washington, D.C.: Government Printing Office, 1923.

[4]Hanna, Rev. Joseph A. *Dr. Whitman and his Ride to Save Oregon.* (Read before the Association of Presbyterian Ministers of Los Angeles, April 8, 1903). Los Angeles, 1903.

[5]Bourne, Edward Gaylord, Professor of History in Yale University. *Essays in Historical Criticism.* "The Legend of Marcus Whitman." Freeport, New York: Books for Libraries Press, Inc., 1901, pp. 80–82.

[6]*The American Peoples Encyclopedia.* Vol. 20. Chicago: Spencer Press, Inc., 1948, pp. 20093–20094.

[7]Maxey, Chester Collins. *Marcus Whitman, 1802–1847: His Courage, His Deeds, and His College.* New York: Newcomon Society in North America, 1950, p. 38.

(vi)   [1]Tibesar, Antoine, OFM (ed.). *Writings of Junipero Serra.* Vol. IV. Washington, D.C.: Academy of American Franciscan History, 1966.

[2]Serra, Junipero. *Title Page of Register Manuscript.* San Gabriel Mission, California.

[3]Morgado, Martin J. *Junipero Serra's Legacy.* Pacific Grove, California: 1987, p. 25.

[4]Ibid.

[5]"Carmel Mission Bible to be used by Reagan," Monterey Peninsula Herald, 28 December, 1966, p. 1.

[6]Morgado, Martin J. *Junipero Serra's Legacy.* p. xix.

[7]Ibid.

[8]Roberts, Mike. *The California Mission Story.* Oakland, CA: Color Productions, 1979, p. 2.

[9]Fogel, Daniel. *Junipero Serra, the Vatican and Enslavement Theology.* San Francisco: Ism Press, 1988, p. 47.

[10]Ibid., pp. 129–132.

[11]Warner, Rita. *Spanish Mission of California Coloring Album.* Meza: MC Creations, 1977.

[12]Morgado, Martin J. *Junipero Serra's Legacy.* p. 97.

[13]Ibid., p. 101.

[14]Geiger, *The Life and Times of Fray Junipero Serra*, O.F.M., 2:392.

Chapter 3

(i)   [1]Independence National Historical Park, Department of the Interior, *Fact Sheet.* Philadelphia.

[2]Ibid.

[3]Millard, Catherine. *God's Signature over the Nation's Capital.* West Wilmington: Sonrise Publications, 1988, p. 171.

(ii)   [1]Dunlop, Becky Norton. (Assistant Secretary for Fish and Wildlife and Parks). *Report.* United States Department of the Interior: January 1, 1989.

[2]Ibid.

(iii) [1]Dunlop, Becky Norton. (Assistant Secretary for Fish and Wildlife and Parks). *Report.* United States Department of the Interior: January 24, 1989.

(iv)   [1]Committee on the Restoration of Independence Hall, Mayor's Office. *Report.* Philadelphia, June 12, 1873, pp. 2, 3.

[2]Ibid.

(v)   [1]Historic Philadelphia Fact Sheet.

[2]Hearings before Subcommittee No. 4 of the Committee of the Judiciary, 85th Congress, 2nd. Session. May 21, 22 & 28, 1958, p. 6.

[3]Ibid., p. 1.

[4]Ibid., p. 135.

[5]Ibid., p. 138.

[6]Ibid.

(vi)   [1]*The Great Organ and the Grand Court.* John Wanamaker, Philadelphia, n.d.

[2]Wanamaker, John. *The Prayers of John Wanamaker.* New York: Fleming H. Revell Company, 1923.

[3]*The Philadelphia Inquirer.* February 22, 1988.

[4]Ibid.

(vii) [1]Morton, Louis. *Robert Carter of Nomini Hall, A Virginia Tobacco Planter of the 18th Century.* Williamsburg: Colonial
Williamsburg, Inc., 1941, p. 63.

[2]Ibid., p. 9.

[3]Ibid.

[4]*Robert Carter to Francis Lee, 15 July 1702.* Wormeley Estate
Papers, 1701-1716. Lancaster County, VA.: Christ Church
Parish.

[5]Wright, Louis B., (ed.) *Letters of Robert Carter, 1720-1727.* San
Marino: The Hunting Library, 1940, p. 25.

[6]Ibid., p. 34.

[7]Ibid., p. 37.

[8]Morton, Louis. *Robert Carter of Nomini Hall.* p. 11.

[9]Ibid., p. 12.

[10]Ibid.

[11]Ibid., p. 13.

[12]Ibid.

[13]Ibid., p. 20.

[14]Ibid., pp. 23, 24.

[15]*Interview with Visitors' Center Docent.* Carters' Grove Plantation. Colonial Williamsburg Foundation, September, 1988.

[16]Historic marker outside original church tower, Jamestown
Island, Virginia.

[17]*Colonial Williamsburg Interpreter's Lecture.* Colonial Williamsburg Foundation, September, 1988.

[18]Hill Carter III, Charles. "Shirley Plantation—Built on a Tradition of Heritage and Hierarchy." *Colonial Williamsburg*
(the Journal of the Colonial Williamsburg Foundation).
Spring 1991, p. 28.

[19]Ibid., p. 29.

(viii) ¹Original Charter, Rare Book Collection, Swem Library. College of William and Mary. Williamsburg, Virginia.

²*Visitors' Guide.* Colonial Williamsburg, Virginia.

³Goodwin, Mary R.M. *Wren Building Interpretative Research Report.* College of William and Mary, Williamsburg, Virginia, p. 7.

⁴Ibid., p. 5.

⁵Ibid., p. 10.

⁶Ibid., p. 41.

⁷Ibid.

⁸Ibid., p. 42.

⁹Ibid.

¹⁰Hood, Graham. Director of Colonial Williamsburg Foundation. *Telephonic interview with author.* October 7, 1987.

¹¹Ingram, John E., Curator, Special Collections, The Colonial Williamsburg Foundation. *Letter to author.* October 25, 1988.

¹²Ibid.

¹³Ibid.

¹⁴Commager, Henry Steele (ed). *Documents of American History.* New York: F.S. Crofts and Company, 1934, p. 1054.

(ix) ¹Commager, Henry Steele (ed). *Documents of American History.* p. 8.

²Ibid.

³Marker outside original Church Tower, Jamestown Island, Virginia.

⁴Marker within reconstructed interior of original church, Jamestown Island, Virginia.

⁵Ibid.

⁶Plaque within reconstructed interior of original church, Jamestown Island, Virginia.

[7]*Replica Sketch of original masterpiece painting of "Pocahontas," by Brooke.* Smithsonian Institution Collection, Washington, D.C.

(x)   [1]*Plaque on front facade of colonial Grace Church.* Yorkhampton Parish, Yorktown, Virginia.

[2]National Park Service, Department of the Interior. *Official Nelson House Script for 1989 Season.*

(xi)   [1]Henry Ford Museum Staff. *Greenfield Village.* New York: Crown Publishers, Inc., 1972, p. 10.

[2]Ibid., p. 6.

[3]Head, Janine. Chief Archivist. *Greenfield Village.* Telephonic interview with author. August 11, 1989.

[4]The Henry Ford Museum Staff. *Greenfield Village.* New York: Crown Publishers, Inc., 1972, p. 10.

[5]Ibid.

[6]Daroczy, Gillian. Letter to author. May 3, 1989.

(xii)   [1]Bartholdi, Frederic Auguste. *The Statue of Liberty Enlightening the World.* (Published for the benefit of the Pedestal Fund), New York: North America Review, 1885.

[2]*Inauguration of the Statue of Liberty Enlightening the World, by the President of the United States.* New York: D. Appleton and Company, 1887, pp. 18–21.

[3]Ibid., p. 23.

(xiii) [1]100th Congress, Approved 98th Congress, 1st Session, S.S. Con. Res. 35, passed July 27, 1983. S. Doc. 99–17. *The Capitol, A Pictorial History of the Capitol and the Congress.* p. 178.

[2]Ibid., pp. 178, 179.

[3]Ibid, p. 179.

[4]*Library of Congress Memorandum.* Submitted by a Senior Librarian to Acting Chief and Supervisor of Division.

[5]Statement of the AFSCME Local 2910 before the Committee on Appropriations, Subcommittee on Legislative Branch

Appropriations, U.S. House of Representatives, February 23, 1987.

[6]Douglas, Howard Grey. *Library of Congress, Washington.* Washington, D.C., 1904, Library of Congress Rare Book Collection, Introduction.

[7]Dart and Bigelow. *Library of Congress.* Washington, D.C., 1897, Library of Congress Rare Book Collection, p. ix.

[8]Ibid., p. vii.

[9]Millard, Catherine. *God's Signature over the Nation's Capital.* West Wilmington, DE: Sonrise Publications, 1988, p. 54.

[10]Foster and Reynolds. *The Library of Congress Mural Paintings, with the colors of the originals, the Library quotations and poems.* Washington, D.C., 1902 (Rare Book Collection).

[11]Ibid.

[12]Ibid.

[13]Ibid.

[14]Millard, Catherine. *God's Signature over the Nation's Capital.* p. 54.

[15]Reynolds, Charles B. *The Library of Congress and the Interior Decorations.* New York: Foster and Reynolds, 1897, Library of Congress Rare Book Collection, pp. 7, 8.

[16]Ibid.

[17]Ibid.

(xiv) [1]Watkinson, M.R., *Minister of the Gospel to Hon. S.P. Chase Secretary of the Treasury.* November 13, 1861.

[2]*Hon. S.P. Chase, Secretary of Treasury to Director of the Mint.* Philadelphia, November 20, 1861.

[3]*Secretary of the Treasury to Director of the Mint.* Philadelphia, December 9, 1863.

(xv) [1]Independence National Historic Park, Department of the Interior. *The Early History of the Supreme Court of the United States (1791–1800).* Philadelphia.

[2]Millard, Catherine. *God's Signature over the Nation's Capital.* p. 34.

[3]Ibid.

[4]Ibid.

[5]Brewer, David J. *The United States a Christian Nation.* Philadelphia: The John C. Winston Company, 1905. (Supreme Court Collection)

Conclusion

[1]Buchanan, Patrick J. *Hidden Agenda of the ACLU, 1988.* PJB Enterprises, Inc.: Chicago Tribune Media Services.

[2]Ibid.

[3]Ibid.

[4]Ibid.

[5]Ibid.

[6]Ibid.

[7]Goff, Kenneth. *Brain-Washing. A Synthesis of the Russian Textbook on Psychopolitics.* P.O. Box 116, Englewood, Colorado, p. 1.

[8]Ibid, pp. 3, 4.

[9]Ibid, p. 2.

[10]Ibid, pp. 6–7.

[11]Ibid, pp. 15, 16.

[12]Ibid, pp. 26, 27.

[13]Ibid, p. 27.

[14]Ibid.

[15]Ibid, pp. 27, 28.

[16]Ibid., p. 39.

[17]Ibid., pp. 41–43.

[18]Ibid., pp. 43, 44.

[19]Ibid., p. 48.

[20]Ibid., p. 49.

[21]Ibid., pp. 52–53.

[22]Ibid., p. 53.

[23]Ibid.

[24]Ibid., pp. 58, 59.

[25]Ibid., pp. 59, 60.

[26]Ibid. p. 60.

[27]Ibid. p. 62.

[28]Ibid. pp. 62, 63.

[29]Ibid. p. 64.

Addendum
Chapter I (vii)

MEMORIAL AND REMONSTRANCE
(Drawn by James Madison, President of the U.S.)

Against the general Assessment, presented to the General Assembly of Virginia, at the Session for the year of our Lord, one thousand seven hundred and eighty five.

TO THE HONOURABLE THE GENERAL ASSEMBLY OF THE COMMONWEALTH OF VIRGINIA
    We the subscribers, citizens of the said Commonwealth, having taken into serious consideration a bill, printed by order of the last session of General Assembly, entitled, "A bill establishing a provision for teachers of the Christian Religion," and conceiving, that the same, if finally armed with the sanction of a law, will be a dangerous abuse of power; are bound, as faithful members of a free State, to remonstrate against it, and to declare the reasons by which we are determined. We remonstrate against the said bill.
    Because we hold it for a fundamental and unalienable truth, that religion, or the duty which we owe to the Creator, and the manner of discharging it, can be directed only by reason and conviction, not by force or violence.* The religion, then, of every man, must be left to the conviction and conscience of every man; and it is the right of every man to exercise it as this may dictate. This right is, in its nature, an unalienable right. It is unalienable, because the opinions of men depending only on the evidence contemplated by their own minds, cannot follow the dictates of other men. It is unalienable, also, because what is here a right towards man, is a duty towards the Creator. It is the duty of every man to render to the Creator such homage, and such only as he believes to be acceptable to him. This duty is precedent both in order and time, and in degree of obligation, to the claims of civil society. Before any man can be considered as a member of civil society, he must be considered as a subject of the Governor of the Universe. And if a member of civil

---

Declaration of Rights, Article 16

society, who enters into any subordinate association, must always do it with a reservation of his duty to the general authority; much more must every man, who becomes a member of any particular civil society, do it with a saving of his allegiance to the Universal Sovereign. We maintain, therefore, that in matters of religion, no man's right is abridged by the institution of civil society; and that religion is wholly exempt from its cognizance. True it is, that no other rule exists by which any question, which may divide society, can be ultimately determined, but by the will of a majority; and it is also true, that the majority may trespass on the rights of the minority.

Because if religion be exempt from the authority of the society at large, still less can it be subject to that of the legislative body. The latter are but the creatures and vicegerents of the former. Their jurisdiction is both derivative and limited. It is limited with regard to the co-ordinate departments; more necessarily, it is limited with regard to the constituents. The preservation of a free government requires, not merely that the metes and bounds which separate each department of power, be invariably maintained; but more especially, that neither of them be suffered to overleap the great barrier which defends the rights of the people. The rulers, who are guilty of such an encroachment, exceed the commission from which they derive their authority, and are tyrants. The people who submit to it, are governed by laws made neither by themselves, nor by an authority derived from them, and are slaves.

Because it is proper to take alarm at the first experiment on our liberties. We hold this prudent jealousy to be the first duty of citizens, and one of the noblest characteristics of the late revolution. The freemen of America did not wait until usurped power had strengthened itself by exercise, and entangled the question in precedents. They saw all the consequences in the principle, and they avoided the consequences by denying the principle. We revere this lesson too much, soon to forget it. Who does not see that the same authority, which can establish Christianity in exclusion of all other religions, may establish, with the same ease, any particular sect of Christians, in exclusion of all other sects; that the same authority, which can force a citizen to contribute threepence only of his property, for the support of any one establishment, may force him to conform to any other establishment, in all cases whatsoever?

Because the bill violates that equality which ought to be the basis of every law; and which is more indispensable in proportion as the validity or expediency of any law is more liable to be impeached. "If all men are, by nature, equally free and independent,"* all men are to be considered as entering into society on equal conditions, as, relinquishing no more, and, therefore, retaining no less one than another, of their natural rights; above all are they to be considered as retaining an *"equal* title to the free exercise of religion according to the dictates of conscience."* Whilst we assert for ourselves a freedom to embrace, to profess, and observe the religion which we believe to be of divine origin, we cannot deny an equal freedom to those, whose minds have not yet yielded to the evidence which has convinced us. If this freedom be abused, it is an offence against God, not against man. To God, therefore, and not to man, must an account of it be rendered.

As the bill violates equality, by subjecting some to peculiar burdens; so it violates the same principle, by granting to others peculiar exemptions. Are the Quakers and Mennonites the only sects who think a compulsive support of their religions unnecessary and unwarrantable? Can their piety alone be entrusted with the care of publick worship? Ought their religions to be endowed, above all others, with extraordinary privileges, by which proselytes may be enticed from all others? We think too favourably of the justice and good sense of these denominations to believe, that they either covert pre-eminences over their fellow citizens, or that they will be seduced by them from the common opposition to the measure.

Because the bill implies, either that the civil magistrate is a competent judge of religious truths, or that he may employ religion as an engine of civil policy. The first is an arrogant pretension, falsified by the extraordinary opinion of rulers, in all ages, and throughout the world; the second, an unhallowed perversion of the means of salvation.

Because the establishment proposed by the bill, is not requisite for the support of the Christian religion itself; for every page of it disavows a dependence on the power of this world; it is a contradiction to fact, for it is known that this religion both existed and flourished, not only without the support of human laws, but in

---

*Declaration of Rights, Article 16

spite of every opposition from them; and not only during the period of miraculous aid, but long after it had been left to its own evidence and the ordinary care of Providence: nay, it is a contradiction in terms; for a religion, not invented by human policy must have pre-existed and been supported before it was established by human policy; it is, moreover, to weaken in those, who profess this religion, a pious confidence in its innate excellence, and the patronage of its Author; and to foster in those, who still reject it, a suspicion that its friends are too conscious of its fallacies, to trust it to its own merits.

Because experience witnesses that ecclesiastical establishments, instead of maintaining the purity and efficacy of religion, have had a contrary operation. During almost fifteen centuries has the legal establishment of Christianity been on trial. What have been its fruits? More or less in all places, pride and indolence in the clergy; ignorance and servility in the laity; in both superstition, bigotry, and persecution. Inquire of the teachers of Christianity for the ages in which it appears in its greatest lustre; those of every sect point to the ages prior to its incorporation with civil policy. Propose a restoration of this primitive state, in which its teachers depended on the voluntary rewards of their flocks, many of them predict its downfall. On which side ought their testimony to have the greatest weight, when for, or when against their interest?

Because the establishment in question is not necessary for the support of civil government, only as it is a means of supporting religion, and it be not necessary for the latter purpose, it cannot be necessary for the former. If religion be not within the cognizance of civil government, how can its legal establishment be said to be necessary to civil government? What influence, in fact, have ecclesiastical establishments had on civil society? In some instances, they have been seen to erect a spiritual tyranny on the ruins of the civil authority; in more instances, have they been seen upholding the thrones of political tyranny; in no instance have they been seen the guardians of the liberties of the people. Rulers who wished to subvert the publick liberty, may have found on established clergy convenient auxiliaries. A just government instituted to secure and perpetuate it, needs them not. Such a government will be best supported by protecting every citizen in the enjoyment of his religion with the same equal hand which protects his person and property; by neither invading the equal rights of any sect, nor suffering any sect to invade those of another.

Because the proposed establishment is a departure from that generous policy, which, offering an asylum to the persecuted and oppressed of every nation and religion, promised a lustre to our country, and an accession to the number of its citizens. What a melancholy mark is the bill, of sudden degeneracy? Instead of holding forth an asylum to the persecuted, it is itself a signal of persecution. It degrades from the equal rank of citizens, all those whose opinions in religion do not bend to those of the legislative authority. Distant as it may be, in its present form, from the inquisition, it differs from it only in degree, the one is the first step, the other the last, in the career of intolerance. The magnanimous sufferer under the cruel scourge in foreign regions, must view the bill as a beacon on our coast, warning him to seek some other haven where liberty and philanthropy in their due extent may offer a more certain repose for his troubles.

Because it will have a like tendency to banish our citizens. The allurements presented by other situations, are every day thinning their number. To superadd a fresh motive to emigration, by revoking the liberty which they now enjoy, would be the same species of folly, which has dishonoured and depopulated flourishing kingdoms.

Because it will destroy that moderation and harmony, which the forbearance of our laws to intermeddle with religion has produced among its several sects. Torrents of blood have been spilt in the old world, by vain attempts of the secular arm to extinguish religious discord, by proscribing all differences in religious opinion. Time has at length revealed the true remedy. Every relaxation of narrow and rigorous policy, wherever it has been tried, has been found to assuage the disease. The American theatre has exhibited proofs, that equal and complete liberty, if it does not wholly eradicate it, sufficiently destroys its malignant influence on the health and prosperity of the State. If with the salutary effects of this system under our own eyes, we begin to contract the bounds of religious freedom, we know no name that will so severely reproach our folly. At least, let warning be taken at the first fruits of the threatened innovation. The very appearance of the bill has transformed "that Christian forbearance, love and charity,"* which of late mutu-

---

Declaration of Rights, Article 16

ally prevailed, into animosities and jealousies, which may not soon be appeased. What mischiefs may not be dreaded, should this enemy to the publick quiet be armed with the force of law?

Because the policy of the bill is adverse to the diffusion of the light of Christianity. The first wish of those, who ought to enjoy this precious gift, ought to be, that it may be imparted to the whole race of mankind. Compare the number of those, who have as yet received it, with the number still remaining under the dominion of false religions, and how small is the former! Does the policy of the bill tend to lessen the disproportion? No; it at once discourages those who are strangers to the light of truth, from coming into the regions of it; and countenances, by example, the nations who continue in darkness, in shutting out those who might convey it to them. Instead of levelling, as far as possible, every obstacle to the victorious progress of truth, the bill, with an ignoble and unchristian timidity, would circumscribe it, with a wall of defence against the encroachments of error.

Because an attempt to enforce by legal sanctions, acts, obnoxious to so great proportion of citizens, tends to enervate the laws in general, and to slacken the bands of society. If it be difficult to execute any law, which is not generally deemed necessary nor salutary, what must be the case when it is deemed invalid and dangerous? And what may be the effect of so striking an example of impotency in the government on its general authority?

Because a measure of such singular magnitude and delicacy, ought not to be imposed without the clearest evidence that it is called for by a majority of citizens; and no satisfactory method is yet proposed, by which the voice of the majority in this case may be determined, or its influence secured. "The people of the respective counties are, indeed, requested to signify their opinion, respecting the adoption of the bill to the next session of Assembly." But the representation must be made equal, before the voice, either of the representatives, or of the counties, will be that of the people. Our hope is that neither of the former will, after due consideration, espouse the dangerous principle of the bill. Should the event disappoint us, it will still leave us in full confidence, that a fair appeal to the latter will reverse the sentence against our liberties.

Because, finally, "the equal right of every citizen to the free exercise of his religion according to the dictates of his conscience" is held by the same tenure with all our other rights. If we recur to its origin, it is equally the gift of nature; if we weight its importance, it cannot be less dear to us; if we consult the "Declaration of those rights which pertain to the good people of Virginia, as the basis and foundation of government," it is enumerated with equal solemnity, or rather with studied emphasis. Either then we must say that the will of the Legislature is the only measure of our authority; and that in the plenitude of this authority, they may sweep away all our fundamental rights; or, that they are bound to leave this particular right untouched and sacred; either we must say, that they may control the freedom of the press; may abolish the trial by jury; may swallow up the executive and judiciary power of the State; nay, that they may annihilate our very right of suffrage, and erect themselves into an independent and hereditary assembly; or we must say that they have no authority to enact into a law, the bill under consideration. We the subscribers say, that the General Assembly of the Commonwealth have no such authority; and that no effort may be omitted on our part against so dangerous an usurpation, we oppose to it this Remonstrance, earnestly praying, as we are in duty bound, that the Supreme Lawgiver of the Universe by illuminating those to whom it is addressed, may, on the one hand, turn their councils from every act which would affront His holy prerogative, or violate the trust committed to them; and, on the other, guide them into every measure which may be worthy of His blessing, may redound to their own praise, and may establish more firmly the liberties, the property, and the happiness of this Commonwealth. (Original document, Rare Book Collection, Library of Congress)

CHAPTER II (i)

Invocation at the Dedication of the Lincoln Memorial
Decoration Day May 30, 1922
By the Rev. Wallace Radcliffe, D.D.
Pastor of the New York Avenue Presbyterian Church

Almighty God, Sovereign among the Nations, God of our fathers, we adore Thee who has been to us as our fathers, the pillar of cloud and fire, and hast endowed us with the heritage of those that fear Thy name. Where Thou didst bring us into the wilderness Thou spokest comfortably to us and didst grant us our vineyards from thence so that the valley of Achor became a door of hope.

Today, we build our Ebenezer saying Hitherto hath Jehovah helped us. We bless Thee for those mighty men of those mighty days who loved righteousness better than life and who because of us and the ages the seers and martyrs for liberty and peace and goodwill. We recount the faith and courage, the patriotism and devotion, the ideals and consecrations, the tears and blood which under their guidance preserved the life and unity of the republic. With special thanksgiving and awesome praise we dedicate this Memorial to that man whom Thou didst ordain that through his leadership and martyrdom there might be the union of the people and the emancipation of the race. Thou has enshrined him in the heart of humanity. In him thou didst cause the little one to become a thousand and the small one a strong nation. We thank Thee for this man of clear eye and high heart who in the fear of God girded on the sword of power and confirmed so enduringly the Nation's trust and hope. We rejoice in the simplicity of his life, in the nobility of his aims, in the fervor of his devotion, in the persistence of his patience, in the rectitude of his motives, in his love of liberty, of man, of God.

Make us faithful to the inheritance of his character and work. Help us, like him, increasingly to recognize Thy presence and purpose, to bring counsel and plan to the light of Thy word, to bow in prayer and trust for the voice of Thy sovereign wisdom that out of all flames of future struggle and martyrdom our people may emerge purified as by fire and born anew into a higher life.

Bless Warren Harding, President of the United States and all associates with him in authority that their lives may be protected especially against hidden evils of malice and wickedness and their minds illumined with heavenly light. Write Thy law upon our statute books and enthrone Thy justice and judgment in our courts. Cast salt into all fountains of influence, civil, social and intellectual and heat the water thereof, that from them may flow streams that shall make glad our city of God. Hold this Nation true to the ideals of the fathers that their high path may not seem too hard for us. Give opportunity and hope to the race emancipated and confirm them in good citizenship, faithful manhood and prosperous lives. Promote unity, brotherhood, justice, right living and Christian patriotism. Deliver us from madness and canker of abused wealth, and luxury and transient glory of power. Give us peace in our time, O Lord, heal the breeches of the land because of which the land shaketh, that Ephraim may no longer envy Judah, nor Judah vex Ephraim. Let our wall be called Salvation, and our gates Praise that the righteous nation which keepeth the truth may enter in. Bless our blessings that all nations may call us blessed and a delightsome land. And may the Lord Jesus Christ go forth in this and in all nations conquering and to conquer in the might of His grace, in the benediction of His peace, in the beauty of His holiness, for the sake of that name that is above every name.

Chapter III (v)

"UNDER GOD"
Sermon preached by
Dr. George M. Docherty,
New York Avenue Presbyterian Church,
on Sunday, February 7, 1954:

The famous city of Sparta was once visited by an ambassador from another kingdom. He expected to find this great city surrounded by thick protecting walls; he was surprised when he saw no battlements at all.

"Where are the walls to defend the city?" he asked of the King of Sparta.

"Here are the walls of Sparta," replied the king, showing him his army of first line crack troops.

Had this ambassador visited our United States today, he would also be surprised to find no wall around our cities. (I should think, as a matter of fact, it would be extremely difficult even for American know-how to build a wall around Los Angeles.) And if our visitor were to ask the question, "Where is the defense of the Nation?", he could be shown something of the awesome power of the mighty American Army, Navy and Air Force; not to mention the enormous economic potential of the country. But the true strength of the United States of America lies deeper, as it lay in Sparta. It is the spirit of both military and people—a flaming devotion to the cause of freedom within these borders.

At this season of anniversary of the birth of Abraham Lincoln, it will not be inappropriate to speak about this freedom, and what is called the American way of life.

Freedom is a subject everyone seems to be talking about without seemingly stopping to ask the rather basic question, "What do we mean by freedom?" In this matter, apparently, we all are experts.

The world of Mr. Lincoln's day is unbelievably different from this modern age. Yet there is a sense in which history is always repeating itself. The issues we face today are precisely the issues he spent his life seeking to resolve. In his day, the issue was sparked by Negro slavery; today, it is sparked by a militantly atheistic communism that has already enclaved 800 million of the peoples of the earth, and now menaces the rest of the free world.

Lincoln, in his day, saw this country as a nation that "was conceived in liberty and dedicated to the proposition that all men are created equal." And the question he asks is the timeless, and timely, one—"whether that Nation, or any nation so conceived and so dedicated, can long endure."

I recall once discussing the "American way of life" with a newspaper editor. He had been using the phrase rather freely. When asked to define the phrase "the American way of life," he became very wordy and verbose. "It is live and let live; it is freedom to act," and other such platitudes.

Let me tell what "the American way of life" is. It is going to the ball game and eating popcorn, and drinking Coca Cola, and rooting for the Senators. It is shopping in Sears, Roebuck. It is losing heart and hat on a roller coaster. It is driving on the right side of the road and putting up at motels on a long journey. It is being bored with television commercials. It is setting off firecrackers with your children on the Fourth of July. It is sitting for 7 hours to see the pageantry of the presidential inauguration.

But, it is deeper than that.

It is gardens with no fences to bar you from the neighborliness of your neighbor. It is the perfume of honeysuckle, and the sound of katydids in the warm night air of summer, when you go out into the garden, the children long ago asleep, and you feel the pulse and throb of nature around you. It is Negro spirituals and colonial architecture. It is Thanksgiving turkey and pumpkin pie. It is the sweep of broad rivers and the sea of wheat and grass. It is a view from the air of the conflux of muddy rivers and neat little excavations and columns of smoke that is the mighty Pittsburgh. It is the canyons of skyscrapers in New York, and the sweep of Lakeshore Drive that is Chicago. It is the lonely, proud statue of Lee on Gettysburg field. It is schoolgirls wearing jeans and schoolboys riding enormous push bikes. It is color comics. It is the Sunday *New York Times.* It is sitting on the porch of a Sunday afternoon, after morning church, rocking in a creaking wicker chair. It is a lad and a lass looking at you intently in the marriage service. It is sickness and a home empty, quieted, and stilled by grief. It is the sound of the bell at the railroad crossing, and children's laughter. It is a solitary bugler playing taps, clear and long-noted, at Arlington.

And where did all this come from?

It has been with us so long, we have to recall it was brought here by people who laid stress on fundamentals. They called themselves Puritans because they wished to live the pure and noble life purged of all idolatry and enslavement of the mind, even by the church. They did not realize that in fleeing from tyranny and setting up a new life in a new world they were to be the fathers of a mighty nation.

These fundamental concepts of life had been given to the world from Sinai, where the moral law was graven upon tables of stone, symbolizing the universal application to all men; and they came from the New Testament, where they heard in the words of Jesus of Nazareth the living Word of God for the world.

This is the American way of life. Lincoln saw this clearly. History for him was the Divine Comedy, though he would not use that phrase. The providence of God was being fulfilled.

Wherefore, he claims that it is under God that this Nation shall know a new birth of freedom. And by implication, it is under God that "government of the people, by the people, and for the people shall not perish from the earth." For Lincoln, since God was in His Heaven, all must ultimately be right for his country.

Now, all this may seem obvious until one sits down and takes these implications of freedom really seriously. For me, it came in a flash one day sometime ago when our children came home from school. Almost casually, I asked what happened at school when they arrived there in the morning. They described to me, in great detail and with strange solemnity, the ritual of the salute to the flag. The children turn to the flag, and with their hand across their heart, they repeat the words:

"I pledge allegiance to the flag of the United States and the Republic for which it stands; one nation, indivisible, with liberty and justice for all."

They were very proud of the pledge; and rightly so.

I don't suppose you fathers would have paid much attention to that as I did. I had the advantage over you. I could listen to those noble words as if for the first time. You have learned them so long ago, like the arithmetic table or the shorter catechism, something you can repeat without realizing what it all really means. But I could sit down and brood upon it, going over each word slowly in my mind.

And I came to a strange conclusion. There was something missing in this pledge, and that which was missing was the characteristic and definitive factor in the American way of life. Indeed, apart from the mention of the phrase, the United States of America, this could be a pledge of any republic. In fact, I could hear little Muscovites repeat a similar pledge to their hammer-and-sickle flag in Moscow with equal solemnity, for Russia is also a republic that claims to have overthrown the tyranny of kingship.

Russia also claims to be indivisible. Mr. Stalin admitted to Sir Winston Churchill that the uniting of the peasants was the most difficult of all tasks. (He did not mention the massacre of the 3 million Kulak farmers in this blood-and-iron unification.)

Russia claims to have liberty. You will never understand the Communist mind until you realize this aberration of their judgment. Marx in his dialectic, makes it clear that the communist state is only an imperfect stage toward world socialism. When that day comes the state will wither away and true socialism will reign forever. Utopia will have dawned. Until that day there must be personal limitations. As the capitalist state limits freedom in the day of war, so must the workers of the world accept this form of restricted freedom. Besides, claims Marx, trouble arises when you give men their unrestricted freedom. Human freedom always proliferates into license and gives rise to greed and war. They might claim that their servitude is perfect freedom.

Again the Communists claim there is justice in Russia. They have their law courts. They have their elections with universal suffrage. When pressed to the point, they will admit there is really only one candidate because the people are so unanimous about that way of life.

They call their way of life "democratic." One of the problems statesmen find in dealing with Russia is one of semantics, of definition. Russia says she is democratic and we are Fascist; we claim to be democratic and call Russia Communist.

What, therefore, is missing in the pledge of allegiance that Americans have been saying off and on since 1892, and officially since 1942? The one fundamental concept that completely and ultimately separates Communist Russia from the democratic institutions of this country. This was seen clearly by Lincoln. Under God this people shall know a new birth of freedom, and "under God" are the definitive words.

Now, Lincoln was not being original in that phrase. He was simply reminding the people of the basis upon which the Nation won its freedom in its Declaration of Independence. He went back to Jefferson as he did in a famous speech delivered at Independence Hall in Philadelphia on February 22, 1861, two years before the Gettysburg Address. "All the political sentiments I entertain have been drawn from the sentiments which originated and were given to the world from this hall. I have never had a feeling politically that did not spring from sentiments embodied in the Declaration of Independence."

Listen again to the fundamentals of this Declaration:

"We hold these truths to be self-evident, that all men are created equal, that they are endowed by their Creator with certain unalienable rights; that among these are life, liberty, and the pursuit of happiness."

At Gettysburg Lincoln poses the question: "Now we are engaged in a great civil war, testing whether that nation, or any nation, so conceived and so dedicated, can long endure."

That is the text of our day and generation also.

The tragedy of the 19th century democratic liberalism, when nation after nation set up parliamentary forms of government, was that two world convulsions shattered the illusion that you can build a nation on human ideas without a fundamental belief in

God's province. Crowns in Europe toppled, not because the people had lost the vision of God.

We face, today, a theological war. It is not basically a conflict between two politician philosophies—Thomas Jefferson's political democracy over against Lenin's communistic state.

Nor is it a conflict fundamentally between two economic systems between, shall we say, Adam Smith's Wealth of Nations and Karl Marx's Das Capital.

It is a fight for freedom of the human personality. It is not simply man's inhumanity to man. It is Armageddon, a battle of the gods. It is the view of man as it comes down to us from Judaio-Christian civilization in mortal combat against modern, secularized, godless humanity.

The pledge of allegiance seems to me to omit this theological implication that is fundamental to the American way of life. It should be "One nation, indivisible, under God." Once "under God," then we can define what we mean by "liberty and justice for all." To omit the words "under God" in the pledge of allegiance is to omit the definitive character of the American way of life.

Some might assert this to be a violation of the first amendment of the Constitution. It is quite the opposite. The first amendment states concerning the question of religion: "Congress shall make no law respecting the establishment of religion."

Now, "establishment of religion" is a technical term. It means Congress will permit no state church in this land such as exists in England. In England the bishops are appointed by Her Majesty. The church, by law, is supported by teinds or rent. The church, therefore, can call upon the support of the law of the land to carry out its own ecclesiastical laws. What the declaration says, in effect, is that no state church shall exist in this land. This is separation of church and state; it is not, and never was meant to be, a separation of church and state; it is not, and never was meant to be, a separation of religion and life. Such objection is a confusion of the first amendment with the First Commandment.

If we were to add the phrase "under the church," that would be different. In fact, it would be dangerous. The question arises, which church? Now, I can give good Methodists an excellent dissertation upon the virtues of the Presbyterian Church, and show how much superior John Knox was to John Wesley. But the whole sad story of church history shows how, of all tyrants, often the church could be the worst for the best of reasons. The Jewish Church persecuted unto death the Christian Church in the first decade of Christianity; and for 1,200 years the Christian Church persecuted the Jewish Church. The Roman Church persecuted the Protestants; and the Protestants, in turn, persecuted the Roman Church; the Presbyterians and the Episcopalians brought low the very name of Christian charity, both in Scotland and America. It is not for nothing that Thomas Jefferson, on his tombstone at Monticello claimed that one of the three achievements of his life was his fight for religious freedom in Virginia—that even above the exalted office of President of the United States. No church is infallible; and no churchman is infallible.

Of course, as Christians, we might include the words "under Jesus Christ" or "under the King of Kings." But one of the glories of this land is that it has opened its gates to all men of every religious faith.

The word of welcome to these shores is epitomized on the Statue of Liberty:

"Give me your tired, your poor,
Your huddled masses yearning to breathe free,
The wretched refuse of your teeming shore,
Send these, the homeless, tempest tossed to me:
I lift my lamp beside the golden door."

There is no religious examination on entering the United States of America—no persecution because a man's faith differs even from the Christian religion. So, it must be "under God," to include the great Jewish community, and the people of Moslem faith, and the myriad of demoninations of Christians in the land.

What then of the honest atheist?

Philosophically speaking, an atheistic American is a contradiction in terms. Now don't misunderstand me. This age has thrown up a new type of man—we call him a secular; he does not believe in God; not because he is a wicked man, but because he is dialectically honest, and would rather walk with the unbelievers than sit hypocritically with people of the faith. These men, and many have I known, are fine in character; and in their obligations as citizens and good neighbors, quite excellent.

But they really are spiritual parasites. And I mean no term of abuse in this. I'm simply classifying them. A parasite is an organism that lives upon the life force of another organism without contributing to the life of the other. These excellent ethical seculars are living upon the accumulated spiritual capital of Judeo-Christian civilization, and at the same time, deny the God who revealed the divine principles upon which the ethics of this country grow. The dilemma of the secular is quite simple.

He cannot deny the Christian revelation and logically live by the Christian ethic.

And if he denies the Christian ethic, he falls short of the American ideal of life.

In Jefferson's phrase, if we deny the existence of the God who gave us life how can we live by the liberty He gave us at the same time? This is a God-fearing nation. On our coins, bearing the imprint of Lincoln and Jefferson, are the words "In God we trust." Congress is opened with prayer. It is upon the Holy Bible the President takes his oath of office. Naturalized citizens, when they take their oath of allegiance, conclude, solemnly, with the words "so help me God."

This is the issue we face today: A freedom that respects the rights of the minorities, but is defined by a fundamental belief in God. A way of life that sees man, not as the ultimate outcome of a mysterious concantenation of evolutionary process, but a sentient being created by God and seeking to know His will, and "Whose soul is restless till he rest in God."

In this land, there is neither Jew nor Greek, neither bond nor free, neither male nor female, for we are one nation indivisible under God, and humbly as God has given us the light we seek liberty and justice for all. This quest is not only within these United States, but to the four corners of the globe wherever man will lift up his head toward the vision of his true and divine manhood.

(Reprinted in the Congressional Record of the 83rd Congress, Second Session, March 8, 1954 at the request of the Honorable Charles G. Oakman of Michigan.)

INDEX

447

Conclusion

U.S. Constitution and Related Documents

Chapter I

THE TEN COMMANDMENTS of Almighty God (Exodus 20)

Chapter I

Chapter III

Thanksgiving—The American Christian Tradition

Chapter I

About the Author

Catherine Millard, B.A., M.A., is the founder and president of Christian Heritage Tours, Inc. She is also the author of *God's Signature Over the Nation's Capital.* Catherine won the 1990 George Washington Honor Medal, sponsored by the Freedoms Foundation at Valley Forge, in recognition of excellence in individual achievement for her many patriotic activities.

If you or your group is going to be in the Washington, D.C. area and would like to take part in an exciting tour that points out the true history of our country, complete with all references to the biblical foundations of our land, contact Christian Heritage Tours, Inc., 6597 Forest Dew Ct., Springfield, VA 22152, or call, (703) 455-0333. Catherine Millard is also available to provide lectures, seminars and multimedia presentations to your organization on the subject of America's Christian heritage. You may contact her through the above address.

For additional copies of
The Rewriting of America's History
contact your local Christian bookstore
or Horizon House.